SECOND EDITION

ESSENTIAL
CISSP

Exam Guide

Updated for the 2018
CISSP Body of Knowledge

SECOND EDITION

ESSENTIAL CISSP

Exam Guide

Updated for the 2018 CISSP Body of Knowledge

Phil Martin

Nearsighted Ninja

Nonce Corp is an independent entity from (ISC)² and is not affiliated with (ISC)² in any manner. This study/training guide and/or material is not sponsored by, endorsed by, or affiliated with (ISC)² in any manner. This publication may be used in assisting students to prepare for the Certified Information Systems Security Professional (CISSP®) exam. Neither (ISC)² nor Nonce Corp warrant that use of this publication will ensure passing any exam. CISSP is a trademark or registered trademark of (ISC)². All other trademarks are trademarks of their respective owners.

An audio version of this print book is available on audible.com!

Essential CISSP Exam Guide

Copyright © 2018 by Nonce Corp. Printed in the United States of America. All rights reserved. Except as permitted under the Copyright Act of 1976, no part of this publication may be reproduced or distributed in any form or by any means, or stored in a database or retrieval system, without the prior written permission of the publisher.

All trademarks or copyrights mentioned herein are the possession of their respective owners and Nonce Corp makes no claim of ownership by the mention of products that contain these marks.

ISBN: 9781723901515

Information has been obtained by Nonce Corp from sources believed to be reliable. However, because of the possibility of human or mechanical error by our sources, Nonce Corp does not guarantee the accuracy, or completeness of any information and is not responsible for any errors or omissions or the results obtained from the use of such information.

Contents

CONTENTS IV
FIGURES XVI
ABOUT 1
    ABOUT THE EXAM 1
    ABOUT THIS BOOK 1

SECTION 1: SECURITY AND RISK MANAGEMENT DOMAIN 2

CHAPTER 1: CIA AND AAA 3
    QUESTIONS 4

CHAPTER 2: FROM VULNERABILITY TO EXPOSURE 5
    QUESTIONS 6

CHAPTER 3: ADMINISTRATIVE, TECHNICAL AND PHYSICAL CONTROLS 7
    QUESTIONS 8

CHAPTER 4: SECURITY FRAMEWORKS 9
    ISO 27000 SERIES 9
    ENTERPRISE ARCHITECTURE DEVELOPMENT 9
    ARCHITECTURE FRAMEWORK TERMS 10
    FRAMEWORKS FOR IMPLEMENTATION 11
    PROCESS DEVELOPMENT 12
    THE PROCESS LIFE CYCLE 13
    QUESTIONS 15

CHAPTER 5: COMPUTER CRIME LAW 16
    LAW 16
    COMPUTER CRIME 16
    TYPES OF LEGAL SYSTEMS 18
    INTELLECTUAL PROPERTY 19
    PRIVACY 21
    QUESTIONS 24

CHAPTER 6: GOALS, STRATEGIES, POLICIES, STANDARDS, BASELINES, GUIDELINES AND PROCEDURES 25
    GOALS AND STRATEGIES 25
    POLICIES 25
    STANDARDS 25
    BASELINES 25
    GUIDELINES 26
    PROCEDURES 26
    QUESTIONS 27

CHAPTER 7: ALL ABOUT RISK MANAGEMENT AND MODELING THREATS 28

Contents

- INFORMATION SYSTEMS RISK MANAGEMENT 28
- THE RISK MANAGEMENT TEAM 28
- THE RISK MANAGEMENT PROCESS 28
- VULNERABILITIES 28
- THREATS 29
- ATTACKS 29
- REDUCTION ANALYSIS 29
- QUESTIONS 31

CHAPTER 8: ASSESSING AND ANALYZING RISK 32

- RISK ANALYSIS TEAM 32
- CALCULATING VALUE 32
- IDENTIFYING VULNERABILITIES AND THREATS 32
- METHODOLOGIES FOR RISK ASSESSMENT 32
- RISK ANALYSIS APPROACHES 33
- PROTECTION MECHANISMS 35
- TOTAL RISK VS. RESIDUAL RISK 35
- OUTSOURCING 36
- QUESTIONS 37

CHAPTER 9: MANAGING RISK 38

- CATEGORIZE INFORMATION SYSTEM 38
- SELECT SECURITY CONTROLS 38
- IMPLEMENT SECURITY CONTROLS 38
- ASSESS SECURITY CONTROLS 38
- AUTHORIZE INFORMATION SYSTEM 38
- MONITOR SECURITY CONTROLS 38
- QUESTIONS 39

CHAPTER 10: BUSINESS CONTINUITY AND DISASTER RECOVERY 40

- STANDARDS AND BEST PRACTICES 40
- MAKING BCM A PART OF THE ENTERPRISE SECURITY PROGRAM 40
- BCP PROJECT COMPONENTS 41
- QUESTIONS 43

CHAPTER 11: PERSONNEL SECURITY 44

- HIRING PRACTICES 44
- TERMINATION 44
- SECURITY-AWARENESS TRAINING 44
- QUESTIONS 46

CHAPTER 12: ETHICS 47

- QUESTIONS 48

SECTION 2: ASSET SECURITY DOMAIN 49

CHAPTER 13: INFORMATION LIFE CYCLE AND CLASSIFICATION 50

THE INFORMATION LIFE CYCLE	50
CLASSIFICATION	50
QUESTIONS	52

CHAPTER 14: LAYERS OF RESPONSIBILITY 53

EXECUTIVE MANAGEMENT	53
DATA OWNER	53
DATA CUSTODIAN	53
SYSTEM OWNER	53
SECURITY ADMINISTRATOR	53
SUPERVISOR	53
CHANGE CONTROL ANALYST	54
DATA ANALYST	54
USER	54
AUDITOR	54
QUESTIONS	55

CHAPTER 15: RETENTION POLICIES 56

QUESTIONS	57

CHAPTER 16: PRIVACY AND ASSET PROTECTION 58

PROTECTING PRIVACY	58
PROTECTING ASSETS	58
DATA LEAKAGE	59
PROTECTING OTHER ASSETS	61
QUESTIONS	62

SECTION 3: SECURITY ARCHITECTURE AND ENGINEERING DOMAIN 63

CHAPTER 17: COMPUTER AND SYSTEM ARCHITECTURE 64

COMPUTER ARCHITECTURE	64
SYSTEM ARCHITECTURE	67
QUESTIONS	69

CHAPTER 18: OPERATING SYSTEMS 70

PROCESS MANAGEMENT	70
THREAD MANAGEMENT	70
PROCESS ACTIVITY	71
MEMORY MANAGEMENT	71
VIRTUAL MEMORY	71
INPUT/OUTPUT DEVICE MANAGEMENT	72
CPU ARCHITECTURE INTEGRATION	72
OPERATING SYSTEM ARCHITECTURES	73
VIRTUAL MACHINES	74
QUESTIONS	75

CHAPTER 19: SYSTEM SECURITY ARCHITECTURE AND MODELS 76

System Security Architecture 76
Security Models 77
Questions 80

CHAPTER 20: SYSTEMS EVALUATION, CERTIFICATION AND ACCREDITATION 81

Evaluation 81
Certification vs. Accreditation 81
Questions 83

CHAPTER 21: DISTRIBUTED SYSTEM SECURITY 84

Cloud Computing 84
Parallel Computing 84
Databases 84
Web Applications 85
Mobile Devices 85
Cyber-Physical Systems 85
Industrial Control Systems 86
Questions 87

CHAPTER 22: A FEW THREATS TO REVIEW 88

Questions 89

CHAPTER 23: CRYPTOGRAPHY 90

The History of Cryptography 90
Kerckhoffs' Principle 91
The Strength of the Cryptosystem 91
Services of Cryptosystems 91
One-Time Pad 91
Running and Concealment Ciphers 92
Steganography 92
Questions 93

CHAPTER 24: ENCRYPTION 94

Types of Ciphers 94
Encryption Methods 94
Questions 99

CHAPTER 25: TYPES OF SYMMETRIC SYSTEMS 100

Data Encryption Standard 100
Triple-DES 100
Advanced Encryption Standard 100
International Data Encryption Algorithm 100
Blowfish 100
RC4 101
RC5 101
RC6 101
Questions 102

CHAPTER 26: TYPES OF ASYMMETRIC SYSTEMS 103

Diffie-Hellman Algorithm 103
RSA 103
El Gamal 104
Elliptic Curve Cryptosystems 104
Knapsack 104
Zero Knowledge Proof 104
Questions 105

CHAPTER 27: MESSAGE INTEGRITY 106

The One-Way Hash 106
MD4 106
MD5 107
SHA-1 107
SHA-2 107
Attacks Against One-Way Hash Functions 107
Digital Signatures 107
Digital Signature Standard 107
Questions 108

CHAPTER 28: PUBLIC KEY INFRASTRUCTURE, KEY MANAGEMENT AND TPM 109

Public Key Infrastructure 109
Key Management 110
Trusted Platform Module 110
Questions 111

CHAPTER 29: ATTACKS ON CRYPTOGRAPHY 112

Ciphertext-Only Attacks 112
Known-Plaintext Attacks 112
Chosen-Plaintext Attacks 112
Chosen-Ciphertext Attacks 112
Differential Cryptanalysis 112
Linear Cryptanalysis 112
Side-Channel Attacks 112
Replay Attacks 113
Analytical Attacks 113
Social Engineering Attacks 113
Meet-in-the-Middle Attacks 113
Questions 114

CHAPTER 30: SITE AND FACILITY SECURITY 115

Physical Security 115
The Site Planning Process 115
Questions 119

CHAPTER 31: PROTECTING ASSETS 120

- Protecting Mobile Devices 120
  - Using Safes 120
  - Questions 121

CHAPTER 32: INTERNAL SUPPORT SYSTEMS 122
  - Electric Power 122
  - Environmental Issues 123
  - Fire Control 123
  - Questions 126

SECTION 4: COMMUNICATION AND NETWORK SECURITY DOMAIN 127

CHAPTER 33: OPEN SYSTEMS INTERCONNECTION REFERENCE MODEL 128
  - Protocol 128
  - Application Layer 129
  - Presentation Layer 129
  - Session Layer 129
  - Transport Layer 130
  - Network Layer 130
  - Data Link Layer 130
  - Physical Layer 131
  - Functions and Protocols in the OSI Model 131
  - Other Protocols 132
  - Questions 133

CHAPTER 34: TCP/IP 134
  - TCP/IP Model 134
  - TCP and UDP 134
  - The TCP Handshake 135
  - Ports 136
  - IPv4 136
  - IPV6 137
  - Layer 2 Security Standards 137
  - Converged Protocols 137
  - Questions 139

CHAPTER 35: TYPES OF TRANSMISSION 140
  - Analog and Digital 140
  - Asynchronous and Synchronous 141
  - Broadband and Baseband 141
  - Pulling It All Together (So Far) 142
  - Questions 143

CHAPTER 36: CABLING 144
  - Coaxial Cable 144
  - Twisted-Pair Cable 144
  - Fiber-Optic Cable 144

    Cabling Problems 145
    Questions 146

CHAPTER 37: NETWORKING 147

    Topologies 147
    Media Access Technologies 147
    Transmission Methods 149
    Network Protocols and Services 149
    Domain Name Service 152
    E-Mail Services 154
    Network Address Translation 155
    Routing Protocols 156
    Questions 158

CHAPTER 38: NETWORKING DEVICES 159

    Repeaters, Hubs, Bridges, Switches and Routers 159
    Gateways 160
    PBXs 161
    Firewalls 161
    Proxy Servers 164
    Honeypots and Tarpits 164
    Unified Threat Management 165
    Content Distribution Networks 165
    Software Defined Networking 165
    Questions 166

CHAPTER 39: INTRANETS, EXTRANETS, LANS, WANS AND MANS 167

    Intranets and Extranets 167
    Local Area Networks 167
    Wide Area Networks 167
    Metropolitan Area Networks 169
    Questions 171

CHAPTER 40: MULTISERVICE ACCESS TECHNOLOGIES 172

    Questions 175

CHAPTER 41: REMOTE CONNECTIVITY 176

    Communication Options 176
    VPNs 177
    Authentication Protocols 178
    Questions 180

CHAPTER 42: WIRELESS NETWORKS 181

    Wireless Communication Techniques 181
    WLAN Architecture 181
    Wireless Standards 183
    Other Wireless Networks 185

Contents

CHAPTER 43: NETWORK ENCRYPTION **188**

    LINK AND END-TO-END ENCRYPTION 188
    EMAIL ENCRYPTION 188
    INTERNET SECURITY 188
    QUESTIONS 190

CHAPTER 44: NETWORK ATTACKS **191**

    DENIAL OF SERVICE 191
    RANSOMWARE 191
    SNIFFING 192
    DNS HIJACKING 192
    DRIVE-BY DOWNLOAD 192
    QUESTIONS 193

SECTION 5: IDENTITY AND ACCESS MANAGEMENT (IAM) DOMAIN **194**

CHAPTER 45: IDENTIFICATION, AUTHENTICATION, AUTHORIZATION, AND ACCOUNTABILITY **195**

    IDENTITY 195
    AUTHENTICATION 196
    AUTHORIZATION 201
    FEDERATION 204
    IDENTITY SERVICES 205
    QUESTIONS 207

CHAPTER 46: ACCESS CONTROL MODELS **208**

    DISCRETIONARY ACCESS CONTROL 208
    MANDATORY ACCESS CONTROL 208
    ROLE-BASED ACCESS CONTROL 209
    ATTRIBUTE-BASED ACCESS CONTROL 209
    QUESTIONS 211

CHAPTER 47: ADMINISTRATING ACCESS CONTROL **212**

    TECHNIQUES AND TECHNOLOGIES 212
    MANAGEMENT 213
    METHODS 214
    QUESTIONS 216

CHAPTER 48: ACCOUNTABILITY AND IMPLEMENTING ACCESS CONTROL **217**

    ACCOUNTABILITY 217
    IMPLEMENTATION 218
    QUESTIONS 219

CHAPTER 49: MONITORING AND REACTING TO ACCESS CONTROL **220**

    QUESTIONS 224

CHAPTER 50: THREATS TO ACCESS CONTROL **225**

    QUESTIONS 227

SECTION 6: SECURITY ASSESSMENT AND TESTING DOMAIN 228

CHAPTER 51: AUDIT STRATEGIES 229

- The Process 229
- Internal Audit Teams 229
- Third-Party (External) Audit teams 230
- Service Organization Controls 230
- Questions 231

CHAPTER 52: AUDITING TECHNICAL CONTROLS 232

- Vulnerability Testing 232
- Penetration testing 233
- War Dialing 234
- Postmortem 234
- Log Reviews 234
- Synthetic Transactions 235
- Misuse Case Testing 235
- Code Reviews 235
- Interface Testing 235
- Questions 237

CHAPTER 53: AUDITING ADMINISTRATION CONTROLS 238

- Account Management 238
- Backup Verification 238
- Disaster Recovery and Business Continuity 239
- Security Training and Security Awareness Training 240
- Key Performance and Risk Indicators 241
- Questions 242

CHAPTER 54: REPORTING AND MANAGEMENT REVIEW 243

- Reporting 243
- Management Review 243
- Questions 245

SECTION 7: SECURITY OPERATIONS DOMAIN 246

CHAPTER 55: ROLES, MANAGEMENT AND ASSURANCE LEVELS 247

- Roles 247
- Administrative Management 247
- Assurance Levels 248
- Questions 249

CHAPTER 56: OPERATIONAL RESPONSIBILITIES 250

- Questions 251

CHAPTER 57: CONFIGURATION MANAGEMENT 252

- Questions 254

CHAPTER 58: PHYSICAL SECURITY 255
Locks 255
Personnel Access Controls 256
External Boundary Protection Mechanisms 256
Auditing Physical Access 258
Questions 259

CHAPTER 59: SECURE RESOURCE PROVISIONING 260
Questions 261

CHAPTER 60: NETWORK AND RESOURCE AVAILABILITY 262
Questions 264

CHAPTER 61: PREVENTATIVE MEASURES 265
Questions 267

CHAPTER 62: MANAGING INCIDENTS 268
Questions 270

CHAPTER 63: DISASTER RECOVERY 271
Business Process Recovery 271
Facility Recovery 271
Supply and Technology Recovery 273
Choosing a Software Backup Facility 273
End-User Environment 273
Data Backup Alternatives 274
Electronic Backup Solutions 274
High Availability 275
Insurance 275
Questions 276

CHAPTER 64: RECOVERY AND RESTORATION 277
Developing Goals for the Plans 277
Implementing Strategies 277
Questions 279

CHAPTER 65: INVESTIGATIONS 280
Computer Forensics and Proper Collection of Evidence 280
Motive, Opportunity and Means 280
Computer Criminal Behavior 281
Incident Investigators 281
The Forensic Investigation Process 281
What is Admissible in Court? 282
Surveillance, Search and Seizure 282
Interviewing Suspects 283
Questions 284

CHAPTER 66: LIABILITY AND ITS RAMIFICATIONS 285
Questions 287

SECTION 8: SOFTWARE DEVELOPMENT SECURITY DOMAIN 288

CHAPTER 67: WHERE DO WE PLACE SECURITY? 289
Environment vs. Application 289
Implementation and Default Issues 289
Defining Good Code 290
Questions 291

CHAPTER 68: SOFTWARE DEVELOPMENT LIFE CYCLE 292
Project Management 292
Requirements Gathering Phase 292
Design Phase 293
Development Phase 293
Testing/Validation Phase 293
Release/Maintenance Phase 294
Questions 296

CHAPTER 69: SOFTWARE DEVELOPMENT MODELS 297
Questions 299

CHAPTER 70: CHANGE CONTROL 300
Questions 301

CHAPTER 71: PROGRAMMING LANGUAGES AND CONCEPTS 302
Assemblers, Compilers, Interpreters 302
Object-Oriented Concepts 303
Questions 305

CHAPTER 72: DISTRIBUTED COMPUTING 306
Distributed Computing Environment 306
CORBA and ORBs 306
COM and DCOM 306
Java Platform, Enterprise Edition 306
Service-Oriented Architecture 306
Mobile Code 307
Questions 308

CHAPTER 73: WEB SECURITY 309
Administrative Interfaces 309
Authentication and Access Control 309
Input Validation 309
Parameter Validation 310
Session Management 311
Web Application Security Best Practices 311

Contents

 Questions 312

CHAPTER 74: DATABASE MANAGEMENT 313

 Database Management Software 313
 Database Models 313
 Database Programming Interfaces 313
 Relational Database Components 313
 Integrity 314
 Data Warehousing and Data Mining 314
 Questions 316

CHAPTER 75: MALICIOUS SOFTWARE (MALWARE) 317

 Viruses 317
 Worms 317
 Rootkit 317
 Spyware and Adware 317
 Botnets 317
 Logic Bombs 318
 Trojan Horses 318
 Spam Detection 318
 Antimalware Programs 318
 Questions 319

ANSWERS 320

INDEX 330

Figures

Figure 1: The Threat Pipeline 5
Figure 2: COBIT Principles 11
Figure 3: ITIL Stages 12
Figure 4: CMMI Levels 12
Figure 5: PDCA 13
Figure 6: From Goals to Procedures 25
Figure 7: Qualitative Impact Matrix 34
Figure 8: Quantitative vs. Qualitative Risk Analysis 35
Figure 9: The CPU 64
Figure 10: Buffer Overflow 66
Figure 11: Operating System Architecture 73
Figure 12: Virtualization 74
Figure 13: Classic Architecture vs. Cloud Computing 84
Figure 14: Symmetric vs. Asymmetric Cryptography 96
Figure 15: Block Cipher 97
Figure 16: Block vs. Stream 97
Figure 17: Symmetric Algorithms 101
Figure 18: Fire Classes and Suppression 125
Figure 19: OSI and Protocol Mapping 131
Figure 20: OSI-TCP Mapping 134
Figure 21: TCP vs. UDP 135
Figure 22: Normal Sine Wave 140
Figure 23: Variable Frequency 140
Figure 24: Variable Amplitude 140
Figure 25: Network Devices 160
Figure 26: Multi-Homed Firewall 163
Figure 27: Various Network Types 167
Figure 28: SIP Handshake 173
Figure 29: Making a SIP call 174
Figure 30: Wireless Standards 185
Figure 31: Kerberos Process 203
Figure 32: Access Control Matrix 212
Figure 33: Capability Table 212
Figure 34: ACL 212
Figure 35: The Evolution of Programming Languages 303

About

About the Exam

The exam consists of 250 multiple-choice, drag and drop, and Hotspot questions that must be answered in 6 hours.

- Multiple Choice – select a single option from many
- Drag and drop – select one or more answers and drag them to a drop area; occasionally the order matters
- Hotspot – click a visual item that does or does not answer the question

There is no penalty for guessing, so be sure not to skip a question. However, you must manage your time well – if you run across a question that you are not sure of, go ahead and guess but then flag it for review. When you have completed all other questions, go back to each flagged question and spend more time on it.

Of the 250 questions, only 225 will be graded – 25 are used for research purposes. Therefore, you may run across questions that are completely unfamiliar or appear to be too vague to answer properly – go ahead and answer them to the best of your ability, but don't worry too much about these critters – they may very well be one of the 25 research questions. Each test taker is given a random sampling of questions pulled from a much larger pool of questions, so you will not be taking the exact same test as the person sitting next to you. You will need to correctly answer 70% of the questions (175 questions).

An important fact to note is that there will be no questions that are specific to a platform (Windows, Linux, etc.). While this book does contain information that is specific to a platform, that content will not be highlighted (see About This Book) – in other words you will not need to remember specifics, just the concept. While most questions are direct, there will be some scenario-based questions that present a situation and then ask one or more questions about that scenario.

Once you have passed the exam, you will still need to provide proof that you possess the experience required to obtain the certification. This will include having a CISSP-certified individual sponsor you.

About This Book

This book has been kept simple on-purpose – no fluff, just the facts - with a few mnemonic devices thrown in to help you remember.

Some simple rules on text formatting:

This is a term you should memorize:

> *Italicized and underlined text*

This is a concept you should remember:

> **Bold text**

This is to help you understand the other two above:

> Normal text

Read normal text at least once, and revisit as often as you need.

After each chapter you will find approximately 5 test questions to gauge how well you have retained the information. While this helps a great deal while reading this book, you will probably want to purchase additional test questions. The companion to this book, *Essential CISSP Test Questions*, is a great resource for this with over 2,000 sample questions that cover all 8 domains.

Answers for all test questions can be found in the back of the book.

Section 1: Security and Risk Management Domain

The goals of security are contained within 3 security principles, commonly referred to in the industry as _CIA_ – confidentiality, integrity and availability.

Chapter 1: CIA and AAA

Confidentiality is achieved when we have a high level of assurance that information is kept from unauthorized parties. Attackers can circumvent confidentiality by social engineering attacks such as shoulder surfing, brute-force password attacks and decrypting packets. Don't worry if these concepts are unfamiliar right now, we'll discuss them later. Confidentiality is usually enforced by encrypting data, or by classifying and restricting that data. Examples of confidentiality are encryption at-rest, encryption in-transit and access controls. Other important confidentiality-related concepts are:

- *Sensitivity*, which is a measure of harm or damage if the information were to be disclosed
- *Discretion*, which is shown by a person when choosing to control disclosure of information to limit damage
- *Criticality*, or how critical to a mission information is
- *Concealment*, or the act of hiding or preventing disclosure
- *Secrecy*, which is the act of keeping something a secret
- *Privacy*, or the act of keeping information confidential that is personally identifiable or that can cause damage if disclosed
- *Seclusion*, which is storing something in an out-of-the-way manner
- *Isolation*, or keeping something separate from others

Integrity is achieved when information remains unaltered (and can be proven to be so) except by authorized parties. We can approach integrity from 3 views:

- Preventing *intentional* unauthorized modifications
- Preventing *accidental* modifications
- Ensuring that the internal and external *consistency* of information remains valid

As an example, if an attacker plants a virus or logic bomb in a system, the integrity of that system has been compromised because it has been altered in an unauthorized manner. Or, an attacker may covertly tamper with data either at-rest or in-transit, meaning that the integrity of the data has not been upheld – in this case hashing can often detect this type of attack. Sometimes loss of integrity can be by mistake, such as an employee accidentally entering the wrong amount to charge a customer, with the result of corrupt data. In this case, implementing the correct input validation can prevent corrupt data from happening. Other examples of Integrity might be managing change control, digital signing, and cyclic redundancy checks (or CRC).

The last attribute in the CIA triad is *availability*, meaning that usable access to a resource is always provided in a timely and uninterrupted manner. For example, applications should perform fast enough to serve all required users and can recover from problems fast enough so that overall productivity is not affected. Likewise, networks must remain up, functional and not susceptible to attacks such as Denial of Service attacks, or DoS. And don't forget about protection against natural disasters or electrical problems – if people can't get to work, or their computers won't turn on, it can be just as damaging as an attack or a major software glitch. At the risk of being obvious, availability is all about making sure things stay available. Other examples of ensuring availability include load balancing, clustering or web farms, making backups, redundant Internet connections or power sources, and warm or hot backup facilities.

Confidentiality and integrity have a two-way relationship – you can't have one without the other. Availability is dependent on both confidentiality and integrity. There is no standardized priority between the three components, but government organizations usually are more interested in confidentiality, while the private sector normally prizes availability above the others.

Now, *AAA* in security refers to authentication, authorization and auditing. However, two other terms always ride along – identification and nonrepudiation.

- *Identification* occurs when a subject claims a specific identity
- *Authentication* happens when a subject proves they are who they claim to be
- *Authorization* is a decision on what the subject can access and how it can be used
- *Auditing* is the recording of activities for a given subject in a log
- *Accountability* occurs when that log is reviewed for compliance

Questions

1. What is the best definition of identification?

A) A subject proves they are who they claim to be

B) A subject claims a specific identity

C) Reviewing logs to check for compliance

D) Recording the activities of a subject in a log

2. What is the best definition of discretion?

A) A high level of assurance that information is kept from unauthorized parties

B) Something shown by a person when choosing to control disclosure of information to limit damage

C) Keeping something separate from others

D) The act of keeping something a secret

3. What does CIA stand for?

A) Confidentiality, Issuance and Availability

B) Confidentiality, Integrity and Availability

C) Concealment, Integrity and Availability

D) Confidentiality, Integrity and Accessibility

4. What is the best definition of isolation?

A) How critical to a mission information is considered to be

B) Keeping something separate from others

C) When information remains unaltered and can be proven to be so

D) The act of keeping information confidential

5. What is the best definition of secrecy?

A) Storing something in an out-of-the-way manner

B) The act of keeping something a secret

C) The act of keeping information confidential

D) Keeping something separate from others

Chapter 2: From Vulnerability to Exposure

When we discuss securing infrastructure or processes, we use terms like vulnerability, threat, threat agent, exploit, risk, and exposure - they are all interrelated.

A _vulnerability_ is a weakness in a system that allows a threat to compromise security. We normally think of this as a software weakness, but it could also be hardware, a process or even a person. Examples of vulnerabilities are:

- A wireless access point without security enabled
- Too many ports on a firewall being open
- An unneeded service running on a server, such as an FTP server that no one uses
- Not keeping sensitive rooms locked
- Not requiring passwords to be changed periodically
- Not performing background checks on new hires

An _exploit_ occurs when a vulnerability is taken advantage of by an attacker. A _threat_ is the danger that a vulnerability might be exploited. A person or process that exploits a vulnerability is called a _threat agent_. Examples of a threat agent might be employees not following proper procedure when shredding documents, an attacker gaining access to data through a network connection or even an automated process that deletes the wrong files. Threats can be natural, manmade or technical in nature.

A _risk_ is the likelihood that a threat agent will exploit a vulnerability combined with the damage that could result. As an example, if an Intrusion Detection System, or IDS, is not implemented on a network, then the risk of an attack going unnoticed goes up.

An _exposure_ is a single real-world instance of a vulnerability being exploited by a threat agent. If you are hacked three times in one year, then you have experienced three different exposures within the last year.

A _control_ (also called a countermeasure or safeguard) is created or put into place to mitigate a risk. Note that a countermeasure does not usually eliminate the risk altogether – it simply reduces the likelihood of a vulnerability being exploited. Examples of controls might be firewalls, encryption, security guards or requiring strong passwords.

Let's put all the definitions together:

A _threat_ is a _vulnerability_ that is _exploited_ by a _threat agent_. The likelihood of this happening coupled with the resulting damage is called a _risk_, and when it does happen we encounter an _exposure_. The way we reduce _risk_ is to implement a _control_.

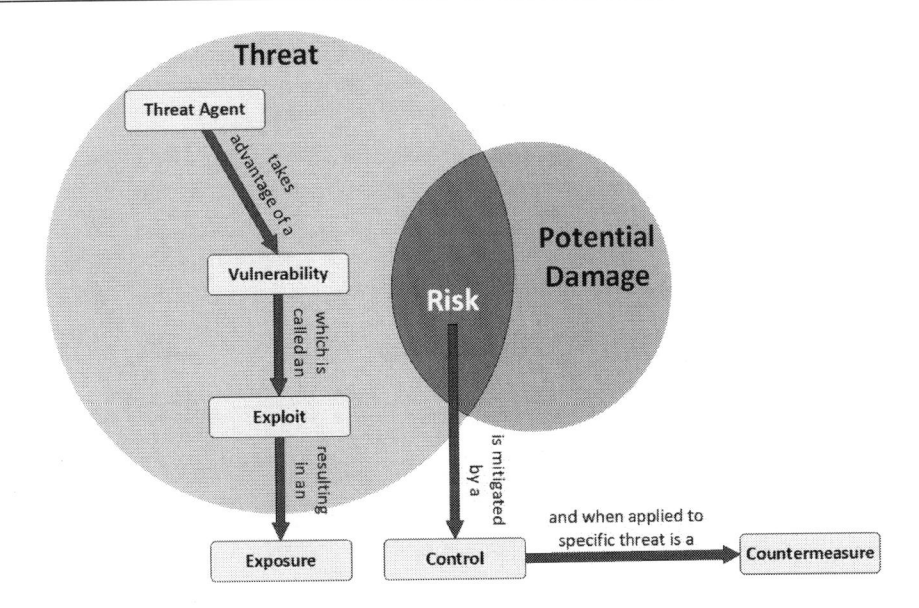

Figure 1: The Threat Pipeline

Chapter 2: From Vulnerability to Exposure

Questions

1. What is the best definition of a threat agent?

A) A weakness in a system that allows a threat to compromise security

B) A person or process that exploits a vulnerability

C) A single real-world instance of a vulnerability being exploited by a threat agent

D) Something that mitigates a risk

2. What is the best definition of a threat?

A) The danger that a vulnerability might be exploited

B) A weakness in a system that allows a threat to compromise security

C) Occurs when a vulnerability is taken advantage of by an attacker

D) A person or process that exploits a vulnerability

3. What is the best definition of a vulnerability?

A) The likelihood that a threat agent will exploit a vulnerability combined with the damage that could result

B) A weakness in a system that allows a threat to compromise security

C) A person or process that exploits a vulnerability

D) The danger that a vulnerability might be exploited

4. What is the best definition of an exploit?

A) The danger that a vulnerability might be exploited

B) Occurs when a vulnerability is taken advantage of by an attacker

C) A weakness in a system that allows a threat to compromise security

D) A single real-world instance of a vulnerability being exploited by a threat agent

5. What is the best definition of a risk?

A) A weakness in a system that allows a threat to compromise security

B) The danger that a vulnerability might be exploited

C) Occurs when a vulnerability is taken advantage of by an attacker

D) The likelihood that a threat agent will exploit a vulnerability combined with the damage that could result

Chapter 3: Administrative, Technical and Physical Controls

Now let's talk about the types of controls we can put in place. There are three _categories_ – administrative, technical and physical.

Administrative controls are usually thought of as management controls and include training, security policies and documentation, and managing risk.

Technical controls (sometimes referred to as logical controls) are software or hardware elements such as hashing or encryption, firewalls and enforcing authentication.

Physical controls might be external lighting, locked doors, fences, card keys and security guards.

Using multiple categories of controls in a layered approach is called _defense-in-depth_ and provides a much better defense, as an attacker would have to go through multiple types of protection.

But, categories are only one way of looking at controls. A second dimension is the _function_ of various controls. The six different functional groups of controls are:

- _Preventative_, in which we avoid an incident.
- _Deterrent_, which discourages an attacker.
- _Detective_, where we identify an intruder.
- _Corrective_, in which a component or system is fixed.
- _Recovery_, where we bring environments back to normal operation.
- _Compensating,_ where an alternative control is substituted if the first choice is unavailable.

The best approach when addressing a vulnerability is to simply prevent something bad from happening. Failing that, be sure you can detect, correct and recover. When trying to determine what functional area a control falls under, always think of the primary purpose and ignore any secondary roles a control might fulfill. For example, a firewall can prevent access, but if an attacker knew it was there, it might act as a deterrent. But what is the primary purpose of a firewall? To prevent an attacker from getting in – that is its primary purpose, and so it is a preventative control. Or what about auditing logs? Attackers hate them, and their presence may act as a deterrent. But their primary purpose is to identify anomalies and track attacks, so they are detective controls.

As an analogy, think of someone breaking into your house. To _prevent_ that from happening, you install locks on all doors. But you know someone could just break down the door, so you decide to hire a security guard to _deter_ would-be burglars. Unfortunately, a security guard costs too much money, so you _compensate_ by buying a guard dog. But, just in case they manage to break down the door and entice your dog to the dark side with some juicy beef steaks, you install motion-activated cameras to _detect_ a break-in. When this happens, the police are automatically called, and they _correct_ the situation by arresting the burglar. You then must _recover_ by repairing the front door.

So, a _compensating control_ is one that is chosen because the first choice is either too expensive or does not meet some business need. In our example, we originally wanted to hire a security guard, but settled for a dog because security guards are expensive. The guard dog was a compensating control.

Now that you know the three categories of controls (administrative, technical and physical) as well as the six functional areas of controls (preventative, deterrent, compensating, detective, corrective and recovery), you should be able to quickly identify each. The good news is that with a little thought you can figure this out instead of having to memorize each possible combination.

Questions

1. Which of the following are examples of a logical control?

A) Training, security policies and documentation, and managing risk

B) External lighting, locked doors, fences, card keys and security guards

C) Ensuring compliance with laws and regulations

D) Software or hardware elements such as hashing or encryption, firewalls and enforcing authentication

2. Which of the following best describes a defense in depth approach?

A) Forcing individuals to reauthenticate multiple times using the same mechanism

B) Using multiple instances of the same control in a layered approach

C) Requiring controls to pass multiple tests before being approved

D) Employing multiple categories of controls in a layered approach

3. Which of the following are examples of an administrative control?

A) Software or hardware elements such as hashing or encryption, firewalls and enforcing authentication

B) External lighting, locked doors, fences, card keys and security guards

C) Ensuring compliance with laws and regulations

D) Training, security policies and documentation, and managing risk

4. Which best describes a corrective control?

A) Fixing a component or system

B) Identifying an intruder

C) Providing an alternative control if the first choice is unavailable

D) Bringing environments back to normal operation

5. Which best describes a deterrent control?

A) Providing an alternative control if the first choice is unavailable

B) Discouraging an attacker

C) Fixing a component or system

D) Identifying an intruder

Chapter 4: Security Frameworks

A security framework is an approach on how to recognize and deal with weaknesses. In this section, we will cover the top 12 frameworks in use today.

ISO 27000 Series

There is only one framework geared specifically to security to speak of, and that is the ISO 27000 series. But first a little bit of history.

This framework started life in 1995 and was called the British Standard 7799, or BS7799 for short. Published by the British Standards Institute, it outlines how an Information Security Management System, also known as an ISMS, should be created and maintained. It was divided into two parts - Part 1 described controls and Part 2 showed how an ISMS could be setup. Part 2 could also be certified against by companies wishing to prove they were compliant with BS7799. A lot of companies adopted this framework, so it became a de facto standard.

Eventually, the need to globalize the standard was recognized so the International Organization for Standardization, more commonly referred to as the ISO, along with the _International Electrotechnical Commission_, or _IEC_, took it upon themselves to create the ISO 27000 series.

As a side note, ISO is a network of national standards institutes from over 160 countries and is responsible for creating a rather large number of standards that we use in everyday life. Ever heard of country codes? That was the ISO. What about language codes? The ISO. Currency codes, date/time formats, you name it – ISO has its fingerprints all over it.

The ISO 27000 series is made of many, many standards, all in the range of 27000-something. The first, ISO 27000, provides an overview and vocabulary used by the rest of the 27000 series. An _ISMS_ is a set of policies, processes and systems to manage risk, and the most well-known is contained in 27001. This provides guidance on establishing an ISMS and is the primary one for which companies gain certifications. _ISO 27002_ provides a code of practice, or general guidelines, for implementing an ISMS. _ISO 27001_ is the golden standard for the creation, implementation, control and improvement of an ISMS.

Enterprise Architecture Development

So, while the ISO 27000 series outlines a framework geared specifically towards security, there are several other frameworks that address the more general structure and behavior of an entire organization – they are called _Enterprise Architecture Frameworks_. These critters are used to build individual architectures that map to specific needs within a business - not the architecture itself, but rather guidance on how to build that architecture. Think of guidelines for creating a blueprint vs. creating the blueprint itself. If we want to build a house, we first must learn how to draw blueprints in general. Then, we create the actual blueprints for a house. The blueprints then tell the construction workers how to build the house. Likewise, an architecture framework tells us how to create an architecture (or how to create the blueprints), which will then instruct us on how operate a business (creating the blueprints). In terms of an ISMS, blueprints are functional definitions of how we integrate technology into our business processes.

One of the biggest advantages of using an enterprise framework is that it allows each group of people within an organization to view the business in terms they can understand. For example, the word 'protocol' means one thing to a software developer, a different thing to a network engineer, and represents a totally different concept to business people. A framework takes the same data or process and presents it in a way that is tailored to each audience's view point. While there are many enterprise architecture frameworks, we are going to cover only the most common 5.

Zachman

One of the earliest architectural frameworks was created by a man named John Zachman in the 1980s, and it carries his name as a result. The _Zachman_ framework is essentially a 2-dimensional matrix with the X-axis containing 5 different audiences, and the Y-axis listing 6 different views. The matrix defines a specific artifact at each intersection of an audience and view. The audiences, also sometimes called perspectives, are Executives, Business Managers, System Architects, Engineers, Technicians and finally, the entire Enterprise. The 6 views are What, How, Where, Who, When and Why.

The Open-Group Architecture Framework

The second framework was created by the US Department of Defense and is called _The Open-Group Architecture Framework_, or _TOGAF_ for short. It defines 4 architecture types, which are Business, Data, Application and Technology. Each type is created by using something called the _Architecture Development Method_, or _ADM_. This is an iterative cycle wherein the last step feeds back into the first step, like a snake eating its own tail. The goal is that after each iteration the overall process has been improved or updated to reflect changing requirements. Each iteration also addresses each of the four views.

Department of Defense Architecture Framework
The third framework was also created by the US government, who often has needs that are unique and don't necessarily translate well into the private sector - specifically the military. The _Department of Defense Architecture Framework_, or _DoDAF_, encompasses such things as command, control, surveillance and reconnaissance, among other things. One of its primary objectives is to ensure a common communication protocol as well as standard payloads.

Ministry of Defence Architecture Framework
Of course, it just wouldn't be right if the British did not have their own version of DoDAF, and so we have the fourth framework called the _Ministry of Defence Architecture Framework_, or _MoDAF_, which is built on top of and extends DoDAF.

Sherwood Applied Business Security Architecture
The last framework is like ISO 27000 in that it is geared towards security and defines an ISMS (also sometimes called an _Enterprise Security Architecture_). This framework goes by the name of _Sherwood Applied Business Security Architecture_, or _SABSA_ for short. It is very similar to the Zachman framework in that is a 2-dimensional matrix with the same X-Axis as Zachman – What, Why, How, Who, Where and When. However, the names are a little different. They are:

- _Assets_ (or What)
- _Motivation_ (or Why)
- _Process_ (How)
- _People_ (or Who)
- _Location_ (or Where)
- _Time_ (or When)

Additionally, the Y-Axis has 6 rows instead of Zachman's 7. They start very wide and narrow the focus as they proceed. In order from the top to the bottom, they are:

- Contextual
- Conceptual
- Logical
- Physical
- Component
- Operational

A notable difference with SABSA is that while it is a framework like the others we have been discussing, it is also a methodology and provides an actual process to follow and is geared toward security specifically. This is a big difference as compared to ISO 27000.

Before moving on it is important to note the distinction between an ISMS – remember that is an acronym for Information Security Management System – and an enterprise security framework. An ISMS specifies the components that need to be put in place to have a complete security program. A security architecture shows you how to integrate these components into the various layers within an organization. In a very simplistic view, the ISMS is a parts list, while the framework is the blueprint to follow when building something with those parts.

This brings us all the way back to the ISO 27000 series, whose primary purpose is to provide a list of required components. The architectures we discussed afterwards provide differing ways of applying the framework. As an example, you would use ISO 27001 to define the controls that are needed for an organization, and you could use TOGAF to implement those controls

Architecture Framework Terms
Regardless of the security framework you choose, there are 4 attributes each must provide to be effective.

Strategic Alignment
The first attribute is _strategic alignment_. An architecture is strategically aligned when it meets the needs of the business as well as all legal or regulatory requirements. Since security is usually a very technology-rich area, it is easy for it to either be ignorant of or ignore the business needs.

Business Enablement
Now, many times the business decision makers view security as being a roadblock to being more productive. Meanwhile, security people view their business counterparts as always trying to get around security. Instead, a good security architecture must enable the business to thrive by not getting in the way, but still providing proper security – this is the second attribute, and it is called _business enablement_. It is accomplished by acknowledging the importance of security measures while

keeping the reason for an organization's existence in mind at all times.

Process Enhancement
A proper balance of security will actually increase an organization's effectiveness, which is usually translated into some type of profit. The third attribute is *process enhancement*, and is achieved when security actually increases an existing process' efficiency. "How can this happen?" you might ask. Well, security forces us to take a closer look at existing processes, and while we are at it, often we find ways to improve efficiency that is not necessarily directly related to security.

Security Effectiveness
The fourth and last attribute that a good architecture should exhibit is called *security effectiveness*. This attribute is the one that is the most quantifiable of the four because it centers on processes that can easily be measured. Examples include return on investments (or ROI), how well the process meets service level agreements (also called SLAs) and providing dashboard views for management to monitor processes with. In short, security effectiveness ensures that the controls an ISMS specifies have been implemented by the architecture in a manner that has achieved the desired results.

We have mentioned several enterprise architectures so far, but we have yet to discuss system architectures. These two architectures are related somewhat but are mostly very different.

An enterprise architecture deals with the structure of an organization while a system architecture addresses software, hardware and networks. One or more system architectures comprise a single enterprise architecture.

Frameworks for Implementation

So, we have discussed the ISO 27000 series which defines an ISMS and the various controls we need. Then we described several architecture frameworks we can use to layout the ISMS controls for an organization, such as Zachman, TOGAF, DoDAF, MoDAF and SABSA. Now let's talk about how we can develop those controls by discussing 3 implementation frameworks.

COBIT
The first implementation framework is the Control Objectives for Information and Related Technologies, or COBIT for a much, much shorter name, which was created by ISACA (which is not an acronym by the way – it is the real name of an organization) working with the IT Governance Institute (ITGI). It defines 17 enterprise and 17 IT goals. At any time, the question "why are we doing this" can be asked, and the answer is an IT goal that points to an enterprise goal, that then points to a stakeholder goal.

It is based on 5 principles:

- Meeting stakeholder needs
- Covering the enterprise end-to-end
- Applying a single integrated framework
- Enabling a holistic approach
- Separating governance from management

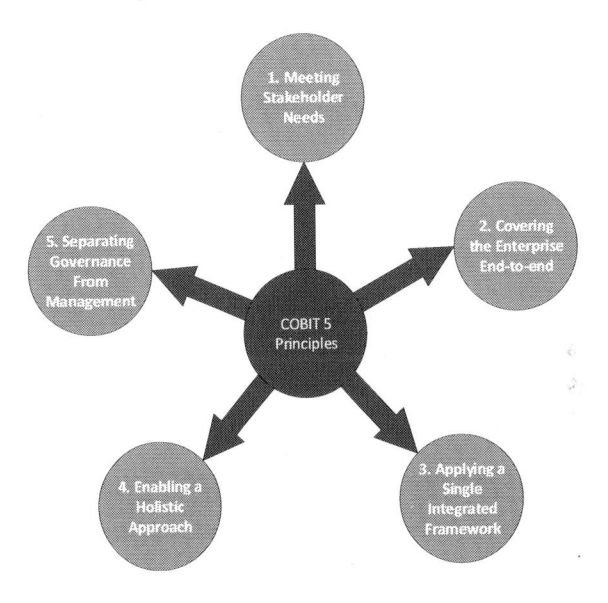

Figure 2: COBIT Principles

Most security compliance audits for private companies are based on COBIT. Note that COBIT is not strictly security-related but addresses many IT-related concerns. In short, COBIT is a framework of control objectives and provides for IT governance.

NIST SP 800-53
Whereas COBIT is primarily concerned with private industries, the US government has its own version created by the *National Institute of Standards and Technology*, or *NIST*. One of its publications is called the *SP 800-53* which is our second implementation framework and specifies the controls that federal agencies must implement. If an agency does not implement these controls, they are not in compliance with the Federal Information Security Management Act of 2002, commonly just called FISMA. SP 800-53 contains a list of 18 control categories. When federal agencies are audited for compliance this publication is heavily referenced.

While COBIT and SP 800-53 are geared for different audiences, private vs. federal, there is a great deal of overlap since they address the same issues. Whereas the private sector categorizes controls as administrative, technical or physical, federal agencies will label them as management, technical or operational. Just remember that administrative is the same as management, and physical is the same as operational. Both sectors use the label technical in the same manner.

COSO

The last implementation framework was created by the *Committee of Sponsoring Organizations*, or *COSO*, and is called *COSO Internal Control,* commonly referred to as *COSO IC*. It identifies 17 control principles grouped into 5 categories:

- Control Environments
- Risk Assessments
- Control Activities
- Information and Communication
- Monitoring Activities

COSO IC was created in the 1980s because of financial fraud and provides *corporate* governance. COBIT was derived from COSO IC, but COBIT provides for *IT* governance instead. In many ways, COBIT is a subset of COSO IC.

Process Development

Now that we have covered how to develop security controls using COBIT, SP 800-53 and COSO IC, we turn our attention to how to manage them. We will look at 3 process management tools.

ITIL

ITIL was developed in the 1980s in the UK and has become the de facto standard for IT management best practices. ITIL bridges the gap between geek-speak and business-speak, by focusing on SLAs between the IT department and its internal customer within an organization. The main stages are design, transition and operation. ITIL tracks efforts beginning with the design and follows the effort as it transitions to full operation. Each stage has between 3 and 5 steps.

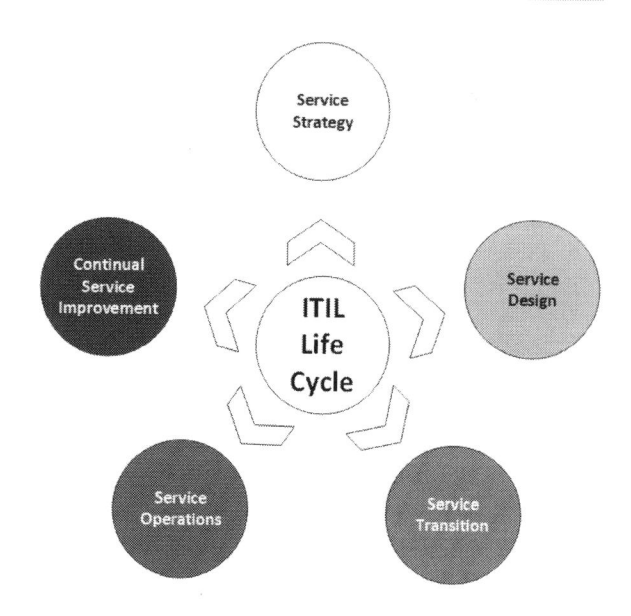

Figure 3: ITIL Stages

Six Sigma

In the 1980s Total Quality Management, or TQM, came on the scene, but was eventually replaced by something called *Six Sigma*. Its primary objective is to measure process quality by using statistical calculations and works to identify and remove defects. A sigma rating is applied to a process to indicate the percentage of defects it contains.

Capability Maturity Model Integration

The last process management tool we will look at is called the *capability maturity model integration*, or *CMMI*. It was created by the Carnegie Mellon University for the US Department of Defense and determines the maturity of an organization's processes. This tool is more heavily used within the security industry than either ITIL or Six Sigma, and CMMI is designed to make improvements in an incremental and standard manner.

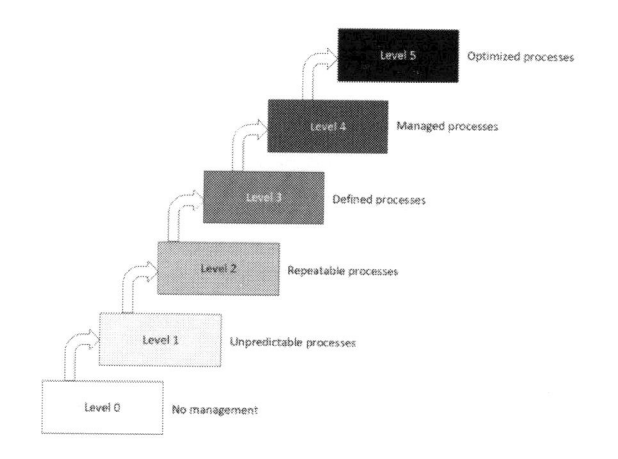

Figure 4: CMMI Levels

CMMI recognizes that it is difficult to become "better", because "better" is hard to quantify or measure. It therefore provides a way to categorize how mature each process is and provides a holistic view of all process maturity side-by-side.

6 levels are defined:

- Level 0, where there is no management.
- Level 1, in which we have unpredictable processes.
- Level 2, where we have repeatable processes.
- Level 3, where we first have defined processes.
- Level 4, which has managed processes.
- Level 5, where we encounter optimized processes.

The Process Life Cycle

Now that we have covered the top three ways to develop processes, we need to discuss how to keep those processes up-to-date and healthy. To do this, we must recognize that the *process life-cycle* has four steps that are another example of the 'snake eating its tail' approach – instead of having a start and stop date, the last step feeds right back into the first step and starts a new iteration. The four steps are plan, implement, operate and evaluate, which starts the plan step all over again.

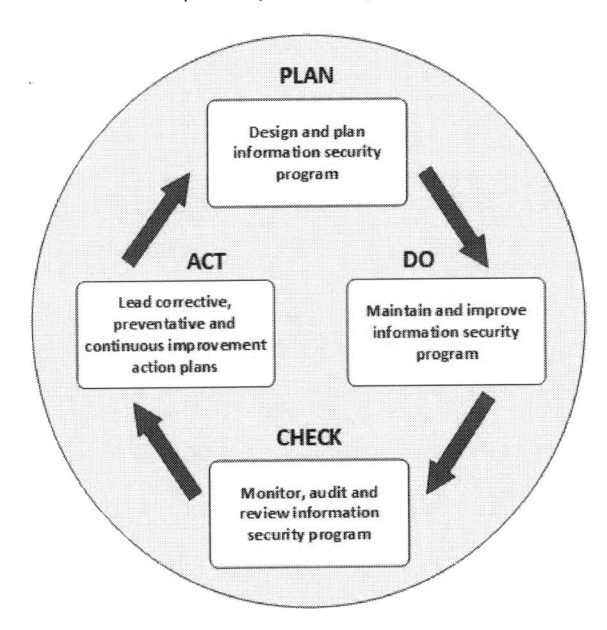

Figure 5: PDCA

Plan

- Establish management and oversight committees
- Identify business drivers and threats
- Perform a risk assessment
- Create security architectures for the business, data, application and infrastructure
- Select possible solutions for the problems identified
- Get management approval to move to the next step

Implement

- Assign duties
- Establish baselines
- Put into operation security policies
- Identify data that needs to be secured
- Create blueprints.
- Implement controls based on the blueprints
- Implement solutions to monitor the controls based on the blueprints
- Establish goals, SLAs and metrics based on the blueprints

Operate

- Follow established procedures to ensure baselines meet the blueprints
- Execute audits
- Execute tasks defined by the blueprints
- Ensure SLAs are met

Evaluate

- Review logs, audit results, metrics and SLAs
- Determine if the blueprint goals have been met
- Hold quarterly meetings with the steering committee
- Identify actions to improve as an input into the first step (which is the Plan step)

Now let's bring all the security framework components we have discussed together in one example. Suppose you are hired to create a comprehensive security program for a company that has virtually nothing in-place. The first thing you would do is to look at the ISO 27000 for guidance on how to create an ISMS, which will give you a shopping list of all the controls that you can or should put into place. Then you choose a security framework to help you create the ISMS – in this example we will go with TOGAF – and you start the process life cycle.

First up you gather the right people to oversee the effort, identify what needs to be done and identify possible solutions – that is the _Plan_ step. Then you create blueprints and implement them – that is the _Implement_ step. All the while you are continuously making sure that the three framework attributes (strategic alignment, business enablement and process enhancement) are being monitored to ensure success. At this point, you have selected and implemented various controls. The categorization of controls into administrative, technical and physical along with the functional grouping (such as preventative, deterrent, etc.) will have been a great help.

Now it is time to go live. Or is it? Ideally, you will have an external party come in, snoop around, and give you a list of everything you did wrong. More than likely the auditor will check your implementation against COBIT to figure this out, since you are not working for a federal agency. In that case NIST SP 800-53 would have been used.

Once you have addressed any audit shortcomings, you will enter the _Maintain_ step. At this point you will want to manage the process using ITIL, Six Sigma or CMMI. This will help you in the _Evaluate_ step, which then feeds back into _Plan_.

Chapter 4: Security Frameworks

Questions

1. Which of the following best describes the Zachman framework?

A) Defines 4 types - Business, Data, Application and Technology - created by the Architecture Development Method (ADM)

B) A 2-dimensional matrix with 5 different audiences on the Y-axis, and 6 different views on the Y-axis

C) Created by the US military and ensure a common communication protocol as well as standard payloads

D) The British version of DoDAF

2. Which of the following best describes ISO 27000 series?

A) Provides a code of practice for implementing an ISMS

B) Geared specifically to security

C) A set of policies, processes and systems to manage risk

D) Sets forward an ISMS

3. Which of the following best describes security effectiveness?

A) Security actually increases an existing process' efficiency

B) Meets the needs of the business as well as all legal or regulatory requirements

C) Ensures that ISMS controls have achieved the desired results

D) Acknowledging the importance of security while not losing sight of the reason for an organization's existence

4. Which of the following best describes ITIL?

A) Provides corporate governance

B) Focuses on SLAs between IT and internal customers

C) Measures process quality using statistical calculations by identifying defects

D) Determines the maturity of an organization's processes by assigning 1 of 6 levels

5. Which of the following best describes SABSA?

A) Similar to Zachman but focused on security

B) A 2-dimensional matrix with 5 different audiences on the Y-axis, and 6 different views on the Y-axis

C) Created by the US military and ensure a common communication protocol as well as standard payloads

D) Defines 4 types - Business, Data, Application and Technology - created by the Architecture Development Method (ADM)

Chapter 5: Computer Crime Law

Law

All the processes, frameworks and architectures we have discussed to this point exist for one overarching reason – we don't want bad things to happen to our organization. Unfortunately, sometimes this happens despite our best efforts, and when it does we need some type of recourse to go after the bad guys. Cyberlaw is the answer, which is a loosely-defined term applied to any law that deals with computer-based crime. The bad news is that because technology moves so quickly the law will never be able to catch up completely. The good news is that that latency has been decreasing each year.

Current law recognizes three different categories of computer crime:

- *Computer-assisted*, or the computer is a tool.
- *Computer-targeted*, or the computer is the victim (and indirectly the computer's owner).
- *Computer is incidental*, or the computer was involved but was not the victim or did not play a significant role in the crime.

An example of a computer-assisted crime is stealing money from a bank across the Internet. The most common example of a computer-targeted attack is a denial of service (or DoS) attack. Sometimes a computer could be viewed simultaneously as a tool and a victim – the litmus test on deciding which should apply is the answer to this question: "Could the crime have been committed before computers existed?" Just because money was stolen across the Internet does not mean it could not have happened before computers existed. Just go to any good old western where bank robbers are holding up a bank in some dusty western town. However, you don't see a whole lot of buffer overflow attacks in the Wild West, and so that would most certainly be a computer-targeted crime. One way in which a computer could be incidental in an attack is if it was used to temporarily store stolen or illegal goods, such as child pornography.

So, why do we need to have these three categories? It all comes down to how existing laws are applied. Based on the role a computer played, existing law could be used to prosecute the perpetrators. This allows us to have applicable laws without having to keep up-to-the-minute with new technologies.

Unfortunately, the Internet affords hackers a lot of anonymity, so prosecution is a lot of times extremely difficult. Oftentimes attacks are carried out by a *botnet*, or a group of compromised systems that are under the hacker's control. These systems are referred to as a *zombie* and the software the hacker has surreptitiously installed on them is called a *bot*. When a botnet is used to carry out an attack, it can be very difficult to unmask the actual perpetrator, as the attacks seem to be coming from somewhere else.

While there are laws that require organizations, particularly financial institutions, to report any security breaches, the clear majority of attacks go unreported. The top reasons are fear of damage to the organization's reputation, interruption of business and potential damages that might need to be paid due to loss of customer data.

As the world becomes more and more reliant on computers, organizations have slowly realized that protecting data is just as important as protecting more tangible assets such as buildings or inventory. Unfortunately, figuring out what is sensitive data and where it should be kept is still a challenge for most.

Computer Crime

In the early days of the Internet, most hacking activities were relatively benign – most were centered on defacing sites, causing problems for some business or in many cases the hacker was in it just for the fun and bragging rights. This created a new class of hackers called *script kiddies*. This group was (and still is) made up of unsophisticated individuals who know just enough about pre-built tools to point them at a network and see what damage they can do.

As more and more sensitive data was accessible across the Internet, however, criminals became increasingly serious about exploiting weaknesses to gain access to data or information. That was soon followed by leveraging computers and networks to cause real-world harm, such as the Stuxnet virus that wiped out Iran's centrifuges around 2010.

There are two types of serious hackers. This first are those that randomly sniff around for weaknesses, and then try to exploit them when found. This is akin to a thief who drives down streets looking for a house with no one home to rob. The second group is far more dangerous – they will target a specific person, group or organization, and will patiently probe for weaknesses, often weeks or months at a time, until the desired access has been gained. This type of criminal is called an *advanced persistent threat*, or *APT*, and is usually a group of individuals who will leave back doors, or covert back channels, on systems that can be later controlled at-will.

Gaining access to an environment normally requires the following steps:

1) Phishing and zero-day attacks to gain a foothold
2) Install back doors on vulnerable machines
3) Lateral movement to other accounts or systems
4) Gather data from servers and prepare for exfiltration
5) Exfiltrate the data via various means to a compromised machine hosted elsewhere

OECD

When cybercrime passes international boundaries, the possibility of prosecution drops significantly. This is due primarily to differing judicial systems, the lack of applicable laws in some countries, and sometimes governments just don't want to cooperate for political or military reasons. The Council of Europe Convention on Cybercrime is one attempt to standardize how international computer crimes are addressed.

Additionally, the *OECD* is an international organization that has provided guidelines on how to deal with data that is transferred between countries. The 8 core principles are:

- *Collection Limitation*, which states that the collection of personal data must be limited and lawful, and with the knowledge of the subject.
- *Data Quality*, which states that personal data should be kept complete and current and be relevant for the purpose.
- *Purpose Specification*, which states that subjects should be notified of the reason for the collection of personal data and should only be used for that purpose.
- *Use Limitation*, which states that if the data is to be used for any other purpose than stated, the subject must give consent or law must provide authority.
- *Security Safeguards*, which states that safeguards should be put into place to protect the collected data.
- *Openness*, which states that practices and policies with regard to personal data should be openly communicated, and subjects should be able to easily determine what data has been collected and where it is stored.
- *Individual Participation*, which states that subjects must be able to find out if an organization has their personal data and should be able to correct errors.
- *Accountability*, which states that organizations should be accountable for complying with measures that support the previous principles.

Safe Harbor

Members of the European Union take privacy concerns much more seriously than most other countries, and this is reflected in the *European Union Principles on Privacy*. The principles and how they must be followed are outlined in the EUs' *Data Protection Directive*. Any company dealing with EU members must follow these principles when it comes to private data.

A special framework has been developed for US and EU data transfer requirements called the *Safe Harbor Privacy Principles* (usually just called *Safe Harbor*) made up of 7 rules that are very similar to the OECD principles.

- *Notice*, meaning that individuals must be notified when personal data is to be collected.
- *Choice*, which states that individuals must be able to opt out of the collection.
- *Onward Transfer*, which requires that transfer of data to third parties happen only if the third party follows adequate data protection principles.
- *Security*, requiring that reasonable effort must be made to prevent loss of collected data.
- *Data Integrity*, which states that collected data must be relevant and reliable for the purpose it was collected for.
- *Access*, which ensures that individuals must be able to access the information held about them and correct errors.
- *Enforcement*, requiring that an effective means of enforcing these rules exists.

Import and Export Law

Each country normally has its own laws regarding goods that can be imported or exported. However, the *Wassenaar Arrangement* is an agreement that currently 41 countries, including the United States, follow in regard to importing and exporting goods. This arrangement is intended to prevent the buildup of military capabilities in any one country such that all countries remain on a relatively equal footing in regard to military capabilities. Of the 9 categories that are defined one, 'Part2: Information Security' deals with the exchange of cryptography, which is a dual-use good, meaning that it has both civilian and military uses. Some countries appear on the 'offensive' list, usually because they are associated with state-sponsored terrorism or have unstable governments with Weapons of Mass Destruction (WMDs). Export of cryptography may be prohibited to these countries. Other countries may restrict import of cryptography because the governments of those countries do not want their citizens to be able to conceal information – this is usually Big Brother countries such as China, Russia, Iran, etc.

Types of Legal Systems

Countries have various legal systems, and it is important to understand the difference between them when dealing with cross-country security concerns. Let's examine 5 different types.

Civil (Code) Law System

The *civil law system*, sometimes called code law, is used in European countries such as France and Spain. It is based on rules, as opposed to precedence as you might find in the United States or the UK. The civil legal system is the most widespread system in the world and the most common in Europe. Lower courts are not compelled to follow the decisions made by upper courts.

Common Law System

The next system is called the *common law system* and is based on precedence, instead of strict rules that you will find in civil legal systems. The United States is based on this type of legal system. Judges and a jury of peers are a prominent feature of this system, and higher court decisions must be recognized by lower courts. The system is broken down into three subsets of law.

Before continuing note that the terms 'common law system' and 'common law' are two different things, as are 'civil law system' and 'civil law'. Don't get them confused.

Criminal

The first of the three law subsets of the Common Law System is called *criminal law* and is based on common law (which are laws based on customs or precedents), statutory law (laws that are written down) or a combination of both. With criminal law, some type of government law has been violated, and the law addresses behavior that is harmful to society and punishment involves loss of freedom and/or monetary fines. To be convicted, guilt beyond reasonable doubt must be established. Cases are usually brought about by government prosecutors with a guilty or not guilty verdict.

Civil/Tort

The second is *civil* law (also called Tort law) which is an offshoot of criminal law and deals with wrongs committed against an individual or company that has resulted in injury or damages. In this case, the defendant is judged by what a 'prudent man' would do in the same situation. If found liable, monetary reparations are usually made by the defendant, but loss of freedom is never a result. Examples of offenses include trespassing, battery, product liability and negligence. Cases are usually brought about by private parties with a liable or not liable for damages verdict.

Administrative

The last type of law under the Common Law system is called *administrative law*, and it addresses issues such as international trade, manufacturing, environment and immigration. Administrative law deals with regulatory standards as defined by government agencies, and is almost always restricted to companies that fall under these regulations.

In summary, *criminal law* deals with an individual breaking a government law, results in a guilty/not guilty verdict, and can involve imprisonment. *Civil law* deals with wrongs committed against an individual or company, uses a prudent man model to decide a liable/not liable verdict, and never involves imprisonment. *Administrative law* deals with regulatory standards and applies only to companies failing under those regulations.

Customary Law System

Now that we have discussed both the Civil Law and Common Law systems, let's move on to the third type called *customary law.* This mainly deals with personal conduct and behavior, and is based on traditions and customs of a specific region. You will very rarely find this type of system operating on its own – instead it is usually mixed with another system, such as in China and India. If found guilty under this system, restitution is normally made in the form of money or services rendered.

Religious Law System

Another system that is becoming more apparent in the world at large is called *religious law*, which is based on religious beliefs of that region. In Islamic countries, the law is based on the Koran, but is different in every Islamic country. Under this system, clerics have a high degree of authority and cover all aspects of human life. Rather than create laws, lawmakers and scholars attempt to discover the truth of law from the accepted religious books. This type of law is commonly found in Muslim countries or regions.

Mixed Law System
And finally, we have the _mixed law_ system, in which two or more of the previously mentioned systems are used together. Examples of countries with this type of system are Holland, Canada and South Africa.

Before we leave this section on law systems, let's revisit the Common Law system one more time to point a few important details. It is possible to be found not guilty under criminal law, but convicted under civil law. This is because criminal law requires proof beyond reasonable doubt, while civil law only requires you to prove the defendant did not act 'prudently'. The O.J. Simpson case is the best example of this outcome, as he was found not guilty of murder under criminal law (and therefore remained free), but was found liable for damages under civil law and was forced to pay reparations to the victim's families. The reason for this is that the burden of proof is lighter in civil law than in criminal law.

Intellectual Property

All the law that we have discussed to this point deals with who is right or wrong. But now we are moving into law that allows individuals or companies to protect what is rightly theirs from illegal duplication or use – this is called _Intellectual Property Law_. To protect intellectual property in a court, a company must be able to show that it exercised due care in protecting the asset in question. For example, if an employee shares some sensitive information with a friend, and then is terminated or prosecuted by their employer, the company must show that it took steps to protect the information and told its employees not to share the information – this is called _due care_, meaning that reasonable steps were taken to secure the information. There are two types of _intellectual property_ – _industrial_, such as inventions or patents, industrial designs and trademarks, and secondly _copyrighted_ property including literary and artistic works.

Trade Secret
Now, a _trade secret_ is something a company creates or owns that is crucial to its survival and profitability. One of the most well-known trade secrets (well, well-known in that everyone knows it exists but not what the actual secret is) is the formula for Coca-Cola. If something is to be called a trade secret then it must be kept, well – secret –

and steps must be taken to ensure its confidentiality. Trade secrets do not expire unless the secret gets out or no longer provides a benefit to the company.

Most companies with trade secrets require employees to sign a Non-Disclosure Agreement (commonly just called an NDA) that prohibits them from revealing the trade secret to anyone, even after they are no longer employed by the company. This agreement is binding and legally enforceable in civil court. Violating an NDA is just cause for terminating an employee.

Copyright
You have probably seen the word _copyright_ any number of places, in recent years probably at the bottom of a website. _Copyright law_ gives the author of a work the rights to control the display, adaptation, reproduction or distribution of that original work – it protects the expression of the idea rather than the idea itself. Whereas trade secrets cover a specific resource and never expire, a copyright is good for a limited amount of time and covers the expression of the idea, which is very nebulous at best. Of course, if you look at what copyright covers it will make a lot more sense why that is – music, sculptures, movies, writings, photos, illustrations, plays, source code and architecture are just a few areas. Any of these can easily be modified or adapted for other use and are covered under the Federal Copyright Act. While the ubiquitous copyright symbol (©) is not required, it is recommended so that innocence cannot be claimed when copying a protected work. Note that copyright law does not cover processes or procedures - that will be covered in patents in just a few minutes.

Specific to the computer industry, copyright law protects both source code and object code. The structure of source code _may_ be protected, but user interfaces certainly fall within the realm of this law. Since the advent of peer-to-peer sharing networks such as Bit Torrent, it has become increasingly difficult to prosecute copyright violations, as law enforcement has finite resources and copyright violators are not at the top of the list. _Warez_ is a term that refers to copyrighted works that are distributed without paying royalties or fees.

Trademark
Whereas copyright law protects original works, _trademark law_ protects a name, symbol, word, sound, shape, color or any combination thereof. A _trademark_ represents a company's brand identity to its potential customers. A number or a common word cannot be trademarked, leaving many companies to create a brand-new word for

their company so that it can be trademarked, such as 'Verizon', 'Exxon' or 'Ikea'. On the other hand, unique colors can be trademarked, such as UPS Brown. International trademark law is overseen by the World Intellectual Property Organization, or WIPO, which is an agency of the United Nations.

Patent
To protect an invention, _patents_ are given to individuals or companies to provide them ownership of the invention and to prevent others from copying or using the invention without permission. A patent is the strongest form of intellectual property protection. To be considered for a patent, an invention must be novel, useful and not obvious, which means that you cannot patent fire or the color yellow. Patents always have an expiration date. This is the reason for generic drugs costing so much less than the brand name – pharmaceutical companies spend huge amounts of money to develop new drugs, and if it were not for patent law they would not be able to make a profit. No profit, no research, and our health declines. To allow companies to recoup their investment, but to prevent a monopoly on much-needed drugs, the patent office grants the patent for 20 years only, after which time any company can manufacture and distribute the drug royalty-free.

In the computer industry, algorithms are commonly patented. Unfortunately, many times another party may write an algorithm from scratch that is so similar to the patented work that the second party is forced to alter it even though no intentional copying took place. Patent infringement prosecution is a matter of everyday life in the computer industry – companies sue and are counter-sued continuously. To make matters worse, a new class of businesses called Non-Practicing Entities, or NPEs buy up patents simply for the opportunity to sue companies who infringe on the patents. These companies are sometimes referred to as 'patent trolls'. Patent research is absolutely required before investing resources into a new technology or methodology.

Protection of Intellectual Property
In addition to protection of intellectual property through litigation means, a company must show due care by properly classify the data and implement sufficient protection. The IT department must ensure there is a proper environment in which to store the data and log all access to the data for subsequent auditing. The data should be available on a need-to-know basis only, and authorized employees must be informed of the expected behavior. If these steps have not been taken, most types of litigation will fail as the company has not shown due care.

Software piracy occurs when protected works or data is duplicated or used without gaining permission from and providing proper compensation to the author. Most commercial software is accompanied by a license that spells out the terms under which the third party may use the software. There are four types of software licensing:

1) _Freeware_, or no restrictions on the use or redistribution of software.
2) _Shareware_ (sometimes called trialware) is software that is free for a period of time, during which some features may be disabled; after the period expires, the user is asked to pay for the continued use.
3) _Commercial_ requires an upfront price to be paid for a copy or a license.
4) _Academic_, which allows for academic purposes at a reduced price.

Commercial software is often sold in bulk licenses, or master agreements, meaning multiple users or seats may use the software simultaneously. Another frequent method is to use an _End User License Agreement_, or _EULA_, to communicate the licensing requirements. A third type is to use software that tracks usage and either charges the user(s) or prevents use accordingly. Violations of licensing agreements may at times find the security officer liable as well as the company.

The Federation Against Software Theft (FAST) and the Business Software Alliance promote the enforcement of software rights to combat piracy. The Asia-Pacific region (which includes India and China among many others) is by far the worst offender when it comes to software piracy rates with losses in the $50 billion to $100 billion range annually.

Many companies think that not delivering source code protects their algorithms. Unfortunately, it is relatively easy to decompile programs and examine the algorithm in detail. The good news is that if someone does this and tries to violate the copyright or patent, the _Digital Millennium Copyright Act_ (_DMCA_) comes into play as it prohibits attempts to circumvent copyright protection mechanisms. This law is a slippery slope however – you can be charged simply if you figure out how to defeat the mechanism even if you did not violate the copyright itself. The European Union has since passed a similar law called the _Copyright Directive_.

Privacy

We previously touched on privacy data when discussing OECD and the Safe Harbor law. At the time, we simply used the term 'private data', but now we need to dive a little bit deeper by talking about _Personally Identifiable Information_, or _PII_.

PII is any data that can be used to uniquely identify, contact or locate an individual, or that can be used with other sources to uniquely identify a person. PII is sensitive data because it is often used to carry out identity theft or other crimes. Different countries have varying definitions of what falls under the PII umbrella.

The US _Office of Management and Budget_ (_OMB_) defines PII as information that can be used to uniquely identify a person – they left out the contact or locate bits we listed earlier. That doesn't mean that an address is not considered to be PII – it simply means that it is included because of the ability to identify a person, not because it allows you to contact them. Some typical PII components are:

- Full Name
- National ID number
- IP Address
- Vehicle registration number
- Driver's license number
- Photo, fingerprints or handwriting
- Credit card numbers
- Digital identities
- Birthdate
- Birthplace
- Genetic information

Federal Privacy Act of 1974

One of the first laws passed to address privacy data was the Federal Privacy Act of 1974, or FPA. The law stated that federal agencies could collect and store information about an individual's academic, medical, financial, criminal and employment history only if the agency had a necessary and relevant need to do so. This data could not be shared with other agencies or private parties without the individual's written permission.

Federal Information Security Management Act of 2002

The Federal Information Security Management Act of 2002, or FISMA as it is usually referred to, built upon FPA by requiring all federal agencies to effectively secure the privacy data by protecting both the information and information systems that had access to the data. This applied not only to the agency itself, but any third-party groups that was allowed access to the data.

FISMA requires high-level officials of each agency to hold annual reviews of the information security programs and report the results to the _OMB_), which in turn reports to congress on the level of compliance achieved. FISMA requires the following:

- Inventory of information systems
- Categorization of the information and information systems according to risk
- Security controls
- Risk assessment
- System security plan
- Certification and accreditation
- Continuous monitoring

If you will recall, NIST SP 800-53, which is an enterprise architecture framework, provides a list of all security controls federal agencies should implement to remain in compliance with FISMA.

Department of Veterans Affairs Information Security Protection Act

Because it is a federal agency, the Department of Veteran Affairs is subject to FISMA regulations. However, in 2006 a laptop with a large amount of very sensitive data was stolen from an employee's home, revealing that the agency was in very poor compliance with FISMA. The government reacted by passing the _Department of Veterans Affairs Information Security Protection Act_ to place additional requirements on that one agency alone due to its extreme failure to remain in compliance.

Health Insurance Portability and Accountability Act

The _Health Insurance Portability and Accountability Act_, or _HIPAA_ as it is more commonly called, is specific to the health care industry, and in particular to patient records. It defines a classification of data known as Patient Health Information, or PHI – this is very close to the same thing as PII, but adds a few details specific to the health industry. This law defines rules for any facility (not just government agencies) that creates, access, shares or destroys patient data.

HIPPA requires steep fines for violations –$100 for each violation up to $1,500,00 per year per standard if mistakes are made. If it is deemed that the act of improper disclosure was intentional by an individual, the fine can be as much as $50,000 and up to one year in prison. If the information is obtained or disclosed under false pretenses, the fine goes up to $250,000 and 10 years in prison. However, HIPAA does not require notification of data breaches.

Health Information Technology for Economic and Clinical Health Act (HITECH)

The Health Information Technology for Economic and Clinical Health Act, or HITECH for short, was created in 2009. Subtitle D deals with the electronic transmission of health information and helps enforce HIPPA rules. It introduces categories of violations with four corresponding penalties, and sets the maximum penalty amount to $1,500,000 for all violations of a single provision. Another important aspect of HITECH is that it directs the US Secretary of Health and Services (HHS) to provide guidance on effective controls to protect data. Companies that comply with this guidance do not have to report data breaches; otherwise data breaches must be reported to HHS and the affect individuals within 60 days of the discovery.

USA Patriot Act

In response to the attacks of 9/11, in 2001 the US Congress passed the very long-titled Uniting and Strengthening America by Providing Tools Required to Intercept and Obstruct Terrorism Act, or simply the PATRIOT act. It was a far-reaching piece of legislation that gave the government many, many powers, including:

- Reduced restrictions on law enforcement when searching electronic records
- Allowed greater foreign intelligence gathering within the US
- Gave the Security of Treasury greater power to regulate financial transactions
- Broadened the ability to detain or deport immigrants suspected of terrorism
- Expanded the definition of terrorism to include domestic terrorism, thereby expanding the PATRIOT Act's reach

The feature of the PATRIOT Act that is most troubling to many is the extent to which the government can now monitor individual's electronic communications at will.

Gramm-Leach-Bliley Act

Going back a few years, in 1999 the _Gramm-Leach-Bliley Act_ was passed, known as _GLBA_ and as the Financial Services Modernization Act of 1999. GLBA requires financial institutions to create privacy notices giving their customers the ability to opt out of sharing their information with third parties. Some major features are:

- _Financial Privacy Rule_, requiring a privacy notice to be provided on how data is used, and allow the customer to opt out.
- _Safeguards Rule_, which requires a written security plan to protect customer data.
- _Pretexting Protection_, which implements safeguards against social engineering.

In the event of a data breach, the financial institution must determine if the customer information has or will be misused, and if so it is required to report the breach to federal regulators, applicable law enforcement and the affected customers.

Personal Information Protection and Electronic Documents Act

Outside of the US, Canada has passed a law called the Personal Information Protection and Electronic Documents Act, or PIPEDA. Its primary goal is to deal with the protection of privacy data collected by businesses, and to provide assurance to other countries doing business with Canada that all data crossing the border is secure (in other words, e-commerce).

Payment Card Industry Data Security Standard

While we are on the subject of e-commerce, the protection of credit card data is the reason that the _Payment Card Industry Data Security Standard_, or _PCI DSS_, or sometimes just PCI, was created. Originally each major credit card company (Visa, MasterCard, American Express and Discover) had their own standards but eventually joined together to create PCI DSS. The PCI Security Standards Council was created to enforce the PCI DSS. Note that this is not a law, but credit card companies will not work with a company that is not PCI compliant. This is a fine example of an industry regulating itself so that government bodies do not have to become involved. Having said that, Minnesota has passed a law requiring PCI compliance where applicable.

PCI DSS applies to any company that processes, transmits, stores or accepts credit card data. It provides 12 primary requirements broken down into six categories. PCI DSS 3.1 no longer recognizes SSL or earlier versions of TLS (earlier than 1.2) to be secure.

Economic Espionage Act of 1996

In 1996, the _Economic Espionage Act_ was passed to define who could investigate data breaches. It also categorized trade secrets into technical, business, engineering, scientific and financial categories. This law specifically protects intellectual property.

The last topic we wish to cover regarding privacy is that of employees. State regulations vary, so a company operating in multiple states must take this into account. The US constitution guarantees a 'reasonable expectation of privacy'. A company can align themselves with this constitutional right by requiring employees to sign an agreement that outlines the company policy.

Now that we have reached the end of the discussion on privacy, let's review rather quickly what we have gone over. The government has passed several laws that are applicable to federal agencies only – FPA, VA Information Security Protection Act, FISMA and the PATRIOT act. Laws applicable to companies are HIPAA, HITECH, GLBA and PIPEDA. The only self-regulation we discussed was PCI DSS. With that, it's time to move on to the subject of data breaches.

International Data Breaches

While the US has a number of laws on the book to address data breaches, the EU has standardized data breach notification as part of the EU Data Protection Regulation, requiring at least a partial notification to take place within 24 hours of discovery, and a complete notification within three days.

There are several countries that do not have any data breach requirements at all, including China, Hong Kong, India, Israel and Russia.

Questions

1. Which of the following promotes the enforcement of software rights in order to combat piracy?

    A) The Copyright Directive

    B) LAST

    C) DMCA

    D) Business Software Alliance

2. What are the three categories of computer crime law?

    A) Computer-actuated, computer-targeted and computer-is-targeted

    B) Computer-actuated, computer-subject and computer-is-incidental

    C) Computer-assisted, computer-subject and computer-is-targeted

    D) Computer-assisted, computer-targeted and computer-is-incidental

3. Which best describes the Security Safeguards OECD principle?

    A) Practices and policies with regard to personal data should be directly communicated, and subjects should be able to easily determine what data has been collected and where it is stored

    B) Measures should be put into place to protect the collected data

    C) Subjects must be able to find out if an organization has their personal data and be able to correct errors

    D) The collection of personal data must be constrained and lawful, and with the knowledge of the subject

4. What are the five types of legal systems?

    A) Civil, Conventional, Customary, Religious and Varied

    B) Domestic, Conventional, Customary, Religious and Varied

    C) Domestic, Common, Customary, Religious and Mixed

    D) Civil, Common, Customary, Religious and Mixed

5. Which best describes literary and artistic works?

    A) Copyright

    B) Industrial Property

    C) Patent

    D) Trademark

Chapter 6: Goals, Strategies, Policies, Standards, Baselines, Guidelines and Procedures

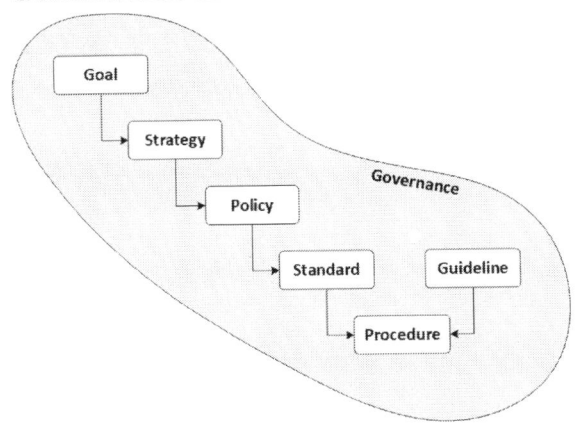

Figure 6: From Goals to Procedures

Goals and Strategies

Put simply – a goal is where we want to be, and a strategy is how we get there. The strategy does not tell us what technology to use or details of how we will execute – it remains very high-level.

Policies

Leaving computer crime law behind us, let's move into discussing security policies. Every company should have a *security policy*, which is a high-level statement that describes how security works within the organization. A security policy can be one of three types. First, there needs to be an *organizational security policy*, also called a *master security policy*, acting as an umbrella for the other two types. This policy dictates how a security program will be constructed, sets the various goals and describes how enforcement will be implemented. This is also where laws and regulations are addressed, and provides direction on the amount of risk management is willing to accept. The organizational security policy should be periodically reviewed and updated, and documentation should be version-controlled and applicable for several years into the future.

Policies underneath the organizational security policy are called *issue-specific policies*, and are sometimes referred to as a *functional policy*. An issue-specific policy provides more detail around areas that need further explanation, such as email use, use-of-Internet policy or physical security. However, security policies must be worded in such a way that they are not reliant on a specific technology or implementation.

The third type of security policy deals with systems, and is called, appropriately enough, a *system-specific policy*. This type of policy is expected to contain details that are specific to a system, but still be sufficiently generic to allow for other technologies and solutions.

Policies can also be categorized in a different manner:

- *Informative* informs employees on a broad range of topics in an unenforceable manner.
- *Regulatory* addresses regulatory requirements for a specific industry such as GLBA, PCI or HIPAA.
- *Advisory* advises employees on enforceable rules governing actions and behaviors.

Standards

Whereas policies establish the corporate strategy, a *standard* provides instruction on how to meet the policy. For example, while a policy may state that 'All employees should be readily identifiable at any time while on-premises" a standard may state "All employees must wear a departmental name badge with photo above the waistline and in full view at all times when moving through secured areas". Standards must always be enforced.

Another way of looking at policies vs. standards is a strategic vs. tactical viewpoint. Policies are strategic – a high-level view of *where* we want to get to. Standards are tactical – they represent specific tools we use to *get* to where want to go.

Baselines

While we're on the subject of getting somewhere, how do you know when you have arrived? If I drive from Los Angeles to New York, I know I have reached my destination when I see the 'Welcome To New York' sign. Whenever I move around New York, if I ever see the same sign, I know that I am leaving the city limits and going the wrong way.

When talking about policies and standards, that sign would be referred to as my baseline. Anytime a change is made, we need to look around and make sure we are not going backwards. Whenever a control has been put in place to mitigate a risk, we need to establish a *baseline* so we can tell later if we have inadvertently increased our risk when changes are made. Keep in mind that baselines do not have to deal with technology – a standard may state that all package deliveries must be made to a specific door – this creates a baseline of protection that can be evaluated from time to time. In summary, a baseline is a minimum level of security an organization wishes to maintain.

Guidelines

In contrast to standards, which are usually expressed in very explicit rules, sometimes we need to be a little more flexible to accommodate unforeseen circumstances. These are called _guidelines_ and reflect recommendations and guides for employees when a specific standard does not really apply.

Procedures

Whereas policies tell us where we want to go, guidelines provide recommendations, and standards provide the tools - _procedures_ give us the step-by-step instructions on how to do it.

Questions

1. Which of the following provides tools on how to meet a policy?

   A) Baselines

   B) Procedures

   C) Guidelines

   D) Standards

2. What are the three policy categories?

   A) Informative, compulsory and suggested

   B) Informative, regulatory and advisory

   C) Informative, controlling and suggested

   D) Educational, regulatory and advisory

3. Which of the following provides more detail around areas that need further explanation?

   A) Organizational security policy

   B) Issues-specific policy

   C) System-specific policy

   D) Security policy

4. Which policy category addresses requirements for a specific industry such as GLBA, PCI or HIPAA?

   A) Informative

   B) Compulsory

   C) Regulatory

   D) Advisory

5. Which of the following is a high-level statement that describes how security works within the organization?

   A) Issues-specific policy

   B) Organizational security policy

   C) Security policy

   D) System-specific policy

Chapter 7: All About Risk Management and Modeling Threats

Earlier we discussed risk in terms of vulnerabilities, threats, exploits and threat agents. The process of identifying, assessing and reducing this risk to an acceptable level is called *risk management*. Among the hacking world there is a saying – 'There is no such thing as a hack-proof system – you can only make it too much trouble'. In the same way, risk management is all about reducing risk to the point where you can live with it.

With regards to information security, risks can come in many flavors – loss of data, application errors, equipment malfunctions, attacks, improper use of data and physical damage are all good examples. *NIST SP 800-53* defines three tiers to risk management:

- *Organizational* is business-wide
- *Business Process* is specific to major business processes within an organization
- *Information Systems* is specific to information systems within a process

So, while risk applies to much more than just information systems, that is where will focus next.

Information Systems Risk Management

An *Information Systems Risk Management policy*, or an *ISRM* policy, is essential to proper risk management. The ISRM belongs to the third tier that SP 800-53 defines, the Information Systems tier, and should address the following elements:

- The objectives of the ISRM team
- What is considered an acceptable level of risk
- How risks will be identified
- How the ISRM policy fits within the organization's strategic planning
- Roles and responsibilities for the ISRM
- Mapping of risk to controls, performance targets and budgets
- How staff behavior and resource allocation will be modified
- How the effectiveness of controls will be monitored

The Risk Management Team

The size of the risk management team depends on the size of the organization – it can be a single person or entire teams. Usually the team is not dedicated 100% of the time to ISRM. Senior management support is crucial so that resources can be allocated to fill the required roles. The team also requires a single leader, who spends approximately 50%-70% of their time on ISRM.

The Risk Management Process

There are four components to managing risk:

- The *Frame* component defines the assumptions, constraints, priorities and the amount of risk the organization can tolerate.
- The *Assess* component determines threats, vulnerabilities and attack vectors.
- The *Respond* component matches the available resources against a prioritized list of risks.
- The *Monitor* component continuously watches the controls to assess their effectiveness against the risk each was designed to protect the organization from.

Before we jump into discussing risk assessment any more, let's stop and discuss the proper way to identify and prioritize risks. We do this through a process called *threat modeling*, which produces a prioritized list of real-world threats. We don't want to spend our time worrying about the possibility of purple aliens stealing our precious data – I suppose that could happen in the future, but we need to stay grounded in the reality of *likely* risks that may take place. Threat modeling is how we stay on-track.

Vulnerabilities

Every information system is comprised of three things – information, processes and people.

Information

Of course, when we say 'information', we are really talking about 'data'. There are three types of data in any given information system:

- *Data at rest* is data persisted to some type of storage device; this data can be stolen, thereby compromising its confidentiality.
- *Data in motion* is data-in-transit from one system to another across some type of network; it can be stolen (compromised confidentiality) or modified (compromised integrity).

- *Data in use* is data after being retrieved and is in-memory; it can be stolen by retrieving it from memory dumps (compromised confidentiality) or deleted (compromised availability).

As a side-note, all major operating systems now support encryption of the entire disk, which is a great way to protect at-rest data.

Processes
After information, the second component of an information system is the various processes. A process can be a block of code executing in-memory, and therefore a vulnerability in a process is also a software vulnerability.

People
When most people think of attacks against information systems, they normally think of a hacker hunched over a laptop in a dark room. But the reality is that people themselves, not computers or networks, have been the attack vector for most high-profile cases. There are three common methods for leveraging people to attack systems:

- *Social engineering* is tricking a person to ignore security policies, usually through email or text messaging.
- *Social networks* are used by an attacker to either blackmail an individual using information found on social networking sites, or by customizing an email with that information to appear to be more legitimate.
- A significant threat is if a person uses weak *passwords* and/or infrequently changes a password.

Threats
ISO 27000 defines threat as a 'potential cause of an unwanted incident, which may result in harm to a system or organization'. As we just mentioned, the first thing that probably comes to your mind when the word *threat* is mentioned will probably be an outside hacker. However, the danger from an insider is greater, who is usually either disgruntled or enticed by financial gain of some type. Ever since Snowden became a verb (as in 'we got Snowdened'), organizations have become increasingly obsessed with actions by deliberate insiders. However, just as common than a deliberate attack are *accidental* inside events.

So, then – threats can come from three sources - deliberate outsiders, deliberate insiders, and accidental insiders.

Attacks
There are two ends of an *attack* – the attacker and the target. If the attacker's means of accessing the target does not exist, then we should not really spend much time addressing this attack. You can also view this triad in a slightly different way as the vulnerability, the attack, and the threat – which essentially defines a threat model. Either way, we are talking about the victim (the target of the attack), the perpetrator (the attacker) and the means (how the attacker will get to the target).

When describing an attack, we must acknowledge that there will be multiple vectors. For example, if you wish to hack into a secure website, an attacker can use the following methods:

- Access site
    - Locally Access the physical server
        - Steal server administrator credentials
        - Brute force credentials
    - Remotely Use valid credentials
        - Social engineering
        - Steal credentials from the network
        - Brute force credentials
    - Remotely Bypass security
        - Exploit hosting vulnerability
        - Take over another system and move laterally

This list is called an *attack tree*. You would start with a leaf node and move to the root, which is the final goal. An *attack chain* or *kill chain* is simply one path in an attack tree – while an attack tree shows multiple paths, and attack chain shows a single path.

Reduction Analysis
The attack tree we just discussed is one of the best ways to discover and define the vulnerability-threat-attack triads. While this tree should be comprehensive, we don't necessarily have to burden ourselves with addressing every possible attack chain – just the most likely ones. So how do we figure out which ones should be addressed and which ones we can accept without mitigation?

This process is called *reduction analysis*, and contains two components:

Chapter 7: All About Risk Management and Modeling Threats

1. Reduce the number of attacks we must consider by identifying commonalities between multiple vectors
2. Reduce the threat posed by attackers – the closer to the root a mitigation is implemented, the more risks it is likely to control.

Questions

1. Which NIST SP 800-53 tier is specific to major business processes within an organization?

    A) Organizational

    B) Business Process

    C) Information Systems

    D) Information Systems Risk Management

2. Which of the following Risk Management Process steps defines the assumptions, constraints, priorities and the amount of risk the organization can tolerate?

    A) Respond

    B) Frame

    C) Monitor

    D) Assess

3. Which of the following best describes the process of risk management?

    A) The process of identifying, assessing and reducing risks to an acceptable level

    B) The process of identifying, prioritizing and planning for risk

    C) The process of prioritizing, reducing and monitoring risk

    D) The process of identifying, assessing and eliminating risk

4. Which of the following is NOT one of three most common methods used to attack people?

    A) Email

    B) Social engineering

    C) Social networks

    D) Passwords

5. Which of the following Risk Management Process steps continuously watches the controls to assess their effectiveness?

    A) Respond

    B) Monitor

    C) Frame

    D) Assess

Chapter 8: Assessing and Analyzing Risk

While a _risk assessment_ results in a list of vulnerabilities and threats, a _risk analysis_ prioritizes that list and assesses the amount of resources to properly mitigate the top threats. It has four main goals:

- Identify and valuate assets
- Identify vulnerabilities and associated threats
- Quantify the likelihood of the threats
- Calculate an economic balance between each threat and the cost of a countermeasure (or control)

A risk analysis produces a _cost/benefit comparison_, which is based on a one-year period. A control should not be implemented if the cost is greater than the benefit. For example, if the loss of equipment is $25,000, then you should not spend more than $25,000 in a single year trying to protect it.

The risk analysis team should first generate a list of assets prioritized by value – taking into account CIA (confidentiality, integrity and availability) - to the company in terms of actual dollar amounts. Senior management must approve this list before proceeding. A budget must then be established to ensure proper scope is created.

Risk Analysis Team

To be successful, the organization must create a _risk analysis team_, which ideally should be made up of individuals from most or all departments – no one understands everything that goes on in a company. Each individual must possess sufficient knowledge about the inner workings of their respective department. Good questions for this team to ask are:

1. What could happen?
2. What would the impact be?
3. How often could it happen?
4. Do we really believe the first three answers?

Calculating Value

The act of calculating currency-based value for each asset, no matter how intangible the asset is – is an absolute requirement to effectively prioritize. An asset might be information, facilities, systems or resources.

While a currency-based number is the ultimate value we need for an asset (in other words, a _quantitative_ value), there is such a thing as a _qualitative_ value. This value represents intangible losses for the organization if an asset was compromised, stolen or lost and should always be factored in to the quantitative value. The following issues should be examined when calculating an asset's value:

- How much did it cost to acquire or develop?
- How much does it cost to maintain and protect?
- What is the value to owners and users?
- What is the value to adversaries?
- What are others willing to pay for it?
- What will it cost to replace?
- What activities will be interrupted if it is lost?
- What liabilities would we have if it were compromised?
- How useful is it to the organization?

After a value has been calculated, the cost to protect the asset needs to be calculated. This allows us to do the following:

- Perform an effective cost/benefit analysis
- Select proper controls
- Determine the amount of insurance to purchase
- Define exactly what is at risk
- Comply with legal and regulatory requirements

Identifying Vulnerabilities and Threats

Beyond intentional and malicious attacks, threats can arise from seemingly innocuous sources such as our own applications and users. For example, an application could have a logic flaw, known as _illogical processing_, which destroys or compromises data or resources. This can then lead to _cascading errors_ wherein a small flaw is passed to another process, which then amplifies the flaw. Or, a user can enter invalid data or even accidently delete important data. User errors can be detected by audits and reviews.

Each risk has a _loss potential_, which simply identifies the loss an organization would incur if a threat agent exploited a vulnerability. Closely related is _delayed loss_, which happens after a vulnerability is exploited. For example, the loss potential may be large if a list of user accounts is stolen, but the delayed loss encountered as your company's reputation takes a hit could even be greater.

Methodologies for Risk Assessment

There are several ways in which we can carry out a risk assessment, and we will cover seven of them.

The first is the _NIST SP 800-30_ guide, which focuses on IT systems instead of organizational strategy, and lists the following steps:

1) Prepare for the assessment
2) Conduct the assessment
    a. Identify threats
    b. Identify vulnerabilities
    c. Determine likelihood
    d. Determine magnitude
    e. Calculate risk
3) Communicate the results
4) Maintain the assessment

A second method for risk assessment is the _facilitated risk analysis process_, or _FRAP_. This method stresses a qualitative measurement of risk instead of trying to calculate a risk value. The scope is restricted to a single system, application or process at a time.

A third method in which we can carry out a risk assessment is to use the operationally critical threat asset and vulnerability evaluation, or OCTAVE for short. The premise of this methodology is that the people involved with a system or process should be the only ones making the decisions on security, as opposed to higher-level or external influences. A facilitator walks the team members through the process, encouraging the team to be self-directed. While FRAP is targeted to single systems or processes, OCTAVE is meant for the entire organization, employs workshops and is commonly used in the commercial industry.

A fourth method is called the _AS/NZS 4360_, and originates from Australia and New Zealand. Whereas NIST SP 800-30 focuses primarily on security, this method focuses on an organization's overall health, but could be used for security.

Let's not forget the ISO 27000 series – _ISO 27005_ describes how risk management should be carried out for ISMS. Whereas NIST SP 800-30 deals with IT and operations, ISO 27005 adds in aspects such as documentation and training. This is the fifth method.

The sixth method we want to consider is the _failure mode and effect analysis_ (_FMEA_), which focuses on identifying functions, their failures and the causes of those failures. This method is usually found in production environments with the goal of identifying likely failure points and addressing them before they happen. It suggests the following steps:

1) Create a block diagram
2) Consider what happens when each block fails
3) Create a table of each failure and the corresponding impact
4) Correct the design and repeat #3 until the system no longer has unacceptable weaknesses
5) Have engineers review the design and table

FMEA excels when examining a single system, but tends to break down when considering multiple systems. In this case, a _fault tree analysis_ can help with complex systems – it is essentially an attack tree but with the root being a failure instead of a successful attack, and leaf nodes being events. Examples of events might be unexpected output, incorrect timing of output, insufficient error handling, false alarms or invalid sequencing of processes.

A seventh, and final, method is the UK-originated Central Computing and Telecommunications Agency Risk Analysis and Management Method, or just CRAMM. It has three stages:

1) Define objectives
2) Assess risk
3) Identify countermeasures

There is nothing special about this methodology other than the fact that Siemens has an automated tool for it, thereby providing a packaged version for immediate use.

To summarize, let's discuss when each methodology would be beneficial to use. If you need to address organizational-wide issues, then use ISO 27005 or OCTAVE. If your focus is solely on IT security issues, use NIST SP 800-30. If you have a small budget and want to examine individual systems or processes, you should choose FRAP. If you want to address security flaws within an existing system, use FMEA or a fault tree analysis. If your focus is the organization's business risk (as opposed to IT) then select AS/NZS 4360. If you want to start out of the gate with an automated tool, then choose CRAMM.

Risk Analysis Approaches

So, we have now looked through how to perform a _risk assessment_. At this point we have gathered a lot of data, but now we need to perform a _risk analysis_ on it – in other words, we need to act on all of that data. As already mentioned, we can analyze data in a quantitative or qualitative approach. A quantitative produces numbers, and is a scientific or mathematical approach. A qualitative approach yields categorizations that are more subjective and more general in nature. For example, a quantitative approach will give you a cost/benefit number. A qualitative approach might give you green, yellow and red categories. First, we're going to discuss the quantitative approach.

Quantitative Risk Analysis

There are several automated quantitative risk assessment tools that can be purchased, but let's go over the basic calculations that each implements.

First, each asset has an *asset value* in currency – the risk assessment phase gives us this value. An *exposure factor*, or EF, is the percentage of loss that a realized threat could have on that asset. For example, if the asset was an assembly line costing $500,000, and the threat was a fire, then we can say that 50% of the assembly line would be damaged by a fire. The EF in this example is 50%.

Now that we have the asset value provided by the risk assessment, and have calculated an EF for that asset, we need to calculate the *single loss expectancy*, or *SLE*. This is the amount of loss per incident and is calculated by the following formula:

SLE = Asset Value x Exposure Factor (EF)

In our example a fire would represent a single loss expectancy of $250,000:

SLE = $500,000 x 50% = $250,000

But what if we have a fire twice within a single year? We can't just double the SLE – the chances of having a fire twice are probably not that great. So, we have to come up with an *annualized rate of occurrence*, or *ARO* – this number is the number of times per year we can expect the threat to take place within a 12-month period. As an example, if we expect a fire to occur once every five years, then the ARO is 1/5, or 0.2. We can now calculate the *annual loss expectancy*, or *ALE* as:

ALE = SLE x ARO

In our example this would be:

ALE = $250,000 x 0.2 = $50,000

So, what do we do with this number? Well, it tells us that we should spend no more than $50,000 per year on fire protection for the assembly line. This in turn helps us to create a budget. However, keep in mind that even though we are dealing with hard numbers, we had to assume certain things when coming up with EF and ARO, so there is still some subjectivity in these numbers. As a result, it is important to record the level of uncertainty the team has in those assumptions as a percentage – 100% means full confidence, while 20% reflects a great deal of skepticism that the numbers can be trusted.

Qualitative Risk Analysis

Now let's discuss qualitative risk analysis, wherein we discuss various scenarios and rank threats and possible controls based on opinions. Each threat is ranked as high, medium or low categories, or on a numeric scale. A matrix is usually used to facilitate this discussion with the Y-Axis being the likelihood of occurrence, and the X-axis representing the impact – the intersection of the two is used to assign a value to the vulnerability/threat. The resulting list is ranked according to the category or numerical ranking. A successful qualitative analysis requires involving people with the correct experience and education evaluating threat scenarios.

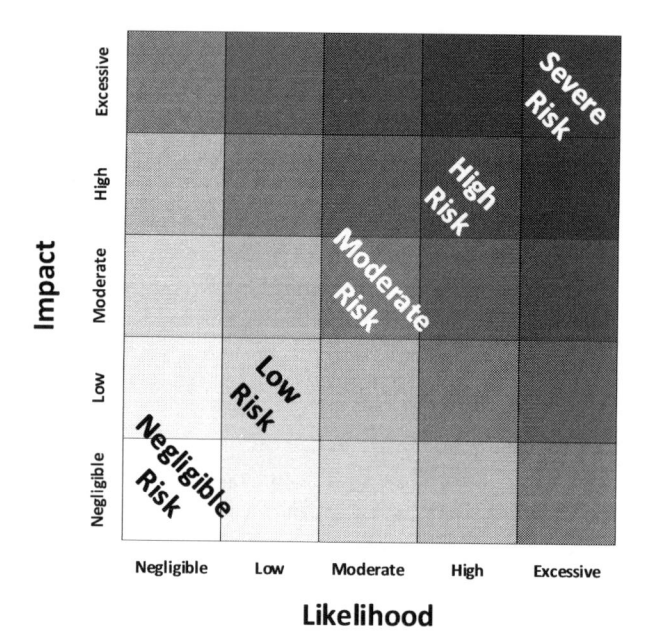

Figure 7: Qualitative Impact Matrix

Oftentimes the *Delphi technique* is used to ensure honest opinions using anonymous communication. With this method, each group member provides a written opinion on each threat and gives the answer to the risk assessment team. The team then compiles the results and distributes it to the group who write down comments anonymously.

The results are then compiled and redistributed until a consensus is reached.

Quantitative vs. Qualitative

Many times, it is most effective to use both approaches simultaneously – quantitative for tangible assets and qualitative for intangible.

	Quantitative	Qualitative
Complex calculations	Yes	No
A lot of guesswork	No	Yes
Can be automated	Yes	No
Requires preliminary work	Yes	No
Has standards	No	No
Is objective	Yes	No
Provides a cost/benefit	Yes	No
Provides support for a budget	Yes	No

Figure 8: Quantitative vs. Qualitative Risk Analysis

Protection Mechanisms

After a risk analysis has been completed, it is time to identify and select controls. The value of a control is calculated by measuring the ALE (annualized loss expectancy) before and after the implementation of a control. For example, if the ALE of the aforementioned assembly line is $50,000 before fire controls are put into place, and the annual cost of the fire control is $10,000, then the value of the control is $40,000, which is a pretty good deal. However, the annual cost of a control is usually not straightforward – some of the hidden costs are:

- The actual product
- Design and planning
- Implementation
- Environment modifications
- Compatibility with other controls
- Maintenance
- Testing
- Repair, replacement or upgrades
- Operating and support
- Negative impacts on productivity
- Subscription
- Time for monitoring and responding to alerts

Following is a list of attributes that should be considered when selecting controls:

- Can be installed without affecting other mechanisms
- Provides uniform protection
- Administrator can override
- Defaults to least privilege
- Ability to enable/disable as desired
- Does not distress users
- Differentiation between user and administrator roles
- Minimum human interaction
- Assets are still protected during a reset
- Easily updated
- Provide sufficient audit trail
- Not have heavy dependence on other components
- Does not introduce heavy barriers for users
- Produce human-readable output
- Easy reset to baseline configuration
- Testable
- Does not introduce compromises
- Does not impact system performance
- Does not require many exceptions across the environment
- Proper alerting
- Does not impact existing assets
- Is not highly-visible

Total Risk vs. Residual Risk

Total risk is the risk an organization takes on if they choose not to put any controls in place. Even if controls are put in place, however, we will always have *residual risk*. We can illustrate these concepts through two formulas:

total risk = threats x vulnerability x asset value

residual risk = total risk x controls gap

You really can't plug in numbers into these formulas – they are conceptual in nature. But, we can derive several truths from this:

- As the value of an asset increases, the total risk increases
- As the number of threats increases, the total risk increases
- As the effectiveness of controls decreases, the residual risk increases

Once we have identified risk, we have four ways to deal with it:

1) *Transfer the risk* – take out insurance; if we encounter an instance, someone else pays for it
2) *Risk avoidance* - terminate the activity that is causing the risk
3) *Risk reduction* – reduce the risk using countermeasures (or controls) until the level of risk is acceptable
4) *Accept the risk* – decide to take the hit if we encounter an instance

Now, there is a big difference between *ignoring* the risk and *accepting* it. If you accept a risk, that means you have gone through the work of assessing and analyzing the risk, and have made a conscious decision to accept the risk.

Ignoring a risk simply means you bury your head in the sand and hope for the best. Even though the decision in both cases is to take no action, there is a huge difference if you get sued. Ignore the risk and you may very well face punitive damages, but if you can show due diligence was taken, your chances of not being found liable goes up significantly.

Outsourcing

Outsourcing risk is not really a viable option unless you can verify that the partner has properly handled the risk. If an occurrence happens, an organization can still be found liable if the outsourcing partner failed to properly mitigate the risk. To facilitate this discovery process, *SAS 70* is an internal controls audit that can be carried out by a third-party.

Questions

1. Which of the following best describes indirect loss occurring after a vulnerability is exploited?

    A) Cascading errors

    B) Illogical processing

    C) Delayed loss

    D) Loss potential

2. What is a technique that charts risk on a graph, with y-axis the likelihood and x-axis the impact level?

    A) Delphi technique

    B) Risk reduction

    C) Risk management frameworks

    D) Qualitative Risk Analysis

3. What risk assessment methodology contains an attack tree with the root as a failure instead of a successful attack?

    A) Fault tree analysis

    B) CRAMM

    C) ISO 27005

    D) FRAP

4. Which of the following best describes AV?

    A) The currency value of an asset calculated during the risk assessment

    B) The percentage of loss a threat could have

    C) The number of times per year we can expect the threat to take place

    D) SLE*ARO

5. What activity results a list of vulnerabilities and threats?

    A) Risk determination

    B) Risk optimization

    C) Risk analysis

    D) Risk assessment

Chapter 9: Managing Risk

We have covered a lot of information regarding risk management. Now it's time to pull it all together using a framework. Don't get these *risk management frameworks* (*RMFs*) confused with architecture frameworks such as Zachman or TOGAF – here we're dealing with frameworks to allow an organization to do three things:

1) Identify and assess risk
2) Reduce it to an acceptable level
3) Ensure the risk remains at an acceptable level

Some commonly used RMFs are:

- *NIST RMF* (*SP 800-37*); as usual, NIST documents apply to federal agencies, but bleed over into the private sector; this framework operates around a systems life-cycle and focuses on certification and accreditation.
- *ISO 31000;* this standard acknowledges that there are things which we cannot control and focuses instead on managing the fallout; it can be broadly applied to an entire organization.
- *ISACA Risk IT*; this framework attempts to integrate NIST, ISO 31000 and COBIT.
- *COSO Enterprise Risk Management–Integrated Framework*; this generic framework takes a top-down approach

We will be focusing on the NIST framework as it incorporates the most important aspects of any framework.

Categorize Information System

The first thing you must do to manage risk is to *categorize* the information system by identifying what an organization has in terms of systems, sub-systems and boundaries. At the end of this first step you should have all the information you will need to select controls that will manage the risk.

Select Security Controls

If you have already performed a risk assessment as part of the first step, you then need to *select* security controls by identifying a number of *common controls*, which together constitute a baseline. As each new system is introduced into the organization, it is assessed from a control point of view to see if existing controls are sufficient, an existing control needs to be modified (a *hybrid control*), or if a new control should be created (*system-specific control*).

Implement Security Controls

Next, you will need to *implement* the security controls. This seems like a no-brainer – if you need a new control, you add it. If you need to modify a control, you modify. Done.

Unfortunately, this step also requires you to create the appropriate documentation as well for two reasons:

1) So everyone will understand the what, where and why of each control
2) It allows the controls to be integrated into an overall assessment and monitoring plan.

Assess Security Controls

Once a control has been implemented, it must then be *assessed* to see how effective it has been. This should be done by an individual or team that did not implement the control. If the control is deemed to be effective, the results are added to the documentation to be referred during the next round of assessments. If the control is not deemed effective, the report should document the results, actions that were taken to address the shortcomings and the outcome of the reassessment.

Authorize Information System

At this point, we forward all documentation and assessment results to the person or the group who can *authorize* integration of the system into the general architecture.

Monitor Security Controls

Once the system is in general operation, it must be *monitored* to ensure it remains effective. If any changes in operation or threats are detected, the system must be updated.

Chapter 9: Managing Risk

Questions

1. Which of the following is a standard that acknowledges there are things which we cannot control and focuses instead on managing the fallout?

    A) SAS 70

    B) COSO Enterprise Risk Management–Integrated Framework

    C) NIST RMF (SP 800-37)

    D) ISO 31000

2. Which of the following is an internal control audit useful with outsourcing?

    A) SAS 70

    B) ISACA Risk IT

    C) ISO 31000

    D) NIST RMF (SP 800-37)

3. Which of the following allows an organization to identify, reduce and monitor risk mitigation?

    A) ISO 31000

    B) SAS 70

    C) ISACA Risk IT

    D) Risk Management Frameworks

4. Which of the following attempts to integrate NIST, ISO 31000 and COBIT?

    A) SAS 70

    B) ISACA Risk IT

    C) COSO Enterprise Risk Management–Integrated Framework

    D) ISO 31000

5. Which of the following is a framework that operates around a systems life-cycle and focuses on certification and accreditation?

    A) ISACA Risk IT

    B) COSO Enterprise Risk Management–Integrated Framework

    C) NIST RMF (SP 800-37)

    D) SAS 70

Chapter 10: Business Continuity and Disaster Recovery

We have spent a god deal of time discussing how to identify, assess and mitigate various risks. Unfortunately, the reality is that no matter how great our best efforts are, at some point something will slip past and cause havoc. It is at that time we must have a plan to maintain some minimal level of acceptable activity and return to full productivity as soon as possible.

<u>Disaster recovery</u> (<u>DR</u>), is how an organization will minimize the effects of a disaster or disruption to business and return to some level of acceptable productivity. This <u>disaster recovery plan</u> (<u>DRP</u>) goes into effect during the emergency while everyone is still scrambling to understand what just happened and how to keep going.

<u>Continuity planning</u>, on the other hand, addresses how the organization will return to full capacity, including backup data centers, spinning up new locations for people to work, or altering processes during the interim. It also involves dealing and communicating with customers, vendors and stakeholders until 'normal' is returned to.

<u>Business continuity management</u> (<u>BCM</u>), encompasses both disaster recovery and continuity planning. BCM must address all three aspects of CIA. For example, during a disaster, you can't just leave a sensitive server sitting in an abandoned building (confidentiality), you can't assume storage media will remain safe and secure (integrity) and you must make sure those resources are back up and running as soon as possible (availability).

BCM is much more than buildings and hardware – you need the right skillset (people) to run the systems, and those people need to know how the original systems were configured. BCM is implemented by a business continuity plan (<u>BCP</u>). A successful BCP contains strategy documents that provide detailed procedures - these procedures ensure critical functions are maintained that will in turn minimize loss. The procedures cover emergency responses, extended backup operations and post-disaster recovery.

It is important to remember that a BCP can quickly become outdated due to employee turnover and undocumented changes, so continuous updating is essential.

Standards and Best Practices

<u>NIST SP 800-34</u> provides the following steps for creating a continuity plan:

1) *Write the continuity planning policy statement* – write a policy and assign authority to carry out the policy tasks
2) *Conduct the business impact analysis (BIA)* – identify critical functions and systems and prioritize the list
3) *Identify preventative controls* – select and implement controls to address the BIA
4) *Create contingency strategies* – make sure systems can be brought online quickly
5) *Develop an information system contingency plan* – write procedures and guidelines on how the organization will remain functional in a crippled state
6) *Ensure plan testing, training and exercises*
7) *Ensure plan maintenance* – put in place steps to ensure the BCP is updated regularly

There are also other standards that address BCM:

- <u>ISO 27031</u>, which describes the concepts of information communication technology (ICT) readiness for business continuity
- <u>ISO 22301</u>, which is the ISO standard for BCM
- Business Continuity Institute's Good Practice Guidelines (GPG)
- DRI International Institute's Professional Practices for Business Continuity Planners

Making BCM a Part of the Enterprise Security Program

For a BCM to be able to rebuild an organization when a disaster hits, it must be built upon a solid understanding not only of how the organization operates, but also the organizational components that are critical to continuing its reason for being. For most companies, making profit is the reason for its existence, but for non-profits and government agencies the answer is quite different. The BCM must understand this to keep the organization functioning.

The Zachman framework is ideal for gaining this understanding, as it looks at everything from the highest level to the smallest detail. But whatever tool is used to generate the BCP, the BCP must be a living entity that is continually revisited and updated as-needed. It should define and prioritize the organization's critical mission and business functions, and provide a sequence for recovery. And, most importantly, it must have management's full support.

BCP Project Components

Once we have management support, a _business continuity coordinator_ should be selected, who then works with management to create a _BCP committee_. The BCP program must then be initiated by allocating a budget, assigning duties, announcing the formation, train skills and start collecting data.

Scope must then be established for the BPC program – should it cover one or all facilities? Should it encompass large threats or smaller ones as well? Senior executives must make these decisions, not the BCP team – executives must also provide final approval of the plan. Often departments are expected to come up with their own plans that fit within the larger umbrella BCP.

A _BCP policy_ must then be constructed that contains its scope, mission, principles, guidelines and standards. Project management is crucial for BCP to ensure it does not run out of funds, and management of scope is one of the key responsibilities of this management. A _SWOT_ analysis is helpful, which looks at the following four areas:

- _Strengths_ (or advantages)
- _Weaknesses_ (or disadvantages)
- _Opportunities_ (opportunities for success)
- _Threats_ (contributions to failure)

These attributes are arranged in quadrants, with items to be considered for scope placed inside the appropriate quadrant. The definition of terms is an important deliverable early in the project plan. Once this project plan has been completed, it should be approved by executives before proceeding.

BCP is important in terms of assigning liability should a disaster occur. _Due diligence_ is defined as doing everything within one's power to prevent a disaster from happening; this is applicable to leaders, laws and regulations. _Due care_ means taking precautions that a reasonable and competent person would have done; this is applicable to everyone. If BCPs are not developed or used, executives could be held liable.

A _business impact analysis_, or _BIA_, is an activity at the beginning of BCP where interviews are executed and data collected to identify and classify business and individual functions. The 8 steps are:

1) Select individuals for interviewing
2) Create data-gathering techniques
3) Identify critical functions
4) Identify resources
5) Calculate how long functions can survive without resources
6) Identify vulnerabilities and threats
7) Calculate risk (risk = threat x impact x probability)
8) Document findings and report to management

During the BIA, each critical system must be examined to see how long the organization can survive without that system. The _maximum tolerable downtime_ (_MTD_), also called the _maximum period time of disruption_ (_MPTD_) must be determined and categorized (these terms will be addressed in more depth later). Understanding the interdependent relationships between functions is critical to BCP success. There are other values calculated during the BIA that will be covered more in depth within the Security Assessment and Testing domain.

In summary, the responsibilities for BCP management are five:

- Committing fully to the BCP
- Setting policy and goals
- Ensuring the required funds and resources are available
- Taking responsibility of the outcome of the BCP
- Appointing a team

The BCP team's responsibilities are:

- Identifying legal and regulatory requirements
- Identifying vulnerabilities and threats
- Estimating threat likelihood and potential loss
- Performing a BIA
- Indicating which functions and processes must be running before others
- Identifying interdependencies
- Developing procedures and steps to resume business after a disaster
- Identifying individuals who will interact with external players

It is crucial that the plans are developed by the people who will be responsible for carrying them out.

Oftentimes a business case must be presented to management before approval may be obtained. This includes the explanation of regulatory and legal requirements, pointing out vulnerabilities and providing solutions.

As part of BCP an *executive succession plan* should be in place. If a senior executive is no longer with the company, or is unexpectedly absent, this plan dictates who will step in until the executive returns or a permanent replacement can be found. Large organizations often dictate that two or more senior executives cannot be exposed to the same risk simultaneously. For example, the CEO and president cannot travel on the same plane together in the event it crashes.

Questions

1. Which term describes how to minimize the effects of a disaster or disruption and return to productivity?

    A) Continuity Planning

    B) Business Continuity Management

    C) Disaster Recovery

    D) Disaster Recovery Plan

2. Which term describes how the organization will return to full capacity after an interruption?

    A) Business Continuity Management

    B) Disaster Recovery Plan

    C) Continuity Planning

    D) Disaster Recovery

3. What defines BCM scope, mission, principles, guidelines and standards?

    A) Business continuity

    B) BCM plan

    C) BCP policy

    D) DRP

4. Which of the following determines long an organization can survive without a given capability?

    A) MTD

    B) RPO

    C) SEL

    D) RTO

5. Which of the following describes doing everything within one's power to prevent a disaster from happening?

    A) Due care

    B) Due reason

    C) Due persistence

    D) Due diligence

Chapter 11: Personnel Security

People are usually the most important aspect of a business, and the weakest link. However, several processes can be put into place to mitigate risks caused by people.

Separation of duties is a process that ensures a single person cannot complete a critical task by himself. For example, an employee who creates user accounts is not allowed to assign permissions to that account; likewise, the employee who is able to grant permissions cannot create user accounts. To create a rogue account, two employees must _collude_ with each other, thereby reducing the likelihood of this happening. Another example is a little more terrifying - before launching a nuclear missile, two people must insert a key – this ensures that a single person cannot purposefully or accidentally cause a disastrous incident. This is also an example of _dual control_. In businesses, separation of duties is usually put into place to prevent fraud in the form of _split knowledge_. As an example, certain information can only be retrieved if two separate people both authenticate into the same system at the same time.

Rotation of duties is an administrative detection control to uncover fraudulent activities. The goal is to move employees around so that each does not have control over the same business function for too long. As employees rotate through functions, they are better able to detect fraud enacted by the previous employee. This protection mechanism is usually found in financial institutions.

For employees operating in sensitive areas, _mandatory vacation_ should be implemented to detect fraud. This forces the employee to vacate the position for a sufficient amount of time for the organization to detect a change in potentially fraudulent activities, or even recurring errors or problems.

Hiring practices

Before hiring new employees, HR should always look into the individual's background for character traits. _Non-disclosure agreements_ (_NDAs_) must be signed by new employees covering conflict of interests and protection of the organization's intellectual property. Behavioral testing and observations are a crucial part of the hiring process. Background checks can include:

- Social security number trace
- County/state criminal history
- Federal criminal history
- Sexual offender registry check
- Employment verification
- Education verification
- Reference verification
- Immigration check
- License or certification validations
- Credit report
- Drug screening

Termination

There should be a _termination_ process defined well before a termination occurs including surrender of ID badges or keys, escort from the premises and immediate disabling of user accounts or other access. Having a severance package dependent upon completion of an exit interview and surrender of company property encourages terminated employees to comply.

Security-Awareness Training

In this book there will occasionally be a reference to something called 'security awareness training'. Your basic _security training_ is the process of teaching security skills to security personnel, while _security awareness training_ is the process of explaining security issues to all members of an organization, so an employee may recognize risky situations and know how to respond. If all employees do not see security as a priority, then an organization will never achieve any appreciable level of security. Promoting security awareness is a preventative control, but it also can be a detective control as it encourages people to identify and report possible security violations.

Remember this phrase: _technology by itself cannot solve any risk_. It must be applied with an equal amount of the proper behavior by people and processes, and altering people's behavior is the biggest win by far.

Proper awareness training starts with the onboarding process for new hires and includes several things. Obviously, we have the training material, which is often administered online. Quizzes are then given to figure out how well people are retaining the training concepts. This is reinforced using reminders such as posters, newsletters and screensavers. There should then be a scheduled refresher of training to bring those lessons back to the front of the brain. In larger organizations, there may be enough mid-level management employees to warrant a special training program. Now, while we have only mentioned employees so far, this training must also extend to all third-party entities who have any level of involvement with the organization's internal processes.

When developing an awareness program several things should be considered, such as who the audience is and what the overall message is intended to be. The communication method will impact how the program is designed, as will the overall structure of the organization. For example, it doesn't make much sense to hold an all-hands meeting to discuss the need to wear badges. On the other hand, if we have a severe problem with phishing emails such a meeting might be warranted.

Successful security awareness training contains the following attributes:

- Repeats the most important messages in different formats
- Up-to-date
- Entertaining and positive
- Simple to understand
- Supported by senior management

There are three audiences for this training:

1) *Management*, which requires a short orientation focusing on how security pertains to corporate assets and financial goals and losses.
2) *Staff*, which receives an overview of policies, procedures, standards and guidelines.
3) *Technical employees*, who require in-depth training on daily activities.

Now, it is possible to implement most of the security efforts described so far and still fail at having an effective security program, all because of the lack of proper oversight, monitoring and measurement. _Security governance_ is the term used to cover these problematic areas, and is a framework providing oversight, accountability and compliance.

Proper oversight means that management has bought into the security mindset from the top down, and it permeates every level of the organization. Proper monitoring ensures that the organization continuously examines the security program, proactively looking for ways to improve it. Of course, it is virtually impossible to determine how well a security program is functioning if you cannot measure it by using metrics.

There are two guidelines for measuring _metrics_ for the effectiveness of a security program:

1) _ISO 27004_; whereas ISO 27001 tells you how to build a security program, ISO 27004 tells you how to measure its effectiveness.
2) _NIST SP 800-55_; this is the government's version of ISO 27004

One last note – all measurements must be aligned so that different controls can be effectively compared.

Chapter 11: Personnel Security

Questions

1. Which term describes ensuring a single person cannot complete a critical task by himself?

    A) Split knowledge

    B) Separation of duties

    C) Dual control

    D) Collusion

2. When should security awareness training be provided?

    A) On the first day of employment

    B) Before hiring

    C) During the hiring process

    D) Within one week of employment

3. Which term describes moving employees around so that each does not have control over the same business function for too long?

    A) Collusion

    B) Rotation of duties

    C) Mandatory vacation

    D) Split knowledge

4. Which of the following is NOT part of good hiring practices?

    A) Background checks

    B) NDAs

    C) Behavioral testing

    D) Access authorization

5. Which term describes the segmentation of responsibilities to prevent fraud?

    A) Dual control

    B) Separation of duties

    C) Split knowledge

    D) Collusion

Chapter 12: Ethics

Every CISSP candidate must understand the (ISC)² *Code of Ethics*. Below is an overview:

- Protect society, the common good, necessary public trust and confidence, and the infrastructure
- Act honorably, justly, responsibly and legally
- Provide diligent and competent services to principals
- Advance and protect the profession

Laws are based on ethics but are strictly applied – ethics comes into play where laws do not cover. More and more regulations are requiring organizations to have an ethical statement and possibly an ethical program.

The *Computer Ethics Institute* is a non-profit organization helping to advance technology by ethical means and has the following Ten Commandments (paraphrased):

1) Thou Shalt Not Use a Computer to Harm Other People.
2) Thou Shalt Not Interfere with Other People's Computer Work.
3) Thou Shalt Not Snoop Around in Other People's Computer Files.
4) Thou Shalt Not Use a Computer to Steal.
5) Thou Shalt Not Use a Computer to Bear False Witness.
6) Thou Shalt Not Copy or Use Proprietary Software for Which You Have Not Paid.
7) Thou Shalt Not Use Other People's Computer Resources Without Authorization or Proper Compensation.
8) Thou Shalt Not Appropriate Other People's Intellectual Output.
9) Thou Shalt Think About the Social Consequences of The Program You Are Writing or The System You Are Designing.
10) Thou Shalt Always Use a Computer In Ways That Insure Consideration And Respect For Your Fellow Humans.

The Internet Architecture Board, or IAB, coordinates design, engineering and management for the Internet. It oversees the Internet Engineering Task Force (IETF), Internet Standards process, and acts as editor for Requests for Comments (RFCs). The IAB also creates ethics-related guidelines for Internet use, and views the Internet as a privilege. In RFC 1087, Ethics and the Internet, the IAB states what it considers to be unethical acts. In summary, when a person:

- Seeks to gain unauthorized access to the resources of the Internet,
- Disrupts the intended use of the Internet,
- Wastes resources (people, capacity, computer) through such actions,
- Destroys the integrity of computer-based information
- Compromises the privacy of users.

Questions

1. What is the name of the non-profit organization who created the Ten Commandments for ethics?

    A) Computer Ethics Institute

    B) Seventh Day Activists

    C) Technology Ethics Institute

    D) IAB

2. Which of the following is NOT part of the (ISC)2 Code of Ethics?

    A) Act honorably, justly, responsibly and legally

    B) Provide diligent and competent services to principals

    C) Advance and protect the profession

    D) Inform the proper parties for illegal activities duties

Section 2: Asset Security Domain

Now it's time to move on to the Asset Security Domain, starting with the information life cycle.

Chapter 13: Information Life Cycle and Classification

Information is created and has value for a time until it is no longer needed – in essence, it has a life-cycle. There are several models that describe information life cycles, but we will focus on one with four progressive stages – acquisition, use, archival and disposal.

The Information Life Cycle

Acquisition

Acquisition occurs when information can be created within or copied into a system. Two things happen at this point – metadata describing the information is attached along with the classification, and information is extracted so that it can be quickly located later, usually by indexing attributes. Sometimes a third step happens – we must apply policy controls to the information. This might require encryption of parts of the data, or we must secure the information behind an authentication/authorization layer or even track changes to support a rollback.

Use

After acquiring data, we must ensure its proper use. The challenge of addressing the CIA triad is mostly concerned with this phase of the lifecycle – while the information is in active *use* it must remain available while still enforcing confidentiality and integrity. An additional item to note is that if an organization duplicates data, the consistency of that duplication must be an enforced process.

Archival

At some point the information in-use will become dated, but will still need to be accessible for a time – this is when we need to archive it. *Archived* information is usually moved to a secondary storage point that is not optimized for reading.

Note that a *backup* is not the same as being archived – backups exist to restore authoritative information that has been compromised or lost, while an archival remains the authoritative source but is no longer in the primary storage location. Backups are not authoritative, but archived data is.

Disposal

Finally, the information reaches a point where it no longer has any use to the owning organization and needs to be *disposed* of. There are two possible steps to disposal – transfer and destruction. If you want to give or sell the information to another organization, then the transfer must be carried out safely. Destruction is more complex than simply performing a delete – depending on the sensitivity of the information, the media may need to be physically destroyed. Additionally, how can you be sure that all copies have been removed? Information must be tracked during the entire life cycle.

Note that encryption is a useful tool at any stage of the life cycle.

Classification

To allow an organization to focus its protection resources on the proper data, it must classify each piece of data by sensitivity, criticality, or both. *Sensitivity* deals with losses incurred if the information were to be revealed to unauthorized sources. *Criticality* measures the impact to the organization's business processes if the data were to be lost. Once these two attributes have been assigned, CIA can be appropriately applied. Each classification level corresponds to the data's value, and should have its own handling and destruction requirements.

Classification Levels

The most common commercial *classification levels* are, from most secure to least secure:

- *Confidential*
- *Private*
- *Sensitive/Proprietary*
- *Public*

The military uses the following classification levels, from most secure to least secure:

- Top secret
- Secret
- Confidential
- Sensitive but unclassified
- *Unclassified*

It is important that whoever is backing up data or has access to back-up data has the necessary clearance level. The format in which the data is stored or the type of media it is stored on should have no impact on the classification. Note that when data is aggregated, the overall aggregation must contain the highest level of classification of any component.

Once the classification levels have been decided on, the organization must write criteria to use when deciding what classification each data element falls under. Attributes may include:

- How the data is related to security
- Legal or regulatory requirements
- How old the data is
- How valuable the data is
- How useful the data is
- How damaging it would be if the data were to be disclosed
- How damaging it would be if the data were to be lost or compromised
- Who can access or copy the data

Applications that store or handle data need to be classified as well.

Classification Controls

There are several attributes that should be considered when dealing with sensitive data and applications such as access granularity, encryption, separation of duties, auditing, periodic review and physical security.

The common procedure for classifying data contains 10 steps:

1) Define the classification levels
2) Define criteria on how to classify
3) Identify those who will be classifying data
4) Identify the data custodian
5) Indicate the security controls required for each classification
6) Document exceptions to the previous step
7) Specify how custody of data may be internally transferred
8) Create a process to periodically review classification and ownership, and communicate any changes to the data custodian
9) Create a process for declassifying data
10) Incorporate the above into the security-awareness training

Chapter 13: Information Life Cycle and Classification

Questions

1. What are the four information life cycle stages?

A) Acquisition, Use, Archival and Disposal

B) Acquisition, Use, Consume and Disposal

C) Procurement, Use, Archival and Decommission

D) Procurement, Consume, File and Decommission

2. Which best describes the information life cycle disposal step?

A) Move authoritative source to a secondary storage point that is not as optimized for reading

B) Information can be created within or copied into a system

C) Information must remain available while still enforcing confidentiality and integrity

D) Transfer and destruction

3. Which best describes the information life cycle acquisition step?

A) Information can be created within or copied into a system

B) Information must remain available while still enforcing confidentiality and integrity

C) Transfer and destruction

D) Move authoritative source to a secondary storage point that is not as optimized for reading

4. Which best describes the information life cycle use step?

A) Information can be created within or copied into a system

B) Transfer and destruction

C) Information must remain available while still enforcing confidentiality and integrity

D) Move authoritative source to a secondary storage point that is not as optimized for reading

5. Which best describes the information life cycle archival step?

A) Information must remain available while still enforcing confidentiality and integrity

B) Transfer and destruction

C) Information can be created within or copied into a system

D) Move authoritative source to a secondary storage point that is not as optimized for reading

Chapter 14: Layers of Responsibility

Enough about information classification – let's talk about the various roles that play a part in organizational security and how each interacts with classification duties. From a very high-level view, there are three layers:

1) *Senior management*, who hold the vision and are ultimately responsible for the entire organization
2) *Functional management* who understand their own department and the roles of individuals
3) *Operational managers* and staff who are closest to the day-to-day operations

We are about to discuss the various roles present in most organizations, regardless of size. However, in smaller organizations, one person normally fills multiple roles simultaneously even if they are not aware of it.

Executive Management

At the top we find *executive management*, which are the "C-suite" positions, such as CEO, CFO, CIO, etc.

The *chief executive officer* (*CEO*) is the highest-ranking officer in the company and acts as the visionary. A CEO can delegate tasks but not responsibility. Due to increasing liability for a company's security from legislation, CEOs are providing more funding for security initiatives.

The *chief financial officer* (*CFO*) is responsible for the financial structure of a company.

The *chief information officer* (*CIO*) oversees information systems and technologies, and is ultimately responsible for the success of the security program.

The *chief privacy officer* (*CPO*) is usually an attorney and ensures the company's data is kept safe. Keep in mind the difference between privacy and security. *Privacy* indicates the amount of control a person should and expect to have over the handling of their data (PII). *Security* represents the mechanisms that enforce this privacy.

The *chief security officer* (*CSO*) is responsible for understand company risks and for mitigating those risks to acceptable levels. This role is more than technology – it extends into the legal and regulatory realm. Sometimes a company will have a *chief Information security officer* (*CISO*) which is more of a technical role that reports to the CSO.

Data Owner

Underneath executive management we find the *data owners*, which are usually members of middle management. This individual will oversee a business unit or department and is responsible for the data owned by that department. Responsibilities include:

- Classification of data
- Ensuring security controls are in place
- Approving disclosure activities and access requests
- Ensuring proper access rights are enforced

If data storage is outsourced, the service contract must include a clause specifying all data remains the property of the company, and should dictate not only how long the storage provider will retain your data after you stop doing business with them, but also how your data will be disposed of.

Data Custodian

The *data custodian* is responsible for storing and keeping the data safe, including backup and restorative duties. Data custodians also ensure that the company's security policy regarding information security and data protection are being enforced. This results in the data custodian being responsible for maintaining controls to enforce classification levels as set by the data owner.

System Owner

The *system owner* is responsible for one or more systems, each of which may contain or process data owned by more than one data owner. A system owner ensures the systems under his or her purview align with the company's policies regarding security controls, authentication, authorization and configurations. The role also ensures the systems have been assessed for vulnerabilities and report incursions to the data owners.

Security Administrator

The *security administrator* implements and maintains security network devices and software, manages user accounts and access and tests security patches. Normally a network administrator keeps the network up and running, while the security administrator keeps the network secure.

Supervisor

The *supervisor*, sometimes called the user manager, is responsible for access and assets for the people under the role's supervision. A supervisor informs the security administrator of new hires or terminations.

Change Control Analyst

The *change control analyst* approves or rejects changes to the network, systems or software.

Data Analyst

The *data analyst* works with data owners and is responsible for ensuring data is stored in a manner that makes sense to the organization's business needs.

User

A *user* uses data for work-related tasks.

Auditor

An *auditor* makes sure all other roles are doing what they are supposed to be doing, and ensures the proper controls are in place and maintained properly.

Questions

1. Which best describes a system owner?

    A) Usually a member of management

    B) Implements and maintains security network devices and software

    C) Is responsible for one or more systems

    D) Responsible for storing and keeping the data safe

2. Which group of organizational security are closest to the day-to-day operations?

    A) Executive management

    B) Operational management

    C) Senior management

    D) Functional management

3. Which of the following is NOT a layer of responsibility in organizational security?

    A) Executive management

    B) Senior management

    C) Operational management

    D) Functional management

4. Which best describes a CISO?

    A) Oversees information systems and technologies

    B) More of a technical role that reports to the CSO

    C) Responsible for the financial structure of a company

    D) The highest-ranking officer in the company and acts as the visionary

5. Which best describes a CIO?

    A) Responsible for the financial structure of a company

    B) Oversees information systems and technologies

    C) Is usually an attorney and ensures the company's data is kept safe

    D) The highest-ranking officer in the company and acts as the visionary

Chapter 15: Retention Policies

Most of the roles just discussed play some part in defining and implementing a _retention policy_. This policy dictates what data should be kept, where it is kept, how it should be stored, and how long it should be stored for. Legal counsel must always be consulted when dictating retention boundaries so that legal, regulatory and operational requirements are considered. Retention policies most importantly drive the transition from the archival stage to the disposal stage of the data life cycle.

Retained data must be kept in a format that is easily accessible. Four issues must be considered:

1) _Taxonomy_ – how classifications are labeled
2) _Classification_ – the classification can affect how the data is archived
3) _Normalization_ – adding attributes to make locating the data easier
4) _Indexing_ – make searches quicker by precomputing indexes on attributes

There are many legal and regulatory requirements for how long data should be retained, but they vary greatly based on the jurisdiction. Some guidelines on how to long to retain data are:

- Permanently – legal correspondence
- 7 years – business documents, accounts payables/receivables, employees who leave
- 5 years – invoices
- 4 years – tax records (after taxes were paid)
- 3 years – candidates who were not hired

The decision to retain data must be deliberate, specific and enforceable. _e-discovery_ is the process of producing electronically stored information (ESI) for a court or external attorney. To facilitate this process, the _electronic discovery reference model_ (_EDRM_) identifies eight steps:

1) _Identification_ of the requested data
2) _Preservation_ of this data while being delivered
3) _Collection_ of the data
4) _Processing_ to ensure the correct format
5) _Review_ of the data
6) _Analysis_ of the data for proper content
7) _Production_ of the final data set
8) _Presentation_ of the data

Chapter 15: Retention Policies

Questions

1. Which of the following best describes classification?

    A) Make searches quicker by precomputing indexes

    B) Adding attributes to make locating the data easier

    C) How classifications are labeled

    D) The classification can affect how the data is archived

2. Which of the following best describes normalization?

    A) Adding attributes to make locating the data easier

    B) The classification can affect how the data is archived

    C) How classifications are labeled

    D) Make searches quicker by precomputing indexes

3. Which of the following best describes taxonomy?

    A) Make searches quicker by precomputing indexes

    B) Adding attributes to make locating the data easier

    C) The classification can affect how the data is archived

    D) How classifications are labeled

4. Which of the following best describes indexing?

    A) Make searches quicker by precomputing indexes

    B) How classifications are labeled

    C) Adding attributes to make locating the data easier

    D) The classification can affect how the data is archived

5. What are the four issues to consider when dealing with retained data?

    A) Taxonomy, classification, categorization and indexing

    B) Taxonomy, classification, normalization and indexing

    C) Taxonomy, categorization, normalization and optimization

    D) Taxonomy, categorization, denormalization and optimization

Chapter 16: Privacy and Asset Protection

Historically, Western democracies have always valued privacy over security. However, after 9/11, the government prioritized security over privacy. Then, after the Snowden leaks in 2013 showing how far the government overstepped reasonable boundaries, privacy has once again become the priority.

Protecting Privacy

Data Owners

As previously noted, *data owners* make decisions regarding who can access their data and when. However, when it comes to privacy data, organization-wide formal written policies should make these decisions, with exceptions well-documented an approved.

Data Processors

Data processors are the users who touch the privacy data daily. The individuals must be properly trained to handle their duties, and routine inspections to ensure their behavior complies with policy must be implemented.

Data Remanence

Data remanence occurs when data is not permanently erased from storage media. Simply hitting the 'delete' button does not erase data – it simply marks the previously-allocated space as free for use, but the data remains. *NIST SP 800-88* 'Guidelines for Media Sanitization' provides guidelines for combating data remanence.

Diving into the details for a minute, when an operating system allocates space on a storage medium, it normally allocates blocks of memory, with each block being referenced in a file allocation table. When you the file is deleted, the blocks are not erased – the pointer is simply removed from the file allocation table. The actual bits and bytes are never overwritten until a new file is saved over the previous data, and in many cases even then some of the original data may remain because the new file does not overwrite the entire block.

To counter data remanence, we have four approaches:

1) *Overwriting* – replacing the 1's and 0's with random data
2) *Degaussing* –applying a powerful magnetic force to magnetic media such as hard drives and tapes
3) *Encryption* – if data is stored in an encrypted fashion, simply deleting the key renders the data unusable
4) *Physical destruction* – the best way is to simply destroy the physical media by shredding, exposing it to destructive chemicals or incineration

Limits on Collection

The US has very few limitations for the private sector on data that can be collected, but as rule only that data which is required for the business to operate should be collected and stored. This policy should be well-documented. Some companies divide privacy collection rules into two documents – one for employee data and one for external customer data.

Protecting Assets

Physical security is designed to counteract the following threats:

- Environment integrity
- Unauthorized access
- Theft
- Interruption to service
- Physical damage
- Compromised systems

The actual loss is almost always a great deal more than the cost of replacing the hardware.

Data Security Controls

There are three states that data may be in – we have already discussed this, but let's go into more detail.

If data is waiting to be used – that is, residing only on some type of secondary storage mechanism such as hard disks, it is called *data at rest*. This data is particularly vulnerable because a thief can steal the storage media if they have physical access. Pretty much the only protection we have in this case is through encryption of the data. Modern operating systems all can decrypt information on-the-fly as it is retrieved from storage and re-encrypt when putting it back.

Due to their mobility, laptops considerably increase the risk of theft. Many organizations encrypt the entire hard drive, and a key must be entered before the OS can even boot. *NIST SP 800-111* 'Guide to Storage Encryption Technologies for End User Devices' provides some decent approaches. Given that countries have varying laws regarding government access to data, an organization's encryption strategy must consider all the locales it will be operating in.

Data in motion describes the state of data as it is traveling across a network – this applies equally well to intranets as well as to the Internet. Again, encryption is the best protection strategy for data in motion with the use of TLS 1.1 or greater, or by using IPSec (which will be discussed later). Note that SSL and TLS 1.0 are not in this list – serious vulnerabilities were discovered in these standards making them unusable. Both TLS and IPSec have multiple cipher suites, with some stronger than others. A common exploit for in-motion data is the man-in-the-middle attack (which will also be discussed later). Beyond encryption, trusted channels such as virtual private networks (VPNs) can also protect data in this state.

The third state, *data in use,* describes data residing in primary storage devices, such as volatile memory, or RAM, memory caches or CPU registers. Data in these locations could remain for a long period of time until power is interrupted. The danger with this state is that the data is almost always in-memory in an unencrypted state, so is particularly vulnerable. So, how could someone get at this data? Often when a catastrophic error is encountered, many operating systems will dump the contents of memory to disk for later analysis, often writing data in an unencrypted format. Anyone with access to this storage medium will have direct access to the vulnerable data. Additionally, rogue processes could access memory in real-time and discover unencrypted information.

A *side-channel attack* exploits information that is being leaked by a cryptosystem. For example, the amount of power being consumed by the CPU or how long it takes a process to read/write data to disk can be used to infer certain types of information.

Media Controls

When discussing *media*, we are referring to any method of storing data, including disks, paper, USB drives, etc. Again, the CIA triad comes into play as we must ensure media is protected with respect to confidentiality, integrity and availability. Some companies have a media library with a librarian in charge of these duties, and users must check out resources. This is often the case when licenses are required for software use.

Media must be properly erased or destroyed (we have already discussed that). When media has been erased, it is said to be *sanitized*. This process is acceptable if the storage device will be used within the same physical environment for the same purposes. But how do we decide if we should destroy media instead of just erasing it? Simply follow this principal: ensure the enemy's cost of recovering the data exceeds its value.

The proper management of media includes the following nine attributes:

- *Audit* - there is a paper trail of who accessed what when
- *Access* – ensure required controls are in place to ensure only authorized people can access media
- *Backups* – we need to track this for two reasons, 1) to be able to restore damaged media and 2) to know what needs to be deleted when the data has reached end-of-life
- *History* – we need to track this for two reasons, 1) to make sure we don't use obsolete versions and 2) to prove due diligence
- *Environment* – physically protect media
- *Integrity* – transfer data to a newer media container before the old one wears out
- *Inventory* – this must be done on a scheduled basis to determine if media has gone missing
- *Disposal* – proper disposal of media that is no longer applicable or needed
- *Labeling* – when and who created it, how long should we keep it, classification, name and version

Data Leakage

The news over the last decade has been replete with stories of companies who have allowed their data to be *leaked* or stolen. It can be devastating to the company when this happens. A single episode can bring about losses including:

- Investigation and remediation
- Contacting individuals
- Penalties and fines
- Contractual liabilities
- Mitigating expenses such as free credit monitoring
- Direct damages to individuals, such as identity theft
- Loss of reputation or customer base

The most common breaches are due to employee negligence, often taking data from a secure environment into an unsecure one. The obvious answer to this risk is better training, but the company must also implement measures to prevent or detect when this type of violation occurs.

Data Leak Prevention

Data leak prevention, or *DLP*, describes all steps a company takes to prevent *unauthorized external* parties from gaining access to *sensitive* data. Note all three italicized words – *unauthorized*, *external* and *sensitive* – all three must apply to be considered part of DLP. DLP is not a technology problem, and neither can it be solved by technology alone.

Also note that the terms *loss* and *leak* are not always interchangeable. *Loss* means we no longer know the location of something, whereas *leak* means the confidentiality of something has been compromised. However, many security professionals use the terms interchangeably.

The first step in properly implementing DLP is to take inventory - figure out what you have and where it lives, starting with the most important assets and working towards less-critical data. The next step is to classify the data (we have already discussed this). Now, it is time to map the pathways through which the data flows. This will tell you where to place automated DLP sensors, which are simply checks that detect when sensitive data passes by. Which begs the question – how does a sensor detect sensitive data? This is normally done by examining file names, extensions, keywords and formats. Unfortunately, this type of detection can easily be defeated using steganography, or hiding data within a container of some type. Encryption can also help leakage get around sensors. Which means that regardless of how hard we try, some leakage will occur.

Therefore, we have to put into place mitigation strategies to handle this:

- *Backups* – we must execute and test backups to resort lost data
- *Life cycle* – ensure the data is safe as it migrates from one stage to the next
- *Physical security* – prevent theft of media
- *Culture* – build security into every aspect of an organization
- *Privacy* – make sure our sensors do not intrude on user's private lives
- *Change* – as organizational changes occur, make sure strategies keep pace

Implementation, Testing and Tuning

DLP requires that sensors be evaluated according to the following criteria:

- *Sensitivity* – how sensitive is the tool to locating protected data? The more in-depth it looks, the fewer false-positives you will have.
- *Policies* – how granular can you adjust the policies? As granularity increases so does complexity and flexibility.
- *Interoperability* – how much integration effort will you have to undertake to make a product work with your existing infrastructure?
- *Accuracy* – this can only be discovered by testing the product in your own environment.

Once a product has been selected, it must be integrated, tested and tuned. Tuning must be done with two aspects in-mind:

1) Make sure existing allowed paths still operate
2) Make sure previously-identified misuse paths are blocked

A successful DLP solution has a mindset of 'when something bad happens' as opposed to 'we hope we catch anything bad before it happens'. Because, bad WILL happen – your network will be penetrated but it must still function even with the perpetrators still inside.

Network DLP

Network DLP, or *NDLP*, is usually implemented inside of a network appliance and examines all traffic as it passes by (data in motion). Due to the high cost, these devices are usually placed at traffic choke points, and therefore cannot see any traffic occurring on network segments not connected directly to the appliance.

Endpoint DLP

An *Endpoint DLP*, or *EDLP*, is software that is installed on devices themselves and applies to local data at rest and in use. This has the advantage of being able to detect protected data when it enters the device or on the decryption/encryption boundary. This is a better solution than NDLP, but does have several drawbacks:

- Complexity – this solution requires many installations
- Cost – usually a license must be paid per device
- Updates – ensuring all devices are updated with new configuration can be expensive

- Circumvention – software can always be disabled, effectively rendering this solution useless

Hybrid DLP

A *Hybrid DLP* approach is to deploy NDLP and EDLP together. This is very costly but effective.

Protecting Other Assets

Aside from electronic data, mobile devices and paper can make very tempting targets for thieves.

Protecting Mobile Devices

Laptops, tablets and phones are a very tempting target for thieves beyond their hardware value. These devices should be configured before use to mitigate the risk of loss or leakage. Some security precautions that should be taken are:

- Inventory all devices (and periodically check to ensure something has not been stolen)
- Harden the OS with a baseline configuration
- Password-protect the BIOS
- Register the device with the vendor (if stolen and sent to the vendor, they can notify you if it appears on their radar)
- Do not check mobile devices when traveling
- Never leave one unattended
- Engrave the device with the serial #
- Use a slot lock cable
- Back up to an organizational repository
- Encrypt all data
- Enable remote wiping

Paper Records

Paper records will probably always be around (even as printed e-mails), and often contain sufficiently sensitive information to warrant controls. Precautions to take are:

- Educate your staff on proper handling
- Minimize the use of paper
- Keep workspaces tidy
- Lock sensitive paperwork away
- Prohibit taking paper home
- Label all paper with its classification
- Conduct random searches of employee bags when leaving
- Use a crosscut shredder

Safes

Many organizations use a safe to store media and paper documents. The types of *safes* are:

- *Wall* – embedded into a wall
- *Floor* – embedded into a floor
- *Chest* – stand-alone
- *Depository* – safes with slots allowing valuables to be added without opening
- *Vault* – large enough to walk inside
- *Passive relocking* – can detect someone trying to tamper with it, and extra bolts fall into place
- *Thermal relocking* – when a certain temperature is reached an extra lock is implemented

Some guidelines for safes:

- Change combinations periodically
- Only a small number of people should have access to the combination or key
- Place in a visible location to deter theft

Questions

1. When properly managing media, which of the following best describes the 'integrity' attribute?

A) Enables us to make sure we don't use obsolete versions and to prove due diligence

B) Physically protecting media

C) Transferring data to a newer media container before the old one wears out

D) Records who created data and when, and how long should we keep it

2. Which of the following terms describes a DLP that is deploy on a network and on computers simultaneously?

A) Hybrid DLP

B) NDLP

C) EDLP

D) Mixed DLP

3. What term is associated with data not permanently being erased from storage media?

A) Remaining data

B) Residual data

C) Data remanence

D) Data retention

4. What are the four attributes used when evaluating sensors for DLP?

A) Performance, availability, ease of use and user acceptance

B) Performance, policies, ease of use and user acceptance

C) Sensitivity, policies, interoperability and accuracy

D) Sensitivity, availability, interoperability and accuracy

5. Which of the following best describes data-at-rest?

A) Data residing in volatile storage devices

B) Data residing in non-volatile storage devices

C) Data traveling across a network

D) Data being actively processed by a computer

Section 3: Security Architecture and Engineering Domain

Let's now move on to the Security Architecture and Engineering *Domain*, which is the task of building security directly into the technology products we use every day. This domain is the second largest for the CISSP BOK and for a good reason – how we engineer security into our systems from the ground-up will either hurt or help the overall security posture of an organization.

Chapter 17: Computer and System Architecture

In general, an _architecture_ is a tool to understand a complex system. In this chapter we are going to examine computer architectures and the resulting system when multiple computers are combined.

Computer Architecture

Computer architecture encompasses all aspects of a physical computer – CPU, memory, storage, logic circuits, buses, etc.

The Central Processing Unit

Inside of a computer is something called the _algorithmic logic unit_, or _ALU_, which is the real brain power. The ALU performs mathematical functions and logical operations on data it gets from computer memory. Now, computers have lots of memory, but the clear majority of it is relatively slow to access, so there is a special type of memory called a _register_ which sits very close to the ALU and is extremely fast. Something must load data from the main memory into the registers for the ALU to operate on, and this is called the _control unit_. Once the control unit has loaded the instructions and data into the registers, it tells the ALU to start processing. Together, the control unit, ALU and registers are collectively referred to as the _central processing unit_, or _CPU_.

The _operating system_ (_OS_) and software that runs on top of the OS are nothing but a list of very complex instructions for the ALU to execute. As blazingly fast as the ALU is, it can only execute one instruction at a time. So how do computers appear to do several things at once? That is because the control unit can switch back and forth between different sets of instructions (in other words, software processes) so that it appears to be doing several things at once.

Now, there are three types of registers. The _general register_ holds variables and temporary results that the ALU will use as it executes instructions. The _program counter register_ points to the next instruction to be executed – when the current instruction has been completed, the control unit will load this register with the memory address to the next instruction, and so forth. _Special registers_ hold information such as things called the stack pointer, the program counter and the _program status word_ (_PSW_).

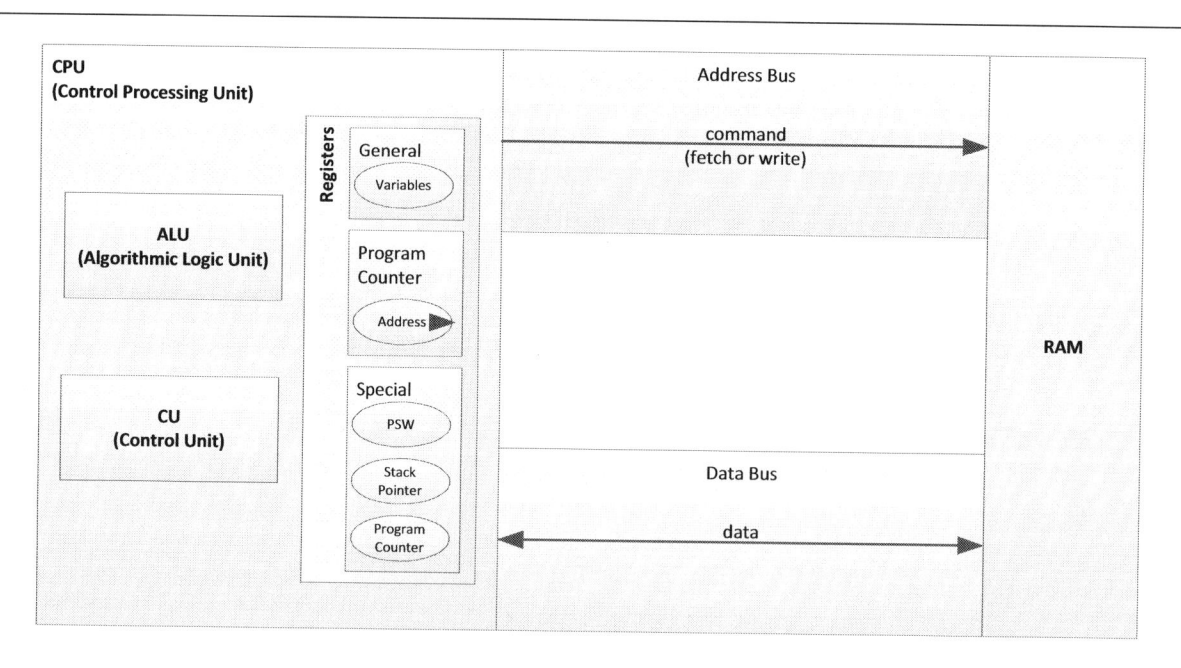

Figure 9: The CPU

The _stack_ is a list of pointers to processes (we will discuss them in a few minutes). As a process invokes another process, a pointer to the first process is put on the stack. When the second process calls another, a pointer to the second process is put on the stack. A _stack pointer_ lets us know where in the whole list we currently are.

The PSW holds different bits that reflect the execution mode the CPU should be operating in. For example, one of the bits indicates if the CPU should be working in _user mode_, also called a _problem state_, or in _privilege mode_, sometimes called _kernel_ or _supervisor mode_. This is a very important concept in security, because when the CPU operates in kernel mode it will pretty much allow anything to happen, whereas in user mode the CPU will keep some functions off-limits.

You might recall that we described registers as being very small and very fast. So how does the CPU operate on large chunks of memory or carry out complex processes? Well, the answer lies in the fact that registers hold addresses to memory locations, not the actual contents themselves. The CPU is connected to general computer memory, or RAM, through a circuit called an _address bus_. Whenever the CPU is ready to execute an instruction or operate on data, it will send a _fetch request_ on the address bus and include the memory address where the information should be sitting – the address comes from the register. The data is located and is returned to the CPU on the _data bus_. If the CPU needs to update the data, it will send the memory address on the address bus, and send the updated data on the data bus along with a WRITE command.

Both the address and data buses can only send a finite number of bits at a time – the more bits sent simultaneously, the faster data can travel. Common sizes (in order of increasing throughput) are 8, 16, 32 and 64-bits wide. The address and data buses are separate, so they can operate simultaneously for even more speed.

Multiprocessing
Now that we have nailed CPUs, let's talk about what happens when you have _multiprocessing_, or when you put more than one CPU into a single computer. Software must be written for a specific CPU architecture, and simply tossing in an additional CPU does not mean software knows what to do with it – the operating system must be written specifically to know how to use more than one processor.

There are two modes that multi-processing units can operate in:

- _Symmetric_ – all processors are load-balanced, and are handed work as each becomes available (most common use)

- _Asymmetric_ – processors may be completely dedicated to a specific task or application (used if time-sensitivity is a must)

Memory Types
There are many different _memory types_, and computers will always use more than one type simultaneously. Memory speed is represented as how long a single operation takes in units of nanoseconds (ns), which is one billionth of a second. The lower the number the faster the memory is.

Random Access memory
Random access memory (_RAM_) is _volatile_, in that it will lose its contents if power is interrupted. _Dynamic RAM_ (_DRAM_) must be continuously refreshed to retain contents, whereas _static RAM_ (_SRAM_) does not, resulting in faster access times. SRAM is more expensive than DRAM, so SRAM is usually used for smaller caches while DRAM makes up the majority of computer memory.

Some other types of RAM are (each require a specific type of controller chip):

- _Synchronous DRAM_ (_SDRAM_) – synchronizes itself with the CPU clock to make communication faster
- _Extended data out DRAM_ (_EDO DRAM_) – whereas DRAM can fetch a single block of data at a time, EDO DRAM can 'look ahead' and fetch the next block at the same time
- _Burst EDO DRAM_ (_BEDO RAM_) – instead of just two blocks like EDO, BEDO can send 4 blocks in a 'burst'
- _Double data rate SDRAM_ (_DDR SDRAM_) – whereas SDRAM carries out one read instruction per clock cycle, DDR SDRAM can execute two

Additionally, some systems can physically segment memory so that only certain processes can access this memory – this increases security and is called _hardware segmentation_.

Read-Only Memory
Read-only memory, or _ROM_, is a non-volatile memory type, meaning that it will retain its contents even when power is lost. ROM cannot be altered once it has been written, and the resulting content is called _firmware_.

Programmable read-only memory, or PROM, can be reprogrammed a single time.

Erasable programmable read-only memory, or *EPROM*, can be reprogrammed any number of times by using a UV light to erase the previous contents. This was replaced by *electrically erasable programmable read-only memory*, or *EEPROM*, which allows for erasing electrically, but only a single byte at a time.

Flash memory is the current technology and is a solid-state device, meaning it does not have any moving parts. It uses a specific voltage to indicate a bit value of 1. It is smaller, lighter and faster than most other non-volatile storage media but is also more expensive.

Cache Memory
Cache memory is a type of memory used for high-speed writing and reading activities. It is more expensive than other types of memory, and is therefore used in small amounts. CPUs usually have some amount of cache memory, as do motherboards. Cache speeds are usually indicated by a level – L1, L2 or L3. L1 and L2 are usually built directly into processors and controllers.

Memory Mapping
The CPU has dedicated circuits to system memory (address and data buses) and therefore deals directly with physical memory addresses, called *absolute addresses*. However, when software wants to use memory, it must use a *logical address* instead – this is required to put a layer of security between software and physical memory, as well as to increase efficiency (as we will discuss).

The security aspect of this layer is very important – you do not want some rogue process wandering off and accessing memory belonging to another application, or worse yet – belonging to the operating system. By requiring a memory mapper to be in the middle of memory reads and writes, this layer of protection is easily and securely enabled. A *relative address* is an offset to another address, whether it is absolute or logical.

Buffer Overflows
Within an application, a process can invoke another process and pass variables to it, which are called *parameters*. The CPU handles this by storing a pointer to the first process at the bottom of something called a *stack*, which is just a list of addresses and data. The CPU will then store each parameter on top of the previous one on the same stack. The second process can modify the parameters passed in and complete its execution, at which point the CPU will retrieve the pointer to the first process from the bottom of the stack and allow it to continue.

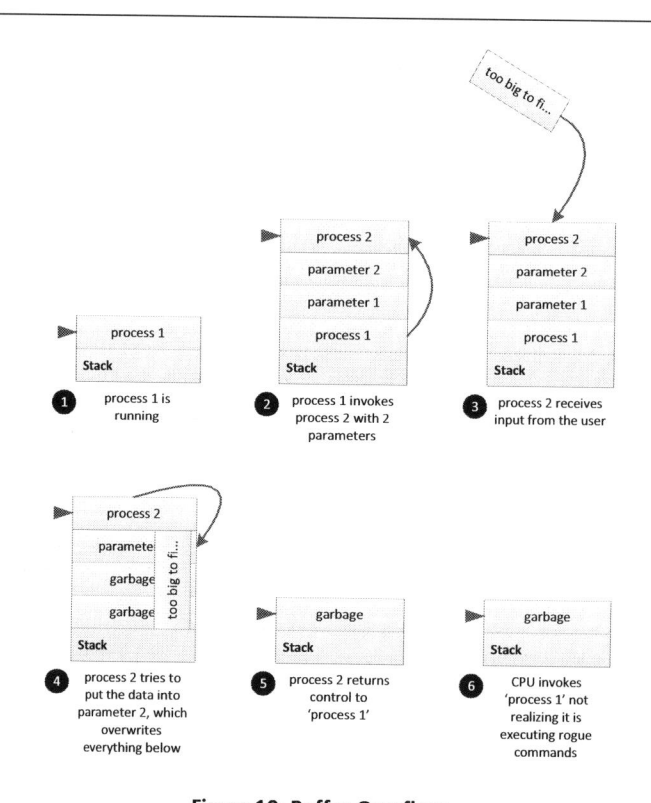

Figure 10: Buffer Overflow

The interesting thing to note is that if the second process were to try and overwrite a parameter on the stack with a new value that was too large to fit into the space allocated for that parameter, it would end up overwriting anything below it. This might be another parameter, or if it itself were the first parameter, it would overwrite the pointer to the first process. This means that when the CPU retrieves the pointer to the first process and executes it, it would be trying to execute instructions in an entirely different location in memory. Parameter values are wrapped in something called a buffer, which is put on the stack. Exceeding the size of this buffer is called _overflowing_. Therefore, this scenario is called a _buffer overflow_.

Now consider this – what if the second process took in some type of user input and tried to store that value into one of the parameters passed in by the first process? No harm – processes do this all the time. But, what if the input exceeded the expected length of that parameter, and the second process did not notice this? Not only do you have a buffer overflow, but now the user is able to insert some rogue data onto the stack. And if the user was really, really clever – say some malicious hacker – they could craft that extra data to force the CPU to execute some of their code. That is a lot of ifs, right? Well, it has happened time and again and is still a major attack vector today. However, the attacker must do three things:

1) Know the size of the buffer to be overflowed
2) Know the addresses that have been assigned to the stack
3) Write a dangerous payload small enough so that it can be passed as a parameter

Some programming languages are more susceptible to buffer overflows than others – primarily lower level languages that require direct memory allocation such as C or C++ are the worst offenders. Since the architecture of the registers change from platform to platform, a specific buffer overflow exploit will normally only work on a single OS combined with a specific hardware platform.

One method for defeating this attack is to introduce _address space layout randomization_ or (_ASLR_), first implemented in OpenBSD. This prevents the same memory addresses from being used each time. Another form of protection is _data execution prevention_, or _DEP_ – this prevents execution of code in certain memory segments.

Memory Leaks
When an application needs to store data, it must request sufficient memory to contain the data from the memory manager. When the application is done, it is supposed to release that memory for use by some other process. Unfortunately, sometimes badly-written code will forget to release the memory resulting in a _memory leak_. Over time, enough of these 'leaky' operations will cause the system to run out of memory and either freeze or slow down so much it becomes unusable. Memory leaks can occur in the operating system, applications or software drivers. Attackers can take advantage of this condition by causing the leaky process to execute repeatedly until the system crashes. One feature that many modern programming languages such as Java and C# include is a _garbage collector_ – this is a background process that ensures all allocated memory is freed up when appropriate.

System Architecture
The term _system architecture_ describes the components of a system and how they interact, and is a tool used to design computer systems such that it meets the goals of all stakeholders. _Development_ refers to the entire life cycle of a system from planning to retirement. A _system_ can be most anything - a computer, an application, a set of computers, a network, etc.

ISO 42010 'Systems and Software Engineering – Architecture Description' outlines the specifications of a system architecture, and is continuing to evolve. This standard defines several terms:

- _Architecture_ – describes a system made up of components, their relationships to each other and their environment, and the principles guiding its design and evolution
- _Architecture Description_ (_AD_) – collection of document types to document an architecture in a formal manner
- _Stakeholder_ – an individual, team or organization with an interest in, or concern about, a system
- _View_ – representation of the entire system from the perspective of a related set of concerns
- _Viewpoint_ – a specification of the conventions for creating and using a view

Stakeholders include users, operators, maintainers, developers and suppliers. Each stakeholder has their own _concerns_ pertaining to the system. Each view describes a different portion of the overall system, and are:

- Functionality
- Performance
- Interoperability
- Security

Decisions made by the architect are communicated using *architecture views*, such as logical, physical, structural, behavioral, management, cost and security. For the remainder of this section, we will focus on security.

Questions

1. Which of the following best describes the program status word?

A) Holds variables and temporary results that the ALU will use

B) Points to the next instruction to be executed

C) Holds the stack pointer, program counter and the PWS

D) Holds different bits that reflect the execution mode the CPU should be operating in

2. Of the following items, which is NOT something an attacker would need to do to cause a buffer overflow?

A) Write a dangerous payload small enough so that it can be passed as a parameter

B) Know the size of the buffer to be overflowed

C) Intercept messages as they pass through the registers

D) Know the addresses that have been assigned to the stack

3. Which of the following best describes EEPROM?

A) Can be reprogrammed any number of times by using a UV light to erase the previous contents

B) Allows for erasing electrically, but only a single byte at a time

C) A solid-state device, uses voltage to indicate '1'

D) Can be reprogrammed one time

4. Which best describes the difference between DRAM and SRAM memory?

A) DRAM memory will not lose the contents if power is interrupted, but SRAM memory must be continuously refreshed to retain contents

B) DRAM memory will lose the contents if power is interrupted, while SRAM memory retains the contents even if power is lost

C) SRAM memory will lose the contents if power is interrupted, while DRAM memory retains the contents even if power is lost

D) DRAM memory will lose the contents if not continuously refreshed, while SRAM memory does not need to be refreshed

5. Which of the following is NOT contained within the CPU?

A) RAM

B) Registers

C) ALU

D) Control Unit

Chapter 18: Operating Systems

An _operating system_ is the software on top of which applications will run. It is very complex and works directly with all processes, memory, input/output devices and the CPU.

Process Management

We have already use the term 'process' several times without really explaining what it means – let's fix that.

Operating systems, applications and software drivers are nothing but lines of code (lists of instructions) for the CPU to carry out. To come to life, they must be loaded into memory and properly initialized. When a portion of an application is initialized and loaded for execution, it is called a _process_, of which a single application may have many. Keep in mind that an application is just a bunch of lines of codes – but the moment it gets loaded into memory and is ready to run it becomes a process.

What does 'ready to run' mean? Well, when a process is being created, the OS assigns whatever resources it needs, such as a memory segment, a CPU time slot, APIs and files that have been requested, and much more. Therefore, a process already has everything it needs to run. As we already stated, the OS has many processes, such as how to display output to the screen, handling print jobs, etc. All modern OS's are capable of _multiprogramming_ – the ability to load multiple applications into memory at the same time. Most modern OS's also provide _multitasking_ – the ability to deal with requests from multiple applications simultaneously. If you have multitasking, then you obviously already can do multiprogramming.

Earlier OS's supported _cooperative multitasking_, in which the application had to volunteer its CPU time for some other application to use – but often time applications were not written to do this. Starting with Windows 95, and in Unix systems, the OS implemented _preemptive multitasking_, meaning the CPU would multitask no matter what the application wanted to do.

Processes can create child processes if they like, and the child process has its own memory space, stack and program counter values, just like the parent process has. A process can be in three different states:

- _Ready_ – the process has not yet sent any instructions to the CPU
- _Running_ – the CPU is executing the process' instructions
- _Blocked_ – the process is waiting for input, such as a keystroke

So how does the OS allow all the different processes to run simultaneously? As we mentioned before, a CPU can only execute one instruction at a time. It would be a big waste to require a single CPU for each process – a modern OS typically has many processes all running at the same time. Instead, the OS will keep track of every single process in a _process table_, which has one entry per process. Each entry contains enough information, such as state, stack pointers, and memory addresses, to be loaded into the CPU at any time so that the CPU can carry out the process' instructions for a little while – this is called a _time slice_, and the CPU is responsible for loading and unloading the information around the time slice. The CPU ensures that all processes get their fair share of CPU time.

However, sometimes an event happens, for example a key was pressed or something comes over the network, and this event needs immediate attention and should not wait until the OS gets around to the interested process' time slice. This is referred to as an _interrupt_ – an event that causes the OS to look the current process schedule, and perhaps move things around a bit to accommodate this new situation. There are two types of interrupts:

- _Maskable_ – assigned to an event that doesn't necessarily have to be taken care of immediately
- _Nonmaskable_ – makes the CPU stop whatever was going on and take care of this event

An example of a nonmaskable interrupt is the _watchdog timer_ – this is a background process that will perform a warm boot if the OS ever hangs.

Thread Management

If you remember, a single application can create many processes, and each process can also create child processes that have their very own memory space, file access and other resources. What we left out is that within each process, you will always find at least one _thread_ – which contains some of the process' instruction sets, and shares the process' memory space and resource. A process can create as many threads as it likes, and if it creates more than one thread, it is called _multithreaded_. This allows a single process to appear as if it is doing several things simultaneously, but in reality, the threads are just being switched around quickly much like the CPU gives each process its own time slice – but an important distinction is that all threads share the owning process' memory space and resources. This can lead to a problem called a *software deadlock*, wherein thread 1 needs a resource that thread 2 has locked, but thread 2 needs a resource that thread 1 has locked – the two threads will sit around forever waiting for the other thread to release the needed resource, which will never happen. If an attack exploits this weakness, it will result in a DoS attack. Normally, the OS will detect this situation and eventually kill the process.

Process Activity

There are several patterns that applications and operating systems follow to ensure proper *process isolation* – making sure that misbehaving processes do not affect other processes. They are:

- *Encapsulation* – making sure that a process does not expose its inner workings – it needs to implement *data hiding* by only communicating through a well-defined interface
- *Time multiplexing* – the OS must manage access to resources that are shared between multiple processes (such as multiple processes all reading from the same file)
- *Naming distinctions* – each process has its own unique ID assigned by the OS
- *Virtual memory mapping* – the OS does not expose physical memory directly – it is mapped through a virtual address, allowing the OS to play memory cop

Memory Management

Let's look at virtual memory mapping in a little more detail. The idea is that an OS provides an *abstraction layer* on top of a resource – this means that the process can't get to the resource directly, but must go through an intermediate layer which can inject security and optimize performance. Memory management is an example of this and provides the following features:

- An abstraction level for programmers
- Optimizes performance with limited physical memory
- Protects the OS and applications loaded into memory

Abstraction means the details are hidden. In the case of memory management, a *memory segment* (a division of the computer's memory into subsections) is exposed to the requesting process, and this is managed by, obviously – the *memory manager*. In short, the memory manager abstracts memory locations away from any process wishing to use the memory. It is responsible for the following:

- *Relocation* - swap memory contents from RAM to the hard drive and hide this from the process
- *Protection* - make sure processes can only access their memory segments
- *Sharing* – ensure CIA with shared memory and allow different levels of access to interact with the same memory
- *Local organization* – segment memory types and provide an addressing scheme, and allow multiple processes to access the same shared DLL*
- *Physical organization* – segment the physical memory for use by the applications and OS processes

* A *DLL* (*dynamic link library*) is a shared set of functions that processes can reuse

So, how does the memory manager make sure a process only accesses its memory segment? When a process creates a thread (and remember that all processes have at least one thread), the CPU uses two registers. The *base register* points to the beginning memory address for the segment, and the *limit register* stores the ending address. Whenever the thread asks the memory manager to access data, the memory manager will make sure the requested memory address falls within the starting and ending addresses.

Just keep in mind that two processes could both have access to the same memory segment but have different access rights. There could also be varying levels of protection assigned to different instruction and data types.

Virtual Memory

Secondary storage is the term we use to describe non-volatile storage (does not lose contents when the power is interrupted) such as hard drives, USB drives and optical discs. When we talk about RAM (which is volatile) and non-volatile memory together, we can collectively refer to that as *virtual memory*. When the system uses all available volatile memory, it can use non-volatile memory to make it appear as if there was more physical memory than there really is. This is done by copying a portion of volatile memory to non-volatile storage, thereby freeing up the volatile memory for use – this process is called *swapping*, and the non-volatile storage is called the _swap space_. Windows uses the pagefile.sys file as the swap space.

So, what happens when a process needs to access the memory that has been swapped to non-volatile memory? The system will load data back into physical memory in units called _pages_ – this is called _virtual memory paging_. Reading from a hard disk will obviously be slower than retrieving the data from physical memory, but it allows the system to provide significantly more memory space than it could otherwise.

This does open a security hole, however – the contents of physical memory remain accessible on the storage media after the OS has already shut down. Any unencrypted data held in memory will then be potentially available on the storage media. Operating systems have routines to ensure this data is deleted, but if an OS crashes, the data may remain in an unencrypted format on disk.

Input/Output Device Management

Remember that the OS must manage input/output devices, such as serial ports and network cards. I/O devices will be either block or character devices. A _block device_ such as a hard drive exposes data in fixed-block sizes, and each block has a unique address. A _character device_, such as a printer, operates using a stream of characters only. When an application needs to use an I/O device, it will communicate with the OS, which then communicates with a device driver. The _device driver_ is very low-level software that knows all the specifics about the device.

We have already described interrupts as events that the OS detects. One source of interrupts are I/O devices – the device will send a single across the bus to the CPU saying 'Hey, I need attention' – that is why we call them interrupts, because they 'interrupt' the CPU and force it to pay attention. However, if the CPU is busy _and_ the device's interrupt is not a higher priority than the job already being worked on, then the CPU simply ignores it.

Operating systems can service I/O devices in several ways:

- _Programmable I/O_ – the CPU will poll the device periodically to see if it is ready; very slow
- _Interrupt-Driven I/O_ – the CPU will send a command, and when the device is ready for another command it sends an interrupt back to the CPU; faster, but still not very fast
- _I/O Using DMA_ – the _direct memory access_ (DMA) controller feeds data to memory that both the DMA and the device share without having to bother the CPU; may also be called _unmapped I/O_.
- _Premapped I/O_ – the CPU gives the physical memory address of the requesting process to the device, and they then communicate directly; fast but insecure
- _Fully Mapped I/O_ – same as premapped I/O, but instead of sharing physical memory addresses, the CPU will only give out logical memory addresses to both the process and device – it does not trust either

CPU Architecture Integration

An operating system is software, while the CPU is hardware. Therefore, for them to work together, the OS must be written exactly for a specific type of CPU. The glue that binds the two together is called an _instruction set_ – a language that both the OS and CPU understand. One example is the x86 instruction set, which works with both Intel and AMD CPUs and Windows, OS X, Linux. All the things that make up the CPU – registers, ALU, cache, logic gates, etc. – are referred to as the _microarchitecture_. The OS talks to the microarchitecture using an instruction set.

Operating systems are made up of multiple layers, with varying degrees of trust. For example, both the memory mapper and registry editors are part of the Windows OS, but Windows must have a higher level of trust in the memory mapper than a registry editor. So how does an OS implement multiple layers of trust, even within its own components? The answer is that the OS has layers we call _rings_. Ring 0 contains the heart of the OS – its kernel – along with access to physical memory, devices, system drivers and some very sensitive configuration parameters. This is the most trusted and protected of all the rings. A process running in Ring 0 is said to be running in _kernel mode_.

The next ring is called Ring 1, then Ring 2, Ring 3 and so forth. The maximum number of rings is dictated by the CPU architecture, but the OS may choose to ignore some rings. For example, Windows uses rings 0 and 3 only, and completely ignores rings 1 and 2. Different OSs will choose to use rings differently, but they all operate on the same basic principle - the higher the ring number, the further away from the core it is, the less trusted it is and the less power processes running there have. Additionally, processes in an outer ring cannot directly contact process in a more inner ring, but processes running in an inner ring can have direct contact with processes in a more outer ring if they wish. Now, a process in Ring 3 can certainly communicate with Ring 0, but not directly - the message must go through a gatekeeper which will inspect the message for security violations first. The gatekeeper is usually called an *application programming interface*, or *API*.

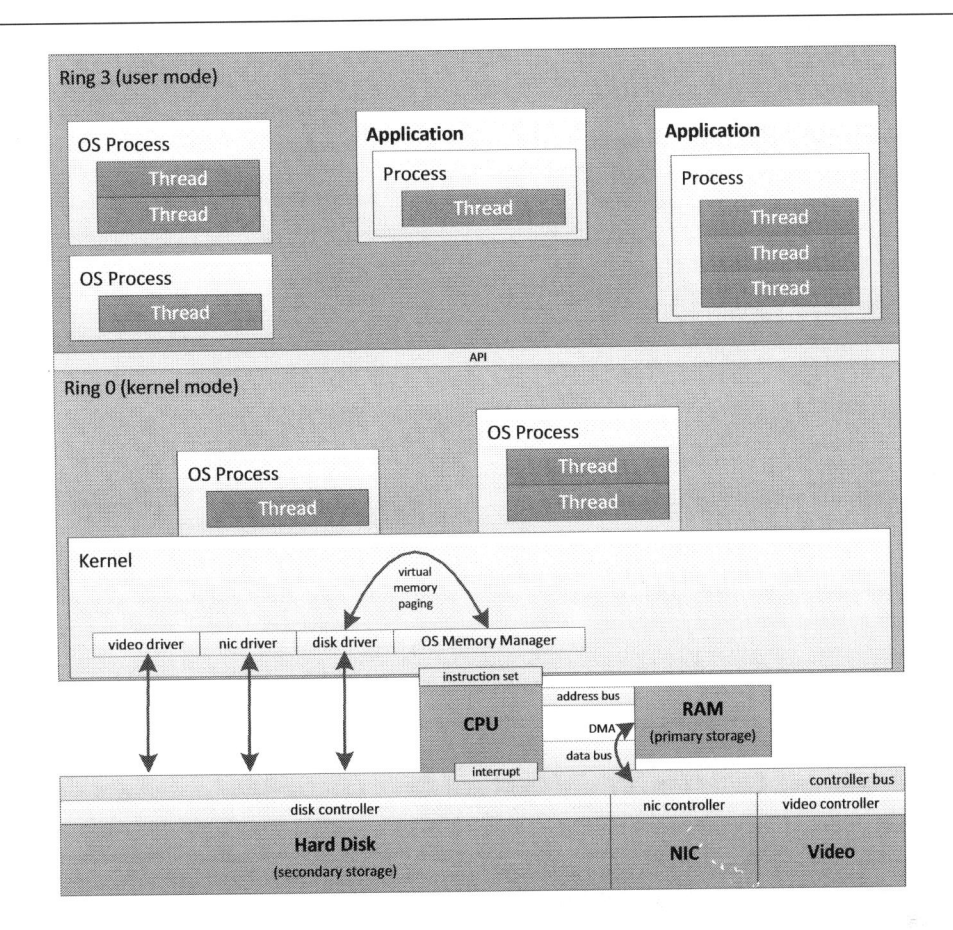

Figure 11: Operating System Architecture

Remember kernel mode? It is used to describe processes running in ring 0. Well, processes running in ring 3 (for Windows, OS X and most versions of Linux) are referred to as running in *user mode*. When a process is registered in the process table, the PSW stores the mode the process is running in – kernel or user. The CPU will then disallow certain instructions based on the mode a process is running under. Obviously, the Holy Grail for attackers is to get their process to load under ring 0 and operate in kernel mode. One method to do this is to replace kernel DLL or modules files with their own code. Once the OS does this, the attacker pretty much has complete control of the system. When we refer to the resources that a process has access to, we are referring to the process' *domain*. The further out a ring is, the larger the domain that process running in that ring have access to.

Operating System Architectures

We previously examined the system architecture, which includes hardware, software and firmware. Now, let's focus on just the operating system architecture. We have already discussed kernel vs user modes, and what components run in each of those modes is really the biggest difference when discussing the various OS architectures. In a *monolithic architecture*, all processes work in kernel mode. Early operating systems such as MS-DOS were monolithic, and suffered from:

- Lack of modularity – difficult to update
- Lack of portability – difficult to port to another hardware platform due to lack of abstraction

- Lack of extensibility – hard to add functionality due again to lack of abstraction
- Unstable and insecure – since everything ran in kernel mode, one process could bring down the entire OS

As a result, architects came up with the *layered operating system*, in which functionality was divided into 5 layers, similar to rings. This addressed the issues of modularity, portability and extensibility, but the entire OS still ran in kernel mode, so it was still somewhat unstable and insecure. However, at least applications resided outside of the OS, providing some type of *data hiding*, or abstraction. Unfortunately, the layered approach had some significant drawbacks – due to the multiple layers performance suffered, it was very complex and security still had not been addressed.

The next OS evolution saw the OS kernel shrink so that only the most critical processes ran in kernel mode, and complexity was reduced as a side-effect. Unfortunately, due to the small size of the kernel, the number of user-to-kernel *mode transitions* was so great that performance became unacceptable.

So, the *hybrid microkernel architecture* was invented. With this architecture, the microkernel remains small to reduce complexity, but it is not the only resident in ring 0 (kernel mode) – the other services in ring 0, called *executive services*, communicate with the microkernel in a type of client-server model. This prevents the user-to-kernel mode transition, but keeps the microkernel small and nimble.

To summarize, we have four different OS architectures:

- *Monolithic* – everything is in kernel mode
- *Layered* – only the OS is in kernel mode and is in layers
- *Microkernel* – a medium-sized kernel is in kernel mode
- *Hybrid microkernel* – a very small kernel and executive services run in kernel mode

Virtual Machines

Many times, software can be run only on certain types of hardware. However, it is possible to create a 'sandbox' on top of an OS to trick the older software into thinking it is running on the hardware it needs. This is called *virtualization* – we are creating a virtual environment for the software to run inside of.

Today we can run storage devices, applications and even entire operating systems in a virtualized environment. Running a virtualized instance of an operating system is called a *virtual machine*. Virtualization allows a single host to execute multiple guests simultaneously – physical resources such as RAM, disk space and processors are shared among the guests by a *hypervisor*, and each guest thinks it is the only one running – it has no awareness of the host. The hypervisor is invisible to the guests, and acts as the abstraction layer between the host and guests.

Beyond being able to run really old software on newer hardware, why do this? It all comes down to economics – it is a lot cheaper to buy a single system with an immense amount of power that can host 48 guest OS's than it is to buy 48 mid-level systems.

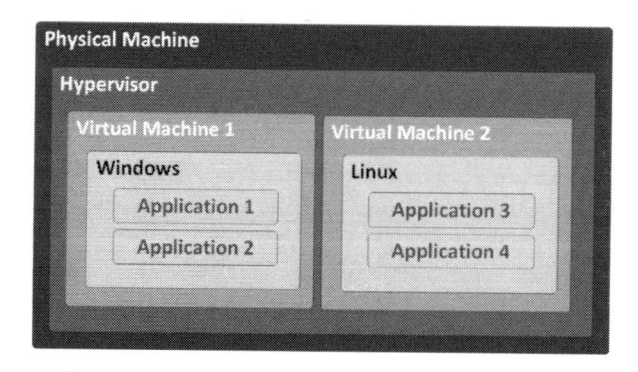

Figure 12: Virtualization

Here are some other reasons:

- Prevents us from having under-utilized systems
- Running legacy applications
- Running untrusted applications in a secure environment (sandboxes)
- Creating systems with limited or guaranteed resources
- Provide the illusion of hardware that does not actually exist
- Hot standbys (running until needed)
- Allows for production debugging
- Ability to inject faults to study application behavior
- Software migration
- Package applications together and running as instances
- Ability to save and restore state
- Create arbitrary test scenarios for QA

Questions

1. Which term represents an interrupt that makes the CPU stop whatever was going on and process the instruction immediately?

    A) Required

    B) Nonmaskable

    C) Primary

    D) Singular

2. Which of the following best describes multiprogramming?

    A) The ability to load multiple applications into memory at the same time

    B) The CPU will multitask no matter what the application wants to do

    C) The ability to deal with requests from multiple applications simultaneously

    D) An application must volunteer its CPU time for some other application to use

3. Which of the following describes a division of the computer's memory into subsections?

    A) Memory segment

    B) Memory allocation

    C) Memory separation

    D) Memory access

4. Which term best describes units used to describe the swap space?

    A) Pages

    B) Virtual memory paging

    C) Swap space

    D) Secondary storage

5. Which best describes all the things that make up the CPU?

    A) Instruction set

    B) Rings

    C) Microarchitecture

    D) Domain

Chapter 19: System Security Architecture and Models

OK – we're done with operating systems, so let's move on now to system security architecture. System architecture has several views, but we're really concerned with security, so let's dive right into system *security* architecture.

System Security Architecture

Security Policy
Security must always start with a policy – otherwise you never know what your end goal is. A _security policy_ defines how sensitive information and resources should be managed and protected.

Security Architecture Requirements
Back in the 1970s when computers were just beginning to support multiple users and networking capabilities, the US government needed a way to instruct vendors on how to create systems the government would then purchase. The biggest item on their shopping list was security – and that is how the _Trusted Computer System Evaluation Criteria_ came into being. At its core are four components.

Trusted Computer Base
The _trusted computer base_, or _TCB_, represents all hardware, software and firmware in a system coupled with how the system enforces security. For the most part, the TCB is the OS kernel, since it incorporates software, hardware and firmware, and is the primary enforcer of security, but can also include other components such as configuration files and some programs. When a user or process communicates with the TCB, we call it a _trusted path_ – the TCB protects resources along this path from being compromised. If someone or some process is working on that path exclusively, then they are said to be in a _trusted shell_ – they cannot break out of that shell and no unauthorized components can break in. Any piece of a system that could be used to compromise the system is part of the TCB, and those components must be developed and controlled with a high level of security in-mind. For example, the memory manager must be tamperproof. When working in kernel mode, the CPU must have the correct logic gates in-place. APIs need to accept only secure requests. And so forth. We have already discussed a 'domain' – within the TCB we call it an _execution domain_ – all TCB components reside in Ring 0 and no one outside of Ring 0 can communicate directly with them.

When a system goes through an evaluation, the TCB is looked at closely, and testing must show how the TCB is protected. The level of detail that a system undergoes is directly proportionate to the rating that the system is trying to achieve – the higher the rating the more granular the review.

Security Perimeter
Between the contents of the TCB (trusted components) and all components outside of the TCB (untrusted components) lives an imaginary wall called the _security perimeter_. Any communication passing through the security perimeter is subject to an extra level of scrutiny to ensure that security is not compromised. Put another way, anytime an untrusted component tries to communicate with a trusted component, we need to inspect that pathway with a great level of scrutiny. In practice, the security perimeter is usually an API sitting between Ring 0 and Ring 3. In this case, 'Ring 3', 'untrusted' and 'outside the TCB' all mean the same thing, as do 'Ring 0', 'trusted' and 'TCB'.

Reference Monitor
So how do we know if an untrusted component is allowed to communicate with the TCB via the security perimeter? That jobs falls to the _reference monitor_, an abstract machine that deals with subjects and objects – a _subject_ wants to access an _object_. To achieve a high level of trust, a system must ensure that all subjects, such as users or processes, are fully authorized before they can access the requested object, such as files, another process or other resources. Keep in mind that the reference monitor is just a concept, not an actual thing, but something a system must implement.

Security Kernel
The _security kernel_ is simply the TCB plus the reference monitor – it is the actual _implementation_ of the reference monitor, and must:

- Provide tamperproof isolation for the processes implementing the reference monitor concept
- Must be invoked for _every_ access attempt and impossible to circumvent
- Must be small enough to be completely tested and verified

The security kernel implements the systems security policy. Policies that prevent flow from a high security level to a lower security level are called _multilevel security policies_.

Security Models

So, we have the concept of a reference monitor, and the actual implementation of the reference monitor called the security kernel. So how do we make the jump from conceptual to actual? Well, it turns out that most patterns of doing that have already been well documented as something called _security models_. Keep in mind that a security model gives us goals of how to implement a reference monitor, but that actual implementation details are still left open for the system vendor. We will go over seven common security models – the primary difference between each is how it addresses the CIA triad.

Each security model has its own set of rules, but there is an easy trick to keep some of them straight:

- The word 'simple' means 'read'
- The word 'star' or the symbol '*' means 'write'

Note: A lot of text editors use the '*' symbol in the title bar to denote that unsaved changes have been made, or that a 'write' needs to take place. Use that little trick to remember the difference between 'simple' and 'star'.

Bell-LaPadula Model

The first model is the _Bell-LaPadula model_, and it provides confidentiality only. It was created in the 1970s to prevent secret information from being unintentionally leaked, and was the first mathematical model of a multilevel security policy. This model is called a _multilevel security system_ because it requires users to have a clearance level, and data to have a classification. The rules are:

- Simple security rule – no read up
- * property rule – no write down
- Strong * property rule – read/write at same level only

Let's use an example to help understand how this model works: Adam is writing a report for a company's shareholders, which must reflect very accurate, factual and reliable information. In fact, Adam uses a fact checker service to make sure his information is always accurate. Eve, who has a lower level of clearance, is also writing a report on the same subject for a different audience, but her report is supposed to reflect her own opinions, which may or may not reflect reality. The simple security rule (no read up) prevents Eve from reading Adam's report – she does not have sufficient clearance to read a shareholder report. The * property rule (no write down) prevents Adam from contributing to Eve's report, just in case he accidentally reveals some confidential information. The strong * property rule prevents Adam and Eve from not only reading each other's report, but also contributing to it.

Biba Model

The _Biba model_ addresses data integrity only – it only wants to make sure data does not lose integrity (write), but doesn't care who can read it. The rules are:

- * integrity axiom – no write up
- Simple integrity axiom – no read down
- Invocation property – cannot invoke a service higher up

Using our example of Adam and Eve, the * integrity axiom says that Eve may not contribute to Adam's report, but she is free to use Adam's content in her own report. The simple integrity axiom says that Adam should not even read Eve's report because it may cause him to introduce opinion-based information into his report. The invocation property would prevent Eve from using the same fact checker service that Adam uses.

Both models discussed so far (Bell-LaPadula and Biba) are only concerned with how data flows from one level to another, but Bell-LaPadula enforces confidentiality while Biba enforces integrity.

Clark-Wilson Model

After the Biba model was around for a few years, the _Clark-Wilson model_ was developed that also enforces integrity, but takes a completely different approach by focusing on transactions and separation of duties. It uses the following elements:

- Users
- Transformation procedures (TPs) – read, write and modify
- _Constrained data items_ (CDIs) – things that can be manipulated only by TPs
- _Unconstrained data items_ (_UDIs_) – things that can be manipulated by users via primitive read and write operations
- _Integrity verification procedures_ (_IVPs_) – processes that check the consistency of CDIs with the real world

So, in short, a user can read and write UDIs only. A TP can read and write a CDI, which is then verified by an IVP.

Here is another way of looking at it:

- The system contains both CDIs (constrained data items) and UDIs (unconstrained data items)
- A User can modify UDIs directly but cannot modify CDIs directly
- Only a TP (transformation procedure) can modify a CDI on behalf of a user
- IVPs watch the work done by a TP and validates the integrity of the result

When a User employs a TP to modify a CDI, we call this an *access triple*. A *well-formed transaction* is the result of an access triple that has been verified by an IVP.

Using our previous example, the Clark-Wilson model would ensure that Eve (User) could not directly insert content into Adam's report (a CDI) – she would instead have to go through his copy writer (TP) first. A fact checker service (IVP) would ensure the new content was indeed factual. However, Eve could setup a meeting with Adam at any time on his calendar (UDI) to discuss content changes without going through any intermediary (TP).

Noninterference Model
When we ensure that actions taking place at a higher security level do not interfere with actions at a lower security level, we have achieved *noninterference*. This model does not worry about how data flows, but rather what a subject knows about the state of the system. For example, if an operation at a higher security level somehow let an operation at a lower level know it something was going on in the higher level, we would have a type of information leakage.

Going back to our Adam/Eve example, let's suppose that neither is allowed to discuss their respective reports with each other, but both have access to a shared network drive. If Adam leaves Eve a message in a text file about his report on the shared drive, this would be an example of communicating through covert channels and the noninterference model would prevent this. Alternatively, if Adam completes his report and sends it to a printer, Eve may be able to view the contents of the printer queue and realize that Adam was done – this too should be prevented by a noninterference model.

By the way, a *covert channel* is anyway to send or receive information in an unauthorized manner. There are two types:

- *Covert storage channel* – communicating through a shared storage system. This does not have to be files containing data – it could simply be the presence or absence of some system feature.
- *Covert timing channel* – communicating through the presence or absence of a system resource in a timed fashion

Brewer and Nash Model
The *Brewer and Nash model* is sometimes called the *Chinese Wall model* and states that a subject can write to an object in data set A only if the subject cannot read an object in data set B. Going back to our Adam/Eve example, let's suppose that if we allowed Eve to read Adam's shareholder report containing earnings information, we want to make sure that she cannot initiate stock market trades based on insider knowledge. Normally, she is free to trade on the stock market, but if she gains access to that insider information (read), we should block her ability to trade shares (write). Under this model access controls change dynamically, thus the 'throwing up a Chinese Wall' under certain conditions.

Graham-Denning Model
So far, all the models we have discussed remain very generic in terms of how to implement the rules each describes. The *Graham-Denning model* attempts to rectify this by defining a set of rights that can be executed:

- How to securely create an object
- How to securely create a subject
- How to securely delete an object
- How to securely delete a subject
- How to securely provide the read access right
- How to securely provide the grant access right
- How to securely provide the delete access right
- How to securely provide transfer access rights

Following this model ensures a system has covered all areas of a secure system. As an example, so far, we have never discussed if Adam can give other people the right to read his report. The Graham-Denning model exposes this security hole.

Harrison-Ruzzo-Ullman Model
The *Harrison-Ruzzo-Ullman* (*HRU*) *model* deals with the access rights of subjects and enforces the integrity of those rights. For example, it is simple to restrict or allow Eve's ability to read Adam's shareholders report. But what if she wanted to get a copy, remove a certain section, save the update, and then print it? If any one of those operations is denied, then the whole sequence should not be allowed. The HRU model is used to ensure that unforeseen vulnerabilities are not introduced.

Chapter 19: System Security Architecture and Models

Recap

Let's quickly review all the models:

- Bell-LaPadula – ensures confidentiality by enforcing no read up, no write down and read/write at the same level only
- Biba – ensures integrity by enforcing no read down and no write up
- Clark-Wilson – ensures integrity by enforcing the access triple, separation of duties and auditing
- Noninterference – ensures that commands and activities at one level are not visible to other levels
- Brewer and Nash (Chinese Wall) – allows for dynamically changing access controls that prevent conflicts of interest
- Graham-Denning – shows how subjects and objects should be created and deleted, and how to assign access rights
- Harrison-Ruzzo-Ullman (HRU) – shows how a finite set of procedures can be used to edit the access rights of a subject

Chapter 19: System Security Architecture and Models

Questions

1. Which of the following describes how sensitive information and resources should be managed and protected?

    A) Infosec attribution

    B) Security policy

    C) Multilevel security policy

    D) Information procedures

2. Which of the following security models shows how a finite set of procedures can be used to edit the access rights of a subject?

    A) Harrison-Ruzzo-Ullman

    B) Biba

    C) Bell-LaPadula

    D) Clark-Wilson

3. Which of the following security models ensures confidentiality by enforcing no read up, no write down and read/write at the same level only?

    A) Biba

    B) Brewer and Nash

    C) Bell-LaPadula

    D) Harrison-Ruzzo-Ullman

4. Which best describes the 'unconstrained data items' element of the Clark-Wilson security model?

    A) Things that can be manipulated by users via primitive read and write operations

    B) Processes that check the consistency of CDIs with the real world

    C) Things that can be manipulated only by TPs

    D) Read, write and modify

5. When dealing with TCSEC, which of the following is the TCB plus the actual implementation of the reference monitor?

    A) Security Kernel

    B) Trusted Components

    C) Reference Monitor

    D) Security Perimeter

Chapter 20: Systems Evaluation, Certification and Accreditation

So, we have just covered all the most common types of security models that a system can implement. But, how can a potential customer know that a given system has been properly implemented from security standpoint?

Evaluation

An *assurance evaluation* looks at all security-relevant portions of a system, and determines the level of protection required and provided by the system. While there have been several methods to determine this, they all have been effectively consolidated under something called the Common Criteria.

ISO created the *Common Criteria* in 1990 as a result of collaboration between the US, Canada, France, Germany, the UK and the Netherlands. The primary goal of this standard is to reduce the complexity of multiple schemes by globally recognizing one. The Common Criteria allows users to specify their requirements, for vendors to make claims on how their systems meet those requirements, and for independent labs to verify vendor claims. The result of this process is an *Evaluation Assurance Level*, or *EAL*, of which there are seven levels – from EAL1 to EAL7, with EAL7 representing the most stringent testing. The levels are (from least stringent to most):

- EAL1 – functionally tested
- EAL2 – structurally tested
- EAL3 – methodically tested and checked
- EAL4 – methodically designed, tested and reviewed
- EAL5 – semi formally designed and tested
- EAL6 – semi formally verified designed and tested
- EAL7 – formally verified design and tested based on a mathematical model that can be proven

Common Criteria uses *protection profiles*, which are a description of the features a product provides, but not how each feature was implemented. Each profile consists of the list of security requirements with definitions, the EAL level that a product must meet, and justifies the need for both. If a consumer cannot find an existing protection profile to meet their needs, that person can just create one. Common criteria can answer two questions:

1) What security does your product provide?
2) Why should I believe you?

Each protection profile typically has the following three sections:

- *Security problem description* – a list of threats the product must address
- *Security objectives* – a list of functionalities the product must provide to address the threats
- *Security requirements* – a list of very specific requirements, detailed enough to be implemented and verified

An EAL rating only applies to the current version and specific configurations of a product. If a customer does not follow the applicable configurations, there is no guarantee the product will meet the awarded EAL level.

Common Criteria has its own language:

- *Protection Profile* (*PP*) – a description of the needed security solution
- *Target of Evaluation* (*TOE*) – the proposed product that meets the *PP*
- *Security target* – the vendor's own explanation of what a *TOE* does and how it does it
- *Security functional requirements* – a list of security functions a *security target* must provide
- *Security assurance requirements* – what the vendor did during product development and evaluation to ensure compliance with *security functional requirements*
- *Packages* – security functional requirements *and* security assurance requirements are *packaged* for reuse; the package describes what must be met to earn a specific EAL level

Common Criteria is codified in *ISO 15408*, which is broken into three parts:

- *ISO 15408-1* – instruction and general model
- *ISO 15408-2* – security functional components
- *ISO 15408-3* – security assurance components

Many companies voluntarily submit their products for Common Criteria evaluation not only because it gives their products a competitive edge for consumers, but also because governments are increasingly requiring Common Criteria evaluations before considering purchases.

Certification vs. Accreditation

While vendors use the Common Criteria system to provide independent evaluation of their products, a given EAL level does not guarantee a good fit for a company. Instead the company must go through a certification process to ensure the product will work in their environment. Certification of a product means that the product is analyzed and tested within a company's environment to make sure it is a good fit. The results of the certification are presented to management who may or may not formally accept the adequacy of a product – if it is accepted then the product has been accredited. *Certification* is the technical review of security mechanisms to evaluate their effectiveness, whereas *accreditation* is management's formal acceptance of the certification's findings. When management extends accreditation to a solution, they are accepting any risk associated with the solution. C&A is a core component of FISMA.

Before we leave this topic, let's talk about open and closed systems. *Open systems* are built on top of standards, interfaces and protocols that have published specifications, allowing different vendors to easily create products that can interoperate with one another. A prime example of an open system is the network standard that allows different operating systems such as Windows, OS X and UNIX to all communicate with each other.

A *closed system* does not follow industry standards and therefore does not as easily communicate well with other systems – it is proprietary. While closed systems can decrease security risks due to operating in a more secluded environment, security through obscurity is never a sound concept.

Questions

1. What does the 'EAL3' evaluation assurance level represent?

    A) Functionally tested

    B) Methodically tested and checked

    C) Methodically designed, tested and reviewed

    D) Structurally tested

2. Which of the following represents a description of the features a product provides, but not how each feature was implemented?

    A) Certification and Accreditation

    B) Common Criteria

    C) Assurance evaluation

    D) Protection profile

3. Which of the following common criteria codes include instructions and the general model?

    A) ISO 15408-4

    B) ISO 15408-1

    C) ISO 15408-2

    D) ISO 15408-3

4. What determines the level of protection required and provided by a system?

    A) Assurance evaluation

    B) Evaluation assurance

    C) System assurance

    D) System assurance

5. Which of the following common criteria terms represents the proposed product that meets the PP?

    A) Security target

    B) Security assurance requirements

    C) Target of Evaluation

    D) Security functional requirements

Chapter 21: Distributed System Security

Now that we have discussed individual systems in-depth, it's time to examine how to tie multiple systems together by covering a lot of subjects rather quickly.

First, a *distributed system* contains multiple computer nodes connected by a network, all working together to accomplish a specific task.

Cloud Computing

Cloud computing is the use of shared, remote servers, usually based on virtual machines. Oftentimes a third-party hosts the services, but more and more companies are creating their own clouds for internal use only. There are three types of services that a cloud can provide:

- *Infrastructure as a Service* (*IaaS*) – the vendor provides the server with the appropriate operating system installed and gives you complete administrative access – the rest is up to you
- *Platform as a Service* (*PaaS*) – the vendor provides a server with the appropriate software installed for you to build on top of, but you don't get administrative access to the OS
- *Software as a Service* (*SaaS*) – the vendor gives you an account for a specific web-based application – you don't have any access to the servers running the application, only the application itself

Keep in mind that when using cloud computing you are outsourcing your security to some extent – be sure the SLAs clearly spell out security-related responsibilities and how your data will be handled.

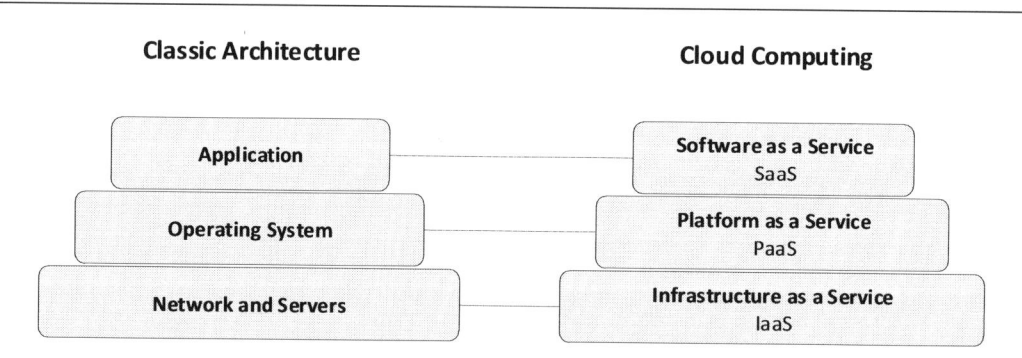

Figure 13: Classic Architecture vs. Cloud Computing

Parallel Computing

If you take multiple computers and have them all work on the same task simultaneously, you wind up with *parallel computing*. This can take place at four levels:

- *Bit-level parallelism* – a CPU operates on multiple bits simultaneously; all CPUs handling bytes can do this
- *Instruction-level parallelism* – multiple CPUs execute multiple instructions simultaneously; almost all multi-CPU computing devices these days have this feature
- *Task-level parallelism* – dividing a program into multiple threads operating simultaneously; modern OSs such as Windows and OS X support this functionality
- *Data-level parallelism* – data is distributed among multiple nodes and processed in parallel; this is called big data

Data-level parallelism is where cloud computing can come into play in a big way, since we can spin up new nodes on-demand and then retire them when the task has completed.

Databases

There are two primary database considerations to take into account from a security point of view. *Aggregation* is process of combining data for a user from separate sources that results in a view the user should not have access to – the combined information has a greater sensitivity than the individual parts. For example, it is OK for a user to see a list of customer addresses, and she can view a list of customers' first names. Neither list can be used to identify a single individual, until they are combined into a list that shows a first name with the address where that person lives – now we have the ability to identify individuals which the user should not have access to. To mitigate this vulnerability, the processes around the data must contain sufficient intelligence to detect when an aggregation has occurred. Auditing must be enabled as well to allow automated processes to detect an attack that is occurring in real-time.

Inference is the intended result of aggregation. For example, perhaps a user is prevented from viewing a list of customers with their home addresses, but if the user can gain access to a mailing list targeting customers who spend more than X dollars per month, and the user knows a specific customer by name is on that list, then he or she can by deduction infer the customer's address if the mailing list is small enough. The mitigation for this vulnerability is to use _context-dependent access controls_. This means that the system keeps track of previous requests by this user and recognizes that the danger exists for that user to infer sensitive information from their latest request. The opposite of a context-dependent access control is a _content-dependent access control_, where only the content is examined when determining access. This is obviously much easier to implement.

There are other ways to mitigate inference attacks. _Cell suppression_ hides specific information that could be used in an attack, while _partitioning_ divides a database into multiple parts, making it harder for an attacker to pull together all required pieces. _Noise and perturbation_ is a technique of inserting bogus information in hopes of confusing an attacker and making the attack not worth the effort.

Web Applications

Some basic guidelines for implementing secure web sites are:

- Keep it as simple as possible
- Never trust input from a user – always sanitize the data
- Sanitize output to minimize information leakage
- Always encrypt traffic
- Always fail securely – when an error occurs display a generic friendly message with no details
- Keep user-facing security measures simple and intuitive
- Never rely on security through obscurity
- Always put a firewall in front

Mobile Devices

Mobile devices are simply smaller computers, and as such represent a risk equal or even greater to desktop computers and laptops. Best practices are:

- Always assume the network is insecure and encrypt your own data
- Always include these devices in the company's security policies
- Only devices that can be centrally managed should be allowed on the corporate network
- Remote policies should be pushed to each device with no capability to locally modify user profiles
- Data encryption, idle timeout locks, screen saver locks, authentication and remote wipe should always be enabled
- Bluetooth should be locked down
- Only allow certain applications to be installed
- Camera policies should be enforced
- Restrictions for social media sites should be enabled
- 802.1X (port authentication) should be implemented on wireless VOIP clients
- Don't forget antivirus software

Cyber-Physical Systems

Anytime a computer controls a physical device, it is called a _cyber-physical system_. There are two types.

An _embedded system_ is a mechanical or electrical device that has a computer embedded into it. Most embedded systems use commercially available processors, but write their own software, so it is very difficult to audit for security compliance. Examination of the network traffic flowing into and out of these devices should be examined and monitored.

The _Internet of Things_, or _IoT_, is the global network of connected embedded systems. What sets these devices apart from your normal embedded systems is that they have Internet connectivity built in and are uniquely addressable. Issues are:

- *Authentication* – IoT devices usually have very poor authentication mechanisms
- *Encryption* – IoT devices with limited processing power seldom include any type of encryption, as it is very expensive in terms of resources
- *Updates* – many IoT vendors do not implement any type of automatic updating of their devices

Recently there have been several reports detailing how network cameras have been turned into zombies to launch DDoS (distributed denial of service) attacks. This type of malicious activity will only escalate going forward until proper authentication mechanisms are implemented in IoT devices.

Industrial Control Systems

An *industrial control system* (*ICS*) is defined as a system using software to control physical devices in industrial processes. Because of their ability to cause physical harm to humans, *NIST SP 800-82* "Guide to ICS Security" was created. There are three major categories of ICS systems.

The first category of devices includes *programmable logic controllers*, or *PLCs*. These computers are programmable and connect to physical devices using standard interfaces such as RS-232 (commonly called serial ports). PLCs are normally network-enabled.

The second category addresses *distributed control systems*, or *DCSs*. A DCS is a small network of PLCs, all orchestrated by higher-level controllers. You normally find a DCS in the same physical proximity, and security has never been seriously considered, as it was felt that if you can control physical access, security concerns are sufficiently mitigated. However, the line between DCSs and our last category is becoming increasingly blurred.

While DCS works well for local processes, it was never meant to operate across large distances, and so the *supervisory control and data acquisition*, or *SCADA*, systems were developed. SCADA systems typically have three types of devices:

- *Endpoints* – remote terminal units (RTU) or PLCs that connect directly to physical components
- *Backends* – data acquisition servers (DAS) that collect data from endpoints
- *User stations* - human-machine interface (HMI) terminals that display data from the endpoints and allows the user to issue commands

Because endpoints are often in areas with poor telecommunications infrastructure, SCADA systems often rely on dedicated cables or radio links over which proprietary protocols and devices are used. This led many to believe SCADA was secure, but again – security through obscurity is never a good idea.

The greatest security vulnerability for ICS is their advancing connectivity to traditional networks. As a result, protocols are converging and becoming less proprietary, and once-private systems are now being exposed on the Internet. NIST SP 800-82 recommends the following:

- Apply a risk management process to ICS
- Put IDS/IPS at the boundaries
- Disable unneeded ports and services on all ICS devices
- Implement least privilege throughout ICS
- Use encryption
- Ensure there is a process for patch management
- Monitor audit trails

Questions

1. Which of the following database countermeasures best describes dividing a database into multiple segments?

    A) Partitioning

    B) Cell suppression

    C) Noise and perturbation

    D) Context-dependent access control

2. Which of the following database attacks combines data from separate sources that results in a view the user should not have access to?

    A) Partitioning

    B) Inference

    C) Aggregation

    D) Cell suppression

3. Which term best describes multiple computer nodes connected by a network, all working together to accomplish a specific task?

    A) Cloud computing

    B) Infrastructure as a Service

    C) Parallel Computing

    D) Distributed system

4. Which term best describes a vendor giving you an account for a specific web-based application, where you have no access to the server?

    A) Platform as a Service

    B) Infrastructure as a Service

    C) Software as a Service

    D) Parallel Computing

5. Which of the following is a system where software is used to control physical devices in industrial processes?

    A) Industrial control system

    B) SCADA

    C) Programmable logic controller

    D) Distributed control system

Chapter 22: A Few Threats to Review

As we have stated before, in the security world one axiom always holds true: an un-hackable system does not exist – the best we can do is to make sure hacking into a system is not worth someone's effort. However, there are a couple of software-related weaknesses that we should routinely avoid.

Developers love to put in _maintenance hooks_, or _backdoors_ that only they supposedly know about. While they may have the best intentions (such as being able to quickly get in and diagnose or fix problems without having to go through the normal channels), once word gets out it becomes a major liability. To mitigate this risk, the foremost protection is regular code reviews to detect back doors being put in. Aside from that we can:

- Use host-based IDS to detect intrusions
- Use file system encryption to protect sensitive information
- Implement auditing to detect back door use

Another weakness is a _time-of-check/time-of-use attack_, or an _asynchronous attack_, abbreviated as a _TOC/TOU attack_. The idea is that code normally implements a two-step process to access resources:

Step 1: Check and see if I can access a resource

Step 2: Access the resource

The attack happens right between steps 1 and 2. For example:

Step 1: A process checks to see if it can access a low-value file

Step 1A: A hacker substitutes a high-value file in place of the low-value file

Step 2: The process opens the file

Step 2A: The attacker reads the contents

A variation on a TOC/TOU attack is a _race condition_, where process 1 should execute before process 2, but an attacker somehow gets process 2 to execute first. For example, authentication is normally followed by authorization – if an attacker could force authorization first, then he could access sensitive resources without having to authenticate at all.

However, keep in mind that a race condition forces two steps to execute out of order, while a classic TOC/TOU attack modifies something in between two steps without altering their order.

These attacks are rare but have happened. To counter these attacks, consider not splitting the two tasks into separate steps that can be altered. Another method is for the OS to apply software locks on the resource being requested so that it cannot be altered or substituted between the two steps.

Questions

1. Which best describes an attack in which the order of execution to gain access is reversed?

    A) Race condition

    B) Maintenance hooks

    C) Time-of-check/time-of-use attack

    D) Substitution scenario

2. Which best describes a non-malicious method put in by developers to gain privileged access after deployment?

    A) Substitution scenario

    B) Race condition

    C) Time-of-check/time-of-use attack

    D) Maintenance hooks

3. Which of the following is a countermeasure for a TOC/TOU attack?

    A) Ensure proper port blocking

    B) Code reviews

    C) Apply a software lock on the requested resource at the OS level

    D) IDS

4. Which best describes an attack in-between 'can I access' and 'access'?

    A) Race condition

    B) Maintenance hooks

    C) Time-of-check/time-of-use attack

    D) Substitution scenario

5. Which of the following is NOT a countermeasure for maintenance hooks?

    A) Ensure proper port blocking

    B) Code reviews

    C) IDS

    D) Encrypt files

Chapter 23: Cryptography

Now we are going to move into a completely different arena – that of providing confidentiality and integrity using cryptography.

Cryptography is the act of storing or transmitting data in a from that only the intended audience can read. The reality is that nothing remains encrypted forever – as in the case of protecting systems, the best we can hope for is to make the effort too great to waste time on.

The History of Cryptography

Around 40 BC the Spartans started using a *scytale cipher* (*skit-a-lee*) – a message was written on a sheet of papyrus wrapped around a stick of a certain thickness – the message could only be read if it were wrapped around a stick of the exact same thickness.

Another early example of cryptography, called *atbash*, is a *substitution cipher* where each character is replaced by a different character. A *monoalphabetic substitution cipher* uses a single alphabet while a *polyalphabetic substitution cipher* uses more than one alphabet. In Rome, Julius Caesar altered the atbash scheme to shift letters by three positions instead of 1, resulting in the *Caesar cipher*. At the time, not many people could read anyway, so it was considered to be highly effective.

In the 16th century, a man named Vigenere invented a polyalphabetic substitution cipher (called the *Vigenere cipher*) for Henry III, which increased the difficulty of the encryption/decryption process by using 27 alphabets with letters being shifted three places.

Beginning with World War II, encryption shifted into high gear due to mechanical and electromechanical technology. The *rotor cipher machine* was invented - a device that substituted letters using multiple rotors within the machine, and paved the way for the most complex cipher machine to date, Germany's Enigma machine. The secret key to this process was the initial setting of the rotors and how they were advanced after each letter.

When computers were invented, encryption took another leap forward by using advanced mathematics. One of the earliest successful projects was developed at IBM and was called *Lucifer*. This project introduced mathematics which was later adopted by the NSA to establish the US *data encryption standard* (*DES*) in 1976. Though DES was later broken, it continues to be used in the form of *triple-DES*.

Cryptanalysis is the science of studying and breaking encryption as well as reverse-engineering algorithms and keys. *Cryptology* is the study of both cryptanalysis and cryptography.

Encryption transforms readable data, called *plaintext*, into a from that appears to be random and is unreadable, called *ciphertext*. A complete *cryptosystem* provides encryption and decryption services and contains at least 4 elements:

- Algorithms
- Keys
- Software
- Protocols

A *key* is a secret value, usually a long string of bits, used by the algorithm to encrypt and decrypt the text. The *algorithm* is a set of rules (also known as the *cipher*) and is usually well-known.

So, if you have plaintext that you want to send to a friend, you would use a cryptosystem to turn it into something unreadable, or ciphertext. But ciphertext is only good if the person you are sending it to can turn it back into plaintext. That is where the key comes in – both you and your friend must have the key for this to work. The cryptosystem runs both the plaintext and the key through an encryption algorithm, resulting in ciphertext. You then send this ciphertext to your friend, who does the reverse – he runs the ciphertext and the key through the decryption algorithm, resulting in your original plaintext. Not only must you both have this secret key, but you also must agree beforehand on the algorithm you are going to use – that does not have to be a secret though. What does it matter if everyone knows the algorithm? Without the key, it is useless.

Now, about that key – we said it is a long string of bits. Are they just a bunch of random bits stuck together? Yes, but the number of random bits in a given key must be well-known. Let's suppose it is only 2 bits in length. Each bit can be 0 or 1. We can calculate the number of all possible key values by raising the number of possible values (which is 2 since it is binary – either 0 or 1) to the number of bits' power (positions^{bits}). That means that 2^2 is 4, so we have 4 possible values, or in crypto-speak, the *keyspace* is 4. Not very secure at all. But if we increase the number of bits in the key to 64, then we have 2^{64} possible values, so the keyspace is 1.8×10^{19}, which is pretty large. The larger the keyspace, the greater the number of possible keys and the more difficult the encryption is to break.

Kerckhoffs' Principle

In 1883, a man named Auguste Kerckhoffs wrote a paper stating that the only secrecy involved with a cryptographic system should be the key, and the algorithm should be publicly known. This paper ignited a debate that is still raging over 130 years later, known as *Kerckhoffs' Principle*. Advocates of public algorithms claim that exposure to more critics makes the algorithm stronger. Detractors – namely governments – claim that if a smaller number of people know an algorithm then a smaller number of people will know how to break it. Going forward, we will agree with Kerckhoffs and assume algorithms are always publicly known.

The Strength of the Cryptosystem

The *strength* of a cryptosystem is defined as how hard it is to discover the secret, whether that is the algorithm, the key or both. The strength comes from five factors:

- Algorithm
- Secrecy of the key
- Length of the key
- Initialization vectors
- How well the first four work together

Cryptosystems are usually broken using a *brute-force method* – trying every possible key until the resulting plaintext is meaningful. The introduction of multi-core processors has made brute-force attacks an even greater risk. Another name for cryptography strength is *work factor* – in other words, how much work is required to break it. Ways to increase the work factor are:

- Use an algorithm without flaws
- Use a large key size (or large keyspace)
- Use all possible values within the keyspace selected as randomly as possible
- Protect the key

Services of Cryptosystems

Cryptosystems provide the following services:

- *Confidentiality* – only authorized entities can read the data
- *Integrity* – proves the data has not been altered
- *Authentication* – verifies the identity of the creator of the information
- *Authorization* – after authentication, the individual is provided with a key or password to allow access
- *Nonrepudiation* – the sender cannot deny sending the message

As an example, suppose you get a message that you have won the lottery. The message is encrypted, so you can be sure it came from the Lottery Commission (authenticity), that no one altered it before you got it (integrity), no one else could read it (confidentiality), and no one can claim they did not send it (nonrepudiation). The message contains a secret key to be used to reply, and so it also provides authorization. We will discuss how each of these work in detail later.

One-Time Pad

A *one-time pad* is considered the perfect encryption scheme and is the only one considered to be unbreakable if properly implemented. It was invented in 1917 by Gilbert Vernam, so is sometimes called the *Vernam cipher*.

It does not use alphabets like the Caesar and Vigenere ciphers, but rather uses a pad (or key) made up of random values. The plaintext message is first converted into bits, and then run through a binary mathematic function known as exclusive-OR, or more commonly called *XOR*. XOR takes into two bits and returns a single bit according to the following rules:

- If the bits are the same, return 0
- If the bits are different, return 1

Let's say you have a plaintext of '1101', and the pad is '1001'. If you XOR these together you wind up with '0100' – that is the cipher text. The receiver must also possess the pad of '1001'. By performing the XOR operation again using the ciphertext and the pad, you get '1101', which is the original plaintext. So, if you XOR A and B to produce C, and then you XOR B and C, you will always get back A. If you XOR A and C, you will always get back B.

The one-time pad is unbreakable only if the following are true:

- The pad must be used one time only
- The pad must be as long as the message
- The pad must be securely delivered to the recipient
- The pad must be protected at both ends
- The pad must be made up of truly random values

You might think that the last requirement of random values would be easy with today's computers. Unfortunately, it is deceptively difficult for computers to generate truly random values. In fact, a computer-based *number generator* is only capable of creating *pseudorandom numbers*. We will discuss why a little later.

So, while the one-time pad sounds great in practice, it is impractical in most situations, primarily when computing power is not available.

Running and Concealment Ciphers

A *running key cipher* uses a key that uses things in the physical world. For example, the sender and receiver could agree to use a specific book that both possess – the key would indicate page, line, word and letter within the book. Unless you know and possess the book, you would be unable to decipher the message.

A *concealment cipher*, also called a *null cipher*, is a message within a message. For example, the sender and receiver agree to use the second letter of every third word in a correspondence letter. This is also a type of steganography method which we will discuss in just a moment.

Both methods use an algorithm, even if it is not computer-based code. Whether it is how to look up a letter in a specific book for the running key cipher, or how many words and letters to skip when using the concealment cipher, an algorithm is still present.

Steganography

Steganography is the art of hiding a message in another type of media such that it is not detected. Only the sender and receiver know to look for the message, usually unencrypted. The containing media could be text, photo, an audio recording or any other medium.

Digital steganography attempts to hide messages within electronic files, programs or protocols. Image and video files are very good choices due to their large size. Steganography involves the following three components:

- *Carrier* – a signal, data stream or file that contains the hidden message
- *Stegomedium* – a medium in which a message is hidden
- *Payload* – the message

One digital method of concealment is to use *least significant bit*, or *LSB*. Many electronic file formats have bits that may be modified without impacting the overall container, most effectively high-resolution graphics or audio files with a high bit rate. The more information that the file contains, the larger the amount of data that can be concealed. Another method is to include a very tiny image of the actual message in a much larger image – this is called *microdot*.

Questions

1. Which term describes the act of storing or transmitting data in a from that only the intended audience can read?

    A) Cryptology

    B) Cryptosystem

    C) Cryptography

    D) Cryptanalysis

2. Which term represents a method that in which a key uses things in the physical world?

    A) Running key cipher

    B) Concealment cipher

    C) Microdot

    D) Steganography

3. Which of the following is NOT a service that a cryptosystem provides?

    A) Authentication

    B) Availability

    C) Confidentiality

    D) Nonrepudiation

4. Which term describes an encryption algorithm that uses more than one alphabet?

    A) Multi-letter cipher

    B) Polyalphabetic substitution cipher

    C) Atbash

    D) Substitution cipher

5. Which of the following is a secret value used by the algorithm to encrypt and decrypt text?

    A) Keyspace

    B) Algorithm

    C) Key

    D) Ciphertext

Chapter 24: Encryption

Types of Ciphers

Symmetric encryption algorithms (both the sender and the receiver must have the same key) come in two flavors.

A *substitution cipher* replaces blocks, characters or bits with different values of equal length – this pattern is dictated by a key describing how the substitution should be carried out. For example, the Caesar cipher's key is to 'shift up three'. Instead of replacing values, a *transposition cipher* puts the bits, characters or blocks in a different order, with the key telling us where to move the value to. Both substitution and transposition ciphers are still used in modern symmetric algorithms, but in significantly more complex ways.

A *frequency analysis* attack looks for common occurrences of the same value, and armed with the knowledge of the most frequently used letters, substitutes a letter for each of those same values. For example, if ciphertext has a value of 'X' that repeats more often than other values, we can assume that 'X' represents 'E', since E is the most common letter. This gives the attacker a leg-up on breaking the encryption. This attack only works against the simplest algorithms, though.

Keys are normally derived from a master key, and are referred to as *subkeys*. *Key Derivation Functions* (*KDFs*) are used to generate keys made from random values.

Encryption Methods

OK, so this next part can get confusing if you don't have a good grasp going into it – so here is your leg-up.

We can describe encryption algorithms in two different ways:

- Keys – symmetric and asymmetric
- Ciphers – block and stream

What does the *key* part mean? *Symmetric algorithms* use a single key for both encryption and decryption. *Asymmetric algorithms* use asymmetric (different) keys – one private and one public.

What does the *cipher* part mean? *Block ciphers* encrypt data in chunks called blocks. A *stream cipher* encrypts data one bit-at-a-time – in a continuous stream.

So, just remember this – a symmetric algorithm can be implemented using either a block or stream cipher.

However, an asymmetric algorithm can only be implemented using a stream cipher. If a public or private key is involved, then it must be a stream cipher.

Got it? Let's continue...

Symmetric Cryptography
Symmetric keys are also called *secret keys*, because they must be kept secret for the algorithm to work securely. Both the sender and receiver must possess the same key, which is not a big deal between two people – we only have to manage two instances of the key. But when the sender wants to send encrypted data to 5 recipients, this would require the management of 6 instances of the key.

Now imagine 10 people wanting to send data back and forth between each other. Each pair would need a key. The equation to calculate the number of keys needed for a symmetric algorithm is:

Number of keys = $n(n-1)/2$ where n is the number of individuals involved

So, 10 people all communicating with each other would result in different 45 keys. This is complicated when you think of how you are going to get all those keys sent securely to each recipient. And then think of the overhead involved when you want to change the keys. Obviously, key management is the Achilles heel of symmetric algorithms. Asymmetric algorithms do not have this problem, as we will see in just a bit. Additionally, symmetric algorithms provide confidentiality, but not integrity and nonrepudiation as asymmetric cryptography does.

If that is the case, then why use symmetric algorithms at all? Because they are extremely fast compared to asymmetric algorithms, and harder to break when used with a large key size, or a large keyspace. Here is a list of symmetric algorithms:

- Data encryption standard (DES)
- Triple-DES (3DES)
- Blowfish
- International data encryption algorithm (IDEA)
- RC4, RC5, and RC6
- Advanced encryption standard (AES)

In summary, symmetric cryptography excels at encrypting large amounts of data and is harder to break, but provides confidentiality only.

Asymmetric Cryptography

The biggest difference between symmetric and asymmetric cryptography: with symmetric both entities use the same key, but with asymmetric each entity uses a different key, or _asymmetric keys_.

A _public key system_ is asymmetric, and each pair of keys are made up of a private key and a public key – both keys are mathematically related so that a private key can decrypt messages encrypted with the public key, and the public key can decrypt messages encrypted with the private key. How that is mathematically possible is a little beyond the scope of our current topic – just accept it. Now, the public key is, well, public – everyone can get to it, and it is not a secret. The private key, however, must absolutely remain secret and is known only by the owner. There is no way to figure out the private key if all you have is the corresponding public key (that is the mathematical magic we are glossing over). Also note that with a _public key pair_, you cannot both encrypt and decrypt a message with the public key alone – you must use one key to encrypt, and the other to decrypt. Either key (public or private) can both encrypt and decrypt, but only one of those in any given exchange. Again, mathematical magic. So, if you encrypt a message with a public key, only its private counterpart can decrypt it. If you encrypt a message with a private key, only its public counterpart can decrypt it.

Let's say that Bob and Joy want to send secure messages to each other. If we go the symmetric route, Bob would have to generate a secret key and somehow get it to Joy without anyone else seeing it. That is a real hassle. But if we use the asymmetric approach, this problem goes away. Here is how that would work.

Bob creates a public/private key pair, and posts his public key on his Facebook profile. Joy does the same with her public/private key pair, posting her public key on her Facebook profile. Bob wants to send a secure message to Joy, so he encrypts his message with Joy's public key and emails it to her. Even if the email was intercepted, no one could decrypt it without Joy's private key. Joy gets the email, decrypts it with her private key, and reads it. She types up a response, encrypts it with Bob's public key, and emails it back. Bob decrypts Joy's message with his private key, and off we go!

But, we have a problem (of course). Remember that we said that asymmetric algorithms are really slow compared to symmetric algorithms? How do we get the ease of public keys with the speed of symmetric cryptography? Here is where it gets a little complicated, but very cool.

Starting the Bob/Joy conversation over, Bob decides he wants to send a message to Joy using both asymmetric and symmetric cryptography – the best of both worlds. To do this, they both must do a little extra work before they start exchanging messages. First, Bob generates a random symmetric secret key to be used only for this exchange with Joy – this is called a _session key_. Then, he encrypts the session key with Joy's public key and sends it to her. Joy decrypts the session key using her private key. Now both Bob and Joy have a shared secret key (the session key) that they can use for symmetric cryptography. Joy needs to acknowledge receipt of the session key – so she encrypts the session key with Bob's private key and sends it back to him. Bob then decrypts the session key with his private key, and checks to make sure they match. If they do, then they can continue by sending symmetrically encrypted messages back and forth.

Note that this example provides for confidentiality, but still does not give us authenticity or nonrepudiation. So, what if Bob includes a 'Hello' message encrypted with his private key and sends it along with the brand-new session key he encrypted with Joy's public key? Now, Joy decrypts the greeting message with Bob's public key, and if the resulting plaintext is 'Hello', she knows for a fact that Bob sent it, because only he could encrypt something with his private key. Then she decrypts the session key using her private key, and we're off! That is how public keys provide authenticity.

What about nonrepudiation? Remember, that is where the sender cannot deny sending the message later. How would we enforce that? Well, we have already done that. Only Bob can encrypt messages with his private key, so if we get a message that can be decrypted with Bob's public key, it could only have come from him. This is all assuming that Bob did not allow his key to get stolen, of course.

Encrypting a message with a private key is called an _open message format_, because anyone with the public key could decrypt it. Sometimes this whole process is called a _digital envelope_.

To summarize the pros and cons of asymmetric cryptography:

- Better key distribution scheme than symmetric
- Better scalability than symmetric due to key management

- Can provide both authentication and nonrepudiation
- Is slower than symmetric
- Mathematically intensive (that is why it is slower)
- Is not a good fit for encrypting large amounts of data

Examples of asymmetric algorithms are:

- RSA
- Elliptic Curve cryptosystem (ECC)
- Diffie-Hellman
- El Gamal
- Digital Signature Algorithm (DSA)

	Symmetric	Asymmetric
Speed	Fast	Slow
Data Size	Large	Small
Scalability	Poor	Good
Key Management	Poor	Good
Authentication	No	Yes
Integrity	No	Yes
Confidentiality	Yes	Yes
Non-Repudiation	No	Yes

Figure 14: Symmetric vs. Asymmetric Cryptography

Block Ciphers

Now that we have keys out of the way, let's discuss how algorithms encrypt data, starting with block ciphers.

A *block cipher* divides the data to be encrypted into blocks of bits. Each block is put through mathematical functions one at a time. For example, a block cipher that uses blocks of 32 bits would chop up a message consisting of 640 bits into 20 different blocks (640/32 = 20), resulting in 20 blocks of ciphertext. Each cipher has two primary attributes – confusion and diffusion. *Confusion* relates to substitution, and *diffusion* is just another term for transposition. A strong cipher will have both attributes. If a slight change to the input of an encryption algorithm causes significant change in the output, then we have witnesses the *avalanche effect* which is highly desirable. Diffusion and the avalanche effect are closely aligned.

Block ciphers operate in several modes, of which we will cover five. The first is *Electronic Code Book mode*, or *ECB* mode. In this mode, a 64-bit block of plaintext is encrypted with a key, producing a 64-bit block of ciphertext. Not all messages can be cleanly divided into 64-bit chunks, so ECB uses padding to make them align nicely. ECB is the fastest mode to use, but does have some drawbacks – namely the lack of randomness. Each block is encrypted with the same key, so if enough ciphertext and plaintext can be collected, the key can be discovered relatively easily. Therefore, ECB is safe for short message blocks only.

The second mode is *Cipher Block Chaining mode* (*CBC*), which is the same as ECB but the ciphertext resulting from the previous block is used to encrypt the next block – this is called *chaining*. This has the effect of removing a large number of repeating patterns that ECB is guilty of (and therefore can handle larger amounts of data), but it does require an *initialization vector* (IV) – we will discuss IVs more in just a bit. For now, just know that since the first block in CBC does not have a previous block to use as random input, we need an IV. For example, we encrypt the first block using the IV and the key, and get back 64-bits of ciphertext. We then use this ciphertext and the key to XOR with the second block, and then use that ciphertext and the key to XOR the third block, and so on.

Now that we have figured out how to handle large amounts of data without repeating ourselves (which is the primary weakness of CBC), what about really small amounts of data? If we only have a few bits of data, say a pin number or 32 bits, we can use the third mode, *Cipher Feedback* (*CFB*). CFB is kind of a cross between a block and stream cipher – we first use an IV and key to create a *keystream*, which is what stream ciphers do. Then we XOR the keystream with the 32-bit plaintext and ship it off. We then use the ciphertext to encrypt the next block. When using CFB we should generate a new IV per message because the message is much smaller.

Both CBC and CFB use the output from the previous block to encrypt the next block. This is great because it reduces randomness, but it also introduces a problem – if even one bit becomes corrupted, all remaining bits suffer as well. What if we created a keystream (using an IV and the key) just like CFB, but did not use previous ciphertext to encrypt the next block of plaintext? We would wind up with the fourth mode called *Output Feedback* (*OFB*) mode. For data that is very sensitive to errors, such as streaming video or audio, OFB should be used instead of CFB.

The last mode is called *Counter* mode, or CTR, and is very close to OFB with two differences –first, the IV is incremented for each block of plaintext, and like OFB, CTR does not use chaining. Without chaining, multiple blocks can be encoded simultaneously, increasing performance. CTR is often used for ATM, IPSec and wireless security such as 802.11i – anything that does not require packets to arrive in order.

	Uses IV	Speed	Random-ness	Parallel	Chaining	Error scope	Data Length	Pre-processing
ECB	No	Very fast	Low	Yes	No	Block	Short	No
CBC	Yes	Fast	High	No	Yes	Message	Long	Yes
CFB	Yes	Fast	High	No	Yes	Message	Short	Yes
OFB	Yes	Moderate	High	No	No	Block	Long	Yes
CTR	Yes	Fast	Moderate	Yes	No	Block	Long	Yes

Figure 15: Block Cipher

Stream Ciphers

A *stream cipher* does not divide the data into blocks or use substitution or transposition. Instead, it views the data as a single stream of bits and performs a mathematical function on each bit individually using a *keystream generator*. This is like a one-pad cipher, in that a key is XOR'd with the plaintext to produce the ciphertext. Keep in mind we're still talking about symmetric algorithms, so both the sender and receiver still need to have the same key.

Block vs. Stream Ciphers

Synchronous cryptosystems use keystreams to encrypt each bit, one at a time – so streaming algorithms are synchronous because the keystream value is 'in-sync' with the plaintext value. On the other hand, *asynchronous algorithms* use previously generated ciphertext to encrypt the next plaintext value – so many block algorithms using chaining are asynchronous.

Symmetric algorithms can use either block or stream ciphers. Asymmetric algorithms can only use stream ciphers.

Initialization Vectors

We mentioned initialization vectors briefly just a moment ago, so let's go back and revisit that topic. If an algorithm

	Block	Stream
Speed	Slow	Fast
Randomness	High	Low
Best Use	Files	Streams
Error Scope	Block	Message
Memory Use	High	Low
Complexity	High	Low
Security	High	Moderate
Asymmetric	No	Yes
Symmetric	Yes	Yes

Figure 16: Block vs. Stream

encrypts the same plaintext value with the same key, it will obviously generate the same ciphertext. This produces a security issue, because anytime a repeating pattern is detected in ciphertext, it makes it much easier to break into. To overcome this weakness, an _initialization vector_ (_IV_) is used with the key to reduce the chance of a repeating pattern – each time the plaintext is encrypted with the key, a different IV is used. Obviously, the recipient must also have this IV so it must be sent along with the ciphertext, but there is no need to encrypt it.

Strong ciphers share the following attributes:

- Easy to implement in hardware
- Long periods of non-repeating ciphertext with keystream values
- No linear relationship between keystream values and the key itself
- Statistically unbiased stream – the number of 0s and 1s should be about the same

Stream ciphers require a lot of randomness and encrypt bits one-at-a-time, and as a result are both slower and less secure than block ciphers. However, when it comes to streaming applications, such as video or audio across a network, stream ciphers are the better choice – and if streaming ciphers are implemented in hardware, they can perform faster and scale better with increased traffic.

One last difference between block and stream ciphers – if a computational error occurs during the encryption process, only a single block is affected with a block cipher, but the entire remaining stream is unusable with a stream cipher.

Strong Encryption Algorithm Techniques
Beyond diffusion (transposition), confusion (substitution), avalanche effects, IVs and generation of random numbers, other techniques that strengthen encryption algorithms (either directly or as a side-effect) include the following:

- _Compression_ – reducing the size of the data before encryption
- _Expansion_ – expand the plaintext to correspond to key sizes
- _Padding_ – adding data to the plaintext before encryption
- _Key mixing_ – using a subkey instead of the entire key – this reduces exposure of the key

Recap
Before we leave this section, let's do a quick test about public keys see if we have really absorbed it.

Question: What is so much better about symmetric encryption than asymmetric encryption?
Answer: Symmetric is so blazingly fast.

Question: If that is true, then why do we even have asymmetric?
Answer: Because managing keys with symmetric is such a pain.

Question: If you encrypt a message with your own private key, what security services are being provided to the recipient?
Answer: Authenticity and Nonrepudiation – only you could have sent the message if it can be decrypted with your public key.

Question: If you encrypt a message with the recipient's public key, what security services are being provided?
Answer: Confidentiality – only the recipient can decrypt the message with their private key.

Question: Why don't we just encrypt the symmetric key with another symmetric key?
Answer: How would you get the second symmetric key to the recipient? We only compounded the problem.

Question: If a sender encrypts data with your private key, what security services are being provided?
Answer: None, and by the way you need to generate a new pair of keys because someone has stolen it!

Question: If you encrypt a message with your own public key, what security services are being provided?
Answer: None – who can read it but you (only you have your own private key)?

Question: What is a session key?
Answer: The session key is a symmetric key that is generated for one conversation and then tossed. How long is a conversation? That is up to you, but anywhere from seconds to days – and conceivably decades.

Question: How many different names can you think of for a symmetric key?
Answer: Secret key, private key, shared key and session key.

Questions

1. Which of the following best describes the difference between block and stream ciphers?

A) Block ciphers output ciphertext in blocks of the same length, while stream ciphers output blocks of varying sizes

B) Block ciphers can only encrypt one block at a time, while a stream cipher can encrypt multiple blocks simultaneously

C) Block ciphers require the plaintext to be fed in blocks, while a stream cipher encrypts can only accept one bit-at-a-time

D) Block ciphers encrypt data in chunks, while a stream cipher encrypts data one bit-at-a-time in a continuous stream

2. Which of the following statements is true?

A) Symmetric algorithms provide integrity while asymmetric do not

B) Both symmetric and asymmetric algorithms provide confidentiality

C) Symmetric algorithms provide nonrepudiation while asymmetric do not

D) Symmetric algorithms provide authentication while asymmetric do not

3. When dealing with encryption ciphers, what is a secret key?

A) Public key

B) Hidden key

C) Symmetric key

D) Private key

4. Which term represents an algorithm using the same key for both encryption and decryption?

A) Sypmotric encryption algorithm

B) Asymmetric encryption algorithm

C) Symmetric encryption algorithm

D) Antisymmetric encryption algorithm

5. Which of the following block cipher modes is just like OFB but increments the IV for each block?

A) Cipher Feedback

B) Electronic Code Book

C) Counter

D) Cipher Block Chaining

Chapter 25: Types of Symmetric Systems

When dealing with symmetric algorithms, you might need to be aware of how these algorithms are described using a shorthand notation of 'w/r/b', where:

- **w** – word size in bits, 16, 32 or 64
- **r** – number of rounds of computation, 0 to 255
- **b** – key size, in bytes

For example, 'RC5-32/12/16' means the RC5 algorithm using 32-bit words – a word is two bytes, so 64-bit block size. It uses 12 rounds of computation, and requires a 126-bit key (16-bytes = 16*8 bits = 128 bits).

Data Encryption Standard

In the early 1970s NIST was looking for encryption algorithms to meet the *data encryption standard* (*DES*) and invited vendors to submit their favorite ones for consideration. IBM submitted a 128-bit algorithm called *Lucifer*, which the NIST accepted, but modified it to use a key size of 64 bits, with 8 bits used for parity, resulting in 56 bits. It met the requirements for DES, so it was named the *data encryption algorithm*, or *DEA*, and became a standard in 1977. Keep in mind that while DES was the standard that DEA fulfilled, we usually refer to the algorithm as DES. It is a symmetric block algorithm – meaning that the output is in terms of blocks of ciphertext, and requires a shared key. Blocks are put through 16 rounds of transposition and substitution.

In 1998, a computer was built that broke DES in three days by executing a brute-force attack until the original key was discovered. This directly led to the adoption of *triple-DES*, or *3DES*.

Triple-DES

After DES was broken, NIST had *double-DES*, but it was easily broken, so the standard quickly moved to *triple-DES* (*3DES*). NIST realized that even 3DES was a stop-gap, but they needed something quickly, so they adopted this until the long-term fix was in.

3DES uses 48 rounds in its algorithm, which makes it secure, but at the expense of being very resource-intensive, meaning it was slow. Instead of the single encryption cycle that DES supported, 3DES has three encryption cycles, and work in several different modes:

- *DES-EEE3* – three keys to encrypt, encrypt, encrypt
- *DES-EDE3* – three keys to encrypt, decrypt, encrypt
- *DES-EEE2* – two keys to encrypt, encrypt, encrypt
- *DES-EDE2* – two keys to encrypt, decrypt, encrypt

For the modes with only 2 keys, the first and third encryption cycle use the same key – the other cycles all use a unique key. Now, when you see the word 'decrypt', we're not actually decrypting ciphertext with the same key used to encrypt it – we are decrypting it with a different key. This 'decryption' results in a jumble of nonsensical data, which is then encrypted again with another key.

Advanced Encryption Standard

Once DES was broken and 3DES was adopted, NIST created a new standard called the *advanced encryption standard*, or *AES*. So, NIST did the same thing it did with DES – it sent out a call to vendors to submit their algorithms for consideration – but one requirement was that it needed to support key sizes of 128, 192 and 256 bits. The winner was the *Rijndael* (pronounced 'rhine-doll') algorithm. The number of rounds depends on the key size used:

- 128 bit key – 10 rounds
- 192 bit key – 12 rounds
- 256 bit key – 14 rounds

Rijndael has relatively low CPU and memory requirements, and defends against timing attacks. Whenever you hear the term 'AES', it means Rijndael.

International Data Encryption Algorithm

The *international data encryption algorithm*, or *IDEA*, is a block cipher and operates on 64-bit blocks, uses 8 rounds of computation and requires a key size of 128 bits. IDEA is faster than DES and to-date has not been broken. PGP (which we will cover later) uses IDEA, but since this algorithm is patented, it has seen limited adoption.

Blowfish

Blowfish is a block cipher and works on 64-bit blocks, uses 16 rounds of computation and supports key sizes from 32 bits to 448 bits. Since it is public domain, anyone is free to use the algorithm.

RC4

<u>RC4</u> is a very common stream cipher with a variable key size. It was a product of RSA Data Security, but after someone posted the source code to a mailing list, the stolen algorithm is sometimes referred to as ARC4 since 'RC4' is trademarked. It was used for SSL, and was very poorly implemented in 802.11 WEP. The algorithm is simple and fast, but does have some vulnerabilities.

RC5

Whereas RC4 is a stream cipher, <u>RC5</u> is a block cipher supporting block sizes of 32, 64 or 128 bits with keys that can go up to a whopping 2,048 bits. The number of computation rounds can go up to 255.

RC6

<u>RC6</u> extended RC5, primarily in speed, and was created to be submitted for the AES consideration.

	Blocks	Words	# Rounds	Key Size	Cipher
DES	64	32	16	64(8 parity)	Block
3DES			48	64(8 parity)	Block
AES	128	64	10,12,14	128,192,256	
IDEA	64	32	8	128	Block
Blowfish	64	32	16	32-488	Block
RC4	64	32		variable	Stream
RC5	32,64,128	16,32,64	255	up to 2048	Block
RC6	32,64,128	16,32,64	255	2,048	Block

Figure 17: Symmetric Algorithms

Questions

1. Which of the following is NOT true of the International Data Encryption Algorithm (IDEA)?

A) PGP uses IDEA

B) It requires a key size of 128 bits

C) In 2008 it was broken in 6 days

D) It is faster than DES

2. Which of the following is NOT true of the Advanced Encryption Standard (AES)?

A) A core requirement was to use 3 key sizes

B) AES has high CPU and memory requirements

C) The number of encryption rounds depends on the key size

D) Rijndael was the winning submission

3. Which of the following is NOT true of the Data Encryption Standard (DES)?

A) DES fulfills the Data Encryption Algorithm (DEA)

B) NIST accepted it with a 64-bit key size

C) In 1998, it was broken in 3 days

D) IBM submitted a 128-bit algorithm called Lucifer

4. Which of the following is NOT true of Triple-DES (3-DES)?

A) When a mode has only 2 keys, a third key is automatically generated

B) It has four different modes

C) It was preceded by Double-DES, which was quickly broken

D) It performs three encryption cycles, making it very slow

5. Which of the following is NOT true of the Blowfish algorithm?

A) It is a block cipher

B) It is in the public domain and is free to use

C) It supports keys sizes ranging from 32 bits to 448 bits

D) It uses 32-bit blocks

Chapter 26: Types of Asymmetric Systems

We know that symmetric algorithms require a shared key – securely and easily sharing that key with the right individual (and only the right individual) is their biggest weakness. That is why we have asymmetric algorithms that support both a private and public key and thereby give us a _confidential_ way to share the key.

Asymmetric algorithms do not rely on complexity to be secure (although some are very complex) but rather the enormous amount of processing power it would take to break it. One day we will have computers powerful enough to render many current asymmetric algorithms useless, but we are betting that day is long off. The idea is that there is an easy path and a hard path – the easy path is to generate the private/public key pairs and to use one of them to encrypt ciphertext – the hard part is to decrypt the ciphertext. This is referred to as a _one-way function_ – creating the result is easy, but reversing it is almost impossible. Think of knocking a drinking glass off a table and seeing it break into hundreds of small shards – that part was easy. Now try to put it back together – good luck with that. One-way functions are the same – the reverse is not impossible, but _is_ impossibly difficult. However, in a one-way function there is a _trapdoor_ – basically the secret to putting the glass back together if you have the required key. That is how we can decrypt the ciphertext if we possess the correct key.

We will be talking about _digital signatures_ soon – all that means is that an encryption algorithm offers nonrepudiation, because we assume something encrypted with a private key can only have come from someone who owned that key. In other words, if I get a message and can successfully decrypt it using a public key, I know that message came from whoever possesses the corresponding private key, and they cannot deny that is true.

Diffie-Hellman Algorithm

The first asymmetric algorithm to try and solve the symmetric key problem was the _Diffie-Hellman algorithm_ and was focused solely on how to securely distribute the symmetric key (confidentiality only). With this algorithm, each party has a private and public key. Both parties take their respective private keys along with the recipient's public key and run them both through the Diffie-Hellman algorithm – this would produce the exact same symmetric key. No need to share the key with each other – they can generate the same key all on their own. This is called _key agreement_, as opposed to _key exchange_.

This algorithm is susceptible to a _man-in-the-middle attack_. Here's how that would work for Bob and Joy (remember them?) – we assume that Dr. Evil is in the middle performing the attack.

- Bob sends his public key to Joy, but Dr. Evil intercepts it, and forwards his public key to Joy instead.
- Joy then sends her public key to Bob, but Dr. Evil intercepts it, and forwards his public key to Bob instead.
- Both Bob and Joy create a symmetric key using their private key combined with Dr. Evil's public key – they think they now have a shared key that only they know, but in reality, Dr. Evil is chuckling to himself because he too has the keys – one for Bob and one for Joy.
- When Bob and Joy send messages to each other, they go to Dr. Evil, who decrypts it with the appropriate key, reads the message, re-encrypts it with the second key, and forwards it on. Bob and Joy never know.

The other vulnerability is that the same key will always be used between two people, whereas what we really want is to generate a key for each session (remember the _session key_)?

Another algorithm called _MQV_ tried to solve this by requiring the attacker to have both party's private keys, but wasn't the real answer.

RSA

So, the Diffie-Hellman algorithm was ground-breaking in its day, but had some obvious flaws – primarily the inability to authenticate the other person before blindly trusting them. A new algorithm, _RSA_, was invented in 1978 to overcome this problem by providing for authentication as well as confidentiality, and is based on prime numbers. RSA is by far the most popular algorithm in the world and has been implemented in all popular operating systems. Keep in mind that RSA can be used as an encryption algorithm _OR_ a key exchange protocol, and with the latter is usually used in conjunction with the symmetric algorithms DES or AES.

El Gamal

Whereas RSA used large prime numbers, _El Gamal_ is based on calculating discrete logarithms in a finite field just like Diffie-Hellman. Basically, if we take two very large numbers and perform logarithmic calculations, it is very difficult to reverse the process. El Gamal performs the same functions as Diffie-Hellman, but is slower because the math involved is more intense.

Elliptic Curve Cryptosystems

An _elliptic curve cryptosystem_, or _ECC_, provides the same services as RSA, Diffie-Hellman and El Gamal, but is much more efficient than any other asymmetric algorithm. Like El Gamal and Diffie-Hellman, ECC uses logarithmic mathematics but on elliptic curves instead of a finite field. Due to its efficiency, you will often find ECC on resource-limited devices such as wireless devices and smartphones. The increased efficiency is due in part to the fact that the ECC algorithm provides the same level of security as RSA but with shorter keys – the shorter the key, the less computations must be performed.

Knapsack

The 'knapsack problem' asks the following question: 'If you have multiple items with each having a different weight, would it be possible to add these items to a knapsack so the knapsack has a specific weight?' Multiple versions of algorithms have been developed around this problem, collectively known as _knapsack algorithms_. Unfortunately, these algorithms were found to be insecure and are no longer used.

Zero Knowledge Proof

One last bit of trivia that applies to all encryption algorithms before we move on. The concept of _zero knowledge proof_ states that you should only reveal exactly what is required and nothing more – don't leak information that can be used to infer anything else. Within cryptography, this means that only the owner of a private key can prove that she has it, but it does not reveal how she got the key or where it is stored.

Chapter 26: Types of Asymmetric Systems

Questions

1. Which of the following is NOT true regarding the Elliptic Curve Cryptosystem?

   A) It is commonly found on resource-limited devices

   B) It is much more efficient than any other asymmetric algorithm

   C) It provides the same services as El Gamal and RSA, but not Diffie-Hellman

   D) It uses shorter keys but provides the same level of security as RSA

2. Which of the following is NOT true regarding the El Gamal algorithm?

   A) It is commonly found on mobile platforms due to its efficiency

   B) It is a slower algorithm due to the mathematics involved

   C) It is based on calculating discrete logarithmic numbers in a finite field

   D) It performs the same functions as Diffie-Hellman

3. Which of the following is NOT true regarding the Diffie-Hellman algorithm?

   A) It was the first to try and solve the symmetric key problem

   B) It was followed by MQV

   C) It was modeled on key agreement, the same as key exchange

   D) It is susceptible to a man-in-the-middle attack

4. Which of the following is NOT true regarding the RSA algorithm?

   A) It provides both authentication and confidentiality

   B) It has been implemented only in hardware token devices

   C) It can be used as an encryption algorithm or a key exchange protocol

   D) It is based on prime numbers

5. Which of the following is NOT true regarding asymmetric systems?

   A) One-way functions have a trap door to allow decryption

   B) Each key is a one-way function in that it cannot decrypt the plaintext it encrypts

   C) Private and public keys must not be mathematically related

   D) They have both a private and public key

Chapter 27: Message Integrity

Encryption algorithms do a lot to ensure confidentiality. But looking back at the security triad (CIA), what about integrity? You could assume if you can decrypt a message successfully, that a certain level of integrity is implied if the message makes sense. But data may have been altered, or encryption errors could have occurred that are not obvious. Let's discuss how we can ensure integrity.

The One-Way Hash

The _one-way hash_ accepts a string of any length and produces a string of a fixed length called a _hash_ - it is always the same length regardless of the input string. The value of a one-way hash comes into play when you want to send a message out and you want the recipient to know if it has been altered or tampered with since you sent it. To do this, you write the message, calculate the one-way hash, and send both to the recipient. He will take the message, perform the same one-way hashing algorithm and compare it to the hash you provided – if they match he can feel confident that no one changed the message before it got to you. Hashing provides integrity only.

Now, this assumes that the hashing algorithm could never result in the same hash from two different messages. Unfortunately, that may not always be true, and when it does happen, we refer to it as a _collision_.

Strong hash functions will have the following attributes:

- The hash is computed over the entire message
- The hash is a one-way function that is not reversible
- Collisions should be impossible
- The function should be resistant to birthday attacks (we'll explain that in just a bit)

The hashing algorithm must be publicly known, and a key is not used. The security comes from the fact that it is extremely difficult to reverse a one-way hash and wind up with the original text, even if no key is required and you know how the algorithm works. However, there is an obvious flaw – someone could intercept the message, alter it, replace the original hash with a hash computed from the new message, and let it continue on its way. The recipient would never know the message was altered. This is where we need to use _message authentication code_, or _MAC_. This allows us to apply a secret key to the hash, but not to the message itself. There are 3 basic types of MAC functions, and all provide authenticity in addition to integrity.

HMAC

If we were to use an _HMAC_ function instead of your ordinary hashing algorithm, we would first concatenate the message with a secret key that the recipient also has, hash this (message+key) and call it the MAC. Then we send the message and the MAC to the recipient. The recipient then also concatenates the message and the secret hash key, hashes it, and compares the result to the original MAC – if they match, the message has not been altered. That way, if some tried to alter the message, they cannot generate the MAC again because they do not possess the secret hash key. Note that the message is never encrypted – it is sent as plain text. Therefore, this method provides integrity and authenticity, but not confidentiality.

CBC-MAC

When a _cipher block chaining message authentication code_, or _CBC-MAC_, is used the message is encrypted with a symmetric block cipher in CBC mode (requiring a secret key), and the output of the final block of ciphertext is used as the MAC. The recipient will perform the same action with their copy of the secret key on the plain text message and compare the two for a match. There is no actual hashing going on. This method provides integrity and authenticity, and has the added advantage that you must possess the secret key to ensure integrity – no one else would know if the message was tampered with or not.

One thing to note is that while this type of MAC provides authentication, it does so at the _system_ level, not the _individual_ level. The possession of a symmetrical key only proves a system has it, but the possession of a private key proves an individual has it. This is called _data origin authentication_, or _system authentication_.

Cipher-Based Message Authentication Code

A few security issues were found with CBC-MAC, so _Cipher-Based Message Authentication Code_, or _CMAC_, was created. This MAC function is the same as CBC-MAC but uses AES or 3DES to create a symmetric key, and subkeys are created – one for each block of ciphertext produced. Like CBC-MAC, the last block of ciphertext is used for the MAC.

MD4

_MD4_ is a one-way hash function that produces a 128-bit _digest value_ (the output of a hashing function – sometimes we just call it the _message digest_, or even just the _hash_). It is not considered to be secure.

MD5

_MD5_ was created to replace MD4 when weaknesses were discovered. It also produces a 128-bit hash, but is more complex and secure. However, MD5 is susceptible to collisions and should not be used for TSL or digital certificates, but is still in limited use.

SHA-1

SHA, similar to MD4, was created by NIST for the _digital signature standard_ (_DSS_). It produces a 160-bit hash (instead of MD4's and MD5's 128-bit hash), which is then run through an asymmetric algorithm to produce the final signature. SHA was improved and renamed SHA-1, which was then found to be vulnerable to collisions.

SHA-2

SHA-1 was replaced by SHA-2, but is referred to a SHA-224, SHA-256, SHA-384 and SHA-512, all considered to be secure for any use.

Attacks Against One-Way Hash Functions

Hashing algorithms should be collision-proof, meaning they never produce the same hash for any two different messages. If an attacker can force a collision, it is called a _birthday attack_. Without going into _why_ it is called that, the attack is based on the knowledge that it is easier to find two matching values in a sea of possibilities than it is to find a match for a specific value. An attack would work like this:

1) Grab a hash value, and toss the original message
2) Craft a message that produces the same hash value (a _collision_)
3) Claim your message is the original one because it matches the hash value

Now, #2 is exceedingly difficult, but possible through a brute-force effort. There is no way to calculate what a message would look like to produce a given hash value, so you just have to run through tons of possibilities, hashing each one until it produces the hash you are targeting. The longer the hash value, the less chance you have of creating a collision – therefore the hashing algorithms with larger outputs are more secure.

Digital Signatures

A digital signature is simply a hash value that has been encrypted with a private key. Here is how that works:

You:

1) Create a message you want to send
2) Hash the message
3) Encrypt the hash with your private key
4) Send the message along with your encrypted hash

The recipient:

1) Decrypts the encrypted hash with your public key
2) Hashes the message
3) Compares the two
4) If they match, we have achieved integrity, authenticity and nonrepudiation

Digital Signature Standard

Earlier we mentioned the _digital signature standard_, or _DSS_. It was created in 1991 and requires the use of SHA along with the DSA, RSA or elliptic curve digital signature algorithm (ECDSA). RSA and DSA (developed by the NSA) are the best known digital signature algorithms.

Chapter 27: Message Integrity

Questions

1. Which of the following is NOT a hash MAC function?

A) CBC-MAC

B) CMAC

C) HCBC

D) HMAC

2. Which of the following is NOT true about a one-way hash?

A) The length of the source text will dictate the length of the output text

B) It cannot be reversed

C) A message authentication code is produced when we apply a secret key to a hash

D) When two different source texts produce the same hash, it is called a collision

3. Which of the following is NOT true regarding the HMAC function?

A) The message is sent as plain text

B) This method also provides confidentiality

C) It is created by concatenating a secret key to the source text

D) A lack of integrity is detected by hashing the message with the secret key and comparing to the hash included with the message

4. Which of the following is NOT a requirement for a strong hashing function?

A) The hash is computed over the entire message twice

B) The function should be resistant to birthday attacks

C) The hash is a one-way function that is not reversible

D) Collisions should be impossible

5. Which of the following is NOT true regarding the CBC-MAC function?

A) This method provides data origin authentication

B) This method applies authentication at both the system and individual levels

C) The MAC is generated using the last block of ciphertext

D) This method does not actually use any hashing

Chapter 28: Public Key Infrastructure, Key Management and TPM

Public Key Infrastructure

We have talked about a lot of different asymmetric algorithms which all require both private and public keys. What we have not discussed is how these keys are managed and discovered, how varying systems coordinate the transfer of messages using the keys, protocols used and how both algorithms work together to provide an actual solution. That is where _public key infrastructure_, or _PKI_, comes into play. PKI is an ISO framework that employs public key cryptography and the X.509 standard (discussed later in more detail), and does not specify actual algorithms or technologies, which is why it is called a framework. It provides confidentiality, authenticity, integrity, nonrepudiation and access control, and uses both symmetric and asymmetric algorithms.

Don't get confused between Public Key Infrastructure and Public Key Cryptography; Public Key Cryptography is another name for the asymmetric algorithms, which are just one component of PKI.

Certificate Authorities

First, someone has to create and manage all of those public/private keys, and vouch for their authenticity. That would be a _certificate authority_, or _CA_. The CA is an organization who creates a digital certificate on behalf of an individual and digitally signs it. When the CA signs it, it binds the individual's identity to the public key. Suppose I want to communicate with you, but you have never heard of me and therefore do not trust me. If I provide a digital certificate signed by Comodo (currently the largest CA) describing myself, then you will probably trust me because Comodo would not sign something that has not been verified in some manner. That verification is carried out by a _registration authority_, or RA. If the RA can verify who you are, it passes the certificate request to a CA, who then issues the certificate to you.

Your certificate the CA gives me will have your public key embedded in it, so I know the key is yours. If I get a message supposedly coming from you (in other words, encrypted with your private key), all I must do is to try and decrypt it with your public key, and if successful I know that you sent it and no one else. Exchanging digital certificates in such a manner prevents a man-in-the-middle attack.

While the CA is usually a third-party company who is trying to make a profit, some larger companies have their own internal CA. When this is done, _cross certification_ might need to take place between two internal CAs in different companies – this is where one CA agrees to trust all certificates issues by another CA.

Beyond creating and maintaining certificates, CAs are also responsible for revoking certificates, by adding the certificate to a _certificate revocation list_, or _CRL_. Unfortunately, browsers do not always check CRLs when setting up an SSL/TLS connection, which represents a significant security concern. The _online certificate status protocol_, or _OCSP_, provides a good alternative in that the provider proactively notifies the browser that a certificate is no longer valid.

Certificates

A digital certificate is used to associate a public key with data sufficient to verify an owner's identity. The standard for this is called X.509, with X.509v3 being the most commonly used version. This standard dictates the various fields that are contained within the certificate and is used by SSL, TLS and other cryptographic protocols. At a minimum, a certificate contains the following attributes:

- Version (of the certificate)
- Serial number
- Signature (algorithm used to sign)
- Issuer (CA who issued the certificate)
- Issuer unique ID (ID of issuing CA)
- Subject (name of owner)
- Subject unique ID
- Validity (dates)
- Public key
- Extensions (optional extensions)

PKI Steps

Let's walk through an example of the entire PKI process we have discussed:

1) Bob makes a request to the RA
2) The RA requests information from Bob to prove who he is
3) The RA sends the request to the CA
4) Bob creates the public/private key pair (usually) and provides it to the CA
5) The CA creates a certificate with Bob's public key and identity info embedded
6) Joy requests Bob's public key from a public directory
7) The directory sends Bob's certificate

8) Joy extracts Bob's public key, creates a session key, encrypts it with Bob's public key, and sends it along with her own certificate to Bob
9) Bob receives the message from Joy, sees that her certificate has been digitally signed by a CA, decrypts the session key using his own private key, and they begin their conversation

Key Management

Cryptography keys used to be physically stored and delivered in person using a courier. Today we have a reliable and trusted infrastructure to do this for us. However, we still must maintain the keys. Common principles and best practices are the following:

- Never store keys in clear text
- Automate all key distribution and maintenance
- Backup copies of keys or escrow them
- Require two or more individuals from different departments to be present when recovering keys from backups (known as *multiparty key recovery* and is an example of *split duties*)
- Key length should be long enough to provide protection
- Keys should be stored and transmitted securely
- Keys should be extremely random
- Algorithms should use the full keyspace
- The more sensitive the data, the shorter the lifetime of the key
- The more the key is used, the shorter the lifetime of the key
- Keys should be properly destroyed when their lifetime ends

Trusted Platform Module

Let's discuss quickly how the encryption technologies we have covered so far can be used to secure hardware. The *trusted platform module*, or *TPM*, is a microchip that can be installed on motherboards to execute dedicated security functions, and was created by the *Trusted Computer Group*, or *TCG*. By embedding this functionality into hardware that can manage digital certificates, passwords and keys, the *Root of Trust* of a system is significantly improved. With this feature enabled, unauthorized changes can be detected and it becomes much harder to access secured information. The TPM is a microcontroller with embedded cryptographic functionality (RSA and SHA-1), and has non-volatile RAM to store data.

The TPM allows the contents of an entire hard drive to be encrypted by *binding* the hard drive. If the TPM chip fails or is compromised, all content on the drive is essentially lost unless a backup copy of the key has been saved.

TPM can also seal a system to a specific hardware/software configuration to prevent tampering. To do this, the TPM generates hashes of the system's configuration files and stores this in its own memory. On boot up, it will allow access only if the configuration files have not been changed.

TPM's memory is divided into 2 types – persistent and versatile.

Persistent memory stores two types of values:

- *Endorsement Key* (*EK*) – a public/private key that is installed by the manufacturer and cannot be modified
- *Storage Root Key* (*SRK*) – the master key used to secure the keys stored in versatile memory

Versatile memory stores three types of values:

- *Attestation Identity Key* (*AIK*) – this key is linked to the TPM's identity by the manufacturer, and ensures the integrity of the EK
- Platform Configuration Registers (PCR) – stores hashes when sealing a system
- *Storage Keys* – keys used to encrypt the system's storage media

Chapter 28: Public Key Infrastructure, Key Management and TPM

Questions

1. Which of the following fields is not a requirement for a certificate?

    A) Signature

    B) Issuer address

    C) Serial number

    D) Subject unique ID

2. What is the term describing TPM encrypting all contents of a hard drive?

    A) Hard encryption

    B) Secure fixture

    C) Binding

    D) Sealing

3. Which of the following is the master key used to secure the keys stored in versatile memory?

    A) SRK

    B) AIK

    C) PCR

    D) EK

4. Which best describes a list of revoked certificates that a CA maintains?

    A) Certificate

    B) OCSP

    C) CRL

    D) X.509

5. Which best describes an ISO framework using public key cryptography and X.509?

    A) CRL

    B) RA

    C) CA

    D) PKI

Chapter 29: Attacks on Cryptography

Now let's discuss how attacks on cryptography systems might take place. A *passive attack* is an attack that does not affect any part of the encryption system, but instead centers on gathering information – these are very difficult to detect so the usual mitigation is to try and prevent them.

An *active attack* includes changing messages, modifying files or pretending to be an individual – the attacker is actively engaged instead of simply gathering data. Cryptography attackers will most commonly focus on people, data, algorithms, implementation and, of course, keys. It should always be assumed that your algorithm is well-known, and that the attacker has plenty of access to ciphertext produced by your system.

The next four attacks will each have a version called 'adaptive-?' where '?' is the name as described. For example, the 'ciphertext-only attack' has a version called the 'adaptive ciphertext-only attack'. All that means is that the result of one attack may cause you to use a different attack next, which is very common.

Ciphertext-Only Attacks

If an attacker only has ciphertext messages generated by the same system, it is called a *ciphertext-only attack*. The goal is to figure out the encryption key – which is very difficult with this limited information.

Known-Plaintext Attacks

But what if the attacker has examples of both the plaintext and resulting ciphertext? This is called a *known-plaintext attack* and has a much greater chance of succeeding. By comparing portions of the plaintext to the ciphertext, reverse-engineering of the key might be possible. The entire content of a message does not have to be known – perhaps only the beginning.

Chosen-Plaintext Attacks

If you can choose the plaintext that gets encrypted, and have access to the resulting ciphertext, you are well on your way to breaking the encryption. This is called a *chosen-plaintext attack*, and you do not have to have control over the encryption process to force your own plaintext to get encrypted – for example, if you provide someone a message that is so important that you know the recipient will run off and send an encrypted version to someone else, then you have effectively chosen the plaintext.

Chosen-Ciphertext Attacks

Suppose you had the ability to force specific ciphertext messages to be decrypted for you, and the resulting plaintext message was put in your hands? A *chosen-ciphertext attack* such as this is more difficult to execute, and often requires access to the cryptosystem. Remember – the goal is not to control the cryptosystem, but rather figure out what key is already being used.

Differential Cryptanalysis

Differential Cryptanalysis is a type of the chosen-plaintext attack, but the attacker analyzes the differences in the resulting ciphertext and computes the probabilities of it being a specific key. This attack was used to break DES in 1998.

Linear Cryptanalysis

Linear Cryptanalysis is very similar to differential cryptanalysis, but the plaintext blocks do not need to be chosen, just known. The analysis is slightly different as well (linear vs. differential).

Side-Channel Attacks

All the attacks we have covered so far center on mathematical analysis. But what about attacks that *infer* something about the key? For example, if you attend a football game and sit in the stands, it is obvious what is occurring on down on the field. What if it was too expensive to buy a ticket and you had to sit in the parking lot – could you figure out what was going on inside the stadium? Well, when the crowd roared you know someone just made a good play. When there was no noise there probably is a timeout or half-time going on. If you see people streaming out of the stadium you could safely conclude that the game was over. The environment around the stadium leaks some information about what is going on inside.

A *side-channel attack* is based on the same concept – instead of using high-powered mathematical tools to figure out the key, perhaps we can figure out something about the key based on changes in the environment. By detecting CPU power consumption or radiation emissions, and measuring how long fluctuations take, we can figure out a good deal. Sound far-fetched? That exact attack was used in the 1990s to figure out RSA private keys by measuring the length of time cryptographic functions took.

Replay Attacks

Sometimes it is better to try and fool a system than to figure out how to beat it. For example, instead of trying to figure out a website's username and password using a brute-force attack, why not just wait till someone signs in and steal their session token? No need to sign in – the token has already been authenticated. A _replay attack_ is very similar – capture some data and send it back to the same system, hoping it will believe you should be able to do something you should not.

To counter replay attacks, two countermeasures are available. By assigning increasing sequence numbers to each packet, a replayed packet would be detected when a packet is received out of sequence. Or, the timeframe in which the system will accept packets from a specific conversation can be limited, so that the packets cannot be replayed later.

Analytical Attacks

If any encryption algorithm is closely analyzed, weaknesses can be discovered. An _algebraic attack_ exploits any mathematical weaknesses found in an algorithm, such as the original RSA algorithm always encrypting a '0' as a '0'. An _analytic attack_ looks for structural weaknesses in the algorithm, which is how 2DES was broken, and why we went from DES straight to 3DES. Finally, a _statistical attack_ looks for values that will be statistically used more than others – this will reduce the number of keys that must be tried.

Social Engineering Attacks

Or, instead of trying to defeat algorithms, many times it is much easier to simply trick people into giving you the key through a _social engineering attack_, such as convincing the victim that you are a person in a position of authority and simply ask them for the information.

Meet-in-the-Middle Attacks

A _meet-in-the-middle attack_ involves working both ends of a cryptographic system simultaneously – both encryption and decryption, and meeting in the middle with the answer.

Questions

1. Which of the following cryptography attacks simply gathers information?

A) Replay attack

B) Active attack

C) Passive attack

D) Adaptive attack

2. Which of the following cryptography attacks figures out something about the key based on changes in the environment during encryption or decryption?

A) Meet-in-the-Middle Attacks

B) Side-Channel Attacks

C) Social Engineering Attacks

D) Replay Attacks

3. Which of the following cryptography attacks figures out the encryption key based on the encryption output only?

A) Chosen-Ciphertext Attacks

B) Known-Plaintext Attacks

C) Chosen-Plaintext Attacks

D) Ciphertext-Only Attacks

4. Which of the following cryptography attacks selects the ciphertext to decrypt?

A) Chosen-Plaintext Attacks

B) Chosen-Ciphertext Attacks

C) Ciphertext-Only Attacks

D) Known-Plaintext Attacks

5. Which of the following cryptography attacks work both ends of a cryptographic system simultaneously?

A) Meet-in-the-Middle Attacks

B) Social Engineering Attacks

C) Replay Attacks

D) Side-Channel Attacks

Chapter 30: Site and Facility Security

OK, we're about to completely shift gears for the remainder of this domain. So far, we have been concerned with very technical aspects of security, but we can't forget about physical security. Some of these topics were covered under the Security and Risk Management domain, but we're taking on a slightly different flavor here.

Physical Security

Physical security is concerned with how people can physically enter a facility and compromise systems or information stored within. There are four types of threats:

- *Natural environment* – floods, storms, earthquakes, fires, etc. – acts of God
- *Supply system* – interruption of power, communication, water, gas, cooling, etc.
- *Manmade* – unauthorized access, disgruntled employees, theft, vandalism, etc.
- *Politically motivated* – riots, employee strikes, terrorist attacks, civil disobedience, etc.

When mitigating physical risks, it is important to value human life above everything else. For example, it may seem prudent to lock doors to the outside, but in case of a fire those doors need to be able to be opened. A *layered defense strategy* should be implemented, meaning that physical controls should work together in layers. For example, outdoor lighting should keep people away from the fence. But, if a light went out, the fence should still cause them problems. If someone climbed over the fence, a locked door should slow them down.

Our old friend the CIA triad is back, because physical security should address:

- Confidentiality of the data and business processes
- Availability of company resources
- Integrity of the assets and the environment

The Site Planning Process

To implement proper physical security, a team needs to be identified that will create or improve an organization's facilities. The security program depends on the level of risk the organization is willing to accept. To do this, the risks must be understood, including the types of adversaries, the tactics these individuals might use, and the potential resulting damage. The program should address the following 5 areas:

- *Deterrence* – fences, warning signs, security guards
- *Delaying mechanisms* – locks, security guards, barriers
- *Detection* – smoke or motion detectors, closed-circuit TV
- *Incident Assessment* – security guards must respond to incidents and assess damage
- *Response procedures* – fire suppression, notification of law enforcement

There are two types of threats – internal and external. External threats are often easier to imagine and protect against, while internal threats are often hidden and much more dangerous. Employees can often undermine the company from within – example controls to mitigate this type of threat are pre-employment background checks, separation of duties, and rotation of duties. A threat that not every company recognizes is their own security officers – these individuals have access to virtually all areas, are supposed to be present when no one else is around and have intimate knowledge of the company's assets. These individuals must be chosen carefully.

A *performance-based approach* should be carried out to monitor the effectiveness of a security program, which provides solid metrics for measurement. Metrics might include the number of successful or unsuccessful crimes and disruptions, how long it took for a criminal to defeat a given control, and the resulting impact to business processes as well as financial health. An initial baseline must be established before progress (or the lack thereof) can be measured.

Crime Prevention Through Environmental Design

Crime prevention through environmental design, or *CPTED*, has as its premise that a physical environment can reduce both crime and the fear of crime. It has been successfully applied to companies as well as neighborhoods. Some examples of the guidelines CPTED provides are:

- Hedges and planters should be no taller than 2.5 feet so they cannot be used to climb into a window
- A data center should be in the center of a building so that the walls will absorb damage from external forces
- Street furnishings encourage people to sit and watch, discouraging criminal activity

- A company's landscaping should not include wooded areas where intruders can hide
- Closed-circuit TVs should be mounted in clear view to let criminals know they are being recorded and to make people feel safer
- Parking garages should allow people to see inside

On the other hand, *target hardening* focuses on preventing access using physical barriers such as locks and fences. The downside of target hardening is that it usually lowers the level of enjoyment that people who work or live in the area enjoy due to the visible signs of enforcement. The best approach is to apply CPTED, and then harden the target afterwards.

CPTED provides three strategies to achieve its objectives, all starting with the term 'natural' to indicate its non-invasive philosophy.

Natural Access Control

Natural access control is the process of guiding people entering or exiting a location by the muted placement of doors, fences, lighting or landscaping. For example, *bollards* are posts outside of entryways that prevent vehicles from driving into a building. But they also can contain lighting to highlight the entrance and to make people feel safer.

CPTED has the concept of *security zones* that are categorized as public, controlled, restricted or sensitive. Access controls prohibit people from freely traveling from one security zone to the next. Guidelines are:

- Limit the number of entry points
- All guests must sign in
- Reduce the number of entry points after business hours
- Implement sidewalks and landscaping to guide the public to the main entrance, and use lighting to highlight it
- For suppliers and delivery vehicles provide a back entrance that is not publicly accessible
- Provide parking in the front so people will be directed to the correct entrance

Natural Surveillance

Natural surveillance is a method for making criminals feel uncomfortable and guests to feel safe by ensuring that all actions will be observed by people in the area. This is achieved by using physical features to maximize visibility. Benches are a favorite use, as people tend to sit and watch their surroundings without even realizing it. Walkways sidewalks can be placed to ensure a steady stream of traffic that will identify criminal activity. Shorter fences, large building windows and additional lighting all have the same effect.

Natural Territory Reinforcement

Natural territory reinforcement creates physical designs that extend the area of a building's area of influence, and enhances the feeling of ownership by legitimate occupants. This can be accomplished using walls, fences, lighting, decorative sidewalks or landscaping. By enhancing the attractiveness of an environment, employees will take pride and ownership of the area and defend it against intruders.

Designing a Physical Security Program

To properly protect a facility, the security team must look at the following elements:

- Materials of wall and ceilings
- Power systems
- Communication infrastructure
- Surrounding environment
  - Hazardous materials
  - Proximity to travel routes
  - Electromagnetic interference
  - Climate
  - Soil
  - Physical barriers
  - Vehicle traffic
  - Neighbors

After performing interviews of pertinent employees, physical surveys and monitoring daily use, the information should be documented and gaps identified. The team must identify any OSHA or EPA regulations the organization must obey. Legal issues such as handicap access and ensuring the environment is physically safe must be addressed. A *facility safety officer* should be identified who understands all the above constraints and understands how to stay in compliance. The result of all this activity is the design of a security program that lists categorized objectives along with how each objective will be achieved.

Facility

When constructing or purchasing a facility, the location should be examined from a security perspective. The purpose of the facility should dictate how visible it is – if it should be easy to find for visitors or the company wants to publicly advertise its existence, buildings usually contain the logo or name of the company. However, when dealing with sensitive infrastructure such as data centers, it is best to make the building as anonymous as possible to not attract potential criminals.

Proximity to emergency infrastructure such as police or fire stations, or medical help should be considered. If electronic eavesdropping is a concern, a location surrounded by hills or mountains might advantageous. Highly sensitive facilities might be built directly into or inside of surrounding terrain to disguise their existence.

Construction

The materials used to construct a facility depend on several factors. If the facility houses equipment that is prone to catching fire, the facility should be built to be extremely fire-retardant or fireproof. If it will primarily house people, some legal requirements come into play regarding the layout of the facility as well as its construction. The weight of the contents must be considered so that walls and floors will not collapse. For outer windows, the opacity, resistance to impact and the ability to filter UV light will depend on the building contents. Raised floors and lowered ceilings (*plenum space*) may be required for accessible wiring. The opening direction of exterior doors, or whether each is bi-directional is dependent upon placement. Fire exits depend on the expected population. The ability to provide ground current for all outlets is important.

When it comes to selecting the building framing, there are several options, listed below in order of increasing resiliency to fire and impact forces, such as an explosion:

- *Light-frame construction* – untreated lumber susceptible to fire
- *Heavy-timber construction* – heavy untreated lumber that is 50% less susceptible to fire as light-frame lumber
- *Incombustible material* - metal that will not burn but can collapse under high temperature
- *Fire-resistant material* – usually steel rods encased in concrete

When dealing with concrete walls, metal rods encased within the concrete call reinforcing bars, or *rebar*, provide extra protection if subjected to an explosive or impact force – while the concrete might crumble, the inside rebar will provide an extra barrier to entry. Double walls also provide an extra layer of security.

Entry Points

Facility entry points must also be properly evaluated and design. These include:

- Doors
- Windows
- Roof Access
- Delivery Access Points
- Fire Escapes
- Chimneys

Secondary entry points, such as internal doors, must also be examined. Ground-level windows should be provided with extra protection as they can be easily broken. Ventilation ducts and utility tunnels within the building can be used to access portions of the building and should be protected by sensors or other access controls.

Doors and windows will normally be attacked first. Let's take doors first.

Door hinges, frames, bolts and material should all provide the same level of protection – what good is a heavy door if it can be easily yanked from its frame? Likewise, a very secure door does no good if someone can just punch a big hole through the wall next to the door. Secured doors should have hinges without removable pins. Panic bars (the horizontal bar that can be pushed in) must be provided on many external doors due to fire codes – be sure sensors are connected to detect when these have been opened.

Doors can be of the following types:

- *Personnel* – large doors designed for heavy traffic
- *Industrial* – heavy steel doors designed for security and not aesthetics
- *Vehicle access* – large doors that normally roll up into the ceiling
- *Bullet-resistant* – made by sandwiching wood and steel veneers
- *Vault* – extremely dense doors designed to withstand explosive force and lock securely
- *Hollow or solid core* – hollow should only be used internally and not used to separate security zones

A *mantrap* is an access control consisting of two doors – a person authenticates and enters the first door, which then locks behind him. He then provides another form of authentication which will unlock the second door – if he fails the second authentication he is trapped. This prevents tail-gaiting or piggybacking, attacks that we will discuss later. Turnstiles provide the same control but are much easier to circumvent, assuming you can jump high or are willing to crawl through.

Many doors have electronic locks that are operated remotely or by a close-by mechanism such as a card swipe. When power is interrupted, the door loses the ability to lock/unlock properly. If the door is _fail-safe_, on power interruption it defaults to being unlocked – people are the priority. A _fail-secure_ is the opposite – security is the priority and in a power-interrupt scenario the door will default to the locked position.

We need to not forget windows, though – here are the various types you can choose from:

- *Standard* – no extra protection
- *Tempered* – glass is heated and suddenly cooled - stronger
- *Acrylic* – plastic instead of glass – even stronger
- *Wired* – a mesh of wires is embedded between two sheets of glass – shatter-resistant
- *Laminated* – a plastic layer is inserted between two glass panels – more shatter-resistant
- *Solar window film* – extra security by tinting and slightly increases strength of glass
- *Security film* – transparent film applied to glass to specifically increase strength

Computer and Equipment Rooms
Now that we have covered doors and windows, let's move inside the building. Modern computer rooms are designed to house equipment, not people. Keep in mind that people do have to occasionally work in these areas for maintenance, so some comfortable accommodations must be provided. Smaller systems can be mounted vertically and wiring should be close to save on cable costs. These rooms should be located near the center of a facility near wiring distribution locations and should not be located directly next to public areas. While fire codes dictate at least two exits, only one door should be used for entry.

Data centers should not be located on a higher floor as this reduces access by fire crews. Below-ground level areas are not ideal due to flooding concerns – if located in a hilly area, below-ground level is relative to surrounding terrain, since the entire area could be flooded if located in a valley. Access door control policies should reflect the sensitivity of the systems held within. Alarms should be activated during off-hours, and combination locks should be changed every 6 months and after an employee who knows the code leaves the company.

Do not use internal compartments to wall off equipment rooms. _Internal compartments_ are thin walls that do not reach all the way into the structural ceiling – they normally stop at the ceiling panels, which are lowered to provide a place for plenum space. An intruder could easily simply climb into a lowered ceiling and climb over these partitions.

Equipment rooms should be located away from any pipes that carry water in the event that a pipe breaks. If there is any type of flooding, the areas should be forcibly dried and cleaned to avoid molds or other contaminates from growing. Water sensors should be located in plenum spaces – under raised floors and lowered ceilings. Vents and ducts leading into the room should have physical barrier bars to prevent access. Rooms should have positive air pressure to prevent contaminates from being pulled into the room. Smoke detectors or fire sensors should be installed along with fire extinguishers.

The proper temperature and humidity must be maintained – high humidity encourages corrosion while low humidity increases the level of static electricity. A _hygrometer_ is used to monitor humidity. The power feed for the area should come from a different source then the rest of the building, and should have a dedicated on-site backup power source.

Many data centers have large glass panes so that all people within the area can be viewed. These panes must act as exterior entry points and should be shatter-resistant. Doors should open out to avoid damaging equipment within the room.

Questions

1. What of the following is NOT a physical threat?

    A) Natural environment

    B) Civil motivation

    C) Manmade

    D) Supply system

2. Which of the following best creates physical designs that extend the area of a building's area of influence, and enhances the feeling of ownership by legitimate occupants?

    A) Natural Territory Reinforcement

    B) Natural Surveillance

    C) Target hardening

    D) Natural Access Control

3. Which door is best described as large doors designed for heavy traffic?

    A) Industrial

    B) Personnel

    C) Vehicle access

    D) Hollow or solid core

4. What type of window is a mesh of wires embedded between two sheets of glass?

    A) Tempered

    B) Wired

    C) Standard

    D) Laminated

5. What access control consists of two doors which trap unauthenticated people inside?

    A) Two-way exit

    B) Trap door

    C) Lock-and-check

    D) Mantrap

Chapter 31: Protecting Assets

Let's quickly go over a list of threats to physical assets. They are:

- Interruption to services
- Theft
- Compromised systems
- Environmental integrity
- Unauthorized access
- Physical damage

The actual loss of an asset is a combination of:

- Replacement cost
- Impact on productivity
- Impact on customer perception
- External consulting fees
- Cost of restoring data or services to production levels

Protecting Mobile Devices

Mobile devices include tablets, smartphones and laptops. Whereas before these devices were stolen for the value of the hardware, they are being increasingly targeted for the value of the data contained within each device. Methods to protect these devices are:

- Inventory all devices including serial numbers
- Harden the operating system
- Password-protect the device
- Never check the device as luggage when flying
- Never leave one unattended, and carry it in a generic case
- Engrave each device with a symbol or number for proper identification
- Use a slot lock for laptops
- Backup data and securely store it
- Use room safes for hotel rooms
- Encrypt all data
- Install tracing software

Tracing software periodically 'phones home' and allows the tracking and possible recovery of the device.

Using Safes

Relating to the security policy, *safes* can be used to store contracts, backup media or other valuables. The types of safes available are (we previously covered these in the Asset Security domain):

- Wall
- Floor
- Chest
- Depositories
- Vaults

Questions

1. Which of the following is NOT considered to be a physical threat?

A) Interruption to services

B) Civil unrest

C) Environmental integrity

D) Theft

Chapter 32: Internal Support Systems

The last topic we are going to cover in this domain relates to support systems such as power and fire suppression. Very few facilities are self-sustaining when it comes to power, water, communication, and sewage services. Physical security must take this into account.

Electric Power

When the power grid is compromised, it is essential for most companies to have a temporary backup plan in-place. Before settling on a solution, the cost of being without power should be calculated down to an hourly basis from past records. Two types of power interruption can take place:

- *Voltage instability* – voltage in the power source fluctuates to a level where equipment starts to malfunction
- *Outage* – all power is no longer accessible

Solutions for outages are generators for a long-term solution measured in days, and *uninterruptible power supplies* (*UPSs*) for a short-term battery-powered solution, measured in hours.

Power protection can be effected in four different ways. First, an *Online UPS* system can be used with continuous power to charge the batteries, with the electrical output from the batteries converted in real-time from DC to AC (via an *inverter*) and used to power equipment even when there is no power loss. This allows the power to be completely interrupted without any detectable voltage drop to the equipment; of course, once this happens the power will continue only as long as the UPS batteries remain charged.

The second method is by using a *Standby UPS* device, which is cheaper than an online UPS. Unfortunately, when power is interrupted with a standby UPS there is a momentary delay while power is switched over from source to the batteries. This delay could be enough to cause some systems to power down.

The third method is by providing for a backup supply of power from a redundant line fed from a different substation than the first. Unfortunately, there is no guarantee that both sources will not be affected by the same event.

The last method is to purchase an onsite generator. If this is done, it must be tested periodically and gas supplies must be monitored.

Even if the power source is constant there is no guarantee that is fit for our purposes. Incoming power must be *clean power* – it must be free from voltage fluctuation. It also must not be subject to interference, or *line noise*. Sources of interference include *electromagnetic interference* (*EMI*) or *radio interference* (*RFI*) – both can cause a disturbance in power as it travels along the power lines. Power lines have three wires – hot, neutral and ground – and together they create a magnetic field. Nearby sources of EMI, such as electrical motors, can interact with this magnetic field and disrupt power flow. RFI can have the same effect, usually from fluorescent lighting. Properly shielded wiring will protect the power flow from both interference sources.

Interference can result in either an increase or decrease in voltage, either of which can be damaging to equipment. There are a few terms we use to describe issues with delivering clean and constant power:

Startup

- *In-rush current* – initial surge of current required to start a load

Momentary:

- *Spike* – high voltage
- *Sag/dip* – low voltage
- *Fault* – power outage

Prolonged:

- *Surge* – high voltage
- *Brownout* – low voltage
- *Blackout* – power outage

An *in-rush* during equipment startup may result in a sag for other devices. You may notice this at home when you turn on a vacuum cleaner and notice the lights dim for a second. The way to avoid this is to ensure that the data center is on a different electrical segment than the rest of the facility.

To protect against these types of power interference, *voltage regulators* and *line conditioners* can be used to ensure clean power.

Best practices for electric power are the following:

- Do not run data or power lines directly over fluorescent lighting
- Do not plug outlet strips and extension cords into each other
- Employ powerline monitors to detect interference
- Use surge protectors, voltage regulators and line conditioners to ensure clean power
- Protect electrical infrastructure with the proper access controls
- Start up and shut down devices in an orderly fashion to avoid damage due to sags
- Use only shielded power lines to protect from EMI and RFI
- Use shielded data cables for long runs
- Always use three-prong connections and never two-prong

Environmental Issues

During construction, all water, gas and steam lines must have readily-accessible shutoff valves, and require positive drains, meaning that contents flow out instead of in. See if you can follow this: computer equipment is especially susceptible to increased temperatures; almost all data center equipment has fans to keep them cool; dust can quickly cause fans to stop operating properly; dust is caused by improper maintenance of HVAC systems. Therefore, even if an HVAC system keeps a data center at the right temperature, if it is not properly maintained it could still damage equipment. Therefore, HAVC systems servicing data centers should be isolated from other systems and maintained properly, including recording activities and annually reviewing these logs.

Fire Control

Let's now talk about fires, which can be one of the most common and devastating risks to facilities. There are 3 aspects you must be aware of – prevention, detection and suppression.

Fire Prevention

Fire prevention includes proper construction and employee training, both subjects which have already been covered in detail. Enough said about that.

Fire Detection

Fire detection is really all about detecting the environmental changes due to fires – smoke and heat. Computer equipment normally does not use enough voltage to start a fire on its own – if a fire starts, it will usually be because of overheated wire insulation or by plastic that ignites because of overheated components. In either case, there will probably be a decent amount of time in which there is smoke before the fire ignites – that is why smoke detection is so important.

There are 2 types of fire detectors. The first, _smoke activated_, is a _photoelectric_ device which detects a change in light intensity. It shines a very narrow beam of light across a detector, and if the light is obstructed by smoke, an alarm sounds. Some devices will draw surrounding air into the device to provide a faster reaction time. The second type of fire detection is called _heat activated_, and as the name implies, detects when there is a rise in temperature. These detectors come in two flavors – fixed temperature and rate-of-rise. _Fixed temperature detectors_ will trigger an alarm when the temperature reaches a specific value, while _rate-of-rise detectors_ detect a change in temperature over time. Rate-of-rise detectors raise the alarm quicker, but can also provide more false positives.

Detectors should be installed above and below dropped ceilings and in raised floors as well. They should also be installed in enclosed spaces and air ducts as smoke can gather in these places without traveling to other areas.

Fire Suppression

There are five classes of fires – A, B, C, D and K – we will cover them in just a second. For now, it is important to know that fire extinguishers are well-marked to indicate the types of fires that extinguisher can be used on. Portable fire extinguishers should be located within 50 feet of electrical equipment as well as near exits, and should be inspected quarterly.

Suppression agents are usually automated systems that engage when a fire is detected and act to extinguish the fire. Each agent has a coverage zone and the chemical used will differ based on the expected type of fire as well as the contents of that zone. It is important to know the five different types of fires, as using the wrong type of chemical may make the fire significantly worse.

First, let's discus what fire is. You may think you know fire, but what would you say if I told you that it really does not exist? Well, it does not. What we typically think of as fire, or flames, is just the byproducts of a chemical reaction under high heat floating away. The crucial ingredient for 'fire' is O_2, or oxygen. Under high heat, oxygen reacts with just about any material, and the result is the destruction of that material. The material is the fuel for the fire, so any fire requires three things – fuel, oxygen and lots of heat. Taking away even one of those ingredients will stop a fire. Again, fire is just oxygen reacting with the fuel when high temperatures are present.

Let's discuss the types of chemicals used for extinguishing fires. First, there is good old H_2O, or water. How would that put out a fire? By removing the heat – water cools down the fuel, and if we can cool it down enough, the fire goes out.

Then we have _foam_, which is usually just water mixed with a foaming agent to allow it to float on top of a burning substance. This acts in two ways – first it can cool down the fuel, but more importantly it smothers the fire – it creates an airtight barrier on top of it and robs the fire of oxygen.

Carbon Dioxide, or CO_2, also puts out a fire by robbing it of oxygen – it will remove oxygen from the air. Unfortunately, CO_2 is an odorless, colorless gas and is equally good at smothering people as it is in smothering fires. Therefore, it is usually only used in unattended facilities. If it is used where people might be, it should be configured to activate a few minutes after alarms start sounding to allow people to exit the area.

Then we have _gases_. We used to use Halon, which simply prevents the chemical reaction from taking place - leaving the fuel and oxygen, and the high heat eventually dissipates. However, due to the negative effects halon has on the ozone layer, it has not been manufactured since 1992. The best replacement is FM-200 which works in the same manner.

We have _dry powders_ to fight fires. There are different dry powders we can use, and each act in one of two ways. Sodium bicarbonate, potassium bicarbonate or calcium carbonate act like FM-200 and prevent the chemical reaction from occurring. Monoammonium phosphate simply deprives the fire of oxygen.

Lastly, we have a _wet chemical_, usually containing potassium acetate, which is designed to put out oil fires, such as are commonly found in kitchens.

Now let's discuss the 5 types of fires and what suppression technique should be used for each. Class A fires are the most common and result from the ignition of wood, paper or laminates. These are easily put out by water or foam, which remove the high heat.

Class B fires are caused when some type of liquid – such as gasoline – catches fire. Water will not do us any good here, since these types of liquids will normally not mix with water. In these cases, we need to use gas, CO_2, foam or dry powders. Basically, just about anything except water. While foam is usually water-based, it can still work because it will lay on top of the fuel and deprive it of oxygen.

Class C fires are fires in electrical equipment or wires. While water could put these fires out, water conducts electricity, and so the cure could be much worse than the disease. A better solution is gas, CO_2, or dry powders. Since foam is water-based, it is not a good idea either.

Class D fires result from the ignition of combustible metals such as magnesium, sodium or potassium. These types of fires usually burn extremely hot and can only be tamed by using dry powders.

Class K fires are specific to commercial kitchens, which are usually cooking oil fires. They should be addressed using wet chemicals.

Since the most common fire is Class A, and water is the best method for extinguishing those fires, it is very common to see water sprinklers peeking out from ceilings. The downside of sprinkler systems is that they can cause water damage and the fact that any live electricity can either make the fire worse or cause harm to people. Therefore, it is important that electricity be cutoff before water sprinklers are allowed to activate. 4 main types of water sprinklers can be installed.

- _Wet Pipe_ – pressurized water is always in the pipe leading to the sprinkler head which activates when elevated temperatures are detected; it is susceptible to burst pipes in freezing weather
- _Dry Pipe_ – same as a wet pipe, but the pipe leading to the sprinkler head contains air pressure which keeps the water in a central storage tank until elevated temperatures are detected
- _Precaution_ – same as a dry pipe, but before the sprinkler head is activated, a thermal-fusible link on the sprinkler head must melt; this gives people time to handle the fire manually and is commonly used in data centers
- _Deluge_ – allows a massive amount of water to be released instead of 'sprinkled'; not used in data centers

One last note – even though we covered this in the Asset Security domain, _plenum space_ is the area under raised floors and lowered ceilings where power and data cabling can be run. _Plenum-rated cabling_ should be used in these areas as they use materials that will not produce toxic fumes when burning.

	Material	Suppression
Class A	Common	Water, foam
Class B	Liquid	Gas, CO_2, foam, dry powders
Class C	Electrical	Gas, CO_2, dry powders
Class D	High-temperature chemicals	Dry powder
Class K	Cooking oils	Wet chemicals

Figure 18: Fire Classes and Suppression

Questions

1. Which type of water sprinkler has pressurized water in the pipe leading to the sprinkler head?

   A) Deluge

   B) Wet Pipe

   C) Precaution

   D) Dry Pipe

2. Which of the following devices operates by detecting a change in light intensity?

   A) Smoke activated

   B) Photoelectric device

   C) Fixed temperature detector

   D) Rate-of-rise detector

3. Which of the following best describes an initial surge of current required to start a load?

   A) In-rush current

   B) Initial load

   C) Upstart spike

   D) Start sag

4. How does sodium bicarbonate put out a fire?

   A) By removing oxygen

   B) By removing both heat and oxygen

   C) By removing heat

   D) By preventing a chemical reaction

5. Which best describes the purpose of an inverter?

   A) Eliminates interference from RF or EMI

   B) Ensures spikes and sags are levelled out

   C) Ensures power lines are noise-free

   D) Converts electrical output from DC to AC

Section 4: Communication and Network Security Domain

The modern Internet today has little resemblance to the Internet of even 15 years ago, when the term 'Web 2.0' was just a gleam. Unfortunately, hackers have changed just as much, and as the Web becomes more sophisticated, so do the attacks.

As we go through this domain, keep in mind that the term *telecommunications* applies to the transmission of data through analog, digital or wireless mediums. It usually applies to telephone systems, Internet service providers (ISPs) and wireless carrier services.

Chapter 33: Open Systems Interconnection Reference Model

In the 1980s when the concept of a global network was still being realized, there were many competing networking standards. ISO attempted to consolidate all the standards by creating a single protocol set to replace them. Unfortunately, it never quite caught on. But, the model of this protocol set, the _Open Systems Interconnection_ model, or _OSI_, was adopted by the entire industry and is still used today to describe how network communication takes place.

At the time, the _Transmission Control Protocol/Internet Protocol_ suite (_TCP/IP_) had its own model that is also still used today. Whereas the OSI model has 7 layers, the TCP/IP model has only 4 layers. Since it is a little more complex, we'll first go over the OSI model and then see how the TCP/IP model maps to it.

Protocol

But, before we start that, it is important to understand a few things. A _network protocol_ is a set of rules that systems use to communicate across a network. Network communication models are vertically stacked layers, and each layer has its own unique protocol that no other layer understands. Here's what happens: you start at the top layer and give it some data. That layer wraps the data with its protocol – just think of the protocol as being a wrapper that encapsulates the data – and hands the protocol-wrapped data to the next layer beneath the first. The next layer doesn't understand what was passed to it – it is just data. So, it wraps that 'data' up into its own protocol and passes to the layer beneath _it_. And so forth, until we get to the bottom of the stack. The bottom layer knows how to ship the entire package off to some other computer, where the entire process is reversed until we wind up with the data originally given to the top layer. This is a severe simplification, but at a 10,000-foot level it works.

The OSI model has 7 layers, with layer 7 being at the top of the stack and layer 1 at the bottom. To help understand how this entire stack works, and hopefully to give you an easy way to remember what each layer is for, let's take a rather simple example and stretch it to the extreme.

Let's say you make some really tasty brownies and post a photo on Instagram. Your friend on the other side of the country - let's say you live in California and she lives in New York – sees it and asks you to send her some. You agree and now you must somehow ship this brownie across the country. Now, brownies tend to crumble so it will need to be wrapped in something to keep it all together - say a paper towel. You know it will take a while to get across the country, so you but the paper towel into a plastic bag to keep it fresh. That brownie is probably going to get beat up on the way, so you are going to need to box it up – but with a bunch of peanuts for protection. You know what I am talking about - those incredibly squeaky and noisy little bits of Styrofoam. So, you pack the peanuts around your plastic bag in a box and tape it shut – and that is what you are going to transport across the country. Of course, the box will go nowhere without a shipping address, so you print off a packing label with the address where the box should be delivered to, and drop it off at the local shipping office, let's say UPS.

UPS will take the box and inspect the package to make sure it has been sealed properly – if it has then it is put it into a larger shipping container filled with other boxes going to the same city. This container gets loaded onto a truck and driven to the airport where it is loaded onto a giant UPS jet. The container is then flown across the country to a UPS shipping hub, where it is put on another truck and delivered to the right city and dropped off at a local distribution center. There the container is opened, and the boxes are loaded onto those big brown trucks for delivery. It is dropped off at your friend's house, where she hears the doorbell ring, brings in the package and opens it up. After getting through the peanuts, plastic bag and napkin, she eats your brownie and posts a big 'THANKS!' on your Facebook page.

And that's it – you now know everything you need to about the OSI model. OK, maybe not yet, but soon you will. Let's turn that example into a trip through the OSI model.

First, you wanted to ship your _data_ brownie across the country. The first thing you did was to wrap the data brownie in a Layer 7 paper towel – Layer 7 contains protocols such as HTTP and FTP – things that holds your data together while it is shipped. This is called the _Application layer_ for some confusing reasons. This is NOT where desktop or web applications live – layer 7 is the top layer that applications talk to. Be sure to not get confused on this matter.

Next, you put your Layer 7-wrapped data brownie into a Layer 6 plastic bag. Layer 6, the _Presentation layer_, is all about taking specific things and packaging them into generic envelopes, such as JPG, MPEG, ASCII, TIFF and so forth. Remember that JPG is a standard format that can contain different implementations, just like plastic bags can hold all sorts of things if they can fit inside of a plastic bag. The term *Presentation* refers to presenting different contents as a single format- it is up to the computer how to handle the contents.

Then you took your Layer 6 plastic back and wrapped it in Layer 5 peanuts. Layer 5 is called the *Session layer* and is all about establishing session connections – for example, VPN tunnels or authentication – it is where one system establishes a conversation with another system, or talks to each other. How does that relate to peanuts? They are squeaky and make noise – you could consider that a form of talking, or establishing a session. OK – it may be a long stretch, but you will probably remember it!

Then you take your Layer 5 peanuts and put them in a Layer 4 box. Layer 4 is the *Transport layer*, and the box is what you are wanting to *transport*. This where the TCP, UDP and SPX protocols all happen.

But before you can ship your Layer 4 box, you must provide a Layer 3 address. Layer 3 is called the *Network layer*, and is where high-level addressing takes place, such as IP, IPX or ICMP. Networks operate because everything has an address.

Now you drop your Layer 3 box off at UPS, where it is placed into a Layer 2 shipping container. But remember there were two things that happened here – first the box was inspected and THEN placed into a container for shipping only if it was sealed properly. Layer 2 actually has two sublayers – the first (*Logical Link Control sublayer*, or *LLC*) checks for errors, and if none are found, wraps it up with all the information required for physical movement, which is the second sublayer called the *Media Access Control sublayer*, or *MAC*. The entire layer is called the *Data Link layer*.

Layer 1 is represented by the trucks and jets. It is the lowest level and about as basic as you can get. Layer 1 physically moves all the encapsulated data from above across network cabling. Occasionally it will encounter routers (UPS distribution hubs, remember?) where it will transfer the contents on to another network (truck to jet to truck). Layer 1 is the *Physical layer*. After that, the entire process is reversed, revealing a tasty data brownie at the end.

Now that we have a good grasp on the overall OSI model, let's take each layer and dive just a bit deeper.

Application Layer

Layer 7 – the *Application layer* (paper towel)– is the top layer that an actual application talks to. An 'actual application' might be a browser, a windows application, a web server, a smartphone app – anything that needs to send data across a network. Layer 7 accepts a chunk of data and wraps it into a high-level networking protocol such as:

- LDP (Line Printer Daemon)
- DNS (Domain Name System)
- HTTP (Hypertext Transfer Protocol)
- IRC (Internet Relay Chat)
- SMTP (Simple Mail Transfer Protocol)

This handoff normally occurs through an API of some kind.

Presentation Layer

Layer 6 – the *Presentation layer* (plastic bag) – wraps more specific content into a generic wrapper that any computer implementing Layer 6 will understand. The Presentation layer also adds compression and encryption. Protocols working at this layer typically are:

- *MIME* (multipurpose internet mail extension)
- TIFF
- GIF
- JPG
- MPEG

Session Layer

Layer 5 – the *session layer* (peanuts) – is concerned with establishing a session between the same application running on two different computers. The session layer can provide this communication in three modes:

- *Simplex* – can communicate in one direction only
- *Half-duplex* – can communicate in both directions, but one at a time
- *Full-duplex* – can communicate in both directions simultaneously

Don't get this confused with the next layer down, the transport layer. Session sets up communication between applications, while the transport layer sets up communication between computers. Interprocess communication, sometimes called a *remote procedure call* or *RPC*, takes place at this layer. RPC is unsecure as it does not provide for authentication, but *Secure RPC, or SRPC,* does. Note that session layer protocols are no longer used very often, and it is considered a best practice to disable them.

Transport Layer

Layer 4 – the *Transport layer* (box) – is all about ensuring data gets to the destination intact. In this layer two computers will agree on:

- How much information to send in a single burst
- How to verify the integrity of the data
- How to determine if some data was lost along the way

This is essentially agreeing on how two computers are going to communicate with each other. In terms of our brownie example, you can think of two computers agreeing on how big the box is and how to make sure it wasn't ripped open and damaged the contents.

Connection-oriented protocols working at this layer, such as the Transmission Control Protocol (TCP), provide reliable data transmission with retries. Contrast this to the User Datagram Protocol (UDP) which is more of a 'fire and forget' mechanism – UDP sends the packet, but doesn't care if it made it. TCP, on the other hand, will send packets and then wait around to see if it made it; if it detects a packet got lost somewhere, it will send it again.

Although we will cover this in greater detail later, the transport layer is where TCP and UDP *ports* are specified, such as port 80 for HTTP, or port 21 for FTP.

Protocols working at this layer are:

- TCP
- UDP

Network Layer

Layer 3 – the *Network layer* (address label) – is all about making sure the packet gets to the correct location. For TCP, UDP and ICMP, this is where the IP address is added. Protocols working at this layer are:

- Internet Protocol (IP)
- Internet Control Message protocol (ICMP)
- Routing Information Protocol (RIP)
- Open Shortest Path First (OSPF)
- Border Gateway Protocol (BGP)
- Internet Group Management Protocol (IGMP)

People often assume an IP address is the only way to address packets across a network, but the truth is that IP is the most *common* but not the only method. The completed network layer 3 envelope is called a *packet*.

Data Link Layer

Layer 2 – the *Data Link layer* (checking for problems before placing into the UPS shipping container) – is probably the most complex of all the layers, because it is split into two sublayers – the *Logical Link Control sublayer* (*LLC*, or checking for problems) and the *Media Access Control sublayer* (*MAC*, or the UPS container).

By the time we get to the Data Link Layer, we are almost to the point of putting data onto the physical 'wire'. The LLC sublayer communicates directly to the network layer above it, and:

- Provides *multiplexing* – allows multiple protocols such as IP and IPX to exist on the network at the same time
- Provides flow control
- Manages errors

Once the LLC sublayer has performed its duties, it will hand the data down to the MAC sublayer, which knows what physical protocol the network is using – Ethernet, Token Ring, ATM, wireless, etc. The MAC sublayer adds a few additional header values right before it is physically sent.

Note that the IEEE standards, such as 802.11 (wireless), 802.3 (Ethernet), 802.5 (Token Ring), etc. all happen at the MAC sublayer.

Protocols working at the Data Link Layer are:

- Point-To-Point (PPP)
- ATM
- Layer 2 Tunneling Protocol (L2PP)
- FDDI
- Ethernet
- Token Ring

Each of the above protocols define the physical medium used to transmit signals. The MAC sublayer takes bits and decides how to turn them into physical signals. For example, if a bit value of '1' needs to be sent over an Ethernet network, the MAC sublayer will tell the physical layer to create a voltage of 0.5 volts. If the same bit needs to be sent over an ATM network the voltage might be 0.9 volts. Just remember that the intelligence of how to create signals using the different protocols happens in the MAC sublayer, and therefore in the Data Link Layer. Actually producing the electrical voltages does not happen yet – just the decision on what the voltage is going to be.

The finished Data Link Layer 2 envelope is called a *frame*.

Physical Layer

Layer 1 – the Physical layer (UPS trucks or jets) – converts the bits into voltages for transmission. The MAC sublayer of the Data Link Layer has already decided what voltage needs to be used, so the physical layer is responsible for creating the voltage. Depending on the physical medium being used, this layer will control synchronization, line noise, data rates and various transmission techniques. Physical optical, electrical and mechanical connectors used for transmission are a part of this layer.

Functions and Protocols in the OSI Model

Although we have already covered a lot of this information, let's list a lot of the functionality and protocols each layer is responsible for:

Application
- File Transfer Protocol (FTP)
- Trivial File Transfer Protocol (TFTP)
- Simple Network Management Protocol (SNMP)
- Simple Mail Transfer Protocol (SMTP)
- Telnet
- Hypertext Transfer Protocol (HTTP)
- Line printer Daemon (LDP)
- Domain Name System (DNS)
- Internet Relay Chat (IRC)

Presentation
- American Standard Code for Information Interchange (ASCII)
- Extended Binary-Coded Decimal Interchange Mode (EBCDIC)
- Tagged Image File Format (TIFF)
- Graphics Interchange Format (GIF)
- Joint Photographic Experts Group (JPEG)
- Portable Network Graphic (PNG)
- Motion Picture Experts Group (MPEG)
- Musical Instruments Digital Interface (MIDI)

Layer 7 Application	HTTP	Telnet
	FTP	LDP
	FTFP	DNS
	SNMP	IRC
	SMTP	
Layer 6 Presentation	ASCII	PNG
	EBCDIC	MPEG
	TIFF	MIDI
	GIF	IRC
	JPEG	
Layer 5 Session	NetBIOS	RPC
	PAP	SRPC
	PPTP	
Layer 4 Transport	TCP	UDP
	SPX	
Layer 3 Network	IP	ICMP
	IGMP	RIP
	OSPF	IPX
Layer 2 Data Link	ARP	RARP
	PPP	SLIP
	802.3	802.5
	802.11	
Layer 1 Physical	10XbaseY	RS/EIA
	TIAS-4XX	ISDN
	DSL	SONET
	FDDI	

Figure 19: OSI and Protocol Mapping

Session
- Network Basic Input Output System (NetBIOS)
- Password Authentication Protocol (PAP)
- Point-to-Point Tunneling Protocol (PPTP)
- Remote Procedure Call (RPC)
- Secure Remote Procedure Call (SRPC)

Transport
- Transmission Control Protocol (TCP)
- User Datagram Protocol (UDP)
- Sequenced Packet Exchange (SPX)

Network
- Internet Protocol (IP)
- Internet Control Message Protocol (ICMP)
- Internet Group Management Protocol (IGMP)
- Routing Information Protocol (RIP)
- Open Shortest Path First (OSPF)
- Internetwork Packet Exchange (IPX)

Data Link
- Address Resolution Protocol (ARP)
- Reverse Address Resolution Protocol (RARP)
- Point-to-Point Protocol (PPP)
- Serial-Line Internet Protocol (SLIP)
- Ethernet (IEEE 802.3)
- Token Ring (IEEE 802.5)
- Wireless Ethernet (IEEE 802.11)

Physical
- 10XBaseY
- RS/EIA/TIAS-4XX
- Integrated Services Digital network (ISDN)
- Digital Subscriber Line (DSL)
- Synchronous Optical Networking (SONET)

Other Protocols

Some older protocols were invented long before anyone thought about putting those protocols on the Internet. As a result, these protocols are particularly unsecure, as the original implementations never thought of having to deal with someone on the other side of the world getting into your 'stuff'. Two protocols stand out due to recent successful attacks.

The first is something called the *distributed network protocol 3*, or *NDP3*. It was designed to be used in SCADA systems, something we have already looked at in the Security Architecture and Engineering domain. There was little need for the 7-layer OSI model – instead a relatively simple 3-layer model called the *enhanced performance architecture*, or *EPA*, was created. It contained absolutely no authentication or encryption, since these systems were supposed to be stand-alone. Overtime the systems were integrated with the Internet, but security was tacked on, and there has never been the concept of network segments. IDS and IPS systems do not understand how the IP and DNP3 protocols interact, and therefore there is very little protection around these networks.

The second protocol that remains very vulnerable is the *controller area network bus*, or *CAN Bus*. This is the network backbone found in vehicles, and was never designed to connect to an external network. Unfortunately, we often see systems such as navigation devices and entertainment systems in modern cars connecting to the Internet via a cellular or wireless connection, and connecting to the CAN bus. The CAN Bus has very little security, so it is possible (although moderately difficult) for a hacker to gain access to a connected car's CAN Bus via these external connections. Vehicle manufacturers are just now starting to take security seriously.

Questions

1. Which of the following is NOT something that two computers agree on at Layer 4?

　A) How much information to send in a single burst

　B) The protocol to use

　C) How to determine if some data was lost along the way

　D) How to verify the integrity of the data

2. Which OSI layer generates electrical signals?

　A) Network Layer

　B) Transport Layer

　C) Physical Layer

　D) Data Link Layer

3. Which of the following is NOT a mode that the session layer can operate in?

　A) Full-duplex

　B) Simplex

　C) Synchronous

　D) Half-duplex

4. Which of the following terms best describes the transmission of data through analog, digital or wireless mediums?

　A) Bandwidth

　B) Throughput

　C) Telecommunications

　D) Network traffic

5. Which OSI layer translates bits into voltage levels?

　A) Layer 3

　B) Layer 2

　C) Layer 1

　D) Layer 4

Chapter 34: TCP/IP

TCP/IP Model

We have already talked about the TCP/IP model when discussing the OSI model. We had stated that the TCP/IP model is a little bit simpler than the OSI model – TCP/IP has 4 layers instead of OSI's 7 – but they map fairly well. The TCP/IP model layers are:

- _Application layer_/Layer 4 – maps to OSI layers 7-5
- _Host-to-Host layer_ /Layer 3 – maps to OSI Transport /Layer 4
- _Internet layer_ /Layer 2 – maps to OSI Network/Layer 3
- _Network Access layer_ /Layer 1 – maps to OSI layers 2-1

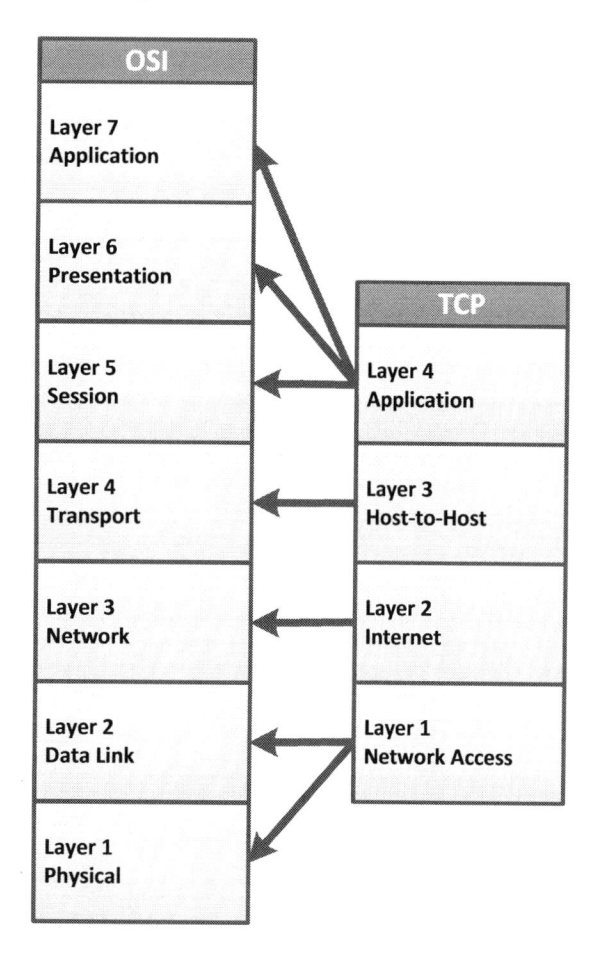

Figure 20: OSI-TCP Mapping

TCP and UDP

Both TCP and UDP operate at the layer 4 Transport layer, just above IP, which operates at the layer 3 Network layer.

The _transport control protocol_ (_TCP_) is a _connection-oriented protocol_, because for communication to happen between two computers some negotiation takes place that establishes how the rest of the conversation takes place – this process is called _handshaking_. The _user datagram protocol_ (_UDP_), on the other hand, is a _connectionless protocol_, because a computer will send the UDP packet without first even checking if the destination IP address is valid or if any process on the other end is listening. It is a 'fire-and-forget' protocol – if the packet never arrives at its destination, no one know or cares.

Developers can choose to send data using either protocol. Due to its reliability and ability to ensure delivery, TCP is most often used. Why then, do we even have UDP? Because TCP also carries with it considerable overhead, and can slow down the process managing it as well as requiring increased bandwidth. If you want to fire off very frequent packets, keep bandwidth use to a minimum, and it's OK if not all packets make it to the destination, then UDP might be the best choice for you.

TCP packets are bigger due to more headers being added to each packet, and thus the increased need for bandwidth. Both TCP and UDP have the following headers in-common:

- Source port
- Destination port
- Checksum
- Data

UDP also has a _Length header_.

TCP has quite a few additional headers:

- Sequence number
- Acknowledgement number
- Offset
- Reserved
- Flags
- Window
- Urgent Pointer
- Options
- Padding

In summary, the differences between TCP and UDP are:

- TCP ensures packets reach their destination, while UDP does not
- TCP is connection-oriented, while UDP is connectionless

- TCP uses sequence numbers to keep packets in-order, there is no guaranteed order to UDP packets
- TCP can slow the transmission rate if data congestion increases, while UDP cannot
- TCP should be used when reliable delivery is required, while UDP is used when it is OK if a few packets are dropped, such as streaming video and audio
- TCP uses more resources and is slower, while UDP is relatively streamlined and faster

If you will remember, each layer in the OSI model wraps the message from the layer above in its own envelope – this process is called *data encapsulation*. The resulting message from each layer has its own name. Before the message gets to the transport layer, it is simply called 'data'. One of the strange things is that when the transport layer wraps up a message for TCP, it is called a 'segment', but when it wraps up the message for UDP, it is called a 'datagram'. After the network layer gets done, it is called a 'packet', and when the data link layer is finished it is called a 'frame'.

	TCP	UDP
Ensures packet reach destination	Yes	No
Connection-oriented	Yes	No
Uses sequence numbers	Yes	No
Can slow transmission rate	Yes	No
Reliable delivery	Yes	No
Resource usage	High	Low

Figure 21: TCP vs. UDP

The TCP Handshake

We mentioned the *handshake* before – when two computers negotiate how the remaining communication will take place. The *TCP handshake* is a 3-step process that uses bits in the Flags header – each bit corresponds to a certain flag. In the TCP handshake, we use two of these flags – ACK and SYN. The process is:

1) The initiating host sends a SYN packet (the SYN flag bit is set to '1')
2) The receiving host sends back a SYN/ACK packet (both SYN and ACK flag bits are set to '1')
3) The initiating host sends back an ACK packet (the ACK flag bit is set to '1')

The three steps are equivalent to this:

1) The initiating host says 'Hey, let's talk'
2) The receiving host says 'OK, I'm free – you want to talk now?'
3) The initiating host says 'Yes, let's talk now'

This SYN-SYN/ACK-ACK process is great for creating a connection, but it can be misused by an attacker. For example, what if an attacker sends packet to some server with the SYN flag set, but sets the source IP address to *your* computer instead of his? That unsuspecting server will then send *you* a SYN/ACK packet, and you are left wondering 'Why is this server telling me it is free to talk – I didn't ask it to talk??' No big deal, right? But what if the attacker sent hundreds of these SYN packets to that server every second? The server would overwhelm your computer, and you would think the server is attacking you. This is a type of *denial of service* (*DoS*) attack and is commonly called a *SYN flood*.

You might have noticed the Sequence number header in a TCP packet. Even though a computer may send out packets in a very strict order, each packet may take different routes across the Internet before it reaches the destination (we will discuss why this can happen later). The side-effect of this reality is that packets can arrive out of order at the destination computer. To be able to put

Chapter 34: TCP/IP

them back in the correct order, each packet contains a sequence number, which is incremented by 1 for each new packet. If a packet is received that does not contain a valid sequence number, the receiving computer will discard it. So, imagine if an attacker could sniff your data cable and get the packet sequence numbers and then create his own packets with the correct sequence numbers and get them ahead of yours? The receiving computer would accept his packets and discard yours. This is call *TCP session hijacking*.

Ports

Both TCP and UDP use *ports* to keep track of multiple conversations that are going on simultaneously. For example, a single server may be running mail services on port 25, a web server on port 80 and an FTP service on port 21. These services communicate simultaneously using the same IP address – by using ports, multiple services can be communicating all at the same time. It is like multiple phone conversations being carried over the same telephone wire simultaneously. Every TCP and UDP packet contains the source IP address and port, and the destination IP address and port. The protocol, IP address and port are collectively referred to as a *socket*.

While we are on the subject of ports, ports are identified by a number ranging from 0 to 65,535. *Well-known ports* are all ports in the range of 0 – 1023. There is not a standards body that manages these well-known ports, they have simply become de-facto standards. Ports in the range of 1,024 – 49,151 are known as *registered ports*, which the Internet Corporation for Assigned Names and Numbers (ICANN) manages. *Dynamic ports* are in the range of 49,152 – 65,535.

Below is list of the most common well-known ports:

- 7 - ECHO
- 20,21 – FTP
- 22 – SSH
- 23 – Telnet
- 25 – SMTP
- 53 – DNS
- 69 - TFTP
- 80 – HTTP
- 110 – POP3
- 161,162 – SNMP
- 194 – IRC
- 389 – LDAP
- 443 - HTTPS

IPv4

There are two versions of IP addresses – IP version 4, or *IPv4*, and IP version 6, called *IPv6*. IPv4 is what most of us are used to, but the available addresses are quickly running out – that is why IPv6 was created. Whereas IPv4 uses 32 bits for addresses, IPv6 uses 128 bits. As we mentioned before, IPv4 is very limited in how may IP addresses are possible. Once this became clear to the powers-that-be, IPv6 was created, but since it required the entire Internet to adopt it before it was possible to use, an interim work-around had to be invented. And that is where *classless interdomain routing*, or *CIDR*, came from – this is also called *supernetting*. This approach defined IP addresses that could be reused within private networks. Interestingly, this temporary 'fix' has been so successful that the adoption of IPv6 has been slowed significantly.

Each IPv4 address has 4 segments, each 8 bits long, and has a *network* and a *host* portion. There are 5 classes of IP addressed based on the range:

- Class A – 0.0.0.0 to 127.255.255.255 – 1 byte for network, 3 bytes for host
- Class B – 128.0.0.0 to 191.255.255.255 – 2 bytes for network, 2 bytes for host
- Class C – 192.0.0.0 to 223.255.255.255 – 3 bytes for network, 1 byte for host
- Class D – 224.0.0.0 to 239.255.255.255 - multicast
- Class E – 240.0.0.0 to 255.255.255.255 - research

For a given network segment, the host segment(s) can be further subdivided to create a *subnet*. Subnets are logical subdivisions within the network, and they are defined by using a *subnet mask*. When normal subnet masks are used, it is referred to as a *classful* or *classical* IP address. However, organizations are free to define the subnet masks within their own network as they see fit and these are called *classless* IP addresses.

IP addresses are great for computers, bit not so great for humans to remember. That is why we usually use hostnames instead, such as WEBSERVER01, or www.mydomain.com. We will discuss how these two methods for specifying destinations are mapped later.

Recall that IP addresses operate at Layer 3, or the Network layer. While IP is a connectionless protocol (TCP takes care of that), it does provide some services such as a *time to live* (*TTL*) value that restricts how long a packet bounces around a network – each time it hits a router, that value is decremented. If it hits 0, the packet is no longer forwarded. IP also provides a type of quality-of-service to ensure certain classes of packets receive priority routing. *Packet fragmentation* is also provided by IP that breaks packets into smaller packets in order to communicate with hosts that can't handle larger packets.

IPV6

IPv6, sometimes called *IP next generation*, or *IPng*, is much more than something that allows more addresses than IPv4. A few of the enhanced features are:

- Provides integrated support for *Internet Protocol Security* (*IPSec*)
- Supports *Quality of Service* (QoS)
- Does not require network address translation (NAT) to extend the address space
- *Multicast* routing is improved and a new *anycast* capability has been added
- Some headers are optional requiring less bandwidth
- Optionally supports authentication, integrity and confidentiality
- Increases packet size from 65K to 4GB (*jumbograms*)

IPv6 is still in the process of being rolled out, so you will find areas of each version here and there, but they still must interoperate until IPv4 is completely gone. Until then IPv4 sometimes encapsulates IPv6, or IPv6 will encapsulate IPv4, depending on the version native to the given network. *Automatic tunneling* allows routers to tunnel this traffic. Some different types are:

- *6to4* - wraps outgoing IPv6 packets in well-known IPv4 anycast addresses, and incoming IPv4 address data in IPv6 packets.
- *Teredo* – uses UDP encapsulation so that NAT is not affected
- Intra-site automatic tunneling addressing protocol (ISATAP) – sees the IPv4 network as a virtual IPv6 local link

Both 6to4 and Teredo are *intersite* mechanisms, and are used to connect two different networks, while ISATAP is used within a network (*intrasite*). Therefore, 6to4 and Teredo are found on the Internet, but ISATAP is found only within intranets. It is important to realize that many devices used to monitor and protect IPv4 networks, such as IDS or IPS, may not be IPv6-aware, and therefore IPv6 traffic may be invisible. Attackers can use this vulnerability to attack your network undetected.

Layer 2 Security Standards

Layer 2 is where *frames* are created and are where network devices frequently operate – if someone were to access a frame in-transit, he could carry out many attacks. *IEEE 802.1AE* is an IEEE MAC Security standard designed to protect MAC-layer traffic, and is commonly called *MACSec*. It provides confidentiality, integrity and authenticity. Don't confuse this with VPN, which protects traffic at a higher level – all of this happens between switches. Here's how it works – each device configured with MACSec allows only other devices that have properly authenticated to talk with it. When a frame arrives, the device (called the *MACSec security entity*, or *SecY*) decrypts it, computes an integrity check value (ICV) and compares it to the ICV sent with the frame. If they match, the device processes the frame normally – otherwise it will deal with the rogue frame according to a preset policy (usually discarding it).

IEEE 802.1AR specifies assigning unique identifiers for each network device and the binding of that identifier to the associated device. *IEEE 802.1AF* carries out key agreement functions for session keys used between the devices. These standards – 802.1AE, 802.1AR and 802.1AF - work together to create the *extensible authentication protocol transport layer security*, or *EAP-TLS*. Within this framework, you can't just connect a device on the network and get it to work. It must authenticate with a RADIUS server, be properly provisioned, exchange keys with other authenticated devices, and THEN it can get to work. This serves 2 purposes:

1) Prevents rogue devices from operating on the network
2) Prevents attackers from sniffing traffic since it is all encrypted

Converged Protocols

When two protocols start off life separately but eventually become one, the result is called a *converged protocol*. Usually one protocol becomes wrapped by the other such as the following three:

- *Multiprotocol label switching* (*MPLS*) – this is sometimes called a layer 2.5 protocol because it operates at both layers 2 and 3; it is used to wrap higher-level protocols and tunnel them
- Fiber channel over Ethernet (FCoE)

- *Internet small computer system interface* (*iSCSI*) – SCSI originally connected peripherals directly to computers only; by encapsulating it in packets, the connection can span across networks

Due to the ubiquitous nature of IP addressing, any time a protocol transitions to ride on top of IP, it is called *IP convergence*.

Chapter 34: TCP/IP

Questions

1. What port does FTP use?

    A) 161 and 162

    B) 22

    C) 20 and 21

    D) 25

2. What are the four layers of the TCP model from top to bottom?

    A) Application, host-to-host, network access, Internet

    B) Application, host-to-host, Internet, network access

    C) Host-to-host, application, Internet, network access

    D) Host-to-host, application, network access, Internet

3. What is the name of an attack in which the attacker guesses the TCP sequence numbers and injects malicious packets instead?

    A) ACK failback

    B) TCP session hijacking

    C) Sequence injection

    D) SYN flood

4. Which is the best definition of a subnet mask?

    A) Defines a subnet

    B) Generates a broadcast domain

    C) Breaks a subnet down into smaller components

    D) Allows multiple networks to appear as one

5. Which of the following protects MAC-layer traffic by providing CIA?

    A) SecY

    B) IEEE 8021AE

    C) EAP-TLS

    D) MPLS

Chapter 35: Types of Transmission

Now let's talk about how data can be physically transmitted. There are three different aspects to data transmission that can be varied, and each can be combined with other aspects to produce multiple methods.

Analog and Digital

First, data can be transmitted as either analog waves or digital signals. A _signal_ is simply a way to communicate some type of information – you can signal a fair catch in baseball by raising your hand, or that you agree with someone by simply nodding your head. The signals we use in data transmission are waves travelling through the air or through cables. A _signal wave_ can be viewed as a squiggly line going past – think of a heart-beat monitor you always see on a TV medical show with peaks and valleys representing your heart beat rhythm. Just smooth the sharp edges of those peaks and valleys out a little until it is a nice curve, and that is what a signal looks like (it is also called a sine wave). A wave can vary by _amplitude_ – how high each peak is,

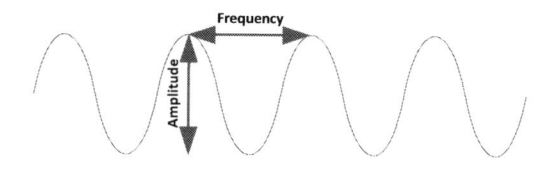

Figure 22: Normal Sine Wave

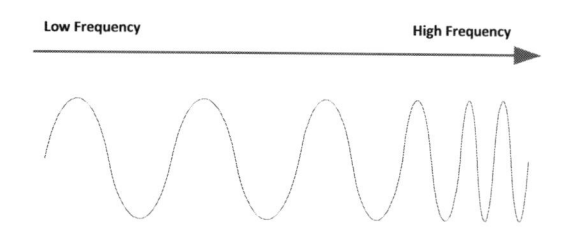

Figure 23: Variable Frequency

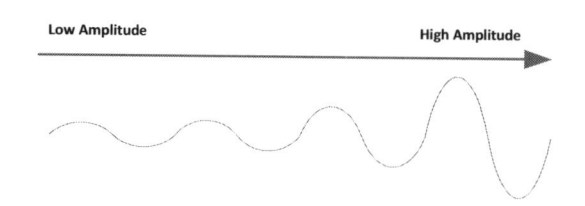

Figure 24: Variable Amplitude

and _frequency_ – how much space there is between peaks. That is where we get the abbreviations _AM_/_FM_ from – they stand for _Amplitude Modulation_ and _Frequency Modulation_.

Data is carried on those signals – for example, with FM we agree that a value is derived from measuring the distance from each peak. So, a radio station will generate an FM wave based on the song currently playing by varying the frequency, and a radio will receive the signal wave and convert it back into a song. Computers can communicate in the same manner. This is called _analog_, and is how the US phone system worked until the 1960s when they were converted to a digital backbone.

Now, a _digital signal_ uses the exact same carrier wave as analog, but encodes its data differently. Instead of an infinite number of values based on the level of amplitude or frequency, digital says 'if the frequency or amplitude is below this number, it is considered to be a 0, but if it is above this number, it is considered to be a 1.' With digital, there are no in-betweens – it is always a 0 or a 1. Think of a TV signal – in the olden days before digital HD TV, a bad signal resulted in a wavy, snowy picture and really bad sound. With digital TV, you pretty much have a great picture or none at all. If the TV can't be sure it is receiving a 0 or a 1, it just gives up and shows a blank screen. Sometimes we see strange artifacts, such as a very pixelated picture, or parts of it that are frozen, but those are a result of compression issues, which we will discuss in just a bit.

As a wave signal travels over longer distances, it starts to degrade and becomes _noisy_. Digital signals are more tolerant of signal loss, since they only care about two values – 0 or 1 – and so perform better over distance than do analog signals. Extracting digital signals from a noisy wave is much easier. Additionally, repeaters work much better with digital signals, as each repeater can 'clean up' the signal by removing noise, whereas analog repeaters amplify the noise right along with the signal.

You might think that analog signals could send more data since it has an infinite range of values, but remember that only a single value can be sent at a time. Compression can be applied to digital signals so they can carry a great deal more information. The actual number of electrical pulses that can be sent over a signal within a given time period is called _bandwidth_ – it measures the capability of a connection to transfer bits per second. However, digital signaling allows us to apply compression before putting the bits on the 'wire' – therefore once the bits are decompressed on the receiving side, our effective _data throughput_ has increased over the available bandwidth. Both bandwidth and data throughput are measured in bits per second, but bandwidth can never exceed data throughput. If no compression is involved, then bandwidth will be effectively the same value as data throughput.

Asynchronous and Synchronous

If you have ever been talking with someone on the phone that had a significant delay, you have experienced _synchronization_ issues. Thinking the other person has completed their sentence, you start talking, only to get interrupted halfway through when you hear the other person continuing the sentence. Them you both start and stop, trying to figure out who should talk. The only way to get past this is by ending your turn by saying something like 'over', as if you were talking over a walkie-talkie.

When you are able to talk without having to resort to saying 'over', you are holding a _synchronous_ conversation – there is no need to signal that you are through talking. When the timing becomes unreliable and you must signal you are done by saying 'over', you are having an _asynchronous_ conversation. Network communications are no different. When two devices are connected to the same physical cable, they can agree to use one of the two modes.

If they use a _synchronous communication method_, both devices agree on a start time (initiated by a clock pulse) and as much data as possible will be sent within a given time window. When that window is done, the receiving system knows the packet has been received in its entirety and can then process the data. This type of communication requires a very stable connection that is used by the two devices exclusively. As a result, a synchronous communication path is ideal for high-volume transmissions and is very reliable, in part due to robust error-checking implemented through cyclic redundancy checking, or CRC.

On the other hand, when a communication link is unreliable in terms of connectivity and available bandwidth, an _asynchronous_ method works much better. Each byte of data is surrounded by a start and stop bit, much like the 'over' stop phrase in our phone conversation example. In addition, a parity bit is usually required to detect errors. As a result, asynchronous communication is not as efficient as synchronous, but is much more forgiving when the communication path is not reliable. In short:

Synchronous:

- Requires a timing agreement
- Supports robust integrity via CRC
- All bits are available for data
- Requires very stable pathway
- Less overhead, more bandwidth

Asynchronous:

- Needs no timing agreement
- Uses a parity bit for error control
- Each byte requires 3 bits for start, stop and parity
- Very forgiving with an unstable pathway
- More overhead, less bandwidth

Broadband and Baseband

So, we've discussed analog vs. digital, and synchronous vs, asynchronous. There is a final component to how physical data is transmitted, and that is broadband vs. baseband.

If data is transmitted over _baseband_, then the entire channel is being used. If the channel has been split up into sub-channels, we are communicating over _broadband_ – this allows us to send different types of data simultaneously. Coaxial cable, such as home TV and Internet connections - is a great example of broadband where TV signals are transmitted on one range of frequencies and Internet connectivity is provided at a different frequency – all at the same time over a single cable, but split up into multiple channels.

Think of a very large, one lane highway where all the traffic flows in one direction – this is a baseband highway. If we were to split the highway into two lanes, we could now have two different types of traffic flowing simultaneously. Unfortunately, each lane could now carry only half of the traffic load, but we have a broadband highway. Let's suppose we split it up into four total lanes – we can now send four different types of traffic through simultaneously. But how do the cars know where to drive?

They simply stay in their lane denoted by painted white stripes – that is the agreed-upon method for knowing where each lane starts and stops.

With physical data pathways, each lane represents a range of frequencies. The lines between each lane are simply a specific frequency based on an agreed-upon standard.

Pulling It All Together (So Far)

Let's take a minute to pull everything we have discussed in this domain so far together. We started with the OSI model, which describes how we package up data for transmission, which is transmitted over signals in an analog or digital format, using asynchronous or synchronous communication methods, over either a baseband or broadband medium.

As a very silly example, let's suppose a spaceship full of aliens land and you are assigned the task of communicating with them. First, you must figure out some type of data you both understand – everyone understands mathematics (you assume), so you settle on using a combination of prime numbers and Sudoku puzzles - why not have fun while avoiding inter-galactic misunderstandings? Both types of 'data' can be encoded using the OSI model all the way down to layer 2.

You then must decide to either speak the 'data' (sound waves through the air - analog) or perhaps perform a tap dance (each tap means a 0 or 1 – digital). Obviously, tap dancing is the better choice. Then, you must decide how the aliens will know when you are done 'speaking' – tap dance as fast as you can for 5 seconds and stop (synchronized) or just add a little bow at the end to let them know you are finished (asynchronous). Finally, since there is so much information to talk to them about, you can have 25 people tap dancing at the same time (broadband) or focus all their attention on a single person (baseband).

Questions

1. Which term represents how high a wave peak is?

    A) Frequency

    B) Data throughput

    C) Amplitude

    D) Bandwidth

2. Which term represents the detection of information based on an infinite degree of AM or FM?

    A) Amplitude

    B) Signal wave

    C) Frequency

    D) Analog signal

3. Which term represents number of electrical pulses that can be sent over a signal within a given time period?

    A) Baseband

    B) Broadband

    C) Data throughput

    D) Bandwidth

4. Which term represents a way to communicate some type of information?

    A) Signal wave

    B) Signal

    C) Analog signal

    D) Digital signal

5. Which term represents two devices communicate based on exact timing?

    A) Analog signal

    B) Asynchronous

    C) Digital signal

    D) Synchronous

Chapter 36: Cabling

Signal waves can be sent in different ways – sound waves travel through either air or water, but we are dealing with _electromagnetic signals_, which we usually only send either through the air (wireless) or suing a physical cable.

Network cabling comes in a variety of flavors, but all carry a consistent naming scheme that indicates the type of wiring, bandwidth and maximum length. As examples, we have 10Base-T, 100Base-TX or 1000Base-T. The first number represents the data throughput, not the bandwidth. 1000Base-T has a bandwidth of 100 MHz (100 million signals per second), but after compression and encoding has a throughput of 1000 MB/sec.

Coaxial Cable

Coaxial cabling has a single, thick copper wire, wrapped by insulation, then a metal shield sheath, and finally an outer covering. Due to the metal sheath, coaxial is less-susceptible to _electromagnetic interference_ (_EMI_), something we covered in more detail in the Security Architecture and Engineering domain when discussing power interruption. Coaxial also supports longer runs and provides more bandwidth than twisted-pair – we'll talk about that in a second. Coaxial used to be used in network cabling, but today it is usually found only while carrying TV cable signals.

Twisted-Pair Cable

Twisted-pair cabling is built using pairs of thin copper wires wrapped in an outer jacket. Each wire in a pair is wrapped tightly around its counterpart, thus the 'twisted-pair' name. This twisting prevents the signal in each wire from degrading, as the wave in one wire balances out the wave in the other – the tighter the twist the more resistant the pair is to outside interference and attenuation. If the wires are each wrapped in an outer foil shielding, it is called a _shielded twisted pair_, or _STP_. If the wire does not have this shielding, it is called an _unshielded twisted pair_, or _UTP_.

UTP comes in 7 categories:

- Category 1 – Voice grade up to 1Mbs
- Category 2 – Up to 4 Mbps
- Category 3 – 10 Mbps for Ethernet and 4 Mbps for Token Ring (10Base-T)
- Category 4 – 16 Mbps – Token Ring networks
- Category 5 – 100 Mbps – most widely used
- Category 6 – 1 Gbps – used in most new installations, required for Gigabyte Ethernet
- Category 7 – 10 Gbps – used in new installations requiring high-speed transmissions

Transmission speed depends on 4 things:

- Quality of the copper core
- Type of insulation
- How tightly twisted the pairs are
- Type of shielding

Twisted pair is cheaper and easier to work with than coaxial, but is less secure because it is more prone to radiating signals.

Fiber-Optic Cable

Coaxial and twisted-pair use copper cores – while copper is relatively cheap it does slow down transmission rates due to resisting the flow of signal. That is why any cabling built around a copper core will have a maximum run length before a repeater is required.

Fiber-optic cabling, on the other hand, can travel very long distances because it is uses a type of glass that carries light signals. All the discussion about wave signals and analog vs. digital goes right out of the window with optics, because light signals are inherently digital – either the light is on or it is off. As a result, we don't have to worry about radiating signals or interference due to EMI, and it is considered to be much more secure than copper core cabling.

Unfortunately, fiber cabling is expensive and difficult to work with – therefore it is usually only used on networks that require very high transmission speeds. Most commonly fiber provides the backbone, and UTP completes the path to computers.

Fiber-optic cables are made of three components:

- _Light source_ – converts electrical signal into a light signal
  - Light-emitting diodes (LED)
  - Diode lasers
- Fiber cable
  - _Single mode_ – small glass core, lower bandwidth, long distance
  - _Multimode_ – larger glass core, higher bandwidth, shorter distances
- _Light detector_ – converts the light signal back into an electrical signal

Cabling Problems

All cabling is susceptible to natural interference. _Noise_ is any undesired addition to the source signal that can interfere with the receiver turning it back into the original information. Analog signals are particularly vulnerable to noise as repeaters amplify the original source as well as noise. Noise can be caused by any type of electrical source such as motors, fluorescent lighting and microwave ovens.

As a signal travels along its medium, it will almost always lose strength – the metal used in cabling is resistant to electrons traveling through it – the longer the wire the signal must travel through, the weaker the signal grows. This signal loss is called _attenuation_ and is why cabling always has a recommended maximum length before the signal needs to be repeated with a stronger signal before continuing. The higher the frequency at which a signal travels, the greater the attenuation becomes. For example, 10Base-T operates at 10 MHz while 100Base-TX runs at an 80 MHz frequency – therefore after 10 feet a signal traveling over 100Base-T will suffer more attenuation than will a signal travelling over a 10Base-T signal. Attenuation can also be caused by cable breaks and manufacturing deformities in a cable.

As we noted before, all cabling produces a certain amount of stray radiation. If a cable is run too close to another cable, this can produce _crosstalk_, or radiation from one cable interfering with the signal in another. Shielding helps to prevent this, so it makes sense that UTP is the most susceptible to this out of all networking cable.

Cabling is usually run above lowered ceilings or beneath raised floors in areas called _plenum space_. Since these spaces are usually out of sight and somewhat isolated from ventilation, fires can start in this space and remain undetected. If the outer wrapping of these cables is made from a toxic material, fumes will be produced that could be harmful to the building's occupants. Therefore, it is important to use only plenum-rated cabling in these areas, which normally have some type of fluoropolymer jacket – _nonplenum cable_ jackets are usually made from PVC which will produce toxic gases when burning.

Chapter 36: Cabling

Questions

1. Which of the following best describes the bandwidth for Category 7 Ethernet cabling?

    A) 1 Gbps

    B) 10 Gbps

    C) 16 Mbps

    D) 100 Mbps

2. Which of the following best describes the bandwidth for Category 2 Ethernet cabling?

    A) 16 Mbps

    B) 10 Mbps for Ethernet and 4 Mbps for Token Ring

    C) Up to 4Mbs

    D) Voice grade up to 1Mbs

3. Which Ethernet cabling is required for Gigabyte Ethernet?

    A) Category 5

    B) Category 7

    C) Category 4

    D) Category 6

4. Which of the following best represents a fiber-optic cable that has a large glass core, provides high bandwidth but can travel only a short distance?

    A) Single mode

    B) Base mode

    C) Multimode

    D) Polymode

5. Which term represents cabling usually found in TV cable?

    A) Coaxial Cable

    B) Twisted-Pair Cable

    C) STP

    D) UTP

Chapter 37: Networking

OK, let's move the discussion on to how cabling is used to create networks.

Topologies

How computers are arranged relative to each other within a network is called a *network topology*. The *physical topology* deals with how the cables are laid out and how they are connected to each computer. The *logical topology* describes how the computers communicate over the physical cabling. Of course, when we say 'cabling', it really should include wireless mechanisms as well.

A *ring topology* describes a network in which each all nodes (computers) are physically connected in a ring – they from an actual circle. In the very simplest form of this topology, if one node goes out, the entire network goes down. Most modern implementations of this topology have redundancy built in, such as an outer and inner ring to provide redundancy. Ring topologies have an advantage in that the rate of traffic flow can be predicted due to the presence of a token – we will discuss tokens in just a bit.

In a *bus topology*, a single cable runs the entire length of the network, with nodes all connected directly to this backbone, or bus. Any frame sent out on the network is visible to all connected nodes - each node decides whether to look at the frame or ignore it. This topology comes in 2 flavors – linear and tree. A *linear bus topology* is the one we have been describing with all nodes attached directly to the bus. A *tree bus topology* has branches connected directly to the bus, with nodes connected to branches. The backbone cable becomes a single point of failure in this topology. Ethernet uses either a bus or a star topology.

'What is a star topology' you ask? A *star topology* requires all nodes to be connected directly to a central device, usually a switch. The switch then becomes the single point of failure, but may be connected to other switches. This topology is the one most used within modern networks.

When all nodes are connected directly to each other, a great deal of reliability and redundancy is achieved, and this is called a *full mesh topology*. Full meshes are impractical for almost any use case, but almost all modern networks implement a *partial mesh topology*. Basically, take any combination of Token Ring, Bus or Star topologies and mix them together, and you have a partial mesh. A partial mesh is almost always a combination of multiple star networks, and this describes the Internet.

Media Access Technologies

Think back to the OSI model for a second and recall that Layer 2, called the Data Link layer, has 2 sublayers called the Logical Link Layer, or LLC, and the Media Access Control layer, or MAC layer. While the LLC pretty much just acts as a translator from the Network layer to the MAC sublayer, the MAC sublayer does a lot of work – it understands everything about Ethernet, Token Ring, FDDI (we will talk more about FDDI later), etc., and it knows how to format the data into something that the Physical layer (Layer 1) can understand. That is where we are going to focus our attention for a few minutes, and this area is collectively referred to as *Media Access technology*.

The one thing that all media access technologies must share is the communication channel – only one computer can be transmitting at a time regardless of the protocol you use. Whether you use a ring, linear bus, tree bus or star topology, they all require that only one computer speaks at a time, the method to determine which computer should be talking at any given time is the whole point of media access control, and there are several methods to choose from. One thing to keep in mind is that when a computer sends a frame on a physical cable, ALL computers connected to that cable receive it – after all we're talking about an electronic signal and there is no way to control which direction that signal travels in or how long it will travel. On ring networks, as a computer receives a signal, it may or may not forward that signal on to the next computer. With bus networks, usually the two ends of the single cable are capped with a device that absorbs signals so they are not reflected back onto the wire. With star networks, a switch will usually absorb the signal. But the media access technologies we will discuss next are *logical* – so when we discuss something like passing a token around, remember that we are referring to a logical construct, not a physical signal.

Token Passing

Sometimes when kids get mad at each other, and start yelling and interrupting each other, the parent will sit them down and say something like 'Here is a spoon – you may not talk until you are holding it, and no one else can interrupt you.' While it drives most kids crazy, it is a very effective mechanism to ensure that everyone gets a chance to speak. Well, computers are no different – they all like to talk at the same time just like kids. However, if we pass around a virtual spoon – let's call it a token – only the computer who possesses the token can speak, and everyone gets their chance to talk in turn. This is called *token passing* and is used by the Token Ring and FDDI networks. The token is a 24-bit control frame, and here is how it works:

- Computer A wants to say something to Computer C on the network, and already possesses the token
- Computer A puts its message inside of the token and sends it out
- Computer B gets the token but ignores it because it is not addressed to it
- Computer C gets the token, sees that it is addressed to itself, extracts the message, flips an 'I got it' bit on the control frame, and sends it out again
- Computer A gets the token back and sees that the 'I got it' bit has been flipped, and so it knows the message was received by Computer C
- Computer A sends an empty token, ready for some other computer to grab it

CSMA

Ethernet approaches media access in a completely different manner using something called _carrier sense multiple access_, or _CSMA_. CSMA has two flavors that deal with collision detection and collision avoidance.

If there is no token to pass around, what would happen if two computers tried to transmit frames at the exact same time? They would both be adding electrical signals to the same wire, resulting in a garbled mess of electrons that make no sense. That situation is called a _collision_ – two or more electronic signals collide and both are corrupted.

When a computer transmits a frame, that transmission is called a _carrier_, because it carries information. Computers who have something to say on Ethernet will wait until there is a lull of traffic on the network and then transmit the data. However, this does not prevent collisions since two computers can both see there is no traffic and transmit at the exact same time, resulting in a collision. If a network has implemented a protocol called _carrier sense multiple access with collision detection_, or _CSMA/CD_, both computers will recognize a collision has occurred, send out a jam signal, and then back off and wait for a random period of time before trying the entire process again. This is why the CSMA/CD has the 'detection' part in it. Ethernet uses CSMA/CD.

A slightly different approach is closer to a token passing method in which a computer listens for a lull, and instead of trying to transmit immediately, sends out a broadcast letting all other computers in the same network know that

it would like to 'speak'. All other computers will back off for a random period of time before transmitting data to ensure collisions do not happen. This is called _collision avoidance_, and the entire protocol is called _carrier sense multiple access with collision avoidance_, or _CSMA/CA_. This method is used with Wi-Fi networks.

Carrier sensing methods such as CSMA/CA and CSMA/CD result in a faster network over token passing methods, until you have a very large number of nodes – the resulting collisions have an increasingly negative effect as the number of nodes increase. To offset this, we can create smaller _collision domains_ by segmented the network with switches, which do not forward frames outside of their network unless they are _supposed_ to go to another network.

So, a collision domain stops at any layer 2 devices, such as hubs, repeaters, switches, bridges or wireless access points. A _broadcast domain_ stops at any layer 3 devices such as routers. One side benefit to creating collision or broadcast domains is that it reduces the amount of data that any one computer has access to – restricting the amount of data an attacker can sniff from a single computer is a good thing. We will cover collision and broadcast domains again later.

Polling

So, we have discussed token passing and CSMA as types of media access technologies. The last type of media access control is called _polling_, and is used primarily in mainframe environments. With this method, a primary station will periodically poll secondary devices on a network, either to monitor or to give permission to communicate on the network. We won't go any further into that subject.

Ethernet

Let's go back to Ethernet for a bit. As we stated before, _Ethernet_ is a network communication standard that is usually used within a star or bus topology. It was invented in the 1970s and is officially defined through the IEEE 802.3 standard. It is a _contention-based technology_, which means that all resources use the same shared medium. It exclusively uses the CSMA/CD access method, employs collision and broadcast domains, supports full-duplex communication and is compatible with coaxial, twisted pair or fiber-optic cabling. We have previously discussed some Ethernet cabling types, but let's revisit them in a little more depth.

By far the most common cabling for Ethernet is UTP. Ethernet cables have 4 pairs of UTP, so it contains 8

Chapter 37: Networking

different wires. Within each pair, one wire is used to transmit data and the other is used to receive data. Ethernet UTP cabling uses RJ-45 connectors (regular telephone connectors are called RJ-11 and are smaller).

Originally, everyone used _10Base-T_, which supports speeds up to 10 Mbps over 100 meters, and is called Category 3.

As bandwidth demands increased, Category 5 _Fast Ethernet_ (_100Base-TX_) was developed that ran over _Cat5_ cable and supported speeds up to 100 Mbps. Both 10 Mbps and 100 Mbps speeds can coexist in the same network if using 10/100 hubs and switches. _Gigabit Ethernet_ (_1000Base-T_) allows for speeds up to 1000 Mbps on Cat5 wire by allowing simultaneous transmission in both directions on all pairs. _Cat5E_ cable is normally used for this application.

Next, Category 6 10GBase-T was invented that supported 10 Gbps over _Cat6_ cabling, but had to do away with the venerable CSMA/CD technology. It has not seen the same wide-spread adoption as Gigabit Ethernet enjoyed due to the poorer cost-to-performance ratio.

FDDI
IEEE 802.4 describes the _fiber distributed data interface_, or _FDDI_, which was developed by ANSI and is a token passing media access technology intended for high-speed networks. It supports up to 100 Mbps and can most commonly be found on fiber network backbones. To provide for redundancy, it has a primary ring traveling clockwise with a secondary ring operating in a counterclockwise direction. The secondary ring is only used if the primary ring goes down, which is triggered by sensors. All nodes are connected to both rings so that if a break in one ring occurs, the two rings can be joined in real-time.

FDDI can be run up to 100 kilometers and allows multiple tokens to be present at the same time, increasing throughput. _FDDI-2_ provided Quality of Service (QoS) capabilities. FDDI was primarily meant for MANs (metro area networks). A variant of FDDI, _copper distributed data interface_ (_CDDI_) provides the same capabilities but over UTP, and is meant for LANs.

Devices that can connect to FDDI are categorized as:

- _Single-attachment station_ (_SAS_) – attaches to only one ring through a concentrator
- _Dual-attachment station_ (_DAS_) – attaches to both rings through a concentrator
- Single-attachment concentrator (SAC) – attaches an SAS device to the primary ring
- Dual-attachment concentrator (DAC) – attaches DAS, SAS and SAC to both rings

Token Ring
IEEE 802.5 defines the _Token Ring_ media access standard, which used to be popular but has been eclipsed by Ethernet. It uses a Token Passing methodology and supports up to 16Mbps. Token Ring uses an _active monitor_ mechanism to remove frames that are continuously circulating when the targeted computer is no longer online. When a computer encounters a problem, it can send a beacon frame, and other computers will attempt to work around the problem – this is called _beaconing_.

Transmission Methods
A packet can be intended for three types of recipients within a specific network:

- _Unicast_ – a single computer
- _Multicast_ – a group of computers
- _Broadcast_ – all computers

Unicast is the transmission method we are usually familiar with. Multicast is like a radio station broadcast with a single source and multiple recipients. So how does a computer on the other side of the country take part in a multicast with 20 routers in between them? Well, the receiving computer tells its router that it wishes to be multicast to, and that router tells the next router, and so forth until the request reaches the router connected directly to the machine with the content to multicast. All 20 routers now know to forward packets from the sender to the recipient. This is all done using the _Internet Group Management Protocol_ (_IGMP_), which has gone through 3 versions – version 2 added the ability to be removed from a group and version 3 allows recipients to specify the multicast sources.

One final note: all above is true for IPv4 – IPv6 completely redid multicasting, but that is a whole other story not in scope for this discussion.

Network Protocols and Services
All right, time to talk about some common protocols that are used to manage networks.

Address Resolution Protocol
When data is traveling between one computer and another, each computer has a _network interface card_, or

NIC, that sends and receives the signals directly from the physical medium. The NIC has a globally unique identifier burned into it at the manufacturer called a *media access control address* (*MAC address*). It is made up of 48 bits – the first 24 bits are unique to the manufacturer and the last 24 bits are unique to any card ever produced from that manufacturer. Guess what OSI layer understands a MAC address? That would be Layer 2 – the Data Link Layer that has a sublayer called, magically enough, the MAC sublayer. When the Data Link Layer receives the raw data, it only knows about MAC addresses – these things called IP addresses are some alien concept as far as Layer 2 is concerned because they are a Layer 3 thing. When frames travel through switches, all the switch cares about is the MAC address as well. So, here's the question – if the upper layer only knows about IP addresses, but switch routing only works at the MAC address level, how do we translate between the IP address and the MAC address?

The answer is to use the *address resolution protocol*, or more commonly called, *ARP*. Here is how it works:

- A Layer 2 device receives a packet containing an IP address
- It looks in an internal cache of IP address to MAC address mapping, and doesn't get a hit
- It then broadcasts a frame with the unknown IP address asking for the owner of that IP address to reply
- The owner replies
- Layer 2 extracts the MAC address from the replied frame, adds it to the cache, and uses that MAC address to send out its frame

What if the owner of the IP address is not in our network? The router we are connected to will recognize that the requested IP is outside the network, and reply on the computer's behalf – the router essentially says, 'Here is my MAC address – go ahead and send the frame to me and I will make sure it gets to where it needs to.'

Now, think what would happen if an attacker's computer could somehow claim that it was the owner of the requested IP when it really was not? The requesting computer would receive two answers – the right one and the attacker's. Normally, the most recent response is cached, so the attacker would need to send a continuous stream of responses of bogus ARP replies. But if it worked, then the attacker would receive all the data intended for the rightful computer. This type of attack is called *ARP table cache poisoning*, or just *ARP poisoning*. ARP does not

have any type of security, so the network must protect it from these attacks, normally by implementing *IDS sensors*.

Dynamic Host Configuration Protocol
Every device on an Ethernet network needs to have a unique IP address assigned to it. If more than one device claims to have the same IP, it causes a lot of routing problems and so this situation needs to be avoided. If devices are manually configured with their IP address, the address is called a *static IP address*. This can work great to ensure there are no conflicts, but the maintenance of such a configuration is not minor.

Instead, many networks using *dynamic IP addresses*. Each device does not have an assigned IP address until it has booted and attempts to connect to the network. A dedicated server hands out dynamic IP addresses as they are needed. Other than configuring that single server, no more configurations are needed, even when adding brand new devices to the network.

As with just about any other mechanism on a network, there is a protocol on how to get this done, and it is called *dynamic host configuration protocol*, or just *DHCP*. The server is called the DHCP server, and devices who are assigned dynamic IPs are called *DHCP clients*. Here is how the whole process works:

- The DHCP client connects to the network and broadcasts out a DHCPDISCOVER message to the entire network
- The DHCP server sees the request, and sends back a DHCPOFFER message containing an available IP address to the client
- The client grabs the IP address and sends a DHCPREQUEST back out
- The server sees the response and sends out a DHCPACK message with information on how long the client can keep the IP address (called a *lease*), completing the exchange
- The client uses the dynamically-assigned IP address

Each time a DHCPDISCOVER message is received by the DHCP server, it will choose from a predetermined range of dynamic IP addresses. This allows a single subnet to support both static and dynamic IP addresses simultaneously. DHCP supports more than just assigning IP addresses though – it also allows the DHCP server to provide IP addresses for the default gateway and DNS servers – everything a device needs to know to operate on a network.

Of course, this protocol is vulnerable in two directions. First, rogue devices can act as if they were a DHCP server – once they convince a client to use the attacker's IP address as their gateway or DNS server IP, they can execute man-in-the-middle attacks and the victim would never know. Secondly, a rogue device can request a dynamic IP address and become part of the network. To prevent this second attack, switches can be configured to allow DHCPDISCOVER requests only from trusted devices based on the device's MAC address – this is called *DHCP snooping*, and prevents trusted DHCP servers from ever receiving the request.

Similar to DHCP is the *reverse address resolution protocol*, or *RARP*. If you recall, the Address Resolution Protocol (ARP) allows clients to send out an IP address and receive back a corresponding MAC address. RARP works in the reverse – the client can send out its MAC address and get back whatever IP address has been previously assigned to the device. While this is not really assigning IP addresses in a *dynamic* manner, it does allow devices to boot up with no knowledge of an IP address and to get one - this is normally used with diskless workstations. The *Bootstrap Protocol*, or *BOOTP*, was added after RARP came on the scene, and added the ability to also retrieve the default gateway and DNS server IP addresses, just like DHCP.

Internet Control Message Protocol
Thinking back to Layer 4 of the OSI model, the Transport layer defined the TCP and UDP protocols – both use ports to create something called a socket. Using a tool like Telnet, you can create a socket connection to a specific IP address and port number, and the tool will show you the contents of the socket in real time. Another frequently used tool is *PING* – you type in an IP address and it will tell you if there is a server at that address. But how does PING work if you never told it a port number? Does it use a predefined port number for PING? The answer is a big NO, because PING works at Layer 3, not Layer 4. Layer 3 knows nothing about ports, so PING must work in some other manner.

It turns out that PING uses another protocol called *internet control message protocol*, or *ICMP* for short. ICMP is a protocol that just about any device understands and can be used to test connectivity, provide status updates and report errors among other things – but the clear majority of time it is used for 'pinging'. Here is how it works:

- Computer A sends an ICMP Echo Request frame to Computer B
- Computer B replies with an ICMP Echo Reply frame
  OR
- Computer B does not reply and Computer A tries a few more times before reporting that the host is unreachable

Routers use ICMP frames to let sending devices know their packet never reached its destination. Note that ICMP is not tied to IP addresses – it works at Layer 3, and any number of addressing protocols work there. There over 40 different types of ICMP messages that can be generated – ECHO Request is type 8 and Echo Reply is type 0.

While ICMP was never designed to hold data, someone was able to figure out how to embed data within an ICMP frame to sneak it into networks undetected – this is called *ICMP tunneling*. This is an example of a covert channel – using an existing communication channel to send data in a way it was never designed.

Another ICMP-based attack is to force routers to redirect traffic in an unauthorized manner. Routers use ICMP messages to communicate with each other, and an attacker could pretend it was a switch and force a legitimate switch to reroute traffic to the attacker or simply send it into oblivion.

Traceroute is a handy diagnostic tool that allows an administrator to look for connection problems. It uses ICMP messages to detect where a connection path has broken, but can also gather a lot of information about the layout of a network. An attacker could obviously find this tool very useful when performing reconnaissance.

To prevent such attacks, an IDS can be used to detect overuse of the ICMP protocol and to properly configure firewalls to block some ICMP messages.

Simple Network Management Protocol
As networks became larger and more complex, a unified method to manage all the devices on a network was needed. *Simple network management protocol* (*SNMP*) was the answer. Released in 1988, SNMP allows a network administrator to monitor and control various devices through a *manager*. The manager is a piece of software running on a central server, while an *agent* is software that runs on network devices. The manager periodically polls agents for status updates and can receive trap messages from agents. A *trap* operation allows an agent to forward information about an event without having to wait for the next poll from the manager.

The agent maintains a _management information base_, or _MIB_, which is simply a small database of objects that the agent keeps track of for the device on which it is installed. The agent collects various metrics for each object and stores it in the MIB, and when the manager asks for it, the agent will forward all the new information to the manager. Therefore, the SNMP manager always has the latest information on every device it monitors. Some of the information SNMP provides are:

- Shares
- Usernames
- Services
- Domain information
- Resource utilization (CPU, memory, etc.)

By default, anyone can ask a device for information via SNMP – obviously that can be a security risk. So, the concept of a _community_ was added, and for an agent to give out information to a manager, the manager must provide a _community string_, which is a fancy word for password. SNMP supports two different types of community strings – read and read-write. If the _read password_ is provided, the querying device can access all sorts of sensitive information about the agent device. If the _read-write password_ is provided, the querying device can modify the contents of the MIB.

SNMP versions 1 and 2 sent both passwords in clear text, so that any attacker who could sniff traffic could discover these values. Version 3 added encryption, message integrity and authentication. SNMP always has default read and read-write passwords set, usually to 'public' and 'private'. Unfortunately, many companies do not bother changing these passwords, creating a vulnerable spot in the network's security. Recommendations for SNMP configuration are:

- Change the read and read-write passwords
- Only use SNMP version 3
- Use different passwords for each network segment
- Lock down ports 161 and 162 and restrict traffic to and from authorized devices on those ports

Domain Name Service

We just barely touched on _domain name services_ (_DNS_) before when discussing DHCP, but let's discuss it in detail a little more. IP networks, and more importantly the Internet, all work based on IP addresses, whether it is IPv4 or IPv6. Computers love IP addresses because they are very logical and make a lot of sense to them. Humans, however, don't think in the same way, and IP addresses are difficult to remember. Imagine having to remember to type in 216.58.194.110 whenever you wanted to Google something – 'typing in 'google.com' is much, much easier. Too bad computers don't think so – they really must have an IP address before they can function properly. So, we need some easy method to turn human-speak into computer-speak, and that is what DNS is all about.

Before getting into the specifics on how that is done, let's look at domain names themselves. If you look at a domain name, such as 'www.mydomain.com', the scope starts very narrow and grows larger with each 'dot' you encounter. The Internet works in the reverse – if you want to find a very specific location, you start at the right, and gradually zero in on where you want to go. So, with 'www.mydomain.com', the first thing you want to figure out is what 'com' means. The first segment of a domain is called the _top-level domain_, and the most common are:

- COM - commercial
- EDU - education
- MIL – US military
- GOV - government
- ORG - organization
- NET – network

DNS servers on the Internet are arranged in a hierarchical fashion with top-level domain servers at the top, second-level domain servers underneath, and so forth. Each DNS server only knows about the level above it, and can communicate with all DNS server beneath it, but doesn't know anything about other DNS servers running at its same level. So, let's follow our example to see how that works.

You are sitting at home, and you type in 'www.mydomain.com' into your favorite browser. The browser knows the first thing it needs to do it to turn that URL into an IP address. Your computer has already been configured with the IP address of a DNS server – that server will be a server run by your Internet Service Provider (ISP). Let's say your service provider is AT&T, so the DNS server assigned to you will be one owned by AT&T. So, your browser will ask the AT&T DNS server 'Hey, tell me the IP address for 'www.mydomain.com'. The AT&T DNS server will have no clue – it only knows about DNS entries inside of the network where it lives – for example, URLs ending with 'att.com'. So, the AT&T DNS server will forward the request up to the next level DNS server it has been configured with, which will more than

Chapter 37: Networking

likely be a *root* DNS server. This server will know the IP address of the DNS server who knows all about 'mydomain.com'. But, that is not the IP address we need – the top DNS server will then forward the request to the DNS server for 'mydomain.com' and ask it for the IP address for 'www.mydomain.com'. The 'mydomain.com' DNS server will look in its entries, retrieve the real IP address for 'www' within its network and return it. Then we unwind the whole stack until the correct IP address is returned to your browser. Then, your browser makes the request using the correct IP address for you.

That was a lot of work just to turn a human-friendly name into a computer-friendly address! But without it, the Internet would be essentially unusable to us mere mortals. Recognizing the overhead of such a mechanism, DNS servers store the results of each resolution they complete, so the next time someone asks for the same URL, they simply pull the IP address from their cache and send it back. Your computer even does the same thing – when it gets back the IP address for 'www.mydomain.com', it will cache the IP address, so the next time you type in that URL, it already knows the IP address instantly without having to ask for it. This process within your computer is called a *DNS resolver*, and can operate in two different modes:

- *Recursive query* – pretty much what we have already discussed
- *Nonrecursive query* – if the computer's DNS server does not know the answer, instead of forwarding the query to another DNS server, it simply fails and returns 'I have no idea'

Most computers also support a *HOSTS file*, which is a text file containing a list of domain names and matching IP addresses – on Windows machines the file is stored in '%systemroot%\system32\drivers\etc' folder, and on Linux machines in the '/etc/hosts' folder. When your computer's local DNS resolver receives a request for an IP address, it will do the following:

- *Check its cache* – if a hit is found, it returns the IP address
- *Check the HOSTS file* – if a hit is found, it is cached and it returns the IP address
- *Ask the DNS Server* – when a hit is returned, it is cached and it returns the IP address

Now, let's talk about some vulnerabilities in the DNS system. First, it is possible for an attacker to just hang around and listen for a DNS resolution request, and quickly jump in and provide the response before the real DNS server answers. The attacker provides an IP address of his own choosing, and from then on, that computer will use the wrong address any time that URL is typed into a browser. This attack works against DNS servers as well when they forward a request to a higher-level DNS server.

There really is only one counter to this problem, and that is to implement some type of authentication and encryption around the DNS request/resolution exchange. *DNS Security* (*DNSSEC*) implements just such an approach, but unfortunately is not easy to roll out casually – all DNS servers taking part in DNSSEC must be configured simultaneously, which has drastically slowed its adoption. However, countries are slowly adopting the standard and ICANN has made plans as well.

Another attack on DNS is for malware that has been maliciously installed on a host system to modify the contents of the HOSTS file, resulting in that content being used for resolving domain names instead of asking a DNS server. A popular use of this attack is to block antivirus software from retrieving updates. Simply making the HOSTS file read-only and implementing a host-based IDS is the most effective counter to an attack of this type.

A third attack vector is not a direct attack against DNS but more of a social engineering attack – that of *URL hiding*. In this approach, a hyperlink containing non-threatening text is linked to a site where an attack is launched. For example, the hyperlink might look like 'www.yourbank.com' but the underlying link goes to 'steal.password.evildomain.com'. Some attackers even encode the actual link so that if anyone bothers to look closer, they cannot tell where the link will take them.

Let's wrap this up with a best practice suggestion – if you host your own DNS server, never put both your external and internal mappings on the same server. For your DNS server to handle external lookups for your public sites, the DNS server must be public-facing, meaning it lives in the DMZ and is accessible from the big, bad Internet. If an attacker manages to compromise that server, and it contains your internal mappings as well, you have given the attacker a substantial head-start. Using two DNS servers – both external and internal – is called *split DNS*.

Before we leave the subject of DNS servers, let's examine two legal issues you need to be aware of. When registering a domain, ICANN implements a first-come-first-serve policy – whoever requests a domain first will get it, regardless of who has a greater need for it. *Cyber squatters* will quickly grab attractive domain names, hoping to sell them for a huge profit to some individual or company who was too slow to act. Once a domain has been registered, you must always watch for re-registration dates. If you forget to re-register your domain, a cyber squatter can grab your domain and force you to pay a hefty premium to get it back. This is called *domain grabbing*. Purchasing domains for a limited time is relatively cheap, so it is always a good idea to buy domains in case you will want them but are not quite sure. It is also a good idea to register nearby domains as well – for example, when buying 'greatness'.com' you might also want to purchase 'great-ness.com' and 'greatness.net'.

E-Mail Services

E-Mail was the original killer Internet app, and continues to be very important. *Simple mail transfer protocol* (*SMTP*) is the protocol all mail servers use for sending email messages, and it runs on top of TCP. When you click the send button, it is SMTP that moves that message from your email client to the email server holding your account. That same protocol allows your email server to forward that email to the recipient's email server. SMTP defines the standard email address format that we all know and love – the ubiquitous 'me@mydomain.com'. There are tons of email clients out there, with Outlook being the most common desktop client, followed by mobile platforms such as iPhone and Android clients. The most common server-based software packages are Sendmail for UNIX servers and Exchange for Windows servers.

SMTP does not provide a whole lot of security, and so *SMTP authentication*, or *SMTP-AUTH* was invented as an extension to SMTP. This allows clients to authenticate with a server before the server will accept a message.

When a message is sent via SMTP, the email server receiving the message will store it in a database waiting for your email client to ask for them. However, the SMTP protocol does not support retrieving messages from a server – it can only send them. That is where the *post office protocol*, or *POP*, comes into play. Whereas SMTP is all about sending email, POP only knows how to download email messages that have been stored on an email server. The annoying thing about POP is that when it retrieves all new messages, they are automatically deleted from the server. You see, back when POP first came out, people had only one computer, and the idea of mobile devices was just a gleam in the Internet's eye. POP asks the server for all messages received since the last time it checked, and all messages are downloaded, leaving nothing on the server.

This worked well back then, but these days we have multiple platforms checking email for a single email account. This means if you use POP to download email on our phone, those messages will not be visible on your desktop.

Originally, POP pretty much had no security until version 3. That is why when we talk about POP, we usually just call it POP3. POP3 introduced support for *simple authentication and security layer* (*SASL*), which is a protocol-independent method for authentication.

POP3's inability to leave messages on the server is why *internet message access protocol* (*IMAP*) was invented. It does everything POP3 can do plus a whole lot more. The most important ability is to download all messages that are new to a client, but leave them on the server. That way, one of your clients (your mobile phone email client, for example) can check in and stay in-sync without affecting your desktop email client. One of the great features of IMAP is that it can mark a message as read from one client, and the other client will automatically get updated to show that message as read as well. Finally, searching all your email messages on the server without having to download them all is a key feature of IMAP.

So, if IMAP is so great, then why do we still have POP3? The big answer is that it takes time to supplant an older protocol. But there are a couple of legitimate reason to use POP3:

- If your email is stored on a server, the server will impose some limits on how much email you can keep.
- If your email is stored on a server, someone else has access to your email. Think Hillary Clinton.

SMTP has a significant vulnerability if an email server is not configured properly. Part of SMTP's capabilities is the feature to *relay* messages to another server. This is crucial for SMTP to forward messages from one server to another, but it can be easily abused to send out spam. If relay is not restricted, anyone can connect to the server using SMTP and say 'I know you don't know who I am, but please forward my spam email to this list of unsuspecting victims' – and the server will do it! Therefore, the email server must be configured to accept relay requests only from certain requestors.

Email spoofing is a technique used by spam authors – they will try to make emails look like they are is coming from a legitimate source by filling in the email header with bogus information. No one likes spam email, and to reduce the number of unwanted messages, the _sender policy framework_ (_SPF_) was created to detect bogus incoming messages from other servers. This system requires an email server's IP address to be registered with the owner's DNS records as an authorized email server. When a recipient email server receives an incoming email message from another server, it will backtrack the domain the email is supposedly coming from, and if the SPF record does not match the sending email server's IP address, the message is rejected. This prevents rogue email servers or clients from trying to pretend to send email messages from someone else's domain.

Phishing is an email-based social engineering attack with the goal of getting a victim to click a link in the email leading to a 'bad' server, or to get the user to reveal sensitive information about themselves. Phishing emails are sent in mass numbers hoping someone will 'bite'. When a bogus email is crafted toward a specific individual, it is called _spear phishing_. When that individual is some 'big fish' in an organization, such as the CEO, CIO, president or board member, it is called a _whaling attack_. Both spear phishing and whaling use finely-tuned information to trick a specific individual into becoming a victim.

Network Address Translation

Going back to IP addresses for a moment, when it became apparent that the world was running out of IPv4 addresses, work began on IPv6. But everyone knew that it would take time to develop and deploy this new addressing standard and a stop-gap was needed. So, _network address translation_ (_NAT_) was created to buy the world more time. And it worked great. Too great in fact – because NAT has caught on so well, the urgency to transition to IPv6 has been greatly abated. To understand NAT, we must understand that there are 3 ranges of private IPv4 addresses. When we say _private_, we mean that they are not publicly routable – you can try and use one of these addresses on the Internet, but chances are you are not going to have much luck. Private addresses are designed to work in private networks, not public ones. Here are the 3 ranges:

- _Class A_ – 10.0.0.0 - 10.255.255.255
- _Class B_ – 172.16.0.0 – 172.131.255.255
- _Class C_ – 192.168.0.0 – 192.168.255.255

The idea behind NAT is that you place a device in the DMZ (short for demilitarized zone – the area in a network where public servers live) that has a public IP address, and all devices in your private network use a private IP address.

Note that for the next example, we are going to completely forget about the domain name to IP address translation that we just covered in excruciating detail. For purposes of this example, domain names are magically getting converted to IP addresses when needed.

Let's say, that you have a laptop on your internal network with an IP address of 10.10.1.1 (which is a private IP address), and the laptop user tries to bring up _www.somedomain.com_ in their browser. So, the laptop will contact the DMZ device and say 'Hey, DMZ device – here is my private IP address, and I am trying to reach www.somedomain.com. Will you contact that server for me and let me know when you get an answer back?' So, the DMZ device reaches out to _www.somedomain.com_ - the server on the other end only sees the DMZ device's public IP, and replies with a web page back to the DMZ device. The DMZ device remembers that 10.10.1.1 was trying to reach _www.somedomain.com_, and sends the web page back to the laptop. That is NATing – the DMZ device is _translating_ a _network address_ from private to public, and back again.

Now, there are 3 types of NATing we can implement. First, we can have _static mapping_, where the NAT software maps a specific public IP address to a specific private IP address. It's a one-to-one mapping, and all we are doing is hiding the internal IP address. This is normally used for servers that need to use the same IP address all the time.

Next, we can use _dynamic mapping_. With this method, the NAT software is assigned a pool of public IP addresses, and they are used as needed – internal devices are assigned a public IP address on a first-come, first-served basis. This requires you to estimate the maximum number of public addresses that will be needed at any given time.

Finally, we can use something called _Port Address Translation_, or _PAT_. With this method, you can use a single public IP address for any number of private computers. To make this work, we must start using ports. In our previous laptop example, the NAT software recorded the laptop's IP address. With PAT, the laptop's outgoing port is recorded as well, and a public port is substituted for it. When the public server at _www.somedomain.com_ sends back a web page, it will send it to the public port. The NAT software (which is also using PAT) will lookup which internal computer was assigned that public port, and then route the web page back to the previously recorded IP address/port. It looks like this:

- The NAT device is configured with a public IP address of 127.43.2.19
- The laptop with a private IP address of 10.10.1.1 contacts the NAT device over port 44,217
- The NAT device assigns this request with an available port of 40,000
- The NAT device contacts *www.somedomain.com* using 127.43.2.19/40,000
- www.somedomain.com replies to 127.43.2.19/40,000 with a web page
- The NAT device looks up the original IP/port corresponding to 127.43.2.19/40,000, which is 10.10.1.1/44,217
- The NAT device sends the web page back to 10.10.1.1/44,217

Both dynamic and PAT implementations of NAT are *stateful* – they must remember the mapping to send responses back to the correct internal address.

Routing Protocols

We previously stated that the Internet is a partial mesh network, meaning that it is made up of a lot of different types of networks. Each of the networks is referred to as an *autonomous system* (*AS*). Within each AS you will find one or more routers, and the communication protocols within that AS will all be the same and are referred to as interior routing protocols. When one AS communicates with another AS, we say it is using an exterior routing protocol.

There are two types of routing protocols – static and dynamic. A *static routing protocol* is manually configured to route packets in a specific manner, and if that path is broken, packets will get lost. When a router is configured to use a *dynamic routing protocol*, it can discover the best path to send packets based on multiple parameters – some parameters are measured by the router, and others are provided to it by other routers. When using a dynamic routing protocol, a router can choose the best path on-the-fly and automatically adapt to changing network conditions, such as routers going down, overloaded traffic in a certain segment, or even a physical line break. When the availability of routers is constantly changing within an AS, we call this *route flapping*. If a router sends packets to a link that is no longer working, the packets are said to have disappeared down a *black hole*.

There are 2 types of interior routing protocols. The *distance-vector routing protocol* is the simplest and only uses the number of hops (distance) and direction (vector) of a given path when calculating the best path to send a packet. On the other hand, a *link-state routing protocol* builds a topological map of the network in memory and looks at number of hops, packet size, link speed, latency, traffic load and historical reliability when calculating the best path. Obviously, the link-state routing protocol results in better path decisions, but also requires more CPU and memory resources, and is slightly slower than distance-vector routing protocols.

There are 6 interior routing protocols we need to discuss:

- *Routing information protocol* (*RIP*) – a very slow distance vector protocol; V1 has no authentication, V2 sends password in clear text or as MD5 hashes, and RIPng adds support for IPv6
- *Open shortest path first* (*OSPF*) – a link-state protocol that supports a backbone link connecting subnets; has mostly replaced RIP, supports authentication and V3 supports IPv6 and IPSec.
- *Interior gateway routing protocol* (*IGRP*) – a Cisco distance-vector protocol that uses 5 metrics (bandwidth, latency, load, reliability and MTU) instead of the usual distance and vector
- Enhanced interior gateway routing protocol (EIGRP) – a successor to IGRP, it adds faster router table updates; V4 supports IPv6
- *Virtual router redundancy protocol* (*VRRP*) – supports a primary and failover router to eliminate a single point of failure
- Intermediate system to intermediate system (IS-IS) – a link-state protocol that is vendor-neutral but does not use IP addresses

There is only one exterior routing protocol to speak of, and that is the *border gateway protocol* (*BGP*). It is commonly used by ISPs, and employs a combination of both distance-vector and link-state algorithms. It creates a map of the network topology like link-state protocols do, but transmits updates to other routers on a periodic basis as distance-vector protocols do, instead of continuous updates. A *routing policy* allows administrators to apply weights to the different metrics measured by the link-state algorithm.

Aside from attempted DoS, attacks on routers almost always focus on trying to force the router to send packets to black holes or to the attacker's location. This is done by the attacker pretending to be another router and sending route table updates. The mitigation for these types of attacks is to ensure that authentication has been enabled on all routers.

A related attack is called a _wormhole attack_, in which one or more packets are captured and transported to another location in the network where another attacker uses the information to gain unauthorized access. To prevent this from happening, a _leash_ should be added to the packet header limiting the use of the data. The leash can be either _geographical_, meaning the packet can be used only within a certain distance of the sender (measured by hops), or _temporal_, meaning the packet must be used within a specific time window before it expires.

Chapter 37: Networking

Questions

1. What is the term describing the use of two different DNS servers – one for external entries and one internal entries?

    A) Segregated DNS

    B) Split DNS

    C) Dual DNS

    D) Double DNS

2. Which of the following is a device that receives a dynamic IP address?

    A) DHCP client

    B) NIC

    C) ARP table cache poisoning

    D) DHCP snooping

3. Which of the following range represents Class B IP addresses?

    A) 172.16.0.0 – 172.131.255.255

    B) 192.168.0.0 – 192.168.255.255

    C) 10.0.0.0 – 10.255.255.255

    D) 1.0.0.0 – 9.255.255.255

4. Which of the following represents the act of removing frames that are continuously circulating?

    A) CDDI

    B) Beaconing

    C) Active monitor

    D) FDDI

5. Which term best describes how computers are arranged relative to each other within a network?

    A) Full mesh topology

    B) Logical topology

    C) Physical topology

    D) Network topology

Chapter 38: Networking Devices

Now we're moving into a discussion of the devices that implement the protocols we just covered.

Repeaters, Hubs, Bridges, Switches and Routers

A network is made of many different types of devices, and the operation of each is very closely related to the OSI layers. We are going to cover all the devices you would normally find in a given network starting with layer 1 and working our way up the stack.

Remember that layer 1 is the physical layer – this is all about getting signals from point A to point B across either some type of cable or perhaps wireless technology. We have already discussed that signal will always lose strength as it travels, and so the first device we encounter is a _repeater_ – a device that simply amplifies a signal and forwards it on. There is very little intelligence in a repeater, but some can clean up noise. Cleaning up a digital signal will be far more effective than trying to clean up an analog signal, because noise can be filtered out with a digital signal. A _hub_ is simply a repeater with multiple ports, and is sometimes referred to as a _concentrator_ because it connects multiple physical devices.

On layer 2 we find a couple of devices – bridges and switches. Now switches can work at layers 2, 3 and 4, but for now we will focus on layer 2 only, which deals with MAC addresses. A _bridge_ connects LAN segments, and examines every frame that comes by. By examining the MAC address, a bridge can decide if the frame should be forwarded to another LAN or simply absorbed (not forwarded). On networks, a bridge separates collision domains – it will not let frames by unless they are addressed to a computer on another network. However, since broadcast packets are a layer 3 thing that works with IP addresses, bridges do not interfere with them and therefore a bridge cannot create separate broadcast domains. There are three types of bridges:

- _Local_ – connects LANs within a local area, usually a building
- _Remote_ – connects LANs over a MAN by using a telecommunications link
- _Translation_ – connects LANs that use different protocols, for example Ethernet and Token Ring

Bridges must know what port each frame should be forwarded to based on the frame's MAC address. Originally, this forwarding table had to be manually entered into each bridge, but this was replaced by _transparent bridging_. This is done by the bridge as it receives frames from each port – it will record the port and the MAC address that just came in, so when a request to send a frame with that MAC address is later received, the switch knows immediately which port it should be forwarded to. Eventually the bridge learns all MAC addresses that are on each network. Of course, to build this table the bridge must be able to figure out where a frame should go if it has not yet encountered the associated MAC address. To do this, it will send a query frame on all ports except for the one that the original frame came in on. The host having the MAC address will respond, and the bridge updates its forwarding table. Some bridges use the _spanning tree algorithm_ (_SPA_), which makes sure that rogue frames do not circulate forever, assigns priorities to certain paths and calculates costs for paths. This results in a more efficient forwarding process.

Sometimes a computer will send out an explorer packet to a destination that will return the path it took, and the computer will insert instructions into the packet header telling the bridge or router the exact path the frame or packet should travel. This is called _source routing_, and is very much frowned upon – we should let the network devices figure out the best path instead of whoever is sending the frame or packet. In fact, attackers will sometimes try to use source routing to get around certain network devices – border routers and firewalls should be configured to discard any such traffic.

A _switch_ is basically a hub combined with a bridge – it amplifies and cleans up signals, AND routes frames based on MAC addresses. However, a layer 2 switch adds a lot of extra intelligence by allowing routing rules to be implemented according to _access control lists_ (_ACLs_) and supporting _virtual LANs_ (_VLANs_). A VLAN allows an administrator to create virtual networks regardless of the physical location of each device. For example, 2 computers on the 2nd floor and 5 computers on the 10th floor can be combined into a single VLAN – as far as the computers can tell they are all physically connected to the same switch. This greatly enhances security as well as management of the network, not to mention scalability because we have just created a separate collision domain – fewer collisions means greater throughput.

In layer 3 we find _routers_, which know all about IP addresses. Remember that broadcast packets are implemented using special IP addresses, so we can create broadcast domains with a router. It can also have ACLs, but based on IP addresses instead of just MAC addresses.

Remember all routing protocols we discussed before? Routers are the network devices that use them – RIP, OSPF, BGP, IGRP, etc., and therefore routers are able to do something switches can't – calculate the best path for packets to take, and work around fluctuations in network congestion. Some networks require smaller packets than others (the _maximum transmission size_, or _MTU_, will specify this), so if a packet needs to be _fragmented_ to meet the MTU requirements, the router is the one who takes care of that. While a switch builds a list of MAC addresses and which port frames should be sent to based on the incoming MAC address, a router builds a table of IP addresses and which port a packet should be sent to.

When should we use each device? Here is a short list to help you decide:

- If you want to send a signal a long distance and don't care about reducing collisions, use a repeater, hub or concentrator
- If you want to create a collision domain, use a bridge, switch or router
- If you want to create a virtual LAN or apply ACLs based on MAC addresses, use a switch
- If you want to create a broadcast domain or apply ACLs based on IP addresses, use a router

While we are still on layer 3, let's return to switches for a moment. Originally switches were only layer 2 devices, as they dealt solely with MAC addresses. But overtime they increased in power and functionality to the point where they are _multilayer devices_ – they can operate at layers 2, 3 and 4. So then, what is the difference between a router and layer 3 switch? A layer 3 switch moves all the routing lookup logic to the hardware where it is much faster, inside an _application-specific integrated circuit_ (_ASIC_).

Because it takes processing power to peel back OSI layers and peek at the contents, layer 3 and 4 switches can add _multiprotocol label switching_ (_MPLS_) tags to packets. What this means in practical terms is that when a switch encounters a packet without an MPLS, it will dig in and extract everything it needs from the packet to decide on how it should be routed, and attach an MPLS tag representing the path it should take. The next switch will see the tag and route the packet according to the MPLS tag without having to take the run-time hit of looking inside the packet. This will considerably speed up routing efficiency. Of course, this opens up a vulnerability, as an attacker could attach a tag to his own packet and trick the switches into forwarding the packet down the path the attacker prefers – this is called a _double tagging attack_. If an attacker understands the tagging values and protocols being used in a network, he can intercept traffic by pretending to be a switch – this is called a _switch spoofing attack_. _VLAN hopping attacks_ occur when an attacker can gain access to traffic in another VLAN.

	Amplifies	Collision Domain	Broadcast Domain	VLAN	MAC ACL	IP Address ACL
Repeater	X					
Hub	X					
Concentrator	X					
Bridge		X				
Switch		X		X	X	
Router		X	X			X

Figure 25: Network Devices

Gateways

A _gateway_ is a piece of software that connects two dissimilar environments. Most often it will translate between two different networking protocols, such as Ethernet/FDDI. A gateway can provide functionality similar to a bridge or a router. For example, an _electronic mail_ *gateway* manages communication between different mail server platforms.

PBXs

A *PBX*, or *private branch exchange*, is a private, company-owned telephone switch located on the company's premises. All in-house telephone lines are serviced by the PBX, which is then connected with the public telephone network via a dedicated line. When looking for security vulnerabilities, many companies overlook PBXs, but these can be a significant vector for attacks as they are almost always connected to the internal network. To make things worse, PBXs often have an attached modem for service personnel to connect to while servicing the PBX – this is called a *hanging modem*. These devices should always be disabled unless a service call is in-progress. Phone hackers (*Phreakers*) used to be very active, but not as much these days.

Firewalls

A firewall is a software package or appliance that examines incoming packets and makes decisions on how to handle each packet based on configurable rules. Modern firewalls blur the line between routers and firewalls, as by definition routers can do the same thing. The biggest difference is that the primary function of a firewall is to protect networks as opposed to simply route packets. *Demilitarized zones* (*DMZs*) are often setup around public servers using firewalls – incoming traffic first hits the external firewall, with some packets being forwarded to the servers in the DMZ. The DMZ servers will usually communicate app servers sitting behind another firewall. IDSs are a common appliance placed in the DMZ as well to watch out for malicious traffic that has gotten past the external firewall. There are 5 different types of firewalls that we will cover, after which we will follow up with a discussion of how to position firewalls within a network.

Packet-Filtering

The first generation of firewalls were *Packet-Filtering* – they were capable of looking at layers 3 and 4 (network and transport) and either allowing the packet through or discarding it. The packet contents examined are:

- Source and destination IP addresses
- Source and destination ports
- Protocols (TCP, UDP etc.)
- Direction (inbound or outbound – also called *ingress* and *egress*)

Packet-Filtering is called a *stateless inspection* because it only looks at individual packets – it does not look at the conversation the packets are involved in. For example, a *stateful inspection* would keep track of the packets exchanged at the socket level over time (remember a *socket* is the combination of an IP address and port). Therefore, a *stateful firewall* keeps tracks of packets until the socket is closed. We'll discuss this more in a just a bit.

Since Packet-Filtering firewalls are stateless, they are unable to detect suspicious behavior – all they can do is to apply their very limited ACLs and either deny or approve packets. As a result, these devices are good at network-level filtering, but not so much when it comes to application-specific filtering. These devices are commonly found at the exterior edge of a network where the 'junk' can be stripped off before being passed through more comprehensive filtering. They have limited logging capabilities, usually do not support advanced authentication functions, and do not recognize packet fragmentation attacks or spoofed addresses.

Stateful

We have already mentioned stateful firewalls – these devices track socket conversations over time so they can apply a much deeper analysis of packets and catch behavioral attacks. Recall for a moment the 3-step handshake that every TCP connection requires of SYN, SYN/ACK, ACK – a specific TCP bit flag is flipped to '1' for both SYN and ACK values, but there are other flags as well. Now, while a Packet-Filtering firewall can reject anomalous things such as all TCP flags being set to 1 (which is highly suspect), when it sees a SYN/ACK come by, it has no idea if a SYN was already sent. A stateful firewall, on the other hand, can simply look back in its log for that socket and see if a SYN was previously sent, and if not discard the packet if a rule says to do so. The TCP states that a firewall can track are (in order) LISTEN, SYN-SENT, SYN-RECEIVED, ESTABLISHED, FIN-WAIT-1, FIN-WAIT-2, CLOSE-WAIT, CLOSING, LAST-ACK, TIME-WAIT and CLOSED. Stateful firewalls will keep track of the overall state of the conversation until it has been closed and then discard all the information it was tracking (log files usually will still retain some of this information). The current packet sequence number is also tracked – while packets out of sequence are a common occurrence, if the frequency for a given conversation is too high, the firewall may act.

UDP packets must also be tracked, but since UDP is by-definition a connectionless protocol, a stateful firewall will have a tougher time detecting anomalies. Since there is not a definitive end to a UDP 'conversation', the firewall will eventually simply decide the connection has timed out after a period of inactivity. While TCP has the ability for a computer to signal the sender to slow down, UDP has no such facility. Instead, UDP relies on ICMP to signal the sending computer to slow down. The firewall must be intelligent enough to allow ICMP packets through if they are associated with a UDP conversation. Stateful firewalls are complicated beasts.

Since stateful firewalls must maintain 'state', it must be stored in memory somewhere, and that opens the device up to additional vulnerabilities. An attacker can simply flood the firewall with all kinds of bogus information in an attempt to fill up its memory and cause it to either freeze or crash – this is a type of _denial of service_ (_DoS_) attack.

Proxy
While both stateless and stateful firewalls simply allow or deny packets from coming in or out, a _proxy firewall_ actually breaks the communication path and talks to each computer itself without allowing the computers to communicate directly with each other. Think of it as a person relaying messages between two people who are just out of ear-shot, but this 'middle-man' is continually looking out for lies or insults and making sure those messages are not relayed. The advantage of a proxy firewall is that it turns the security model upside down. Where packets going through a stateless or stateful firewall might default to getting through if they do not match a rule, packets going through a proxy firewall must make sense to the proxy before it can be translated on the other side – this provides extra security.

Proxy firewalls only operate at the higher OSI layers (5-7). A _circuit-level_ proxy works at layer 5 (the Session layer), and therefore cannot look too deeply into each packet since it does not understand anything above layer 5. _Application-level proxies_ work at layer 7 (the Application layer) and have much more intelligence, but are also slower since they must dig through more data that is available at layer 7. For example, a circuit-level proxy can inspect FTP packets but won't be able to notice most issues because it doesn't understand FTP, while an application-level proxy can tell the difference between an FTP GET or PUT command. Unfortunately, in addition to being slow, application-level proxies are more expensive to maintain since each can only monitor a single application-level protocol such as FTP, HTTP, SMTP, etc. Circuit-level proxies can handle just about any type of traffic, but lack in intelligence. _SOCKS_ is one example of a circuit-level protocol, and is used to provide a secure channel between two computers. Because SOCKS is a circuit-level protocol, it is widely-supported and many applications communicate over this protocol.

Dynamic Packet-Filtering
When client computers connect to an external server, they will choose a random, high-numbered port that they will ask the external server to connect back to them on. For example, when you visit a web site from your laptop, it will randomly select a port such as 20,110 and then connect to the web server over port 80 – which is a well-known port for HTTP. Your computer will send not only your own IP address, but port 20,110 as well as the address the web server should return the web page to. When the web server has prepared the content to send back, it will establish a socket connection back to your computer over port 20,110.

However, if there is a firewall in-place, we would have to open port 20,110 for this to work. To make matters worse, the firewall has no knowledge of which random port your computer will choose, so it would have to open, let's assume, ports 18,000 through 30,000. If we must do this, then what is the point of a firewall - we just opened ourselves up to be attacked on those ports. Instead, a _dynamic packet-filtering firewall_ will keep these high-numbered ports closed until a computer within its network tries to use one. Then, the firewall will open the port up and monitor the connection – when the connection has been closed, it will close the port as well. This allows any type of traffic outbound, while still limiting inbound traffic.

Kernel Proxy
There are many software firewall packages that can run on common operating systems such as Windows and Linux. However, the more complex a system, the more vulnerabilities it will have. Because firewalls are the first line of defense, they must be extremely stable and secure from attacks. Therefore, most modern-day firewalls are implemented in _appliances_, which are dedicated hardware/software platforms that exist solely to create a firewall.

However, fifth-generation firewalls take it one step further and put the packet inspection intelligence inside of the kernel itself, providing a magnitude of speed increase over software whose packet inspection is placed outside of the kernel. These systems are called _kernel proxy firewall_, and because of their speed boost can load virtual network stacks for each packet inspection process that is customized to the packet's protocol. Kernel proxy firewalls provide the same level of features as the other firewalls we have already discussed.

Next-Generation

Next-generation firewalls (*NGFWs*) provide the best features of all firewalls we have discussed thus far, plus one huge advantage – they implement an *Intrusion Prevention System* (*IPS*) that can detect attacks or malicious behavior based on *signatures*, or detectable patterns that have been seen elsewhere. NGFWs update their signature list dynamically based on attacks other NGFWs from the same vendor have reported. They also reduce the potential for misconfiguration by connecting to Active Directory, whitelists and blacklists, and policy servers. They are very expensive to purchase and maintain, but offer state of the art protection.

Firewall Architectures

Some companies place a firewall at the edge of their network and feel safe. Unfortunately, most firewalls are relatively insecure at their default settings, and even when properly configured do not offer as much protection as many think. That is why defense in depth is so important – this is the implementation of multiple layers of security. The idea is that if an attacker gets past one layer, they then must contend with another – the more layers of defense, the more secure a network is.

If a packet-filtering firewall is placed at the outer edges of the network, every device connected to that firewall is referred to as being a *screened host*. Often, the screened host will be an application-level firewall – the first firewall filters out all the noise, so that the screened application-level firewall can concentrate on deeper interrogation of incoming packets that make it past the first firewall.

An even better architecture is to place another firewall between the screened host firewall and the rest of your network – this creates a DMZ (demilitarized zone) in which the public-facing servers can be placed. If an attacker makes it past the packet-filtering firewall, manages to get past the application-level firewall and then can take over a server in the DMZ, he *still* has to make it past another firewall before he gets to the good stuff. The DMZ network is called a *screened subnet*, and this is a perfect example of defense in depth. You might encounter some other terms referencing this architecture:

- Single-tiered configuration –same as single firewall
- Two-tiered configuration –same as a screened host
- Three-tiered configuration –same as a screened subnet

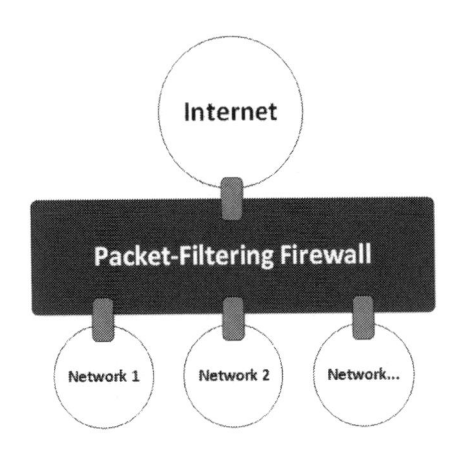

Figure 26: Multi-Homed Firewall

Firewalls are normally at least *dual-homed* – they have at least two network interfaces – one for the external network and one for the internal network. In this case, packet forwarding and routing should be turned off so that all packets are forced to be filtered through the ACLs. Higher-end firewalls will be *multi-homed*, with 3 or more network cards – this allows a single device to create multiple DMZs. However, multi-homed firewalls are a single point of failure, and as such the network should have hot or warm standbys ready in case of failure. Servers in DMZs must be *bastion hosts,* meaning that they must be hardened against attacks because they will be hit first.

Because of increasing hardware performance, it has become more economical for companies to virtualize servers instead of rolling out dedicated hardware for each OS. Routers and firewalls are no different – instead of appliances, often these devices are being implemented as virtual machines. An interesting side-effect is the need for *virtual firewalls* – not firewalls that are simply implemented *on* virtual machines, but firewalls that sit *between* virtual machines. Virtual firewalls can provide bridge functionality and monitor traffic links between virtual machines, or they can be integrated directly into the hypervisor.

Let's go over some best practices on configuring firewalls. Be sure and implement a *deny first policy* - in other words, if there is no rule to accept a packet then discard it. Any incoming packet caught masquerading or spoofing an internal IP address should be discarded. Likewise, any *outgoing* packet not having an internal source IP address should be discarded. In this case, the source is probably a *zombie* computer – a computer that has been infected and is being forced to attack other computers outside of its network in a *distributed denial of service* (*DDoS*) attack. Always reassemble fragmented packets before making a decision – attackers sometimes purposefully fragment packets in order to conceal what is going on. Any incoming packet with source routing should be discarded.

Common rules that are implemented in firewalls are:

- _Silent rule_ – drop 'noisy' traffic without logging it; otherwise the logs might fill up too quickly
- _Stealth rule_ – do not allow access to the firewall software except from authorized systems
- _Cleanup rule_ – any packet that does not meet a rule should be discarded
- Negate rule – same as 'deny first'

When rolling out firewall protection, you should be aware of the major things that a firewall will _not_ provide:

- One firewall is not good enough (defense in depth)
- A firewall can be a traffic bottleneck and a single point of failure – plan accordingly
- Firewalls will not recognize malware and can be fooled by sophisticated attacks
- They do not protect against sniffers, rogue wireless access points (which can bypass most firewalls) or insider attacks (the attacker is already inside of the network)

Before we leave the subject of firewalls, let's briefly discuss common fragmentation attacks – you will see why it is important to reassemble packet fragments before letting the assembled packet through. An _IP fragmentation attack_ is executed when an attacker crafts packet fragments that cannot be reassembled – this can result in a software crash or an out of memory condition. A _teardrop attack_ occurs when reassembled fragments exploit a software issue causing the system to become unstable. An _overlapping fragment attack_ is carried out when an attacker sneaks past firewalls that do not reassemble fragments before approving – in this case an already approved fragment is overwritten and is used to carry out the attack on the victim.

Proxy Servers

We have previously discussed proxy firewalls, which connect to two different networks and communicate on behalf of both, dealing for the most part in protocols. A _proxy server_ is similar but takes it to the next level – it understands the software that is running on the computers, not just network protocols. Proxy servers often implement request caching to increase performance.

A _forwarding proxy_ allows the client to indicate which server it wishes to speak to. An _open proxy_ is a forwarding proxy that is available for anyone to use. An _anonymous open proxy_ is a server that allows users to remain anonymous by concealing their real IP address. A _reverse proxy_ hides the servers behind it so the client never knows they exist.

There is a very fine line between a forward and reverse proxy. They both sit between the client and the server. The difference is in what the client knows about the servers behind the proxy:

- When using a forward proxy, the client is actively choosing to use the proxy instead of contacting the servers directly – the client tells the proxy "I want to get to server X, so please be the middle man"; this is usually done to circumvent access restrictions or to remain anonymous
- With a reverse proxy, the client has no choice but to go through the reverse proxy and doesn't even know the servers exist

Reverse proxy servers can act as load balancers, encryption acceleration, security and caching.

Honeypots and Tarpits

How do you slow down a bear? You throw a pot of honey in front of him. And that is exactly what a _honeypot_ is – it is an attractive target for attackers, but is designed to slow them down and distract them for two purposes:

- Get them to leave more important system alone
- To give you time to monitor them and figure what they are up to

Honeypots are configured with attractive services left enabled that look like a live system but really are not connected to anything important. Activity is heavily logged to alert network administrators to the activity, but also for proof in case of subsequent prosecution. These systems need to be placed in the DMZ, and if more than one honeypot is put into place, it is called a _Honeynet_.

Another approach is to create something called a _Tarpit_ – this also is a system attractive to attackers, but is purposefully handicapped to be very slow in responding. This not only takes up an attacker's valuable time but also causes many tools to conclude the site is not worth the effort.

Unified Threat Management

In a bid to offer a simpler way to manage all the network threats we have been discussing, a type of appliance called *unified threat management* (*UTM*) is sometimes purchased and applied to a network. This appliance implements a firewall, anti-malware, anti-spam, IDS and IPS, VPN support, information leak prevention and content filtering. The actual list of features varies by vendor, but the tradeoff for simplicity is that a single appliance becomes a potential bottleneck and a single point of failure, and somewhat violates the principal of defense in depth.

Content Distribution Networks

When a service offering on the Internet implements caching at various geographical places around the world to speed delivery and reduce latency, it is creating a *content distribution network* (*CDN*). CDNs also reduce the vulnerability to DoS/DDoS attacks.

Software Defined Networking

As virtualizing servers takes off, the need to provide dynamic management of the network is needed as well. It is one thing to spin up new instances of a virtual server on-demand, but to properly route traffic to these instances and ensure security is quite another. *Software-defined networking* (*SDN*) meets this need by implementing network management as distributed software that can react quickly to a changing environment. SDN has two concepts associated with it – control and forwarding planes.

The *control plane* is where routing paths are tracked, discovered and discarded. This responsibility within SDN is located in a centralized controller. The *forwarding plane* functions take place in individual network devices and is where actual forwarding decision are made based on the paths tracked by the control plane. Forwarding planes are usually implemented in hardware (ASICs). So, the control plane is centralized while the forwarding plane is decentralized.

There are 3 different approaches to implementing SDN. The most common is the *open* approach, which relies on open-source code and standards to create the components of SDN. An open source package called *OpenFlow* is used for communication between the devices implementing the forward plane and the controller. The various components communicate using RESTful or Java APIs.

The second approach, the one preferred by Cisco, is called *API*, and extends OpenFlow to allow deeper packet inspection and works with Cisco's proprietary devices.

The third approach, *overlays*, is to virtualize all nodes and view the resulting virtualized network architecture as simply being overlaid on top of the physical network. The SDN is then seen as simply a virtual overlay on top of the physical network.

Questions

1. Which of the following is a circuit-level protocol used to create a secure channel between two computers?

   A) CICR

   B) SOCKS

   C) Circuit-level proxy

   D) Application-level proxy

2. Which device amplifies a signal?

   A) Hub

   B) Concentrator

   C) Repeater

   D) Bridge

3. Which term best describes a device with 2 NICs - internal and external?

   A) Dual-homed

   B) Multi-homed

   C) Virtual firewall

   D) Bastion host

4. Which term best describes an inspection that only looks at individual packets, not the entire conversation?

   A) Ingres

   B) Stateful

   C) Egress

   D) Stateless

5. Which of the following describes the maximum size that a packet can be?

   A) Fragmenting

   B) MTU

   C) Source routing

   D) Transparent bridging

Chapter 39: Intranets, Extranets, LANs, WANs and MANs

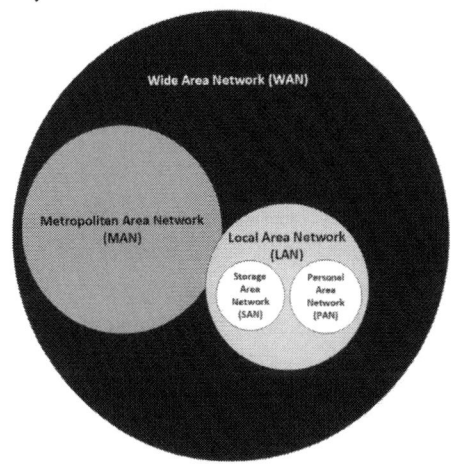

Figure 27: Various Network Types

Intranets and Extranets

Most companies maintain an *intranet* – an internal network of servers and clients that are inaccessible outside of the company's network. Intranets are normally based on the HTML and XML standards built on top of TCP/IP protocols. If two companies from a partnership, they often will setup an *extranet* – a network only between the two companies that allows real-time communication. It used to be that companies would have a dedicated transmission line, but it is now more common for the extranet to operate over the Internet, perhaps with a VPN connection. *Electronic data interchange* (*EDI*) is the term used when automated processes exchange data, usually between two different infrastructures. Both networks agree on a common data format going both ways, so that each company is free to implement their own network according to their own needs.

Instead of sharing an extranet, sometimes companies will connect through a *value-added network* (*VAN*). This is a network created and hosted by a third-party that allows two companies to connect in real-time. For example, a retailer will order inventory through the VAN, and the supplier will receive the order from the VAN. This third-party charges fees to both companies for use of the VAN. The common technologies used in VANs are SOAP or RESTful web services.

Local Area Networks

A *local area network* (*LAN*) is defined by a small geographical region covered by a single network. Of course, the phrase 'small geographical region' can be interpreted many ways – in most cases it means a single building, but could include a network that spans multiple buildings. A LAN has its own addressing scheme, broadcast domain and communication mechanisms. When two LANs are connected by a router, it is called an *internetwork*. If two LANs are connected by a different layer 2 technology, such as frame relay or ATM, it is considered to be a *wide-area network* (*WAN*).

Wide Area Networks

So, let's talk about the technologies that make WANs possible by looking back in time. When telephones were first invented, each telephone line was capable of carrying a single conversation. Later, phone companies figured out how to make a single telephone line can carry multiple conversations simultaneously, and that was called *multiplexing* - a single transmission path is broken up into multiple channels. Digital lines arrived in the 1960s, and a single call could take place over a 64K connection. A T1 line which carried 24 calls over a single pair of twisted copper wires, and resulted in 64*24 = 1.544 Mbps transmission rate (we're rounding values here so the math may not be 100% precise). Then T3 lines came along, which bundled 28 T1 lines together, resulting in 1.544*28 = 43 Mbps. T1s and T3s are collectively called *T-carriers* and carry both voice and data. T-carriers achieve multiplexing not by using various frequencies, but by using something called *time-division multiplexing* (*TDM*). TDM essentially uses a single transmission channel, but intersperses multiple data channels into 'time-slots' within that transmission channel. For example, if I have 24 calls all going on simultaneously, I will add 8 bits from the first call, followed by 8 bits from the second call, and continue until I have 24 8-bit chunks of data, and then I send that chunk off and start on the next chunk. Because of the high cost of T lines, *fractional T lines* are sometimes sold where multiple companies all share the same T line. Dedicated T lines are expensive to install, and rent, and are very inflexible when physical locations are moved.

European countries have a somewhat equivalent technology called *E-carriers*, with E-carrier lines being called E1 and E3.

Before discussing the next evolutionary step in WANS, let's pause and consider some other methods for multiplexing. We have already discussed TDM, which T-carriers use. T lines also can employ a specialized version of TDM called *statistical time-division multiplexing* (*STDM*). Instead of packing in 8-bits of data per channel regardless of whether a channel is being used, STDM will dynamically include channels based on each channel's historical usage. Therefore, if a certain source is a resource hog, STDM can allocate more room for that channel over one that is seldom used. While TDM and STDM use a constant frequency but variable amplitudes, *frequency-division multiplexing* (*FDM*) will insert additional frequencies to allow even more data to be carried. This is normally found in wireless communication mediums such as radio or video broadcasts.

Now back to our WAN evolution story - after high-speed copper lines were adopted, fiber eventually came along with the most basic unit being called 'OC-1' (OC is short for optical carrier), which provided a bandwidth of 52 Mbps, and OC-3 providing 155 Mbps (roughly 52*3). Other values of the 'OC' definition apply, and are just multipliers of the OC-1 52 Mbps bandwidth. OC-12 connections are common for larger companies, while OC-48 lines are used by ISPs. OC-192 (10 Gbps) is commonly used for the Internet backbone.

However, we had to figure out how to make US copper and optical transmission lines work together, and so the *synchronous optical network* (*SONET*) standard was developed. Europe has different infrastructure, and so they developed the *synchronous digital hierarchy* (*SDH*) standard. As a result, North America uses SONET while the rest of the world uses SDH – for the two to communicate a gateway s required.

Once SONET was firmly established, a newer standard was desired that used a fixed-size for frames to achieve greater efficiency and to reduce the need for error handling. *Asynchronous transfer mode* (*ATM*) was the answer, and was created specifically with SONET in mind (more on ATM later).

So, all this technology – T1s, T3s, OC-1s, OC-3s, SONET and ATM – is where WANs live. So, how do LANs and WANs connect? Two pieces of equipment are required here – first we need to convert our LANs' frames into something the WAN can understand – that is the job of the *data service unit* (*DSU*). The DSU is responsible for converting voltage levels appropriately before signals are sent by the *channel service unit* (*CSU*). The CSU provides the physical connection between the LAN and the WAN. Since both jobs are so closely aligned – convert and send – we refer to them as a single device – the *channel service unit/data service unit* (*CSU/DSU*). Just remember we must convert the LAN's *data* before putting it on the WAN's *channel*. For the carrier's point of view, it happens in the reverse – the WAN's channel sends signals, where the signal is converted into LAN data – that is why it is called the CSU/DSU and not the other way around.

The CSU/DSU is not always a stand-alone device but always lives within the company's network. Any device within the company's network that is directly attached to the CSU/DSU is called *data terminal equipment* (*DTE*). Any device belonging to the carrier that is attached to the CSU/DSU is called *data-circuit terminating equipment* (*DCE*), with the carrier's switch being an example. So remember the path starting with a company's network - a DTE connects to a CSU/DSU which connects to a DCE. The carrier owns the circuit, and so its equipment is called the data-*circuit* terminating equipment, or DCE.

So far, we have pretty much glossed over any details of how packets travel between networks – we have only acknowledged that there are connections between the networks made up of various types of switches and routers. But when many networks are involved, and there are multiple ways to get from Point A to Point B, how do we decide how those packets are going to travel? The answer is two-fold – circuit switching and packet switching.

When a constant stream of data is required – such as when making a live voice call over the phone – we cannot afford to have packets wander around and arrive out of order because some went this way, and some went that-a-way. In these cases, we want to use *circuit-switching* and decide before any real data is sent how all packets will get from Point A to Point B. When each voice call starts, the network is examined and a single path (that may include many switches and routers) is chosen – all packets for that call will follow the same route. This ensures the orderly arrival of packets in a timely fashion, and this type of connection is sometimes called a dedicated virtual link.

On the other hand, sometimes we send data and don't really care if the packets arrive out of order or there is a variable latency, as long as everything eventually arrives intact. In this case, we want to use *packet switching,* which X.25 (which is what the Internet is built on) and frame relay use. With packet switching, the data is broken up into multiple packets, and each is assigned a *frame check sequence* (*FCS*). At the receiving end, the various packets are assembled back into the original data using the FCS numbers. Whereas circuit switching provides a constant stream rate but sacrifices reliability, packet switching emphasizes redundancy and reliability of timeliness.

For a long time, companies relied on dedicated links to communicate with other companies. There was a lot of wasted bandwidth on these lines because a company might experience peak usage during a specific time every day, but the rest of the time 90% of that bandwidth might be wasted. Therefore, companies started searching for a way to share a dedicated line with other companies to defray the costs. That is why _frame relay_ was invented – it allows more than one party to share in a single dedicated line across a WAN. It operates at the data link layer and uses packet switching for transmission – the cost to each company is loosely based on the amount of bandwidth needed, as opposed to the distance between the two endpoints. Note that the cost is not based on the actual bandwidth used – only on how much bandwidth is guaranteed. This guaranteed bandwidth is called the _committed information rate_, or _CIR_. All of this magic happens in the _frame relay cloud_, which is a simply a collection of DCEs which gets the packets from Point A to Point B. Note that frame relay is an older technology and is not used as much these days.

A _virtual circuit_ is used when frame relay or X.25 needs to send data across a WAN or MAN link. Each virtual circuit can be programmed into the devices directly, resulting in a _permanent virtual circuit_ (_PVC_), which is the equivalent of a CIR. We can also have a _switched virtual circuit_ (_SVC_) which is built on-the-fly and torn down when it is no longer needed. SVCs are often used for teleconferencing, voice calls, or temporary remote connections. However, SVCs do not provide a guaranteed bandwidth, and while PVCs do, PVCs require a minimum of hours to setup.

Metropolitan Area Networks

A _metropolitan-area network_ (_MAN_) is usually a backbone that connects LANS, WANs, the Internet and other telecommunications and cable networks. It is almost always based on the _synchronous optical network_ (_SONET_) standard running over T1, fractional T1 or T3 lines. MANs communicate over FDDI or Metro Ethernet, connect multiple companies or geographic locations, and are implemented in a ring topology. SONET requires multiple rings and is _self-healing,_ in that if a break occurs, traffic can continue in a back-up ring. Slower SONET networks often feed into faster SONET networks, much like slower highways feed into faster ones. Since Layer 2 and 3 technologies operate in MANs, VLANs can be created as-needed.

When Ethernet is used in MANs, it is called _Metro Ethernet_. With Metro Ethernet, Pure Ethernet can be used to keep costs down, but it is less reliable and scalable than if MPLS (Multiprotocol Label Switching) is used as well, so large service providers normally include MPLS in their architecture. At the customer's site, a CSU/DSU device will connect the LAN/WAN to the MAN, where it is routed to the aggregated network closest to the destination network, where another CSU/DSU on the destination network will accept the traffic and place it back on the LAN/WAN. A _virtual private LAN service_ (_VPLS_) can be used to create a distributed LAN over a MAN, but the MAN needs to implement MPLS for this to work. VPLSs are implemented by layer 2 Ethernet bridges.

We have already gone over frame relay in depth. We also mentioned X.25 and ATM but did not offer too many details – let's fix that. _X.25_ is an older WAN protocol that defines how networks establish and maintain connections, and uses packet switching like frame relay. X.25 allows many parties to use the service simultaneously, and each pays according to the amount of _actual_ bandwidth used. At the bit-level, X.25 looks a lot like frame relay – it uses 128 bytes encapsulated in a High-level Data Link Control frame. However, x.25 was created back in the 1970s when networks were relatively unstable, so it was designed to compensate by adding error checking and correcting as well as fault tolerance. This makes X.25 have a lot of overhead and as a result is much less efficient than ATM.

Asynchronous Transfer Mode (_ATM_) is also a switching technology but uses cells instead of packets, and is a connection-oriented technology like frame relay – this means it is ATM's job to make sure packets arrive at their destination. ATM's data is put into a fixed size packet of 53 bytes, which provides an efficient delivery for data, and uses virtual circuits so that guaranteed bandwidth is possible. This all means that ATM is a great choice for audio and video transmission and provides QoS. ATM is the core technology used in the Internet backbone and by carriers and ISPs, but some companies use it internally as well. ATM can be very cost-efficient because companies are billed based on the bandwidth used instead of by the line for T-carrier lines.

We just mentioned that ATM can provide QoS – well, what is that? _Quality of Service_ (_QoS_) is a capability that some protocols provide, enabling them to distinguish between different types of traffic and assign delivery priority levels. For example, if a packet is tagged as being real-time video, the protocol can make sure it gets the first crack at the best path on the network. QoS first appeared in ATM, which defined 4 different types of services. In the following list, the bit rate is a measure of how many bits are transferred within a given time (i.e. it is a measure of bandwidth).

- *Unspecified bit rate service* (*UBR*) – a connectionless channel that pretty much promises nothing
- *Variable bit rate service* (*VBR*) – a connection-oriented channel that does not guarantee a minimum latency and provides a peak and sustained data rate; good for delay-insensitive applications
- *Available bit rate service* (*ABR*) - a connection-oriented channel that allows the bit rate to be adjusted to match whatever bandwidth is available
- *Constant bit rate service* (*CBR*) – a connection-oriented channel that is based on a bandwidth requirement that is specified when the connection is started; good for voice and video applications

While ATM was the first to offer QoS, other protocols have since included QoS in 3 basic levels:

- *Best-effort service* – no promises whatsoever – just best effort after all other classes have been served; most traffic on the Internet falls under this classification
- *Differentiated service* – no promises other than that this class gets priority over best-effort service
- Guaranteed service – promises a guaranteed speed

Administrators can set the classification priorities for traffic, which is called *traffic shaping*.

Back in the 1970s IBM was selling mainframe hosts to work with a systems network architecture (SNA), and synchronous data link control (SDLC) was the protocol used for these types of networks. SDLC was a bit-oriented, synchronous protocol that allowed mainframes to communicate with remote locations through a polling mechanism. As mainframes started dying out, so did SDLC. However, a very similar offshoot of SDLC – high-level data link control (HDLC), manage to survive and evolve. HDLC is used for communication between two devices on a WAN and works at the OSI data link layer (Layer 2).

Similar to HDLC is *point-to-point protocol* (*PPP*) – both implementing framing and encapsulation for a Point A to Point B connection. PPP encapsulates dissimilar protocols so that two different networks can communicate, and contains the following:

- *Link control protocol* (*LCP*) – establishes, configures and maintains a connection
- Network control protocol (NCP) – configures the network layer
- User authentication:
    - Password authentication protocol (PAP)
    - Challenge handshake authentication protocol (CHAP)
    - Extensible authentication protocol (EAP)

In short, PPP uses LCP to set up the communication channel, and one of several NCPs to move traffic over that channel. For each network protocol such as IP, IPX, AppleTalk, etc. there will be a corresponding NCP.

For ATM or frame relay to be used on top of routers and multiplexers, we need some kind of a common interface that works at the physical layer (Layer 1) – *high-speed serial interface* (*HSSI*) provides this.

Questions

1. Which ATM QoS service is a connection-oriented channel that allows the bit rate to be adjusted to match whatever bandwidth is available?

    A) VBR

    B) ABR

    C) UBR

    D) CBR

2. Which best describes a network created and hosted by a third-party that allows two companies to connect in real-time?

    A) Extranet

    B) VAN

    C) Internetwork

    D) MAN

3. Which of the following best describes an automated process exchanging data with other processes?

    A) Traffic shaping

    B) Multiplexing

    C) Metro Ethernet

    D) EDI

4. Which type of line consists of fiber and runs at 155 Mbps?

    A) OC-1

    B) OC-3

    C) OC-7

    D) T3

5. Which method requires all packets to follow the same path?

    A) Frame-switching

    B) Packet-switching

    C) Toggle-switching

    D) Circuit-switching

Chapter 40: Multiservice Access Technologies

When you pick up a phone that is connected to an RJ-11 cable in the wall (it looks like an Ethernet port, but skinnier) you are using the _public-switched telephone network_ (_PSTN_). During a call, switches are selected up-front, and for the duration of the call all data packets go through the exact same path. This ensures that all audio is consistently delivered with minimal latency, and is implemented using the _signaling system 7_ (_SS7_) protocol.

However, as voice and data networks converge, we start to encounter _multiservice access technologies_ where a single transmission line is used to carry several types of communication categories – voice, data and video. More and more companies are switching over from PSTN to _voice over IP_ (_VoIP_) technologies for everyday phone calls - the primary advantage for moving in this direction is that a company only has to pay for one network instead of two. VoIP allows phone calls to be routed as IP packets (using either TCP or UDP at the transport layer) across networks but without the latency and inconsistency normally found in 'bursty' transmission paths. VoIP uses the _session initiation protocol_ (_SIP_) to setup and tear down conversation sessions, which is exactly what SS7 did for PSTN calls. SIP is responsible for dialing a number, ringing the remote phone, busy signals and other call features we take for granted. PSTN expects the end-user device to be dumb, whereas VoIP allows the end-user device to support advanced software and hardware features. VoIP technology uses very high-quality compression, and is based on packet-switching technologies. Because packet-switching does not guarantee packets will arrive in order or with the same latency, VoIP calls can sometimes encounter _jitter_, but VoIP has protocols in-place to handle this type of scenario. Time-sensitive applications such as VoIP need to run over an _isochronous network_, or a network that contains the required devices and protocols to ensure a consistent bandwidth availability.

VoIP requires 4 components:

- _IP telephony device_ – the end-user software or hardware responsible for digitizing analog signals such as audio, and turning digital signals back into audio
- _Voice gateway_ – routes packets and provides links to legacy and backup voice systems
- Call-processing manager – initiates and accepts calls
- _Voicemail system_ – stores messages, forwards calls and provides direct lookup capabilities

Now let's go back and address _jitter_ – that is the tendency for voice traffic sent over an IP network to not arrive in a consistent manner – IP is a connectionless protocol, and by nature it is 'bursty' – the data will get there, but no promises are made for consistency or timeliness. That sounds like a terrible vehicle to use for live voice calls, doesn't it? On the other hand, protocols like frame relay and ATM, which are connection-oriented (and have the capability for circuit-switching instead of packet-switching) sound ideal. Unfortunately, calls normally originate and end on LANs, which are almost always going to be Ethernet, and so IP will be the network protocol. Finally, we are getting to the point where we can see the need for these different protocols – what if we ran voice over IP on the LAN, which then piggy-backed our IP traffic on top of frame relay or ATM on the WAN/MAN? We get the best of both worlds! A connectionless protocol with low overhead on the local networks, but circuit switching on the fat pipe in between the two networks to minimize latency and guarantee packets arrive in the correct order! Remember PVCs (permanent virtual circuits) and SVCs (switched virtual circuits)? SVCs sounds like just the thing we need – temporary circuit-switching that is setup and torn down on a per-call basis. It's a win-win because of leveraging of the right protocol in the right place.

Let's look a little deeper into SIP – the signaling protocol that VoIP uses. SIP has two logical components – the _user agent client_ (_UAC_) and the _user agent server_ (_UAS_). The _UAC_ sits with the end-user and is a piece of user-facing software that may or may not be running on dedicated hardware. The UAS is the SIP server which takes care of all routing and signaling. Here is the process flow for setting up a call when user UAC **A** is calling user UAC **B** – note that all communication is taking place invisibly through a UAS:

1) A sends an **INVITE** message to B
2) A gets back a **TRYING** message
3) When B receives the INVITE, A gets back a **RINGING** message
4) When B answers, B sends an **OK** to A
5) A sends an **ACK** back to B
6) _The call starts over RTP_ (we'll cover RTP in a second)
7) A hangs up, so A sends a **BYE** to B
8) B sends back an **OK** to A

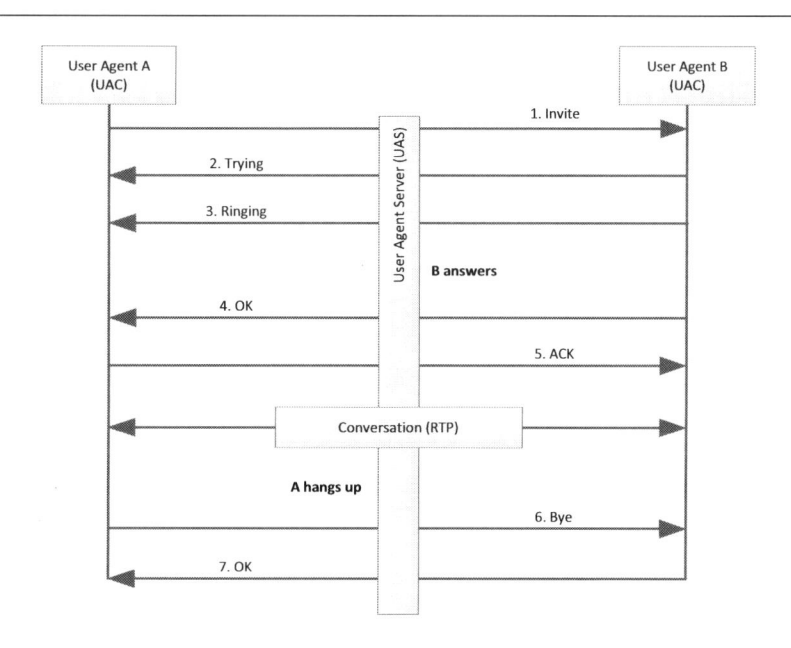

Figure 28: SIP Handshake

Note that SIP does not actually carry out the conversation when it finally starts – SIP is simply a signaling protocol that gives the go-ahead to the _real-time transport protocol_ (_RTP_) to start streaming audio. RTP is a session-layer (Layer 5) protocol and normally uses UDP to send data. _RTP control protocol_ (_RTCP_) is used with RTP to provide the information required to deliver QoS.

So that is the messaging pattern that SIP follows. The SIP server architecture which implements the messaging pattern consists of 3 components:

- _Proxy server_ – relays signals between the UAC and UAS
- _Registrar server_ – tracks the addresses of all participants
- _Redirect server_ – allows SIP devices to be physically move without having to change identities

When a VoIP device moves, this is covered under an intra-organizational configuration – SIP traffic can be dynamically routed without having to use a PSTN or external network.

Here is how the 3 servers work when establishing a call – note that the UAC and UAS signaling we previously discussed is still taking place, we are just looking at the same process from a network view instead of signals. To make this easier to understand, this configuration will have each caller's domain owning a separate instance of both the both proxy and registrar servers, while there is only a single instance of the redirect server running for both domains.

1) A's UAC sends a request to A's proxy server to call B
2) A's proxy server asks the redirect server for the address to B's proxy server
3) A's proxy server sends a call request to B's proxy server
4) B's proxy server asks B's registrar server for B's IP address
5) B's proxy server forwards the request to B's UAC
6) B's UAC sends messages back to A's UAC

This is how your typical VoIP infrastructure will work. Skype, however, is a slightly different animal that relies on a peer-to-peer infrastructure rather than a centralized one.

VoIP is great, and is slowly but surely replacing PSTN. Naturally, it also has security issues largely in part due to its reliance on TCP/IP. This doesn't mean that TCP/IP is inherently less secure than other protocols, but it is by far the most popular in use today, and therefore is the most targeted by hackers - so hackers can target VoIP with an already-mature packet of tools and experience. Stealing call-time is a financial lure, and the fact that VoIP devices have an OS architecture like desktop computers makes them even more vulnerable. SIP signaling protocols do not include any type of authentication or encryption, so hackers can gain access to login IDs, passwords and phone numbers, resulting in tool fraud, which is the greatest threat VoIP faces.

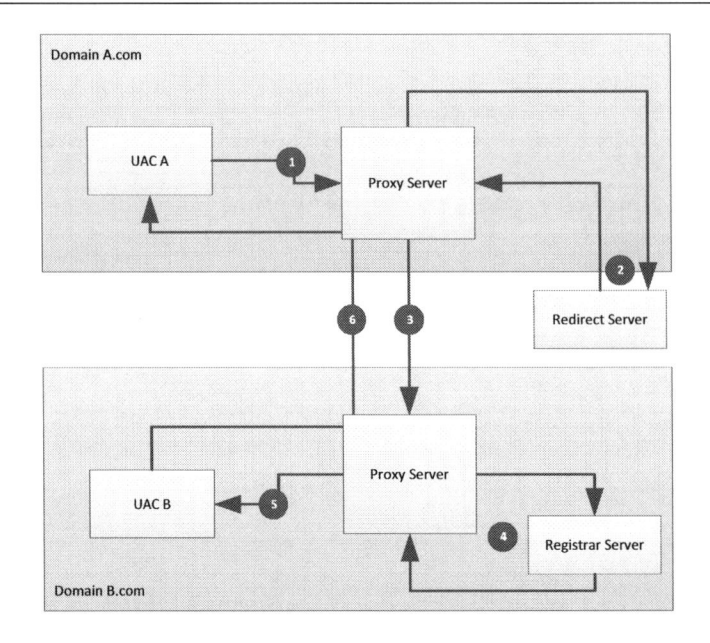

Figure 29: Making a SIP call

Attackers can also steal identities so that calls are routed to themselves without the caller's knowledge. DoS attacks against VoIP devices are a real vulnerability – for example an attacker could flood an RTP server with call requests. Since VoIP phones usually use a standard Ethernet cable, laptops can easily be plugged into these lines and simulate a VoIP client. Of course, attackers can sniff out RTP packets and even inject their own data under the right conditions. By impersonating a server an attacker could interrupt calls by issuing BYE, CHECKSYNC or RESET commands to VoIP devices. A CHECKSYNC command can cause a client device to reboot, while a RESET command sent to a server could cause it to reset itself an interrupt all in-progress communications. A variant of spam called _spam over internet telephony_ (_SPIT_) is possible on VoIP networks when an attacker sends a voice message to a voicemail server – because clients must play the entire message before it can be deleted, it can not only be a real nuisance but eat up bandwidth on the network.

To mitigate these risks, authentication must be enforced to prevent rogue devices on the network. Device identification via MAC addresses is also a useful control. Finally, SIP and RTP data must be encrypted using TLS to prevent sniffing.

Questions

1. Which describes storing messages, forwarding calls and providing direct lookup capabilities?

    A) Call-processing manager

    B) Multiservice access technologies

    C) Voice gateway

    D) Voicemail system

2. Which of the following is a user-facing software client?

    A) RTP

    B) UAC

    C) SIP

    D) UAS

3. Which describes a single transmission line used to carry several types of communication categories?

    A) Voicemail system

    B) Multiservice access technologies

    C) Voice gateway

    D) Call-processing manager

4. Which of the following describes an attacker sending a voice message to a voicemail server?

    A) SPIT

    B) SS7

    C) Jitter

    D) PSTN

5. Which of the following relays VoIP signals between the UAC and UAS?

    A) Redirect server

    B) IP telephony device

    C) Proxy server

    D) Registrar server

Chapter 41: Remote Connectivity

Let's talk about remote connectivity into a network for a moment.

Communication Options

A _modem_ (modulator-demodulator) is a device connected to a PSTN connection allowing a remote device to connect to the network. The modem takes the computer's digital signal and converts it into an analog signal that can travel over UTP. _War dialing_ is the process of configuring a computer to automatically dial through a list of phone numbers, looking for a networked modem to answer. While modems are a mostly antiquated technology, they still do exist as backups, and the following security precautions should always be followed:

- Always have the server call back on the same phone number instead of allowing the remote caller to establish a connection directly
- Disable, or better yet, remove modems that are no longer required
- Consolidate all modems centrally and manage them together
- Require two-factor authentication, VPNS and firewalls on all remote connections

Modems were the first mainstream manner used to connect homes and small businesses to the Internet, but _integrated services digital network_ (_ISDN_) began appearing in the late 1990s. ISDN was the first truly digital connection for the masses to travel over copper phone lines. Telephone companies had gone digital years before up to the _central office_ (_CO_) - the telephone company's neighborhood infrastructure), but the 'last mile' (the phone lines from the local loop to residential houses) were still analog. With ISDN, it became truly digital end-to-end, using circuit-switching. The standard has 2 types of channels – a B channel running at 64 Kbps and a D Chanel with 16 Kbps – the D channel is an out-of-band communications path and is used to setup the call, while the B channel handles all the data.

There are 3 ISDN implementations:

- _Basic rate interface ISDN_ (_BRI_) – 2 x 64 Kbps B channels and 1 x 16 Kbps D channel for 144 Kbps total; used for home and small offices
- _Primary rate interface ISDN_ (_PRI_) – 23 x 64 Kbps B channels and 1 x 16 Kbps D channel for 1.544 Mbps total; companies with higher bandwidth requirements
- _Broadband ISDN_ (_BISDN_) – used within a backbone and ATM and SONET is employed

While ISDN used to be state-of-the-art, it is now commonly used only as a backup channel in case faster links go down. However, some companies do still use ISDN for WAN links for small amounts of traffic only.

After ISDN had been around for a few years, _digital subscriber line_ (_DSL_) took off. It operates over the same phone lines as ISDN but at rates up to 52 Mbps – the actual speed depends on how far from the CO the DSL modem is due to signal attenuation - the maximum distance is 2.5 miles. DSL achieves these higher rates because it uses all available frequencies on a UTP line. Normally a service provider will remove low and high frequencies on analog lines, but for DSL lines it is left untouched so that the DSL modem can utilize those frequencies. DSL comes in five different flavors:

- _Asymmetric DSL_ (_ADSL_) – 768 Kbps down and 128-384 Kbps up; residential
- _Symmetric DSL_ (_SDSL_) – 192-1100 Kbps down and up; businesses
- _High-bit-rate DSL_ (_HDSL_) – T1 speeds (1.544 Mbps); requires 2 UTP
- Very High-bit-rate DSL (VDSL) – 13 Mbps down and 2 Mbps up
- _Rate-Adaptive DSL_ (_RADSL_) – rates adjust to match the signal quality

Cable companies already have coaxial cable delivering TV channels to homes and small businesses, with each TV channel being delivered on its own frequency. One or more of those 'channels' have been dedicated to delivering data, so both TV and Internet services run on the same cable simultaneously. One of the downsides of this type of infrastructure is that all homes within a neighborhood same share the same cable, resulting in two side effects:

- There is only a finite bandwidth, so as simultaneous usage increases, everyone experiences slower speeds – whenever people start arriving home from work, the performance can be abysmal
- Since everyone is sharing the same network lines, sniffing packets becomes very easy; cable companies have started encrypting data at the data link layer to combat this

To address the security issue, most cable companies follow the *data-over-cable service interface specifications* (*DOCSIS*) which addresses how to provide high-speed data over existing cable TV networks, and includes MAC layer security.

One last difference to note between these remote connection technologies – dial-up and ISDN connect as-needed, while DSL and cable modems are an 'always on' connection. Having a connection that is live 24x7 is convenient, but it does open the owner to additional security concerns as it makes their home computers more likely targets for attacks.

VPNs

While the Internet is a fantastic and ubiquitous thing, it is inherently unsecure at its core. When IP was invented, no one was thinking "You know, in about 30 years the entire world will be built on top of this protocol – we should probably build in some security". Security has had to be bolted on top of it a little at a time. One of the ways this has been done is to create *virtual private networks* (*VPNs*) – a mechanism that allows two trusted networks to communicate over untrusted infrastructure (i.e. the Internet). To do this, the industry invented something we have already discussed – point-to-point (PPP) connections – this allows us to create VPNs across the Internet.

Unfortunately, PPP and IP traffic are incompatible, so we had to figure out how to send PPP packets across an IP network – therefore 'tunneling' was invented. Imagine driving your car from London to Paris – if you know your geography even just a little, you know that there is a lot of water separating the two. That is why the Channel Tunnel (or 'Chunnel') was created – it allows cars to 'tunnel' from London to Paris through stuff that would normally be very unfriendly to vehicles – namely, water. Tunneling across the Internet work the same way – we simply create a virtual tunnel through which data can travel.

Microsoft built the *point-to-point tunneling protocol* (*PPTP*) into Windows and it subsequently became the de facto standard for tunneling. While the original intent for PPTP was to simply tunnel PPP connection through an IP network, PPTP was usually accompanied by some type of encryption security. PPTP wraps protected packets inside of the *generic routing encapsulation* (*GRE*) and the TCP protocol. With Microsoft's implementation of PPTP, authentication can be handled in one of 4 ways: PAP, CHAP, MS-CHAP and EAP-TLS. Encryption is carried out using *Microsoft's point-to-point encryption* (*MPPE*) –

unfortunately MPPE used RC4 such that the payload could be modified, and the symmetric keys could even be discovered. A significant limitation to PPTP is that it only supports system-to-system communication, not gateway-to-gateway – therefore only a single desktop can leverage it at any given time. While PPTP addressed the need for routing packets incompatible with IP over the Internet, security needed some more work.

About the same time Cisco came along and invented something called *layer 2 forwarding* (*L2F*) – this was a PPP protocol very similar to PPTP, but they went even further and wrapped it in the *layer 2 tunneling protocol* (*L2TP*). Unlike PPTP, L2TP could route traffic over non-IP networks as well such as ATM, X.25, etc. Neither protocol has addressed security concerns sufficiently, but L2TP integrates with other protocols that *do* provide acceptable levels of security – it implements PPP authentication and works with IPSec to deliver confidentiality, integrity and even more authentication above and beyond that which PPP offered. While PPP allowed users to authenticate, T2LP allows *systems* to authenticate.

So, in summary – Microsoft's PPTP is a system-to-system PPP connection for IP traffic which uses the insecure RC4 for encryption. Cisco's L2TP supports PPP over multiple types of traffic, and works with IPSec.

So, let's dive into *internet protocol security* (*IPSec*). As we previously noted, IPv4 had no security and IPSec was invented to provide that missing security for the IP protocol only. It works in the layer above PPTP and L2TP – they work at the data link layer, while IPSec works at the network layer – which makes sense since that layer is the only one that understands IP. IPSec has 4 main protocols:

- *Authentication Header* (*AH*) – a hash that provides integrity and system authentication, and protects from replay attacks
- *Encapsulating security payload* (*ESP*) – encryption that provides confidentiality, integrity and authentication
- Internet security association and key management protocol (ISAKMP) – controls the management and storage of all the possible variables with a connection
- *Internet key exchange* (*IKE*) - allows for key creation and secure exchange for ISAKMP

AH and ESP can be used together or separately, but only ESP can provide encryption (confidentiality). When two routers want to communicate over IPSec, they must first agree on a number of options such as hashing algorithms, encryption algorithms, tunnel modes, etc. When a router receives these parameters, they are stored in a _security association_ (_SA_) – each router will have one SA per connection describing the parameters that the remote router has specified. The NSA has created a protocol encryptor based on IPSec called _high assurance internet protocol encryptor_ (_HAIPE_, pronounced 'hay-p'). It is usually implemented as a device and has largely replaced link layer encryption technologies.

Transport adjacency happens when more than one security protocol is being used together in IPSec, such as using both AH and ESP at the same time. Sometimes IPSec will be used over multiple network segments with each segment requiring different levels of security. For example, perhaps IPSec is being used within an intranet with AH enabled for integrity, but once it hits a public router, it needs to be wrapped in ESP for confidentiality. You can't simply flip on the ESP flag for this public segment – instead you must wrap the original IPSec packet in another IPSec packet with ESP enabled. This is called _iterated tunneling_.

Everyone is probably familiar with SSL – usually in association with browsers and web sites. SSL is now considered to be insecure, and has been superseded by _transport level security_ (_TLS_). However, TLS v1.0 was pretty much the same as SSL v3.0 and has a lot of security issues. Only TLS v1.1 and v1.2 should be used.

TLS works at the session layer, meaning it can provide more granular control than IPSec since it lives at a higher OSI layer (and therefore knows more about the packet's contents). It is primarily used for HTTP traffic such as email and web-based traffic. It can secure only a small number of protocols, and creates a VPN. There are two different implementations commonly used:

- _TLS portal VPN_ – a single user connects to a web site acting as a gateway into more services; this is what a browser normally uses
- _TLS tunnel VPN_ – a single browser connects to multiple non-web-based network services

So, to recap – PPP allows us to create VPNs, but PPP is incompatible with other protocols. So, we use PPTP or L2TP to 'tunnel' PPP across other networks – PPTP for IP networks only, and L2TP for just about any network. But neither provides acceptable security. So, we have to layer on another protocol to provide security – that would be IPSec. Obviously IPSec only works for IP traffic, so if L2TP is used to traverse a non-IP network, some other security

protocol must be used. Finally, we can leverage TLS on top of other protocols to provide more intelligent security at a higher layer.

Authentication Protocols

We have already mentioned in passing things like PAP, CHAP and EAP without really discussing what they are – these are various protocols used for authentication across PPP connections. _Password Authentication Protocol_ (_PAP_) requires the user to first create a connection, and then enter a username and password, which is then sent to an authentication server where the credentials are compared against an authorized list. Unfortunately, PAP sends passwords in clear text and really should no longer be used. However, when two routers start negotiating parameters and are unable to agree on an authentication protocol, PAP is chosen as the default – this option should be disabled. PAP also is vulnerable to man-in-the-middle attacks.

A step up from PAP is _Challenge Handshake Authentication Protocol_ (_CHAP_). Instead of sending the password, CHAP implements the following for authentication:

1) Local (router) sends an authentication request (username) to remote (router)
2) Remote generates a nonce (a random one-time use number) and sends it to local
3) Local encrypts the nonce with the user's password and sends it back to remote
4) Remote decrypts the password and compares it to the stored value
5) If the two match authentication is allowed

Once a connection has been established, you might think that CHAP is vulnerable to man-in-the-middle attacks, but it will randomly force re-authentication throughout the session just to check that the other end is still who it claims to be. This is done programmatically – the user doesn't have to keep typing in his or her password. _MS-CHAP_ is Microsoft's version of CHAP, and allows both routers to authenticate with each other. There are two incompatible versions of MS-CHAP in the wild.

Finally, the most secure protocol is called _Extensible Authentication Protocol_ (_EAP_). The name is a little misleading, because unlike real protocols like PAP and CHAP, EAP is more of a framework to host authentication protocols – it _extends_ the possibilities. EAP works with a broad range of technologies including PPP, PPTP, L2TP, and both wired and wireless networks. When talking about a specific protocol working within EAP, it is called EAP-*XXX*. For example, some possibilities are:

- Lightweight EAP (LEAP) – Cisco's wireless protocol
- *EAP-TLS* – digital certificated-based
- *EAP-MD5* – hashed (weak)
- *EAP-PSK* – symmetric key mutual authentication
- *EAP-TTLS* – extends EAP-TLS
- *EAP-IKE2* – asymmetric or symmetric mutual authentication
- *PEAP-v0*/EAP-MSCHAPv2 – like EAP-TTLS but requires a server certificate
- *PEAPv1*/EAP-GTC – based on Cisco's Generic Token Card (GTC)
- *EAP-FAST* – Cisco's replacement for LEAP
- *EAP-SIM* – used for GSM cell SIM cards (cellular networks)
- *EAP-AKA* – used for UMTS cell SIM cards (cellular networks)
- *EAP-GSS* – Kerberos with Generic Security Service (GSS)

Questions

1. Which best describes a single user connecting to a web site acting as a gateway into more services?

    A) Transport adjacency

    B) TLS portal VPN

    C) Iterated tunneling

    D) TLS tunnel VPN

2. Which type of DSL provides 192-1100 Kbps down and up?

    A) VDSL

    B) HDSL

    C) ADSL

    D) SDSL

3. Which of the following tunnels PPP connections through an IP network?

    A) VPN

    B) PPTP

    C) IPSec

    D) GRE

4. Which of the following IPSec protocols provides a hash that provides integrity and system authentication, and protects from replay attacks?

    A) SA

    B) AH

    C) IKE

    D) ESP

5. What is a device connected to a PSTN connection that allows a remote device to connect to the network?

    A) Modulator

    B) Modem

    C) Analog traffic

    D) Demodulator

Chapter 42: Wireless Networks

Wireless networks move electromagnetic signals with variable _frequencies_ and _amplitudes_ through air and space. As the frequency of a signal increases, the more data it can carry but the distance it can carry that data decreases. So, you can send a little bit of data over long distances or a lot of data over short distances. While wireless networks don't use cables, they are constrained by many of the same issues the affect wired networks. For example, the wireless frequencies available for use are limited just as they are in a single cable. Collisions can occur in wireless traffic just like on an Ethernet network. If you recall, Ethernet uses CSMA/CD (collision _detection_) to handle collisions while wireless networks use CSMA/CA (collision _avoidance_). Most new technology advancements in the wireless area center on increasing data throughput or reliability.

Wireless Communication Techniques

One of the approaches to achieving these goals is to use _spread spectrum_ technologies. The FCC decides what frequencies are available for certain usage, so wireless network technology has a range of frequencies to play with. When spread spectrum is used, the devices communicating use more than a single frequency. _Frequency Hopping Spread Spectrum_ (_FHSS_) splits up the available frequencies into channels, and only a single channel is used at any given time, and only for a short burst. After the burst of data has been sent, the device will 'hop' onto a different channel. Both devices – sending and receiving – must agree on both the timing and hop sequence in order for this to work. The idea is that if the devices are constantly changing frequencies, the impact of interference on a given frequency is diminished. This allows multiple conversations from different devices to happen simultaneously as each conversation will have its own timing and hop sequence. FHSS reduces the likelihood of collisions by continuously hopping frequencies.

Direct Sequence Spread Spectrum (_DSSS_) takes a different approach to handling collisions – instead of trying to avoid them, DSSS simply encodes enough extra information that the receiver can rebuild the information if a collision occurs. In other words, DSS does not divide the available frequencies into channels like FHSS – it uses all available frequencies all time. It just uses some of the bandwidth to provide redundancy by adding _chips_ (extra bits) to each packet of data. The pattern of applying the chips to data is called the _chipping code_, and both the sender and receiver must agree on this as well as the timing.

802.11 first used FHSS, and provided bandwidth in the 1 to 2 Mbps range. Since DSSS uses all available frequencies, it achieves a bandwidth up to 11 Mbps – 802.11b uses DSSS.

The next wireless technology to come along abandoned spread spectrum altogether and instead focused on multiplexing the available frequency range into channels that are used simultaneously. While FHSS created multiple channels, it only used one at a time, so it is technically not multiplexing like _Orthogonal Frequency-Division Multiplexing_ (_OFDM_). Each channel used by ODFM is orthogonal (perpendicular) to the channel next to it so that they do not interfere with each other – this allows each channel to be a very narrow band. ODFM is used with digital television, DSL, audio broadcasting, wireless networks and 4G cellular networks.

WLAN Architecture

A Wireless LAN (WLAN) is just what the name implies – a LAN connected not with cables but wirelessly. Just as computers on an Ethernet network must have a _network interface card_ (_NIC_) to which the Ethernet cable is attached, computers on a wireless network must have a wireless card that connects to the signals that are sent and received. At its simplest, a wireless network is made up of two computers talking to each other over their wireless cards – this is called an _ad hoc_ WLAN. If a wireless _access point_ (_AP_) is involved, then both computers are connected to the AP instead of each other, and we have a _stand-alone WLAN_. If the AP is also connected to another network (either wired or wireless), then it is referred to as an _infrastructure WLAN_.

For devices to communicate on a WLAN, they must all be configured to use the same frequency range, or _channel_. A group of devices communicating in infrastructure mode from a _basic service set_ (_BSS_), which is assigned a human-friendly name, such as 'myHomeNetwork'. This name is called the _service set ID_ (_SSID_). All of this was defined in the original 802.11 standard.

When wireless networks first started appearing, there was very little security – you only had to know the SSID and authenticate using an extremely weak protocol named _wired equivalent protocol_ (_WEP_). Based on an RC4 algorithm, WEP made no grandiose promises – it only claimed to provide protection equivalent to unsecured traffic traveling over a physical Ethernet cable.

Unfortunately, people assumed more and the standard has since been much aligned.

WEP clients can authenticate using 1 of 2 methods:

- Open system authentication (OSA) – requires only the SSID, no encryption
- *Shared kay authentication* (*SKA*) – the AP and client possess a shared key and use a CHAP method for authentication

Beyond the complete lack of security with OSA, WEP has significant weaknesses even when using SKA:

1) Both the AP and client must use a shared key with no built-in infrastructure to update those keys – the result is that keys very seldom get changed
2) The WEP implementation did not properly randomize IVs (initialization vectors); that in combination with seldom-changing keys meant that detectable patterns in the encrypted packets emerged enabling discovery of the shared key
3) WEP uses an *integrity check value* (*ICV*) to ensure integrity – unfortunately it is possible to make changes to the data and result in the same ICV

Needless to say, that while WEP is still around, it should never be used – it can be broken in a matter of minutes with modern tools. When the weaknesses of WEP became blatantly clear, standards bodies began work on a new standard called *Wi-Fi protected access* (*WPA*). While it was still in the draft stage, the pressure to create a replacement for WEP was so extreme that the standard was released before it was properly defined. As a result, while much better than WEP, WPA incorporated some of the same weaknesses that its predecessor was guilty of.

WPA introduced the temporal key integrity protocol (TKIP), which does the following:

- Generates a new key for every frame that is transmitted
- Provides a sequence counter to protect against replay attacks
- Provides a message integrity check mechanism

WPA kept the RC4 algorithm and made sure it was backwards-compatible with existing hardware that WEP ran on. WPA also implemented both EAP and 802.1X port authentication (we'll cover this more in just a bit) – these two standards worked together to enforce mutual authentication between the two devices. Let's take each of the 3 vulnerabilities in WEP and see how WPA (and specifically TKIP) compare:

1) Shared key: Addressed through 802.1X
2) Non-random IV: The IV was lengthened and every frame has a unique IV; this is combined with the WEP key and the device's MAC address, resulting in a truly random encryption key
3) ICV: Instead of using an ICV, a MIC (similar to a MAC hash) is used instead, in which the hash is calculated and then encrypted

Once the WPA standard was ratified, *WPA2* was released – this was WPA as it was intended, and is referred to as a *robust security network*. WPA2's major contribution over WPA was encryption – it used AES in counter mode instead of RC4, and CBC-MAC (CCMP) instead of TKIP. WPA2 defaults to CCMP but can downgrade to TKIP and RC4 if needed to provide backwards compatibility with WPA.

When WPA came out, 802.11 was replaced by the *802.11i* standard. This new standard defines 3 components in 2 layers – at the lower layer we find TKIP and CCMP, which are not used together – choose one or the other. In the upper layer, we have 802.1X, which we kind of glossed over a few paragraphs back, but this is important stuff.

First, 802.1X is not a wireless standard – it doesn't care about the physical medium on which it is currently riding. In a nutshell, 802.1X ensures that a user cannot make a full network connection until authentication has properly happened – this is called *port-based network access*. Contrast that to WEP which only required that a *system* authenticate instead of a *user*. Why is this distinction important? Consider if you have a smartphone that is connected to the corporate network using WEP. Anyone who steals your phone can gain access to the network because the WEP shared key is cached. But if 802.1X is used, not only does your device must know the shared key, but you also have to provide your username and password before you can even connect to the network. That is the beauty of port-based network access. To do this, it defines 3 roles – the *supplicant* (the wireless client), the *authenticator* (the AP) and the *authentication server* (usually RADIUS). The authenticator remains dumb in this conversation so that it can focus on being the middleman and push packets around. The main responsibility it has in this authentication process is to ensure the client cannot access the network until fully authenticated by the authentication server.

But 802.11i doesn't stop there. It also allows _mutual authentication_ – whereas WEP only required the client to authenticate to the AP, 802.11i requires the AP and client to authenticate to each other, preventing rogue clients from connecting to the network and sniffing traffic. Now, 802.11i doesn't implement mutual authentication – it simply provides the framework to plug in your favorite EAP module, which does all heavy lifting – you can use tokens, passwords, Kerberos, smart cards, certificates – whatever your favorite flavor of EAP might be. Of course, both the authentication server and the client must have the appropriate EAP modules plugged in for this to work. This 'framework' approach allows 802.11i to stay focused on the data link layer, letting EAP modules take care of higher functionality.

We have already iterated the possible EAP implementations, but let's revisit some of the most important ones and see how well they work with 802.11i. Cisco uses LEAP, which is a simple password-based approach. Other vendors use EAP-TLS which requires both parties to have digital certificates – this can be a pain because of the overhead involved in distributing certificates to clients. PEAP solves this somewhat, because it only requires the server to have a certificate, but at the cost of mutual authentication. EAP-TTLS has all the power of EAP-TLS but without requiring client certificates. Both EAP-TLS and PEAP require some type of public key infrastructure (PKI) to be installed.

Let's end this section with a quick summary. WLANs are comprised of a group of devices, which from a BSS, which is assigned an SSID. WEP, a very poor implementation of wireless security, is built on RC4 and supports two authentication modes – OSA and SKA, of which SKA is really the only realistic choice. WAP was introduced to replace WEP before the standard was ready, and addressed almost all WEP weaknesses, mostly by introducing TKIP and supporting 802.1X – but was still based on RC4. Whereas WEP required system-based authentication, WPA requires user-based authentication. WPA2 was the officially released version of WPA, and replaced RC4 with AES and CCMP. 802.11i defines two layers, the first with either TKIP or CCMP, and the second layer with 802.1X. 802.1X ensures port-based network access, meaning you can't access the network until you authenticate, and defines 3 roles – _supplicant_, _authenticator_ and _authentication server_. 802.1X works at the data link layer, and relies on EAP extensions to perform higher-level authentication. Of those EAP modules, LEAP is Cisco's super-simple implementation, PEAP requires only a server cert, EAP-TLS is strong but requires everyone to have a cert, and EAP-TTLS is just a strong as EAP-TLS but only requires the server to have a cert.

Now, let's discuss some best practices for securing WLANs:

- Change the default SSID
- Implement port access with WPA2 and 802.1X – this requires user authentication
- If you cannot implement WPA2 and 802.1X, use a different WLAN for guests that is on the outside of your network perimeter
- Use separate VLANs for each class of users just like you would on a wired network
- Deploy a Wireless Intrusion Detection System (WIDS)
- Place the AP in the physical center of the building to prevent signal leaking
- Place the AP in a DMZ
- Only allow known MAC addresses to connect to the AP
- Implement VPN for wireless devices
- Pen test over the WLAN

Wireless Standards

All right, let's go over the ga-jillion wireless standards that exist – all named '802.11_something_'.

_802.11_ originally came out in 1997 and leveraged the 2.4 Ghz frequency range since it was free to use (it is called the Industrial, Scientific and Medical (ISM) band) – this provided about 1 -2 Mbps bandwidth. Soon thereafter, work was started on 802.11a, but was delayed due to the technical complexity. So, _802.11b_ was also started and was released _before_ 802.11a. 802.11b increased the transfer rate to 11 Mbps by using DSSS, and was backwards-compatible with 802.11.

_802.11a_ was subsequently released, using ODFM in the 5 GHz frequency range, resulting in speeds up to 54 Mbps. Remember the rule that the higher the frequency, the more data you can push but over shorter distances. That is why 802.11a had significantly increased bandwidth capabilities, but suffered from a shorter maximum range of 25 feet. 2.4 GHz was also considered to be a 'dirty' range because other devices such as microwaves and cordless phones also used this range, causing a lot of noise to deal with. 802.11a products are not guaranteed to work outside of the US because not all countries include the 5 GHz range in the frequencies allocated for WLAN traffic. Because of the significant differences, it was not compatible with 802.11 or 802.11b. Some devices (called AB devices) were created that could work with both standards, but the device had to be able to intelligently sense the standard being used.

Up to this point QoS was not a concern, and as a result timeliness of packet delivery was not very reliable. *802.11e* addressed this by adding support for QoS and multimedia traffic.

APs have a relatively short range, and originally once you move out of that area you would have to authenticate with another AP to stay connected. *802.11f* introduced the concept of *roaming* to allow devices to seamlessly move from AP to AP. Note that both 802.11e and 802.11f added functionality to existing standards and were not implemented as a stand-alone standard – therefore you will never hear of an '802.11f access point'.

802.11g was designed to provide the same speeds as 802.11a but be backwards-compatible with both 802.11 and 802.11b. It stayed in the 2.4 Ghz spectrum and provided speeds up to 54 Mbps.

802.11h addresses the concern that 802.11a will not work well outside of the US (primarily European countries) due to its implementation in the 5 GHz range.

802.11j was not a released standard but more of a task group that worked to better align standards among various countries to allow for more interoperability in all countries.

802.11n almost doubled the bandwidth of earlier standards to 100 Mbps, but solely in the 5 GHz range. The increase was due to leveraging *multiple in, multiple out* (*MIMO*) by using two pairs of antennas to double the overall throughput.

Finally, *802.11ac* is the current standard to rule all other standards – it is backwards compatible with 802.11a, 802.11b, 802.11g and 802.11n, but if you enable this compatibility mode it will slow everything down to the slowest standard. When not in compatibility mode it provides up to 1.3 Gbps and uses *beamforming* to shape and direct radio signals to improve performance – this overcomes the 'shorter ranges at higher frequencies' conundrum.

OK, so all above 802.11 standards are specific to WLANs. But there are wireless standards that address other types of networks. *802.16* defines broadband access for a MAN – essentially how to provide wireless connectivity over a geographically large area - 'large' being relative to the very small areas that a WLAN can cover. The standard supports speeds anywhere from 2 Mbps up to 155 Mbps. WiMAX is a coalition of wireless organizations that support the 802.16 and ensures compatibility between vendor devices. Somewhat related to 802.16 is *optical wireless*. This technology uses a laser system called *free-space optics* (*FSO*) to transmit light across open air in a point-to-point connection requiring a clear line of sight. The signals are very hard to intercept and weather is not a factor.

On the other side of WLAN's 'geographical area' from 802.16, we find 802.15.4 which defines a *wireless personal area network* (*WPAN*). This wireless network connects devices surrounding a person such as a keyboard, headset, cell phone, etc. 802.15.4 uses the 2.4 GHz band over a maximum of 100 meters. It is typically used for Internet of Things (IoT) devices. ZigBee is the most popular 802.15.4 protocol and supports transfer rates up to 250 Kbps with 128-bit symmetric encryption.

Another small network standard is *Bluetooth* which works in the 2.4 GHz range and provides 1 Mbps to 3 Mbps rates and supports distances at intervals of 1, 10 and 100 meters. Bluetooth provides a real security vulnerability because its traffic can be captured by any device within range. *Bluejacking* occurs when someone sends an unsolicited message to a device that has Bluetooth enabled – the attacker must be within a short distance for this to work. The countermeasure to this attack is to make sure Bluetooth is in non-discoverable mode. While Bluejacking is more of an annoyance, *Bluesnarking* allows the attacker to retrieve data from the victim's device, such as calendar events, contacts, text messages, photos and videos.

	Frequency (Ghz)	Speed (Mbps)	Notes
802.11	2.4	2	
802.11b	2.4	11	
802.11a	5	54	
802.11e	-	-	added QoS
802.11f	-	-	added roaming
802.11g	2.4	54	
802.11h	-	-	amended 802.11e
802.11j	-	-	just a task group
802.11n	5	100	added MIMO
802.11ac	2.4 and 5	1300	added beamforming
802.15.4	2.4	250K	WPAN
802.16	-	155	MAN, WiMAX

Figure 30: Wireless Standards

Other Wireless Networks

In terms of communication, a *satellite* is a communications relay that is placed into a low-earth orbit and simply receives a signal from one location on the earth, amplifies it and then transmits it to a different location on earth. Satellites require a clear line of sight to dish antennas that fall within the satellite's *footprint*, or the area covered by (visible to) a satellite. Satellites are capable of one-way or two-way transmissions – Internet connectivity requires two-way – and speeds can range from a few Kbps to several Mbps. While these satellites are placed in a low orbit to minimize latency, relative to wires or wireless networks the latency is still very high. Normally a *very small aperture terminal* (*VSAT*) will be used to link a remote site to a service provider's gateway facility.

Cellular networks are probably the largest type network of any kind on the planet. These networks are based on radio networks connected to PSTN. Radio networks traditionally broadcast information in a one-way fashion, but cell networks use two-way radio transmissions to allow bi-directional traffic. Mobile phone calls would be very short indeed if they were only one-sided. *Cellular networks* are called that because they are divided into 'cells' – smaller geographical areas, usually less than 1 mile in diameter in densely-populated areas. Because frequency ranges are limited, each cell will operate at a different frequency than any of its neighbors, but that same frequency can be reused 1 or 2 cells away. As you travel from one cell to another, the cellular network will seamlessly hand responsibility for your call to the nearest cell tower.

To squeeze more and more bandwidth out of a finite frequency range, cellular networks have employed several 'multiple access' technologies. In 1980, the first multiple access technology appeared, known as *frequency division multiple access* (*FDMA*). FDMA divided the available frequency range into channels called sub-bands, with each channel being assigned to a single subscriber making a phone call (a single connected mobile phone device). During the call, no other subscriber could use that channel. FDMA represent the first generation of cellular networks, or 1G, and supported voice calls only at 19.2 Kbps. Some 1G implementations include *advanced mobile phone* system (*AMPS*), *total access communication system* (*TACS*) and *Nordic mobile telephone* (*NMT*).

In 1995 cell providers came up with *time division multiple access* (*TDMA*) which divided the FDMA channels into time slots so that multiple subscribers could share the same channel. Systems such as *global system for mobile communication* (*GSM*), D-AMPS and PDC used TDMA. About the same time *personal communications service* (*PCS*) was created that provided management of voice combined with data.

TDMA, GSM and PCS represented the second generation of cellular networks, called 2G. Most notably, 2G added the ability to send and receive data in addition to voice calls, including encrypted data and short message service (SMS, or more commonly known as text messaging). Caller ID and voice mail were added, but data bandwidth was stuck in the 120 Kbps range.

Code division multiple access (*CDMA*) arrived in 2000. CDMA assigns a unique code to each call or data stream so that they can be mixed in with all other traffic on all channels. In addition, each cell can interact with other cells simultaneously. CDMA was the basis for 3G, where circuit switching was replaced with packet switching and a real Internet experience finally arrived on mobile devices. Data bandwidth hovered around the 2 Mbps mark, and wireless and Bluetooth support was common for mobile devices. *Multimedia messaging service* (*MMS*) was added to SMS, and very low-quality video was now possible. Follow-on enhancements, called 3.5G, were grouped together as the *third generation partner project* (*3GPP*) and included *enhanced data rates for GSM evolution* (*EDGE*), *high-speed downlink packet access* (*HSPDA*), CDMA2000 and WiMAX. This provided data bandwidth speeds up to 10 Mbps.

Orthogonal frequency division multiple access (*OFDMA*) appeared in 2010, and combines both FDMA and TDMA. By using perpendicular frequencies on adjacent channels, the room between each channel can be reduced, and each channel can be separated into multiple subchannels. MIMO can be used to transmit on each subchannel simultaneously resulting in a much higher bandwidth. These 4G technologies are based on OFDMA and include WiMAX and *Long-Term Evolution* (*LTE*). 4G uses packet switching technologies in the entire path, so 4G devices are IPv6-based on top of OFDMA. High-definition video is possible and data bandwidth is supported up to 100 Mbps if the device is moving, and 1 Gbps if it is stationary.

Let's review the various cellular generations quickly.

- *1G* – voice calls only, analog, circuit-switched
- *2G* – added paging support, caller ID and low-speed data (email)
- *2.5G* – added always on for email and pages, increased bandwidth
- *3G* – true Internet connectivity, changed to packet-switching
- *3.5G* –OFDMA, increased bandwidth
- *4G* – all IP, increased bandwidth (100 Mbps to 1 Gbps)
- *5G* – being developed

Chapter 42: Wireless Networks

Questions

1. Which of the following wireless security protocols kept RC4 but added TKIP, EAP and 9021X port authentication?

    A) WAP

    B) WEP

    C) WPA

    D) WPA2

2. What wireless standard supports 5Ghz, 100Mbps?

    A) 802.11e

    B) 802.11g

    C) 802.11ac

    D) 802.11n

3. What is the term describing two devices authenticating to each other?

    A) Mutual authentication

    B) Dual authentication

    C) Supplicant/authenticator

    D) Two-way authentication

4. Which multiple access technology added 3G and packet switching?

    A) CDMA

    B) TDMA

    C) FDMA

    D) OFDMA

5. What is best term for electromagnetic signals consisting of both frequency and amplitude traveling through air and space?

    A) Wireless networks

    B) Free channels

    C) Variable networks

    D) Variable channels

Chapter 43: Network Encryption

Link and End-to-End Encryption

Now let's move past all of those wireless technologies, and talk about network security in general, and encryption more specifically. There are two types of network encryption – link encryption and end-to-end encryption. The name implies the OSI layer at which the encryption is implemented. *Link encryption* happens at the data link layer so that all data in layer 2 and above are encrypted. Link encryption is sometimes called *online encryption*, and is great because:

- None of the data can be sniffed (traffic-flow security)
- Applications do not have to worry about encrypting traffic

Of course, there are some downsides:

- Every frame must be decrypted at each Layer 2 device (switches and routers), examined and re-encrypted
- All Layer 2 devices require key management
- More encrypt/decrypt steps mean more opportunities for exploitation

End-to-end encryption happens by the application generating the traffic (the application is the 'end point'). This too is great because:

- Applications have more control over encryption
- Layer 2 devices do not require key management
- Network performance is increased because Layer 2 devices do not need to perform decryption/encryption

And, of course the downsides:

- Applications must implement their own encryption
- Attackers can see routing information

There are more encryption opportunities than link or end-to-end. For example, TLS takes place at the session layer, while PPTP also take places at the data link layer. But those are specific examples, whereas link and end-to-end encryption are recognized categories.

Email Encryption

The *multipurpose internet mail extension* (*MIME*) is a specification on how systems should handle email binary attachments. When an email arrives with an attachment, the email header will contain a MIME type for that attachment, indicating what type of file it is, and if it is using a common format. If the receiving computer understands that format and has an application that indicates it knows how to process such a MIME type, the email client will invoke this application when the user tries to open it. Browsers use this same method to handle downloaded files.

In 1991 Phil Zimmerman created the *Pretty Good Privacy* (*PGP*) program to encrypt email. It was the first widely-adopted public key encryption program, and provides the entire infrastructure needed for an end-to-end solution – thus it is an entire cryptosystem. PGP uses RSA public key encryption for key management and the IDEA symmetric cipher for data encryption, although the user can select a different algorithm. PGP provides:

- Integrity – MD5 hashing
- Confidentiality – IDEA encryption
- Nonrepudiation – cryptographically-signed messages
- Authentication – public key certificates

Since PGP uses a self-contained certificate management instead of PKI, it relies on a 'web of trust' – a user publishes their public key, and other users sign that key. Remember that PKI uses CAs and RAs to provide trust, so PGP uses a more peer-to-peer process to provide the same level of trust. The more users that have signed a key, the more trusted the owner of the public key becomes. Contrast this to a PKI, in which no one trusts anyone else except for the CA.

Each PGP user keeps a list of public keys that have been received inside a file called a *key ring*. Each public key has an accompanying level of trust that allows a user to make an informed decision on whether to communicate with that key's owner or not. In the case of a lost key, PGP supports key revocation, but there is no guarantee that everyone will receive this notice.

Internet Security

The Internet, at its simplest, is a mesh of servers offering various services to consuming devices, all sitting on top of a vast TCP/IP network. There are many common and ubiquitous service types based on accepted standards.

Chapter 43: Network Encryption

One of the most common is HTTP, which lives at Layer 7 of the OSI model. *Hypertext Transfer Protocol* (*HTTP*) is a connectionless protocol – for every operation the server and client create and destroy a unique connection. HTTP is how browsers request web pages and submit web forms. Everything is sent in clear text and there is absolutely no concept of integrity, confidentiality, authentication or nonrepudiation with HTTP.

Which is why we have *HTTP Secure* (HTTPS) – which is HTTP wrapped in either secure sockets layer (SSL) or transport layer security (TLS). Both protocols are almost identical in terms of infrastructure, but differ in terms of algorithms. While SSL is no longer trusted, and has several serious vulnerabilities, it is still being used in many places, so let's discuss it first.

SSL uses public key encryption and provides encryption, integrity, server authentication and optional user authentication. The conversation between a client and an SSL-secured server goes something like this:

- Server tells the client a secure session is required
- Client sends its security requirements
- Server validates the client security requirements and returns a digital certificate containing the server's public key
- Client generates a session key, encrypts it with the server's public key and sends it to the server
- Server decrypts the session key with its private key
- Both client and server encrypt all messages with the session key

If this sounds just like the Bob and Joy conversation we had earlier about public keys – that it because it *is* the exact same thing – only we have replaced Bob and Joy with a browser and a web server.

SSL only ensures the identity of the server and that the data exchanged remains hidden and unaltered. When used in a browser, the URL will begin with an 'https://' – this indicates a secure session has been established. SSL operates at both the Session and Transport layers, but for the exam the correct answer is the Transport layer.

SSL v3.0, which is a proprietary protocol, was replaced with TLS v1.0 as an open-community protocol, meaning that TLS can be extended by the community at-large. In 2014, an attack called the P*adding Oracle on Downgraded Legacy Encryption* (or with the adorable acronym *POODLE*) permanently demonstrated that SSL was fundamentally flawed, whereas TLS v1.0 did not have the susceptibility. TLS v1.0 did have another different flaw, sadly, so only TLS 1.1 and 1.2 are considered secure. TLS is currently at v1.2.

A *cookie* is a file that a browser stores on the local computer's hard drive. The contents of this file are specified by a web server, and the cookie will persist as long as the server desires unless the local user intentionally deletes it. A server can only access cookies that it created in the first place, so it should not be a concern that other sites can steal the data. However, there is no restriction on the type of data that can be stored inside of a cookie, and if it contains sensitive information such as username and password, anyone with access to the browser's file system could discover this information. Cookies are often used to track behavior patterns, so the more paranoid among us will often turn cookies off. Unfortunately, many sites require cookies to be enabled to work properly.

Secure shell (*SSH*) is a tunneling mechanism that allows remote users to execute commands as if they were physically on the target computer, and allows secure file transfers and port redirection. SSH is normally used for remote administration, but can be easily abused by an attacker if not properly secured. Other similar functions that are less secure include Telnet, FTP, rsh, rexec and rlogin. When communicating via SSH, both computers use Diffie-Hellman to exchange session keys that are used to encrypt all traffic exchanged between the two.

Questions

1. What is HTTP encrypted by SSL or TLS called?

A) SHTTP

B) HTTPS

C) SSL

D) TLS v1.2

2. Which of the following is NOT a disadvantage of link encryption?

A) More encrypt/decrypt steps mean more opportunities for exploitation

B) All Layer 2 devices require key management

C) Every frame must be decrypted at each Layer 2 device

D) Attackers can see routing information

3. Which type of network encryption is carried out in Layer 2 devices?

A) Level 2

B) Switch-level

C) Link

D) Connection

4. What is the current version of TLS, considered to be secure?

A) TLS v1.3

B) TLS v1.2

C) TLS v2.0

D) TLS v1.0

5. Which of the following is a specification on how systems should handle email binary attachments?

A) HTTP

B) SSH

C) MIME

D) PGP

Chapter 44: Network Attacks

Now that we have discussed the basics of encryption and network security, let's talk about the methods attackers will use to defeat those security measures.

Denial of Service

At the bottom of the pile is the crude but very effective method of denying the use of services to legitimate users – this is called _Denial of Service_ (_DoS_). Back when network standards were new and not yet hardened, the most common attacks were centered on malformed packets as they caused these new services to misbehave. The most famous was the _Ping of Death_, a DoS that would send a single ICMP Echo Request that exceeded the expected maximum size of 65,536 bytes, causing the OS to crash. This attack has not been viable for a long time, but the use of malformed packets is still alive and well. Since new vulnerabilities are always being discovered, the best defense is to monitor network traffic for anomalies and to subscribe to feeds that alert on new types of attacks being discovered.

Instead of trying to attack a specific vulnerability, many DoS attacks are carried out by _flooding_ a computer with so much traffic that it is unable to respond to new requests. If you think back to the TCP 3-way handshake, it follows a SYN, SYN/ACK, ACK pattern before a conversation can begin. For that to take place, the receiving device must track the packet progression, and therefore for every SYN packet that is received, the device must allocate a little bit of memory and wait for the ACK. Well, what happens if an attacker sends a whole bunch of SYN packets but never bothers to answer with an ACK to complete the handshake? The device will fill up its memory and either crash or be unable to accept new connections. This is called a _SYN flood_.

Of course, memory is cheap, so to execute a successful SYN flood attack the attacker needs to generate an insane number of SYN packets. A single computer over one network connection will unlikely be able to generate sufficient traffic to overwhelm the device, because the device will start clearing out old unfinished handshakes after just a few seconds. But if a whole bunch of computers could somehow be coordinated to execute the attack against a single victim at the same time over multiple network connection, then the attack stands a very good chance of succeeding. And this is where a _Distributed Denial of Service_ (_DDoS_) attack comes into play, and here is how one scenario might play out:

1) Launch a phishing campaign to trick users into downloading malware onto their computer
2) The malware connects to a _command and control_ (_C&C_) network which the attacker owns
3) The victim computer is now a _zombie_ or _bot_, and is part of a _botnet_
4) The attacker sends out a command to all bots instructing them to launch a SYN flood attack against the target server
5) The target server receives a flood of SYN packets from all over the Internet and dies

Of course, phishing is not the only way to get malware on the zombie computer – any number of ways can be used, but the result is that the attacker's software is running unnoticed on all zombie bots. Unfortunately, you no longer have to build your own botnet – there are many 'dark' organizations across the world more than willing to rent their botnets to you for a short time. There are several countermeasures to DDoS attacks:

- Detect and block the attacking IP address – not very useful when the attack is coming from legitimate IP addresses due to zombies
- Configure switches and routers to throttle any traffic coming from IPs that are particularly noisy
- For SYN flood attacks, configure servers to use _delayed binding_ – a half-open connection is not bound to a socket until it has completed the 3-way handshake – this reduces memory consumption
- Use a _content distribution network_ (_CDN_) to distribute content and services across the internet – this forces an attacker to launch a massive campaign to take out all services simultaneously which will make it not worth the effort for all but the most determined attackers

Ransomware

A new trend in recent years is the use of _ransomware_ to blackmail victims into paying a fee. It follows the same entry point as other attacks – getting someone to download malware. Ransomware does not attempt to turn your computer into a zombie though – it will encrypt files on the victim computer's storage, followed by a message to the victim that they must pay a certain dollar amount to get their files back. The files never leave the computer – they are simply encrypted, but without the key are rendered completely inaccessible to the owner. Once the fee has been paid (often in Bitcoins), the attacker sends the encryption key with instructions on how to decrypt the files. Ransomware attackers almost always keep their word upon payment, because it would do them no good to keep the key (the victim will not pay twice) and the ransomware 'industry' wants the victim to be assured that payment will allow them to access their files.

To mitigate this attack, use the common controls to prevent malware from being installed. However, the best way to mitigate the effect of this type of attack is to back up your data often and keep several weeks' worth archived – restoring your unencrypted data is a great way to avoid paying the ransom.

Sniffing

The ability to eavesdrop on passing network packets is called _sniffing_. To do this, a computer's NIC must be put into _promiscuous mode_, meaning it will look into every frame received, not just frames addressed to the NIC's MAC address. NICs operating in this mode can be detected if someone is explicitly looking for it, but sniffing on a network is a very common tool for troubleshooting problems – so network administrators seldom routinely look for this type of behavior. To be able to sniff inside a network, the attacker must be able to physically connect to it, so physical countermeasures often make this type of attack difficult.

DNS Hijacking

DNS hijacking forces a user to unknowingly use a malicious DNS server. This attack is normally carried out with the goal getting you to visit the attacker's fake web site which looks just like the real site – the victim enters logon credentials that are then captured, or they download malware.

We have touched on DNS attacks earlier, but let's go into more detail. DNS attacks can be 1 of 3 types. The first is a _host based attack_ where the attacker modifies the DNS settings a computer uses to point to the attacker's own server. The attacker can then redirect the victim to whatever server he wishes and the user could never tell any difference. This attack can only be carried out if the attacker can gain a foothold on the victim's computer, so any type of countermeasure to protect against that vector will prevent this.

The second type is a _network based attack_– the attacker redirects DNS traffic to his own server using tactics such as ARP table poisoning. This works at the IP address level, and instead of the attacker trying to fool the host-name to IP address lookup, he simply convinces the computer that he owns the IP address in question when the victim's computer sends out an ARP request. To counteract this threat, most popular network intrusion detection systems (NIDS) can detect this type of behavior.

The third type is _server based attack._ With this type, the attacker convinces a legitimate DNS server that his own DNS server is authoritative for the victim domain. Then when a browser attempts to resolve the host name to an IP address, the attacker's DNS server will be allowed to perform the resolution activity and send back his own custom IP address. To mitigate this attack, make sure your DNS servers are properly configured to require authentication with other DNS servers. We covered this topic extensively in the Domain Name Service section earlier.

Drive-by Download

One of the most dangerous types of attacks is a _drive-by-download_ – all the victim must do is to visit a single page on an infected website, and malware could be downloaded and installed on the victim's computer. The site could be perfectly legitimate but simply vulnerable to an attacker that uploaded the malware and configured one or more pages to download the malware when visited. The download is done via browser vulnerabilities, or more commonly through a browser plug-in that has a specific vulnerability. The countermeasure against this threat is ensure plug-ins are disabled by default and that all active plug-ins are updated to the latest version.

Questions

1. Which of the following is NOT a DoS attack?

A) SYN flood

B) ACK silence

C) Ping of Death

D) Flooding

2. What describes malware that locks some resource and blackmails victims into paying a fee to unlock it?

A) Sniffing

B) Promiscuous

C) Loose

D) Ransomware

3. Which term describes forcing a user to unknowingly use a malicious DNS server?

A) Server based attack

B) Network based attack

C) Host based attack

D) DNS Hijacking

4. Which attack sends a computer so much traffic that it is unable to respond to new requests?

A) SYN flood

B) Flooding

C) ACK silence

D) Ping of Death

5. What is a term describing a computer that has malware installed that carries out central instructions?

A) Hood

B) C&C

C) Botnet

D) Zombie

Section 5: Identity and Access Management (IAM) Domain

Whenever we think of controlling access to some type of IT resource, we normally think of limiting a person's access. However, we might also need to limit a server's ability to accidentally drop a database or prevent a printer from printing certain restricted materials. That is why when we discuss *access controls* we use terms like 'subject' and 'object'.

Access is the flow of information between a subject and an object. A *subject* is an active entity that requests access to an object, and can be a user, program or process. An *object* is passive entity that contains the desired information or functionality. *Access control* is a security feature that controls how subjects access objects. For example, consider the scenario in which Mike needs to make a duplicate of a document on a copier, and must enter his password. Mike is the subject, the copier is the object, and the access control is the requirement to enter a password.

A lot of times when discussing authentication and authorization people resort to using users (people) as an example, but that can be misleading. Within networks, and specifically server-to-server communication, access control is just as important as enforcing user logins, but people are not involved. For example, a web server needs to connect to a database – this is a fine example of hidden authentication and authorization at work. Therefore, we will always use the term 'subject' to refer to people, machines or processes that need access to an object. We will make an exception here and there when people require extra attention, but it will be explicitly called out.

Chapter 45: Identification, Authentication, Authorization, and Accountability

We have already discussed the CIA triad (confidentiality, integrity and availability) in another domain, but let's quickly review it again in terms of subjects and objects:

- *Confidentiality* is the assurance that information is not disclosed to an unauthorized subject
- *Integrity* is the assurance that information has not been altered by an unauthorized subject
- *Availability* is the assurance that an object is available when a subject needs it

To properly implement access control, 4 steps must be executed.

1) The subject must provide an *identity*, which should be public information such as a username or account number
2) The subject must *authenticate* they are who they claim to be by providing private information such as a password or smart token
3) The system validates the identity and authentication information, and then checks to see if the subject is *authorized* to access the object
4) The system records all activities between the subject and object for future *accountability*

Logical access controls are technical tools (usually software components) used to carry out identification, authentication, authorization and accountability. Note that the terms 'logical' and 'technical' are interchangeable in this context. While operating systems always implement the above access controls, it is important to understand that software applications riding on top of OSs also may do this – sometimes simply extending the OSs capabilities, and sometimes implementing their own through stand-alone infrastructure. Whichever the case may be, the principles described in this section equally apply.

Identity

An *identity* uniquely represents a subject within a given environment. When creating and issuing an identity, 3 attributes should be addressed:

- *Uniqueness* – the identity should represent something unique about the subject
- *Non-descriptive* – the identity name should not describe the role or purpose of the account
- *Issuance* – how the identity is issued to the subject is important (email, ID card, etc.)

Best practices for identities are:

- Each value should be unique for accountability
- A standard naming scheme should be followed
- The name should not describe the position or task
- The name should not be shared among multiple subjects

Identity Management

Identity Management (*IdM*) is the process of creating, managing and retiring identities. This undertaking can be a huge task, and there are many software tools on the market today to help. We are going to cover the various types of technologies required to properly manage identities.

Directories

A *directory* is a central location where all subjects and objects are tracked (*everything* in a directory is called an 'object', so don't get confused between directory-lingo and access management lingo), along with authentication and authorization details. Most directories follow the *X.500* standard which defines a hierarchical format, and the *Lightweight Directory Access Protocol* (*LDAP*) which allows other applications to interact with the directory. The objects in a directory are managed by a *directory service* and are labeled and identified using a *namespace* – a hierarchical naming convention that uniquely identifies a location or object. When using X.500 and LDAP, the directory service assigns a *common name* (*CN*) and a *distinguished name* (*DN*) to each object. The object's DN identifies that object uniquely in the directory, but the object's CN is not required to be unique. The DN is made up of several objects called *domain components* (*DC*) – each DC is not unique by itself, but when you combine all DCs within a DN, you get back something that is unique in the entire directory. For example, to identify a user with an email address of 'george.washington@whitehouse.us.gov' we could have:

DN: cn=george.washington, dc=whitehouse, dc=us, dc=gov
CN: George Washington

An X.500 directory database follows certain rules:

- All objects are arranged in a hierarchical parent-child relationship
- Every object has a unique name made up of unique identifiers called 'distinguished names'
- The supported attributes for objects are defined by a schema

In a Windows network environment, a user will log into a *domain controller* (*DC*) that contains a hierarchical database. The DC is running a directory service called 'Active Directory' that will authenticate and authorize a user.

A directory is basically a centralized database, but is not necessarily the authority on the data it contains. For example, an employee's office number might be contained with some other HR database, while authentication information could be stored in a Kerberos server, while the user roles a user belongs to is stored in the directory itself. In this case, the directory is a *meta-directory* – it aggregates information from multiple sources and presents a unified view. The directory is responsible for remaining in-sync with each authoritative data source that it aggregates. If a directory does not aggregate the data into its own database, but instead simply points to the external databases containing the information, it is called a *virtual directory*.

Web Access Management

Web Access Management (*WAM*) is a software layer that controls authentication and authorization within a web-based environment. It can be proprietary logic built into a web site or a plug-in module that facilitates the process using external systems, but most often is associated with a *single sign-on* (*SSO*) experience. For example, a user logs on to the company intranet for the latest corporate news, switches to a help desk application, and then accesses the company directory to locate a fellow employee. All 3 of those sites are completely different web applications running on different servers and know nothing about each other, yet only one log in was required. This is an example of SSO and is why we have WAM. In this example, WAM is coordinating the authentication and authorization with external systems behind the scene, and all 3 web applications are aware of these internal systems. The most common method of implementing WAM is that after the initial authentication, WAM stores a cookie on the user's computer containing some type of session identifier. Each web application will use WAM to retrieve this cookie and validate that it is still valid – if so, the user does not need to log in again. This assumes that all web applications are accessed using the same sub-domain (the sub-domain is the 'mydomain.com' part of 'www.mydomain.com') – different sub-domains cannot access each other's cookies. This cookie is checked every time the browser requests a new page or resource from the web server.

Authentication

Identification and Authentication require two different pieces of information (public and private information), but are used together to *authenticate* a subject. *Authentication* is the process of the subject proving it is who it claims to be. With machine authentication, this will usually be a digital certificate or a password; with users, it can be a number of things - people can authenticate with 3 different 'factors':

- *Something a person knows* – something a person stores in their memory, such as a password, pin, entry code for a vehicle or combination for a lock; an attacker could acquire this knowledge
- *Something a person has* – a physical possession, such as a swipe card, a smart token, keys or an access badge; an attacker could steal this
- *Something a person is* – a unique physical attribute, such as fingerprint, retina pattern, their gait or voice print; an attacker could physically emulate this

While most authentication is single factor (requires only one factor from the list above), *strong authentication*, or *multifactor authentication*, requires at least 2 factors. Most commonly only a password is required, which is among the weakest type of authentications.

Managing Passwords

If password is the sole authentication factor used within an environment to access systems (and it almost always is except for the most secure facilities), then how passwords are managed becomes very important. There is a balance that needs to be struck between stringent policies and usability. For example, if a company requires passwords to be so strong that they cannot be easily memorized and must be changed every other week, users will resort to writing them down which will defeat having strong passwords to begin with. On the other hand, having change password and strength policies that are too lax may make users happy, but will weaken the company's security posture significantly and introduce unacceptable vulnerabilities.

Adding to the problem is the lack of supporting a single set of credentials across multiple systems – if each system requires a unique password (and possibly a unique identity), you are guaranteed that users will write these passwords down somewhere. To avoid this a company can implement *password synchronization* – having multiple systems update their respective passwords at the same time. If the password remains constant, the user can memorize a stronger password. The downside of this is that by stealing one set of credentials, an attacker can have access to multiple systems. But a stronger password offsets this and strikes an acceptable balance.

Another potential problem with password management is the ability to manage forgotten passwords – a manual reset process requiring IT personnel will be a serious resource drain and fraught with mistakes – an automated solution needs to be implemented but with the proper level of identification controls to ensure fraud does not take place.

Self-Service Password Reset

One answer is a self-service password reset, and is a 3-step process:

1) The user provides an alternative means of authentication:
    a. The user answers a personal question (something they know); the correct answer was provided when the original account was setup
    b. The user provides a smart card, access card or token (something they have)
    c. The user provides a fingerprint or retina scan (something they are)
2) *An email is sent with a link* to reset the password to the email address on file – this provides another layer of security as only that person should be able to access that email; the link contains a random globally-unique identifier (GUID) that is tied to the password reset request
3) *The link is clicked* and the system allows the user to enter a new password

Assisted Password Reset

Another option is the *assisted password reset* – this uses the same information as the self-service password reset, but instead of interacting with a system the user interacts with a helpdesk person, who enters the answers to the security questions into an application. At this point, a new password is generated known to both the helpdesk person and the user, but when the user logs in the next time, the system requires a new valid password to be provided before access will be granted.

Single Sign-On

A third option is *single sign-on* (*SSO*). Like password synchronization, SSO keeps all passwords the same across multiple systems. But where password synchronization requires each system to maintain its own credential set (just kept in-synch), SSO provides a single infrastructure to manage credentials that all system leverage. SSO is not without its problems though – it can be very expensive to implement, and becomes a single point of failure and possible bottleneck. Older systems may also lack the hooks to plug in an SSO solution. And like password synchronization, SSO creates a vulnerability in which an attacker can access multiple systems with a single set of credentials.

While we are on the subject of SSO, let's think back to the idea of directory services we touched on in Identity Management. A directory service provides the single infrastructure required for SSO – if it is based on the X.500 standard, the LDAP protocol can be used to authenticate and manage the credentials.

Thin clients that do not possess the required amounts of local storage or memory can also take advantage of SSO – on boot up the device prompts the user for credentials, which are then authenticated using SSO to a central server or mainframe – this allows the thin client to use multiple services with a single authentication step visible to the user.

Managing Accounts

Account management is the process of creating, modifying and decommissioning user accounts on all appropriate systems. When this is carried out manually, accounts are left in-place too long and too much power is handed out. Some type of automated process is required to effectively manage this activity – one that leverages workflows to model the desired process and can transparently update multiple systems without requiring any type of manual intervention. This results in the following benefits:

- Reduces errors caused by manual data entry
- Each step in the process is tracked and logged (accountability)
- Ensures the appropriate amount of privileges are assigned
- Eliminates orphaned user accounts when employees leave the company
- Makes auditors happy

The downside is that these types of systems are very expensive to implement. But if a longer-term view is taken, the return on investment (ROI) for such a system almost always outweighs the short-term costs.

While account management deals with user accounts, *user provisioning* is the act of creating user objects and attributes – a 'user account' includes other metadata including passwords and auditing, while user objects simply represent the user. Normally a *profile* is created to accompany a user account, containing such things as addresses, phone numbers and email addresses. If a user can update their own profile information, then the system offers self-service.

Biometrics

Biometrics is the act of verifying an individual's identity based on physiological or behavioral attributes. *Physiological traits* are physical attributes that are unique to the individual such as fingerprints, voice print or retina scan. A *behavioral trait* is a characteristic of an individual that is not guaranteed to be unique among all people, but sufficiently unique to be used in conjunction with another authentication method. Behavioral traits include handwriting signature, height or a walking gait. A physiological trait is 'what you are' while a behavioral trait is 'what you do'.

A biometric system measures the trait in real-time and compares it to a record created during an earlier enrollment process. The results must be very sensitive yet reliable. When a biometric system fails to properly identify an individual, it can result in two types of errors:

- *Type 1 error* – rejects an authorized individual
- *Type 2 error* – accepts an unauthorized individual

The frequency of a type 1 error results in a number called a *false rejection rate* (*FRR*). Type 2 frequencies result in a *false acceptance rate* (*FAR*). While the goal is to keep both numbers low, type 2 errors are much more concerning – it is far better for authorized individuals to be occasionally forced to repeat the authentication step, than it is to occasionally provide unauthorized individuals access to the protected resource or facility.

When comparing the accuracy of various biometric systems, it is helpful to have some kind of objective way to measure their respective performance. That is why each system provides a *crossover error rate* (*CER*), which measures the point at which the FRR equals the FAR and is expressed as a percentage. For example, a system could be configured to be so sensitive that the FAR is 0%, but at that level the FRR might be 90% - that means no unauthorized individuals are accepted, but it also means that 90% of authorized individuals are rejected as well. The closer to 0% the CER is the better the overall accuracy. A system with a CER of 3% is better than a system with a CER of 4%. However, an organization very concerned with security might purchase a biometric system with a CER of 3, but tweak it after installation to lower the FAR to 1% at the expense of raising the FRR to 10% - fewer unauthorized false positives at the expense of more authorized false negatives.

During the enrollment process, the biometric system measures the individual's trait and converts that information into a digital signature which may be hashed. During authentication, the measurement is repeated, and the two values are compared. Obtaining a 100% match rate is unreasonable as many environmental factors such as smudges, misaligned sensors or lighting may affect results from day-to-day.

The various types of biometric data are:

- *Fingerprints* – a complete record of ridges and valley on a finger
- *Finger scan* – certain features of a fingerprint
- *Palm scan* – fingerprint and the creases, ridges and grooves of the palm
- *Hand geometry* – the shape, length and width of hand and fingers
- *Retina scan* – blood-vessel patterns on the back of an eyeball (most invasive)
- *Iris scan* - the colored portion surrounding the pupil (most accurate)
- *Signature Dynamics* – the speed and movements produced when signing a name
- *Keystroke dynamics* – the speed and pauses between each keypress as a password is typed
- *Voice print* – a number of words are recorded during enrollment; during authentication, the words are jumbled and the user repeats them to prevent a recording from being played
- *Facial scan* – bone structure, nose ridge, eye widths, forehead size and chin shape are measured
- *Hand topography* - a side camera captures the contour of the palm and fingers; not unique enough to be used alone but can often be used with hand geometry

While it may be a little morose, some biometrics check for a pulse and heat of a body part to ensure it has not been cut off.

The downsides of biometric systems are:

- *User acceptance* – many people feel uncomfortable
- *Enrollment timeframe* – the enrollment phase may take a long time to reach an acceptable CER level due to required tweaking
- *Throughput* – biometric systems can greatly increase the time required before access is granted; an acceptable elapsed time from start to response is 5 to 10 seconds
- *Accuracy over time* – living things change

Passwords

As we said earlier, passwords are probably the most common – and weakest – forms of authentication. An attacker will try the following tactics to get a password:

- *Electronic monitoring* – sniffing network traffic or recording keystrokes; if an attacker can capture the network packet containing the encrypted password, he might be able to simply replay the packet later to gain access
- *Password file* – the authentication server usually stores passwords in a file of some type; if the attacker can gain access to that file, she has the password
- *Brute-force attack* – using an automated tool to try and login by cycling through many possible combinations of characters, numbers and symbols until a match is found
- *Dictionary attack* – words in the native language are used to guess the password
- *Rainbow table* – using all likely passwords in a table already hashed (much quicker than a brute-force or dictionary attack)
- *Social engineering* – convincing the owner to reveal their password

There are a number of tactics and policies that can be implemented to mitigate vulnerabilities:

- After login, show the date/time of the prior successful login attempt, how many unsuccessful attempts were made and the location of the login; the user will be alerted to a possible attack
- After X number of failed attempts within the last Y seconds, lock the account for Z minutes (this is called the *clipping level*, and temporary locking prevents brute-force, dictionary or rainbow attacks)
- Record an audit trail capturing both successful and unsuccessful login attempts, including the date/time, the user ID and the location where the attempt was made
- Limit the lifetime of a password - force the user to change it at recurring intervals (this is called *password aging*)
- Do not allow previously used passwords to be chosen when changing a password; the last 5-10 passwords should be stored to prevent this.

A *password checker* should be employed by security to check the strength of passwords but only after obtaining the proper management permission. The same tool may be used by an attacker but then it is called a *password cracker*. Systems should never send passwords in clear text – it should hash them if encryption is not involved. Unix/Linux hashes passwords and stores them in a *shadow file*, and might add a *salt* before encryption to further randomize encryption keys.

There are several methods for a user entering a password to authenticate. We have previously discussed *cognitive passwords* when discussing resetting passwords – these are opinion-based questions that a user answers during enrollment, such as 'What color was your first car?" This is *authentication by knowledge*, which could be a password, pin, cognitive password, personal history information, or *CAPTCHA*. CAPTCHA forces a person to enter information about a graphical image that is very difficult for computers to process, such as a photo of a house number, and the person must enter the correct string of digits. This proves that a real person is entering information instead of a computer-based automated process.

A *one-time password* (*OTP*) is – you guessed it – good for a one-time use only. If someone steals it as it is being entered, it does no good because it is immediately invalid. OTPs come in 2 types: asynchronous and synchronous, and in 3 formats – physical, a smartphone app or as a text message.

The physical format is called a *token device* and is a hand-held password generator with a small screen and sometimes a keyboard. It is a *synchronized device*, so it must be synchronized with the authentication server, with the result that both generate the same passwords simultaneously. The user will read the screen and type the password into some type of user interface (usually a web browser). Because the password is one-time only, it is good only for a short time. A _counter-synchronized device_ requires the user to push a button, forcing both the token device and the authentication service to advance to the next password. With either the synchronous or counter-synchronized method, both the device and the authentication services must share the same secret base key. To summarize, a synchronous token OTP device can be time-based, or counter based (also called _event-based_). The SecureID from RSA Security is the most common implementation of a time-based token.

An _asynchronous OTP_ method uses a challenge/response scheme, wherein the authentication service sends a random value called a _nonce_ to the user. The user enters the nonce into the token device, which encrypts the nonce with a secret key. The user then sends the encrypted nonce to the authentication service, which attempts to decrypt it with the shared secret key – if the original and encrypted nonce result in the same value, the user is authenticated.

When using a synchronous or asynchronous device, the obvious weakness is if someone gains access to the device. Requiring a pin to be entered into the device (something the user knows) before using the device to generate a token (something a person has) increases security – this is strong authentication. The token-generating devices are not susceptible to eavesdropping, sniffing or password guessing – at least until the user enters the value into a remote user interface, and the value travels over a network. Note that the device may be software running on some type of hardware not dedicated to being a token device, such as a smartphone app – in this case the token is called a _soft token_.

A highly-secure way to authenticate is to use a private/public key, or a digital certificate, also called a _cryptographic key_. We have covered this extensively when discussing PKI infrastructure, but let's quickly summarize in case you have forgotten how this could work. A user has both a public and private key. The authentication service provides a nonce, the user encrypts the nonce with their private key, sends the encrypted nonce and their digital certificate to the authentication service, which then decrypts the nonce using the public key from the digital certificate. If the decryption is successful, the service knows who is on the other end – the valid owner of the digital certificate.

A _passphrase_ is made up of multiple words, which is then reduced down via hashing or encryption into a simpler

from. In almost all cases, the only difference between using a password and a phrase is the 'reduction' step. A passphrase is considered more secure than a password because it is longer and easier for the user to remember.

Cards

There are two type of cards used for authentication. A _memory card_ is the simpler of the two, and is capable only of storing data. Examples are cards that are swiped to gain entrance through locked doors, magnetic ATM or credit cards. Stealing a memory card effectively means the thief can use the card with impunity. Many systems require the user to enter a PIN when using a memory card – the transaction is authorized only if the PIN matches the number stored on the card – this is considered 2-factor authentication. However, if the data contents of the memory card are not properly encrypted, it is often easy for a thief to read the card and discover the required PIN. Not that when entering a PIN the memory card does not process the PIN – an external authentication system must compare the PIN from the value residing on the card.

If you take a memory card and add a tiny computer, you wind up with a _smart card_. The most recent examples are credit cards containing on-board chips. One advantage a smart card has over memory cards is that a PIN number can be required before the data can be read – this on-board computer processes the PIN as opposed to a memory card which requires an external system to perform the validation. If tampering is detected, some smart cards will erase the information they contain. While smart cards cost more than simple memory cards, the decrease in fraudulent activities more than pays for the increased cost.

Because computers require power - even tiny ones – a method must exist to power the on-board chip without resorting to batteries which run out and add unwanted bulk. There are two methods used to power smart cards – contact and contactless. The first method is used with _contact cards_ – the card must be inserted into a reader which connects with the chip via an external contact point on the surface of the card – this provides power to the chip as well as establishes a 2-way communication path between the reader and card. The second is a _contactless_ card which has an antenna running the entire perimeter of the card – when the antenna comes very near an electromagnetic field, the field provides power and a communication path. This is an example of using _radio frequency identification_ (_RFID_), which usually is not encrypted due to the high-power processing requirements encryption normally requires. Smart cards may or may not employ encryption depending on their purpose.

In some cases, a card will have one chip but support both contact and contactless methods, and is called a *combi card*. Some cards will even have two chips – one for each contact method – and is called a *hybrid card*.

When used within organizations, the ability to standardize procedures inside of smart cards can be beneficial instead of having to roll out the same logic among multiple systems. However, the increased complexity does provide more opportunities for exploitation – remember, security loves simplicity. Smart-card specific attacks are usually carried out by inducing various conditions and watching how the card behaves. For example – enter a correct PIN, and then enter an incorrect PIN and note any differences. Some common attacks are:

- Non-invasive
    - Side-channel attacks – leave the environment alone and:
        - Differential power analysis – watch the power emissions during processing
        - Electromagnetic analysis – watch the frequencies emitted
        - *Timing* – watch how long a process takes
    - *Software attacks* - provide instructions that exploits a vulnerability
- Invasive
    - *Fault generation* – change the environment of the card (voltage, temperature, clock rate) and watch for differences
    - *Microprobing* – access the internal circuitry directly

Memory and Smart Cards have an IEEE standard – ISO 14443 which contains 3 sections:

- ISO 14443-1 – Physical attributes
- ISO 14443-2 – Initialization and anti-collision
- ISO 14443-3 – Transmission protocol

Authorization

Thus far we have covered the first two steps in implementing access control – identity and authentication. Both of the first steps work in tandem to ensure that the subject is who it claims to be. But once we, as a system implementing access control, believe you are who you claim to be, we now have to figure if you are allowed to carry out the action you are requesting – this is what *authorization* is all about.

Access Criteria

At the heart of authorization are access criteria – what are the rules used to determine if a subject has access to an object? *Roles* are a great way to represent access rights based on the tasks a subject might need to perform. For example, a front-desk receptionist might need to be able to search for employees and their office assignments, but it would not make sense to give her the ability to edit those employee accounts. Instead of associating a role directly with a subject, a *group* can be used instead to allow more effective management. For example, the receptionist might belong to the 'General Employee' group, which can perform employee searches as well as to enter time into a resource-tracking system.

For information that should only be accessed from certain devices, we can use physical or logical location to restrict access. *Physical location restriction* would be managed by restricting access to a device, while *logical location restrictions* might be based on an IP address. It often makes sense to restrict access based on the *time of day restrictions* – perhaps certain functions are accessible only during business hours or week days. *Temporal restrictions* would allow access based on an absolute date or time – for example, log in access is terminated after the employee's record indicates he no longer works at the company. *Transaction-type restrictions* limit access to features or data depending on the activity that the subject is engaged in. One example is a bank customer attempting to withdraw money more than twice in one day, or a retail employee requiring management approval for returns over $200.

Default to No Access

An important philosophy that all access control mechanisms should be built upon is to *default to no access*. Many systems assume that because most features should be available by default, the security model should also assume features are granted unless indicated otherwise. The problem with this type of behavior is that is a mistake is made and a sensitive feature is not explicitly dis-allowed, no one will know about it until an attack happens and the damage has already taken place. On the other hand, if a system implements the rule that no features are allowed unless explicitly indicated, two things will happen:

1) It will take more work to properly configure the system for the first time
2) There will be a significant drop in the number of accidental security 'holes'

The advantages of this approach far outweigh the additional configuration work required. Most _access control lists_ (_ACLs_) on routers and firewalls use the Default to No Access ruleset. _Need-to-know_ and _least-privilege_ are almost identical – both state that subjects should be given only just enough access to get a job done, and no more. Often, administrators will give users more access than they need to avoid having to tweak access every time the user's job description changes. _Authorization creep_ refers to the tendency for an employee to gain more and more access over time as she changes positions, even if the old levels of access are no longer needed. This is typically a result of the lack of well-defined tasks and roles that can be modeled in an access management system. As an employee changes roles, she should be removed from the current role/group and assigned to a new one that matches her new responsibilities. It is up to management to define these tasks and roles, and a security administrator is responsible for ensuring the roles and groups are assigned based on those management decisions. _Sarbanes-Oxley_ (_SOX_) is a regulatory law that requires review of this process on an annual basis.

Kerberos

One of the most common implementations for SSO revolves around a protocol called _Kerberos_. It was originally developed in the 1980s and is currently implemented on all major OSs, and many commercial non-OS products implement it as well. In a nutshell, Kerberos was designed to eliminate the need to send passwords across the network, uses shared keys as well as session keys, provides access controls and is the de facto standard in mixed networks. The main components in Kerberos are:

- Key Distribution Center (KDC) – the Kerberos server made up of:
    o Authentication Service (AS) – authenticates a principal
    o Ticket Granting Service (TGS) – creates a ticket for a principal
- _Principals_ - a user, application or network service
- _Tickets_ – proof of identity passed from principal to principal

The whole idea of Kerberos is that principals don't trust each other, but everyone trusts the KDC. So, if the KDC says 'Hey, I know this guy can be trusted, and since you trust me, you should trust this guy too' then everyone gets along. Let's say Bob (a principal) wants to log in and send something to a printer (another principal) – here is how that would work with Kerberos:

1. Bob logs into his Windows workstation
2. Bob's desktop sends his username to the KDC's AS, which looks up the associated password, generates a random session key, encrypts it with Bob's password and sends it back – this is an AS ticket
3. Bob's desktop will decrypt the session key using the password Bob entered – if successful, Bob has signed into his machine – now the KDC and Bob's desktop share a session key
4. Bob tries to send something to a printer
5. Bob's desktop sends the AS ticket obtained during login to the KDC's TGS and asks for a ticket allowing it to print to the printer
6. After the KDC validates Bob's AS ticket, the KDC's TGS generates a new random session key, and sends back two copies to Bob's desktop – one encrypted with Bob's secret key (Bob's password) and one encrypted with the printer's secret key. It also contains an _authenticator_* encrypted with the printer's secret key.
7. Bob's desktop receives this new print ticket, decrypts the session key using Bob's password, adds its own authenticator*, and sends the print ticket to the printer
8. The printer receives the ticket and decrypts the session key and the KDC's authenticator using its secret key; if the decryption succeeds, it knows the ticket came from the KDC; if the decrypted authenticator matches Bob's desktop authenticator*, it knows Bob's machine sent the message
9. The printer prints the document

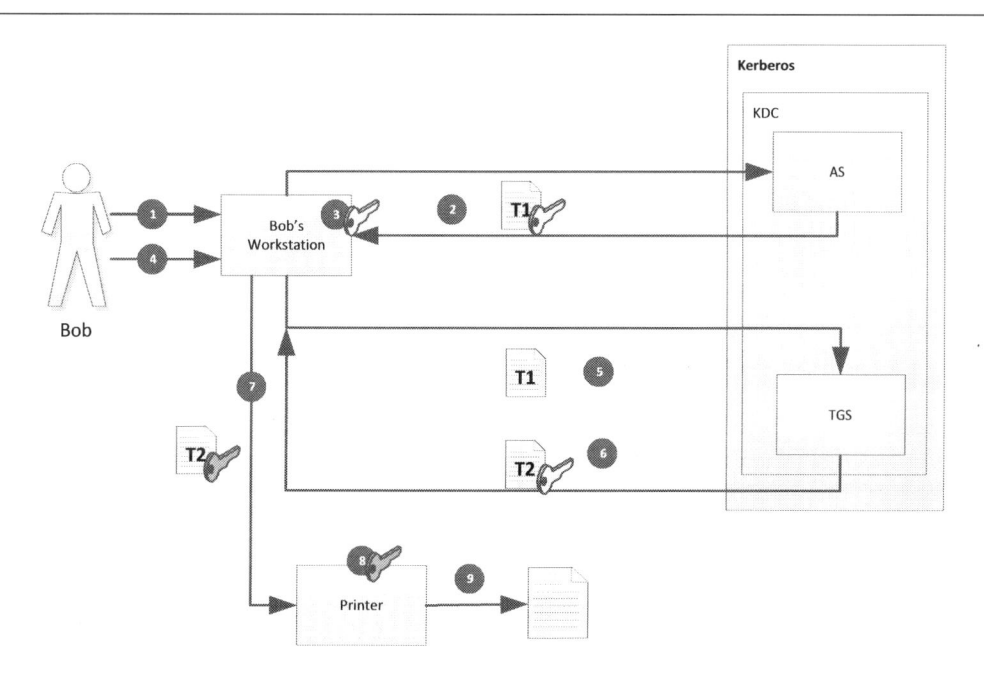

Figure 31: Kerberos Process

* An *authenticator* is simply a packet of data containing a principal's information, the principal's IP address, a timestamp and a sequence number; the timestamps and sequence numbers help protect against replay attacks.

For Kerberos, a set of principals is called a *realm*. A KDC can be responsible for one or more realms. So how does Kerberos help us implement SSO? By eliminating the need to authenticate multiple times. After the first system authenticates, it will use a ticket from then on to represent the user's identity and authentication. As the user moves from system to system, all we have to do is to pass the ticket along, and the authentication session will move with it.

Of course, no system is without weaknesses (mitigations are in parenthesis):

- The KDC can be a single point of failure (provide failover)
- The KDC can be a bottleneck (provide sufficient hardware)
- Both secret and shared keys are temporarily stored on machines acting on behalf of the principal and could be stolen (normal security precautions)

- Kerberos is susceptible to password guessing (OS will protect – see below)
- Data not in tickets are not encrypted (ensure network traffic is encrypted)
- Short keys can be susceptible to brute-force attacks (enforce long keys by policy and configuration)
- Kerberos requires all server and client clocks to be synchronized (normal network administration)

OSs always implement protection against password guessing attacks – that is why Kerberos does not include such protection. Proper security management will take care of clear-text data and key length problems. The 4 attributes for any authentication mechanism are:

1) *Transparent* (user should not be aware of it)
2) *Scalable* (does not create bottlenecks)
3) *Reliable* (no single point of failure)
4) *Secure* (provides authentication and confidentiality)

Security Domains

When dealing with resources that fall under the same security umbrella, we often talk in terms of *security domains*, which are simply logical groupings of resources that are managed by the same security policy and the same group who manages them. A resource within a security domain may be a physical asset such as a server or a network, data, subnets, or one or more processes. Security domains are usually segmented by the level of trust that subjects within that domain need, and are often arranged hierarchically. For example, a wireless user domain normally has very limited access, but a telecommuter domain has all access granted to the wireless user domain plus access to the intranet. The Payroll security domain will have all grants the telecommuter domain has plus access to employee records. Instead of having to define access levels from scratch for each domain, building upon lower domains is a much easier method, but does require forethought.

Federation

If you have ever signed into one site, and then visited a partner site owned by a different organization which used your same set of credentials, you just experienced a federated identity relationship. A *federated identity* is a portable identity (along with any access rights) that can be used across organizational boundaries. This is different than SSO, which is constrained to be used within an organization's own boundaries. A federation requires two organizations to enter into a partnership who share information in real-time. Many times, the end result of this partnership is a web portal – a single page that is made up of *portlets*, or browser-based plug-ins that are self-contained buckets of functionality, usually served up by different organizations. For all portlets to work correctly, they must all share the identity of the authenticated user and there must be a high level of trust between all owners of the portlets.

Access Control and Markup Languages

In the beginning (back in the 1980s) we had something called generalized markup language (GML), from which standard generalized markup language (SGML) was created, and from SGML we created hypertext markup language (HTML). We all know and love HTML – it is the standard on which all browsers operate. Later, these markup languages were gathered together under the eXtensible Markup Language (XML) umbrella. Today we commonly talk about HTML and XML – raw XML is almost always used for data representation, while HTML is normally used to create browser-based user interfaces.

Since XML is the granddaddy of all markup languages, it only makes sense that other languages other than HTML would evolve over time. In fact, when we discuss access control, *service provisioning markup language* (*SMPL*) will eventually come up. SMPL provides a vehicle for automated configuration of users and entitlements. It has 3 main entities:

- *Requesting authority* (*RA*) – the software sending a change request to a PSP
- *Provisioning service provider* (*PSP*) – the software that will validate and distribute the change request to one or more PSTs
- Provisioning service target (PST) – the system acting on the change request

For example, when a new employee is hired, an HR person will enter the information into an RA, which will create an SMPL message and send it to the PSP. The PSP will in turn examine the request, and if it is valid will forward it to all PSTs that need to carry out the tasks. Each PST will setup the requested account and apply the proper entitlement configuration. On termination of the employee, the same process is followed. SMPL is the language that is used to ensure consistent account management.

Another XML format used for real-time authentication in a federation is the *security assertion markup language* (*SAML*). The idea here is that if a user wants to authenticate with Party 1 using Party 2's credentials, SAML is used to carry out this request using the browser as the middle man. For example, if Sally wants to sign into Big Bob's website using her credentials from Little Jimmy's website, the following will take place:

1) Sally clicks the sign-in link on Big Bob's
2) Big Bob's website generates a SAML request, and redirects the browser to Little Jimmy's sign in page (the SAML request rides along)
3) Little Jimmy's web site accepts the SAML request, prompts Sally for her credentials, authenticates, returns the SAML response and redirects the browser back to Big Bob's website
4) Big Bob's website verifies the SAML response Little Jimmy's website sent and logs Sally in

Both websites obviously must have some sort of contractual agreement beforehand in order for this to work. But, even if we have an agreement in-place, what if the two sites are not configured the same, and their access policies are quite different? How does Big Bob's website figure out what Little Jimmy's website says that Sally can do if they do not speak the same language? This is where *extensible access control markup language* (*XACML*) comes in - it is a standardized way of communicating access rights and security policies.

Of course, SAML does not have to always go through a browser, and XACML is designed for direct server-to-server communication. Both SAML and XACML can use _web services_ – services that are accessible using HTTP across the web. There are two primary technologies used for HTTP web services:

- _Representational state transfer_ (_REST_) – a very simple format that has low overhead but provides no security
- _Simple object access protocol_ (_SOAP_) – a very heavy format that has considerable security built in

SOAP and REST are not used together – you choose one or the other. Because of its simplicity, REST is starting to overtake SOAP, except for industries where security is very important (such as for banks). How does SAML, HTTP and SOAP/REST work together? SAML is wrapped in SOAP/REST, which is transmitted over HTTP.

Effective web services are usually patterned after a _service oriented approach_ (_SOA_). SOA is not a technology, but rather a pattern for creating independent services across business domains that can work together. For example, a company may have a set of HR SOA web services built on Microsoft .Net, and another set of Java-based SOA web services for IT infrastructure. Because they both follow the SOA pattern, they look the same and can easily be integrated into other applications – in fact, if done properly applications have no idea they are running on 2 completely different platforms.

OpenID
Going back to Sally's authentication predicament for a moment, let's say that Big Bob and Little Jimmy don't know or trust each other, but they want to create a great user experience for Sally. How can they both leverage the same set of credentials without having to trust each other? This sounds a lot like PKI – no one trusts anyone else but the CA. As it turns out, _OpenID_ is the solution, and it does act like a CA in this scenario. OpenID uses a communication method very similar to SAML by defining the following 3 entities:

- End user – Sally
- Resource party – Big Bob or Little Jimmy
- _OpenID provider_ – the system in which Sally already has an account, and which Big Bob and Little Jimmy both support

If you have ever tried to sign into a site and one of the options was to authenticate using your Facebook credentials, you just saw OpenID in action. In your example, Facebook was the OpenID provider, you were the end user, and the resource party was the site you were trying to sign into.

It is important to note that OpenID was designed to solve the authentication problem, but does not have anything to say about authorization. That is why the _OAuth_ standard was created – it allows a website to access authorization information contained in another website. For example, using OAuth, Sally can let Big Bob's website access her order history on Little Jimmy's website – assuming both sites support OAuth. The flow can be a little complicated:

1) Sally visits Big Bob's website and clicks a link indicating that she wants to allow Big Bob to access her order history on Little Jimmy's website
2) Big Bob redirects the browser to Little Jimmy's website, where Little Jimmy asks Sally to give permission
3) Sally selects the access she wants Big Bob to have to Little Jimmy's information
4) Little Jimmy's website sends an authorization code to Big Bob's website
5) Big Bob's website returns the authorization code (and proves to Little Jimmy that it is Big Bob's website talking) to Little Jimmy's website
6) Little Jimmy's website records the authorization; Sally can revoke this authorization at any time by visiting Little Jimmy's website
7) Little Jimmy's site redirects Sally back to Big Bob's site

OAuth2 (OAuth version 2) combines both authentication and authorization, and is quickly supplanting the need for OpenID.

Identity Services
More companies are beginning to outsource identity management to _Identity as a Service_ (_IaaS_) providers. IaaS normally offers SSO, federated IdM and password-management services. While this relieves the subscribing company of a lot of effort, it does have its drawbacks:

- Some regulated industries may be in non-compliance as the provider may not be able to meet all regulatory requirements
- IdM is among the most sensitive data a company maintains – and that data just moved outside of the company's own control
- Integration of legacy applications is not always straightforward or even possible

Regardless of whether a company implements identity services in-house or outsources it, two key objectives must be considered:

- Connectivity – all connection points must be encrypted and monitored via IDS/IPS – only IdM traffic should pass through these connection points; firewalls and PKI must be properly configured
- Incremental rollout – implement a portion and test before continuing – this will uncover unforeseen issues and help isolate where a problem is occurring

Chapter 45: Identification, Authentication, Authorization, and Accountability

Questions

1. Which of the following creates a ticket for a Kerberos principal?

    A) KDC

    B) DAS

    C) AS

    D) TGS

2. Which attack sniffs network traffic or records keystrokes?

    A) Electronic surveillance

    B) Electronic monitoring

    C) Hidden recording

    D) Packet sniffing

3. Which of the following password management techniques allows multiple systems to use a common authentication mechanism?

    A) Password synchronization

    B) Assisted password reset

    C) Self-service password reset

    D) Single sign on

4. Which of the following is NOT a step required to properly implement access control?

    A) Authorization

    B) Authentication

    C) Access

    D) Identification

5. Which of the following best describes a contactless card that is normally not encrypted due to power requirements?

    A) Hybrid card

    B) Contact card

    C) Contactless card

    D) RFID

Chapter 46: Access Control Models

To this point we have referenced 'access controls' quite a bit, but have never really talked about what that term means. In short, to 'control access' means to enforce the rules and objectives of a given model – of course, you can't really control access until you know what the rules are. An _access control model_ defines those rules and how they are applied to subjects and objects. There are 5 different models to choose from, and we will visit all of them in turn. It is important to know that the model is implemented in the kernel of all operating systems, and which model an organization chooses is very dependent upon their prioritized business model. In other words, the chosen access control model should reflect the organization's priorities.

Discretionary Access Control

The first model is called _discretionary access control_ (_DAC_). If you have used a common desktop operating system such as Windows, OS X or Linux, you have used DAC. For example, you create a Word document and place it on a network share that only you can get to, but you want James in Accounting to see it – so you edit the network shares' properties and add James' account as read-only. You have just adjusted access at your own 'discretion'. DAC allows each user to control access to anything that user owns. If you give 'full control' rights to another person, then that person effectively 'owns' that object as well. Rights can be given to either named users or groups. Desktops commonly allow the following access permissions:

- No Access
- Read (r)
- Write (w)
- Execute (x)
- Delete (d)
- Change (c)
- Full Control

DAC internally operates using _access control lists_ (_ACLs_). An ACL for an object contains a list of subjects who may access the object, and the permissions available for that subject. ACLs with DAC systems are commonly inheritable – an ACL for a parent is automatically applied to children as they are added. The inheritance can always be overridden, but is normally automatically applied. DAC systems also provide a lot of flexibility, but at the expense of security. For example, if a user accidentally installs malware, then that malware can act as if it was the currently logged-in user.

Mandatory Access Control

The opposite of discretionary is _nondiscretionary_, which means that the user cannot make any decisions on access. On this end of the spectrum from DAC we have _mandatory access controls_ (_MAC_), in which users have absolutely no ability to change the level of access granted to other users. MAC systems are usually only found in highly-sensitive areas where security is paramount, such as in government systems. Every subject and object contains a _security label_ (also sometimes called _sensitivity labels_), which provides two pieces of information:

- A single classification (clearance level)
- One or more categories

Classifications and clearance levels have the same possible values – but when dealing with subjects the usual term is 'clearance level' and when dealing with objects it is 'classification' – when referring to both we will use the term 'classification'. Classifications are hierarchical (such as top secret, secret, confidential, etc.), and the level above is more trusted than the level below. If a MAC system allows a subject to access an object at a different classification, the system is called a _multilevel security system_ (_MLS_). In these cases, a subject can access an object if the subject's security clearance _dominates_ the object's classification (the object's classification is at or below the subject's clearance).

Categories can contain any number of values and can change over time. However, they usually map to departments, projects or management levels, and provide the vehicle to enforce need-to-know rules. For example, if an object has a classification of 'secret', it does not mean any subject with a clearance of 'secret' should be allowed access to the object – access should be granted only if the subject and object have at least one category in-common.

Care must be taken in MAC systems when communication takes place between two systems with different levels of security – for example, when a system with a lower security level communicates with a system having a higher security level. In such cases, hardware or _software-based guards_ should be put in place to monitor the exchange of information and ensure only appropriate data is transferred between the two systems. A guard between email servers is a common use of this precaution.

An operating system cannot switch from DAC to MAC – it is one or the other. _SE Linux_ is a MAC OS released by the NSA and SecureComputing. _Trusted Solaris_ is another common MAC system. Because users within a MAC system cannot install software, malware is much less of a threat, but at the cost of significantly decreased usability. This is why MAC systems are very specific in nature to high-sensitivity environments.

Role-Based Access Control

While DAC provides maximum flexibility for the user, it also makes centralized management and enforcing security policies a headache. MAC over-rotates by taking away virtually all flexibility in favor of centralized management and enforcing security policies.

So, what if we modified DAC just a little to find some common middle-ground by:

- Taking away ACLs (that fixes out-of-control security policies)
- Only allow centrally managed groups (users can no longer create them)

We are left with something called _role-based access control_ (_RBAC_), where a role is nothing but a DAC group that only an administrator can manage. A role represents a task within an organization, and rights (permissions) are no longer assigned via an ACL to a user – rights are assigned directly to a role, and users are assigned to a role. This means that rights are then assigned _implicitly_ to users via a role instead of _explicitly_ via an ACL. RBAC is a great fit for companies with a high turn-over rate – instead of having to figure out what a new employee should have access to the administrator just assigns them to a role that fits their tasks.

There are two components to RBAC. The first is the _core RBAC_, which is included with every RBAC implementation as it is the very foundation of the model. When a user logs in (referred to as creating a _session_), the core RBAC will gather all possible roles and permissions granted via those roles and make them available for access decisions. Because this is a centralized process, other factors such as time of day or day of the week can be used to limit or extend the permission set.

The second component is the _hierarchical RBAC_, and allows the administrator to model the roles based on the actual organizational structure. The benefit of such a model is that we can then apply a hierarchical relationship between the roles to make management even easier. For example, a 'dock worker' role can access lock codes for loading bay doors, and the 'manifest clerk' role can enter shipping data. A dock supervisor role would inherit access rights from both the 'dock worker' and the 'manifest clerk' roles plus additional rights. Hierarchical RBAC comes in 2 flavors:

- _Limited hierarchies_ – inheritance only once (Role 1 inherits from Role 2 but not from any other role)
- _General hierarchies_ – inheritance is allowed for multiple levels simultaneously (Role 1 inherits from Role 2 AND from Role 3)

Separation of duties is an important security tool to prevent fraud, and hierarchical RBAC can help in 2 ways:

- _Static separation of duty_ (_SSD_) – constrains the combination of privileges (for example a user cannot be a member of both 'dock worker' and 'manifest clerk')
- _Dynamic separation of duty_ (_DSD_) – constrains the combination of privileges that can be active within the same session (for example a user can belong to both 'dock worker' and 'manifest clerk', but not at the same time)

RBAC can be managed in 4 different manners:

- _Non-RBAC_ – no roles; users are mapped directly to applications and no roles are used
- _Limited RBAC_ – roles + no roles; users are mapped to multiple roles as well as being mapped to application that do not have role-based support
- _Hybrid RBAC_ – pseudo roles; users are mapped to roles for multiple applications with only selected rights assigned
- _Full RBAC_ – enterprise roles; users are mapped to enterprise roles

DAC, MAC and RBAC do not really provide a good vehicle for protecting data such as PHI or PII within a given sensitivity level, but a version of RBAC called _privacy-aware RBAC_ does.

Attribute-Based Access Control

RBAC is a good compromise between DAC and MAC, but we still have one problem – the flexibility of decisions is still mostly centered on membership in a given role. While we did say that RBAC has some limited ability to take into consideration other factors such as time of day and day of week, when we dive into more complex scenarios such as 'If the user is a member of group A and the file has not been accessed in the last 3 days and the user has not transferred more than 30 MB in the last 24 hours and the company is not currently under attack by Godzilla, then...' – well, RBAC is just out of luck.

This is when we bring in our last access control model, called *attribute-based access control,* or *ABAC*. This approach is sometimes called rule-based role-based access control, or RB-RBAC, and is built right on top of RBAC by extending the capabilities to include if...then coding. The model can completely ignore the identity of the user if it likes, whereas the other models must examine the identity. ABAC uses policies that look at a combination of attributes to arrive at the level of access a given user will be provided. Each attribute can come from a variety of sources, such as users, resources, objects, or environments. The policy will dictate the attributes to look at, along with how each attribute value is consumed. As an example, a policy could dictate that read access for a given resource is granted only if a user has an 'Administrator' flag set, the resource does not have its 'Top Secret' flag set, and the computer from which the request is coming from is NOT part of the 'Guest' domain. Just remember – the primary difference between ABAC and RBAC is that ABAC uses policies that can be simple or complex, whereas RBAC uses roles only.

Questions

1. Which term represents a definition of access rules and how they are applied to subjects and objects?

    A) Authorization approval models

    B) Access control models

    C) Security access models

    D) Authentication approval models

2. What term means that an object's classification is at or below the subject's clearance, and can therefore be accessed?

    A) Dominate

    B) Accessible

    C) Permissible

    D) Allow

3. Within RBAC, what concept constrains the combination of privileges that can be active within the same session?

    A) General hierarchies

    B) SSD

    C) DSD

    D) Limited hierarchies

4. Which access control model extends capabilities to include if...then coding?

    A) ABAC

    B) RBAC

    C) MAC

    D) DAC

5. What RBAC component allows the roles to be modeled on an actual organizational structure?

    A) Core RBAC

    B) Hierarchical RBAC

    C) Access RBAC

    D) Tree RBAC

Chapter 47: Administrating Access Control

Techniques and Technologies

Once we have figured out which access control model we want to use, the next step is to put into place technologies and techniques that will support that access control model. There are 4 considerations that should be examined.

The first is the user interface that can limit a user's ability to access data or functionality – this is called a *constrained user interface*. The primary methods for constraining a user interface are:

- *Menu* – limit the options the user can chose from
- *Shell* – limit the commands available when a shell (virtual environment) opens
- *Database view* – limit the data that can be viewed by creating a virtual view of the data
- *Physical constraint* – limit the physical controls the user can access such as keys or touch-screen buttons

The second is an *access control matrix* that is a table of subjects and objects on opposite axis – the intersection of each row and column dictates the level of access a subject has to the object. This is normally used with DAC systems, and there are 2 types of matrices that can be used. A *capability table* specifies the rights a subject has to a specific object, and a *capability* can take the form of a token, ticket or key. Kerberos is an example of a capability table system. When a subject wants to access an object, it presents a *capability component* (the name of the object, for example) to the system, which will then return a capability representing the rights the subject has to the object. This is the same as a user's machine asking the KDC TGS to create a ticket (capability) so the machine can talk to the printer (capability component) – the KDC TGS uses a capability table to determine access. The second type of matrices that can be used is an ACL (access control list). It is important to understand the fundamental difference between a capability table and an ACL:

- Capability table – for a given subject and a given object, the subject's access rights for that object
- ACL – for a given object, a list of all subjects and their corresponding rights

So, a given capability table will contain the same number of ACLs as there are objects – one ACL for each object, and each ACL will contain a list of all subjects with the subject's rights to the

	File A	File B	File C
Larry	Read	Full	Read
Moe	Read, Write	Full	Read, Write
Curly	Full	No Access	No Access

Figure 32: Access Control Matrix

	File A	File B	File C
Larry	Read	Full	Read
Moe	Read, Write	Full	Read, Write
Curly	Full	No Access	No Access

Figure 33: Capability Table

	File A	File B	File C
Larry	Read	Full	Read
Moe	Read, Write	Full	Read, Write
Curly	Full	No Access	No Access

Figure 34: ACL

object to which the ACL applies. A capability table is represented by a row while an ACL is represented by a column.

The third consideration for access control techniques is to control access based on the content of an object – this is called *content-based access control*. An example this technique is to filter a database view based on the values contained within a record. Email filters employ this technique when searching email text for keywords such as 'social security number', 'confidential' or 'secret'. Filtering web content can also be done to determine if employees are engaged in non-approved behavior.

One drawback to content-based access control is that the technique has no context on which to base decisions. For example, a web page that is flagged for containing the word 'craps' may not be considered gambling if the site is recognized as being from 'www.amazon.com'. *Context-*

based access controls can dig deeper to understand the context in which information is being used. Stateful firewalls use this technique to determine if a SYN attack is underway. Another use for this technique is to prevent a user from being able to piece together information he should not have access to based on seemingly-innocuous data bits. For example, the following bits of information do not seem to be overly-sensitive:

- The company recently reported a 30% drop in revenue
- The CEO is meeting tomorrow with individuals from a competitor from overseas
- Yesterday a board meeting was scheduled for tonight

However, someone who is paying attention may recognize that a hostile takeover is in the works and use this inside information to leak news to the media. A context-based access control system could recognize that a single individual searched for this information all within 2 hours and prevent information from being revealed.

Management

Now that we have selected the access control techniques and technologies, we need to figure out how an organization will manage the access control model. We have two choices – centralized or decentralized.

Centralized Access Control Administration

The _centralized access control administration_ method requires that a single individual or department control all access to resources. While this ensures a consistent method to controlling access, it also becomes a bottleneck to request changes as that single entity must process all requests. We are about to discuss in detail several methods of implementing a centralized control method, and each of them follow the _AAA_ protocol – authentication, authorization and auditing.

Remote authentication dial-in user service (_RADIUS_) is a well-established network protocol that provides authentication and authorization services to remote clients. It is normally used in conjunction with an access server that communicates directly with a client desiring remote connectivity. The process follows:

1) A remote client contacts the access server via PPP and provides credentials
2) The access server forwards the credentials to the RADUIS server using the RADIUS protocol
3) After the RADIUS server authenticates and authorizes the client, the access server assigns an IP address to the client

RADIUS has served its purpose well, but there are several design limitations. For example, it uses UDP for communication, so it must contain a considerable amount of overhead to ensure proper delivery of data over a connectionless protocol. RADIUS combines the authentication and authorization steps together, which effectively reduces flexibility in how those processes are implemented outside of RADIUS. Passwords are encrypted when communicating between the access server and the RADIUS server, but all other data is sent in clear text, which is an invitation for replay attacks. Only the PPP protocol is supported and RADIUS is implemented in a client/server architecture, which means that only the client can initiate communication – the server has to wait until someone pays attention to it before it can speak. Access control systems normally implement a flexible list of permissions called _attribute value pairs_ (_AVPs_), and RADIUS is no different – bit it does not support a very large number of AVPS, and so it is useful only for answering an allow-or-deny question, not for more granular rights.

A competing standard, the terminal access controller access control system (TACACS) protocol, really did not address any of the issues that RADIUS has. However, extended TACACS (XTACACS) separated the authentication and authorization steps, so that helped a little. But things got a lot better with the last version of TACAS, called simply TACACS+. Because TACACS+ is not backwards-compatible with TACACS or XTACACS, it really is not simply a new version, but it does provide everything the originals had plus a whole lot more. It started using TCP instead of UDP, so all that connection-oriented overhead was removed from the standard. all data between the client and server started to be encrypted (instead of just the password), and it supported a very large number of AVPs – this meant that it could support very granular access rights instead of just an allow/deny answer. Instead of just PPP, TACACS+ allowed other protocols such as AppleTalk, NetBIOS and IPX. Support for 2-factor authorization was finally added, as well as one-time (dynamic) passwords. It still was based on a client/server model, however.

More recently, a new protocol called _Diameter_ has been gaining traction. Diameter is meant to replace RADIUS – the name implies it is much better because a 'diameter is twice the radius' – these people were being really clever. Diameter provided pretty much all advantages of TACACS+ with quite a few additional features – so you can assume that if TACACS+ had it, so does Diameter. It is based on a peer-to-peer model, so the server can initiate communication with Diameter clients at any time. While it is not backwards-compatible with RADIUS or TACACS+, it does provide a clear upgrade path and brings much better network stability due to added error handling. This new protocol divided its functionality into two components – the base protocol and extensions.

The base protocol provides the following:

- Secure communication between Diameter entities
- Feature discovery
- Version negotiation
- Header formats
- Security options
- A list of commands
- A large number of AVPs

The *extensions* component allows different technologies to leverage the protocol using AAA. It supports authentication for VoIP, Fax over IP (FoIP), Mobile IP, wireless and cellular traffic. For each of the As in AAA, Diameter provides the following support:

- Authentication
    - PAP, CHAP, EAP
    - End-to-end encryption
    - Replay attack protection
- Authorization
    - Supports redirects, secure proxies, relays, and brokers
    - Reauthorization on-demand
    - Unsolicited disconnects
    - State reconciliation
- Auditing
    - Reporting, roaming operations (ROAMOPS) accounting, monitoring

We just mentioned Mobile IP – let's take a second to define what that is. *Mobile IP* is a technology that allows a mobile device to move from network to network without changing its IP address. That might not make sense at first, since by definition two networks must have different IP addresses, but this is supported by assigning a quasi-permanent *home IP address* to the mobile device that all traffic can be sent to. The Mobile IP server tracks the current address of the mobile device, called the *care-of address*, and forwards all traffic sent to the home IP address to the care-of address in real-time.

Decentralized Access Control Administration
A company may decide that the decisions on who has access to what are better made by the various individuals or departments who are closest to the 'what'. In other words, I own some data, so shouldn't I know best who has need to access the data? If properly managed, this information access could be funneled through a centralized process as we just discussed, but a central process can add considerable overhead. May organizations decide to trust the data owners to take care of managing access, and implement *decentralized access control administration*. This removes potential bottlenecks and red tape, but for larger organizations can significantly increase the likelihood that employees will gain unneeded access, and that when an employee leaves the company, the ability of that ex-employee to access data or services will not be properly removed.

Methods

Access controls come in many forms, shapes and sizes, but all fit within 1 of 3 categories – administrative, physical or technological. It is important to be able to identify the category each fits into.

Administrative controls deal with personnel policies, employee training and periodic testing to make sure all controls are in-place and effective. Senior management is responsible for providing the security goals but delegates the actual implementation. They also indicate the personnel controls that should be used, and specify how testing of the controls are to be carried out. Some administrative controls are:

- *Policies and procedures* – confirms the existence of appropriate policies and procedures, and that they are well-documented and kept up-to-date
- *Personnel controls* – covers the hiring, promotion, movement, suspension, and termination of employees; addresses how employees should interact with the various security mechanisms and what will happen if an employee does not follow the policies
- *Supervisory controls* – ensures that every employee has a supervisor, and that supervisor is responsible for the employee's actions
- *Security-awareness training* – recognizes that people are the weakest link, so employees need to understand the proper use of security controls, why they exist and the consequences of bypassing them

- *Testing* – defines how often periodic testing will be carried out; tests include drills to test physical disruptions (such as network or power outages), penetration testing for various applications, quizzing employees to vet policy knowledge and the required review of procedures to ensure relevancy

<u>Physical controls</u> must work in tandem with both administrative and technical controls, and deal with physically securing assets such as:

- *Network segregation* – designing a network to require all hardware to be placed in a restricted area behind secured doors, normally requiring access cards
- *Perimeter security* – provides protection for individuals, facilities and components inside the facilities by requiring identification badges, closed-circuit TV (CCTV), fences, deterrent lighting, motion detectors, window and door sensors, and alarms; the location and appearance of a building can also act as an indirect deterrent
- *Computer controls* – protects computer hardware by providing cover locks, removal of USB and optical drives to prevent unauthorized copying, and dampening of electrical emissions to prevent wireless eavesdropping
- *Work area separation* – restricting physical access to a walled-off area to only a few authorized people; for example, labs, server rooms, wiring closets, vaults, etc.
- *Data backups* – providing a secure method for the transfer and storage of data backups

- *Cabling* – properly shielded to prevent emissions and crosstalk, and concealed to prevent tampering and physical damage, either purposeful or accidental
- *Control zones* – division of the physical facility into security zones with applicable access controls

<u>Technical controls</u> may have a hardware component, but almost always have a software component, and are used to restrict access. The control may live in the kernel of an OS, as an add-on package or application on top of the OS, inside of network devices, and as protocols or encryption mechanisms. It could also be the implementation of access control matrices working at multiple OSI layers. Technical controls ensure confidentiality, integrity and availability. Areas include:

- *System access* – includes access control models (MAC/DAC/RBAC/RB-RBAC), username/password mechanisms, Kerberos implementations, biometrics devices, PKI, or RADIUS/TACACS/TACACS+/Diameter servers
- *Network architecture* – logically separating network components by using subnets and DMZs; implementing IDS/IPS
- *Network access* – logical access controls implemented in routers, switches, firewalls, and gateways
- *Encryption and protocols* – preserves the confidentiality and integrity of data, and enforces specific paths for communication
- *Auditing* – tracking activity within a network, network device or computer; auditing is not proactive or reactive, but is used to point out weaknesses to be fixed

Questions

1. When dealing with TACACS+, which of the following is everything but AAA?

    A) Segments

    B) Byproduct

    C) Base protocol

    D) Extensions

2. Which of the following is a flexible list of permissions implemented by access control systems?

    A) AVP

    B) RADIUS

    C) TACACS

    D) XTACACS

3. When controlling access, which approach uses the UI to limit a user's ability to access data or functionality?

    A) Limited user interface

    B) Constrained user interface

    C) Access control matrix

    D) Content-based access control

4. When using an access control matrix, which of the following is an object that a subject wishes to access?

    A) Capability component

    B) Capability

    C) Capability module

    D) Capability table

5. Which constrained user interface limits the commands available when a virtual environment opens?

    A) Database views

    B) Shells

    C) Physical constraints

    D) Menus

Chapter 48: Accountability and Implementing Access Control

Accountability

Accountability is the result of implementing audit tracking – recording the who, what, when, and where of activity within a company's infrastructure. Accountability allows the company to:

- Detect intrusions
- Track unauthorized activities back to the user
- Reconstruct events and system conditions
- Create problem reports
- Provide material for legal actions

Audit logs usually contain a huge amount of information, but are only of value if the data can be filtered down to the pertinent information. Auditing captures three data points (with examples):

- User actions
    - Logon attempts
    - Security violations
    - Resources and services used
    - Commands executed
- Application events
    - Error messages
    - Files modified
    - Security violations
- System activities
    - Performance
    - Logon attempts (ID, date/time)
    - Lockouts of users and terminals
    - Use of utilities
    - Files altered
    - Peripherals accessed

From an availability standpoint, the logs allow system administrators to monitor the health of a system or application, as well as to reconstruct events that lead to a system crash. From a security perspective, the logs can be used to alert the administrator to suspicious activities to be investigated at a later time, and after an attack has occurred, they can be informative on how long/far an attack went on and what damage may have been done.

One of the most common tactics for an attacker is to *scrub* logs as the last step of carrying out an intrusion. The attacker will try and remove any information from log files that will alert an administrator to his presence or activity.

That is why it is important to properly protect log files by implementing the following best practices:

- Store on a remote host (not where the log file is generated)
- No one should be able to view, modify or delete log files except for an administrator
- Integrity must be ensured by using digital signatures, hashing and implementing proper access controls
- Loss of the data must be prevented by secure storage and committing to write-once media (such as CD-ROM)
- Any unauthorized attempt to access logs should be captured and reported
- A chain of custody should be securely stored to prove who had access to audit logs and when for legal reasons

More severe possibilities that can be warranted in some very security-conscious environments include:

- Implement *simplex communication* – this is physically severing the "receive" pairs in an Ethernet cable to force one-way communication only to prevent retrieval of log information by the source who is writing the data
- Replicate log files to ensure a backup in case of deletion of the primary copy
- Implement *cryptographic hash chaining* - each log entry contains the hash of the previous entry, allowing the removal or modification of previous entries to become detectable

Clipping refers to applying the proper level of filtering such that only important details are logged – this reduces the impact of logging on system/application performance and keeps log file sizes down. Once the proper logs are being automatically generated, they must be reviewed to gain insight. There are three types of reviews:

- *Event-oriented* – results from a disruption or security breach
- *Audit trails* – periodic reviews to detect unusual behaviors from users, applications or systems
- *Real-time analysis* – an automated system correlates logs from various systems (SEM or SIEM)

Even with proper clipping, logs are usually very verbose. An *audit-reduction tool* discards irrelevant data to make reviews easier. When dealing with multiple systems, companies often use a *security event management* (*SEM*) or *security information and event management* (*SIEM*) system to automate the sifting and correlation of all logs - which are usually in different formats - resulting in reports or alerts that the company is interested in. This results in a *situational awareness*, or the ability to make sense of the current state despite a large number of data points and complex relationships.

Keystroke monitoring deserves a special mention. This technique captures each keystroke on a keyboard and records the resulting characters in a file. This type of logging is unusual, and is normally only done in cases in which an employee is suspected of wrong-doing. It can be implemented either through software or by using a hardware *dongle* – a device inserted between a wired keyboard connection and the computer. Companies must use this logging method with care, because it can constitute a violation of an employee's privacy if it has not been clearly spelled out in some type of employee training or an on-screen banner that monitoring of this type may take place. Attackers often use the same technique to capture credentials, but are almost always implemented through a Trojan horse.

Implementation

Once access controls are put into place, they must be maintained. Following is a list of 'must do' items that span the range of controls – these are best practices:

- Ensure that access criteria is well-defined and strict
- Enforce need-to-know and least-privilege patterns
- Reduce and monitor any type of unlimited access
- Look for and remove redundant access rules, user accounts and roles
- Audit user, application and system logs on a recurring basis
- Protect audit logs properly
- Only known and non-anonymous accounts should be given access
- Limit and monitor usage by highly-privileged accounts
- Enforce lockouts after unsuccessful login attempts
- Never leave default passwords
- Make sure that passwords are required to be changed periodically, only strong passwords are allowed, are not shared and are always encrypted both in-transit and at-rest
- Ensure accounts are removed that are no longer required after an employee leaves
- Suspend inactive accounts after 30 to 60 days
- Disable ports, feature and services that are not absolutely required

Most security measures around networks and computer systems are designed to prevent unauthorized disclosure of information. The most common attacks to circumvent access controls are:

- Social engineering
- Covert channels
- Malicious code
- Sniffing (wired and wireless)
- Object reuse (not properly erasing previous contents)
- Capturing electromagnetic emissions

Let's dive into the last item - capturing electromagnetic emissions – a little more in-depth. All electrical equipment will produce some amount of electromagnetic noise. There are actual cases in which an intruder has been able to capture the data displayed on a computer monitor by listening to the 'noise' it produces. More recently, the ability to capture keystrokes simply by watching how hand movements interrupt Wi-Fi signals is being explored.

To combat this risk, the Department of Defense (DoD) created the *TEMPEST* standard. Any equipment that meets this standard limits electrical emissions by wrapping the product in a metal shield called a *Faraday cage* - this cage prevents the signals from leaking out. This is a very expensive process and only highly-secured installations such as government facilities normally use this technology. There are two alternatives to TEMPEST – white noise and control zones. *White noise* is created when random electrical signals are created across the entire communication band. An attacker is unable to distinguish valid signals from the background noise. The other mitigation approach is to house rooms or perhaps even buildings in a Faraday cage, instead of individual pieces of equipment, resulting in a *control zone* from which usable signals cannot escape.

Questions

1. Which term describes an attacker deleting log file entries after an attack?

A) Erasing

B) Scouring

C) Scrubbing

D) Cleaning

2. Which of the following tools provides the ability to make sense of the current state in spite of a large number of data points and complex relationships?

A) SEM

B) Situational awareness

C) Dongle

D) Audit-reduction tool

3. What term best describes applying the proper level of filtering such that only important details are logged?

A) Elimination

B) Elevated filtering

C) Clipping

D) Snipping

4. Which term best describes the result of implementing audit tracking?

A) Secure stance

B) Awareness

C) Traceability

D) Accountability

5. Which type of log review uses an automated capability to correlate logs from multiple systems?

A) Real-time analysis

B) Event-oriented

C) Exceptional event

D) Audit trail

Chapter 49: Monitoring and Reacting to Access Control

Some access controls are designed to detect and protect assets. There are three primary types of technological tools designed specifically for this task – Intrusion Detection Systems (IDSs), Intrusion Protection Systems (IPSs), and honeypots.

An *intrusion detection system* (*IDS*), simply put, detects intrusion attempts, which are the unauthorized use of, or attack upon, a network or devices attached to the network. An IDS is a passive component that does not take any action other than generating alerts. It looks for passing traffic that is suspicious, or monitors logs in real-time, and any anomalous behavior can trigger an alarm. IDSs always contain 3 components:

- *Sensor* – collects information which is sent to the analyzer
- *Analyzer* – looks for suspicious activity and sends alerts to the administration interface
- *Administration interface* – processes alerts, which can result in an email, text message, phone call, a visual alert on a screen or sending a message to some other system

An IDS is used to alert an administrator to an on-going attack or to produce data after-the-fact that can be used to:

- Highlight vulnerabilities in a network
- Expose techniques used by an attacker
- Produce evidence for subsequent legal action

There are 3 types of IDSs – network-based, host-based and application-based.

A *Network-based IDS* (*NIDS*) watches network traffic. Its sensors are dedicated hardware devices or software installed on a server, but in either case an NIDS requires the sensor to have a NIC that is in *promiscuous mode*, which captures all traffic whether it was intended for that device or not. The sensor *sniffs* packets as they pass by, and uses a *protocol analyzer* (a fancy name for software that understands various protocols) to examine each packet based on the protocol the packet is using. NIDSs cannot see anything going on inside of a server or workstation – it can only view network traffic.

A *Host-based IDS* (*HIDS*) is the exact opposite – it cannot see network traffic, but can see pretty much anything it wants to that goes on inside of an operating system running on a 'host' computer. It is always some type of software installed on the host, and watches for anything suspicious happening on that machine, such as system file deletion, reconfiguration of important settings or other actions the HIDS is configure to monitor. Because of the high cost of maintenance and the amount of resources required to run, HIDS are normally installed only on servers.

Even more specific are *Application-based IDSs* (*AIDS*), which, as the name implies, are very specific to certain software applications running on a host. AIDSs have very intimate knowledge of the inner-workings of a given application, and don't worry about anything happening outside of that application. AIDSs are useful if the application uses encryption that would hide activity from NIDS or HIDS.

Let's focus in on the NIDS for a while. It supports 3 different detection types – signature-based, anomaly-based and rule-based.

A *signature-based* (also known as *knowledge-based* or *pattern-matching*) IDS is the most popular detection type, but requires that its 'signatures' be constantly updated in order to remain effective, which means that it cannot detect 'zero-day' attacks. This detection type simply compares traffic patterns in real-time to a list of patterns known to represent an attack, and if a match is found it will generate an alert. The known patterns represent attacks seen 'in the wild' – meaning they have already been encountered in production environments. The vendor of the IDS is responsible for collecting these signatures and continuously disseminating updates to all its devices currently running (this requires a subscription – meaning that it costs money to keep the IDS up-to-date).

The great thing about signature-based IDSs is that they have a very low false-positive (reporting that an attack is underway when there really is not one happening), and the IDS can provide a ton of information on an attack when one is detected. The downside is that the false-negative (missing a real attack) runs very high, especially if the list of signature profiles is not constantly kept up-to-date. This is why signature-based IDSs cannot detect new attacks – because a signature has not yet been created for it. Examples of attacks that a signature-based IDS can detect are a *Land attack* where the source and destination IP addresses are the same, and a *Xmas attack*, which sets all TCP header flags to '1' (it turns on all Christmas lights).

As an aside, there is one permutation of a signature-based IDS that is called _stateful matching_. It is used for host-based IDSs only because it monitors the contents of memory on a host. Stateful matching will take continuous snapshots, called a _state_, of the contents of volatile and non-volatile memory within a host and compare it with the last captured state. The difference between the two states is then compared to a database and if the changes match a pattern, an alert is generated. So, a _stateful-matching IDS_ is simply a pattern-matching IDS that is being applied to host memory states instead of network traffic.

Instead of simply comparing network traffic patterns to a constantly changing list, an _anomaly-based IDS_ (also called a _behavioral-based IDS_) compares those patterns against a baseline that is considered to be 'normal'. When an anomaly-based IDS is first installed, it is put into a learning mode for a while, where it watches all traffic passing by and assumes the traffic is 'normal'. It creates a database of these normal traffic patterns, and when it is taken out of learning mode, it will alert if the network traffic deviates from this baseline. Obviously, the network administrator must ensure during the 'learning' period that no attacks are underway – otherwise the IDS would consider them to be normal. The longer the IDS is left in learning mode, the fewer false positives it will generate. The advantage of such an IDS is that it can detect new attacks; the disadvantage is that any alert requires a very skilled engineer to analyze the data to determine if the anomaly is indeed an attack. Because the IDS is simply reporting rogue packets, it has no idea of the type of possible attack and can only provide raw data when reporting the issue.

Diving a little deeper into the statistical algorithm used by an anomaly-based IDS, when the IDS detects patterns outside of the norm, it will assign a degree of irregularity to the pattern and continue to monitor it; if the pattern continues the assigned degree increases to the point at which it passes a given threshold, resulting in an alert. Because of this algorithm, anomaly-based IDSs can detect 'low and slow' patterns – attacks that are designed to fly under the radar to avoid attention. When dealing with false-positives and false-negatives, anomaly-based IDSs have the opposite problem of a signature-based IDS – any anomaly rising above a certain threshold is reported as an attack, resulting in a high number of false-positives with a low number of false-negatives. Fine-tuning the threshold is crucial to achieving a reliable ratio.

In addition to watching overall traffic patterns, an anomaly-based IDS can include two additional filters – protocol filtering and traffic filtering.

If protocol filtering is applied, the IDS is called a _protocol anomaly-based IDS_ and it will understand the various protocols passing by, allowing it to dig a little deeper and add some context to patterns. This is a very useful filter to enable because most attacks happen at the protocol level as opposed to being contained within application software. Of course, protocols as defined by their respective RFCs and how they are implemented in the real world never quite align perfectly, so most IDSs are configured with protocol profiles that are somewhere in between the two. Some examples of attacks that a protocol filter can uncover are:

- Data Link Layer - _ARP poisoning_, where a rogue client pretends to own an IP that it does not
- Network Layer - _Loki attacks_, where ICMP packets are used to hide data
- Transport Layer – _session hijacking_, where an attacker uses sequence numbers to jump in and take over a socket connection

The second type of filter is a traffic filter. A _traffic anomaly-based IDS_ will watch for changes in relative patterns. This can be a little confusing over your basic anomaly-based IDS, so here is the difference – a simple anomaly-based IDS looks for patterns it has never seen, while a traffic anomaly-based IDS looks for acceptable patterns that do match the normal frequency or time range. For example, it might notice login activity in the middle of the night and generate an alert that would be ignored in the middle of a week day. Or it notices a significant increase in traffic that is usually considered to be normal, but decides that a DoS attack is underway.

So far, we have discussed signature-based and anomaly-based IDSs. The last type of IDS is called a _rule-based IDS_, sometimes referred to as a _heuristic-based IDS_. This is an _expert system_ and has the following components:

- _Facts_ – data that comes in from a sensor or system that is being monitored
- _Knowledge base_ – 'if...then' rules that analyze facts and acts
- _Inference engine_ – uses 5th generation programming languages (artificial intelligence) that can infer relationships

Rule-based IDSs collect facts, and then applies any number of rules to the facts in the form of 'if...then' statements. While this makes the system very flexible and extensible, the real power comes when the inference engine kicks in. This capability 'infers' knowledge – it can learn based on facts as they come in and the relationships that are apparent. For example, a very simple inference might be 'if A is B, and C is B, then A is C'. That might not seem so special to us humans, but when that type of awareness is combined with a computer's processing speed a whole new level of detection is achieved, resulting in improved levels of false-positives and false-negatives. However, it should be noted that rule-based IDSs cannot detect new attacks, and if the rules are overly complex it will result in excessive resource consumption in terms of CPU and memory requirements.

The latest approach to identifying malware (malicious software) is called _behavior blocking_. With this approach, vendors allow malicious software to execute on a host and then gather the changes that were made to the system. Antimalware systems then can use this 'behavior' to detect malicious activity. This is a proactive approach, and can detect zero-day vulnerabilities.

We have discussed in-depth about NIDSs and how they process network traffic, but we pretty much glossed over how that network traffic is collected – in other words, NIDS sensors deserve some attention. An NIDS can be self-contained within a firewall or other dedicated device, but normally it is a distributed solution with various sensors scattered across the network at strategic points. It is good practice to place a sensor in the DMZ, and one inside of the intranet, and perhaps at sensitive entry points such as a wireless AP connection. In this configuration, each sensor contains everything required to gather data, analyze the data and decide if an alert is warranted. Alerts are then sent to an administrator interface where it is handled according to predefined rules, such as sending a text message, an email, creating a visual alert on a monitor, or perhaps sending a signal to some other system.

A sensor might be a dedicated device or simply software installed on a server. In either case, the sensor can only examine packets that pass by if its NIC is set to promiscuous mode, meaning that all packets will be opened and looked at regardless of who it is addressed to. Unfortunately for the IDS, it is a very rare network that does not segment data using switches, meaning that not all data will pass by the sensor. To overcome this, switches often must enable a spanning port – a port where all data is sent regardless of destination or rules; the IDS sensor can then be connected to this port and access all traffic the switch handles. Depending on how deep a sensor digs into each passing packet, the required processing power can easily be overwhelmed if traffic increases significantly. That is why it might be a good idea to place multiple sensors in each location, with each sensor analyzing packets for a subset of signatures or patterns.

An attacker will normally try and figure out if an IDS is in-use, and if so she will try and identify the brand so she can adjust the attack to avoid discovery. If that is not possible, she might launch a DoS attack to force the IDS offline. Or, she could flood the network with bogus data to distract the IDS while the actual attack proceeds undetected.

So, that pretty much covers IDSs. You might have noticed that an IDS is only good enough to let us know something bad is taking place. Why not just allow the IDS to act on its own sometimes? For example, if a DoS attack is coming from a single IP address, why not just stop accepting traffic from that IP address? Or, in the case of a DDoS, perhaps we can have it update some firewall rules to not allow any ICMP echo requests for the next 10 minutes? That is exactly what an _intrusion prevention system_ (_IPS_) does. It basically is an IDS which, instead of just reporting an attack, acts according to some predefined rules. In fact, it is not uncommon for the only difference between and IDS and an IPS to be a simple configuration flag that must be turned on to enable reactive behavior.

We have one more tool in our network protection belt that we can pull out – a _honeypot_. This is a server that has purposefully been left vulnerable to attacks just enough to make a hacker think that he has stumbled upon a victim worthy of his time. The server contains no data or services that is of value to the company, and is not connected to any other systems except for the ability to let a network administrator know that it is being attacked. Why would we do this? For several reasons:

- It distracts the attacker so that our real systems are left alone
- It allows us to study the attack in real-time so that we can harden other areas on-the-fly based on the activities
- It gives us time to discover the identity of the attacker
- We can collect evidence from the attack for subsequent legal action

Of course, we must be careful how this is done – there is a very fine line between enticing an attacker to hit up a honeypot and entrapment. There is nothing wrong with *enticing* an attacker – we are simply redirecting their efforts that he or she has already determined to carry out.

But if we convince an attacker to act by encouraging or tricking them, when they may not have been planning on attacking us, it is called *entrapment* and is quite illegal. Always consult a legal team before setting up a honeypot.

Questions

1. Which IDS component looks for suspicious activity and sends alerts to the administration interface?

   A) Analyzer

   B) Inference engine

   C) Sifter

   D) BL engine

2. Which best describes a vendor allowing malicious software to execute on a host and then gathering the changes that were made to the system?

   A) Behavior block

   B) Sniff

   C) Promiscuous

   D) Protocol analyzer

3. Which term best represents a device that detects intrusion attempts against a network or network devices?

   A) HIDS

   B) IDS

   C) AIDS

   D) NIDS

4. Which of the following is an attack in which all TCP header flags are set to '1'?

   A) Session hijacking

   B) Xmas attack

   C) Land attack

   D) Loki attack

5. Which anomaly-based IDS filter contains an expert system?

   A) Protocol anomaly-based

   B) Source-based

   C) Traffic anomaly-based

   D) Rule-based

Chapter 50: Threats to Access Control

Gaining access to credentials is a primary goal of an attacker. While social engineering is often used, we are going to focus on computer-based attacks. There are two approaches an attacker can use to figure out passwords – the first is to make attempt to login using the standard user interface provided by an application. A program will automatically populate the password field with chosen values and submit the request until it succeeds.

The second approach is to gain access to a list of passwords stored in a database or file. Obviously, if the passwords are stored in clear text the attacker is very fortunate indeed, but the values are usually either encrypted or hashed, most often hashed. In the case the values are hashed, the attacker's program will choose a value, compute its hash, and then compare it against all known hashed password values. If a match is found, the attacker has effectively discovered the password that produced the hash. The following attacks work with either approach unless otherwise noted.

A *dictionary attack* is carried out by a program that is fed a list of commonly used words or combinations of characters. The program will iterate through all possible combinations and attempt to guess the password. Countermeasures against dictionary attacks are:

- Perform dictionary attacks to find weak passwords, and force the user to change it
- Require strong passwords
- Require passwords to be changed frequently
- For attacks against a user interface:
    - Use lockout thresholds
    - Use one-time password tokens
    - Use an IDS to detect this type of activity
- For attacks directly against a file:
    - Never store passwords in clear text – encrypt or hash
    - Protect password files

A *brute-force attack* (also called an *exhaustive attack*) iterates through every possible character (uppercase letter, lowercase letter, number and symbol) in increasing lengths until a match is found. This takes much longer than a dictionary attack, but given enough time is guaranteed to be 100% successful. Countermeasures are the same as with a dictionary attack, but an administrator should carry out brute-force attacks to discover weak passwords instead of the using a dictionary attack.

War-dialing (automatically dialing through a list of phone numbers until a modem answers) is a form of a brute-force attack. Countermeasures are:

- Perform brute-force attacks against all company phone number ranges to find hanging modems
- Make sure only necessary phone numbers are public

A *hybrid attack* is a combination of dictionary and brute-force attacks. A dictionary attack is used to discover at least a part of the password, and then a brute-force attack is used to discover the remaining portion.

A *rainbow attack* can be either a dictionary or brute-force attack, but instead of using raw values and computing the hash in real-time, the hashes for all relevant values are pre-computed into a 'rainbow table'. This allows the attack to be carried out much faster, but is really only useful against files.

A completely different approach is to try and steal the password directly from the user by *spoofing at logon*. This requires a malicious program to be installed on a workstation or server. When an unsuspecting user attempts to login, the malicious program will prompt for credentials instead of the OS logon screen – since the false logon screen looks just like the real thing, the user enters the correct credentials. The malicious program claims that the credentials were invalid and immediately hands control over to OS, which then shows the real logon screen. The user, thinking that he or she simply mistyped the password, tries again which succeeds. The end result is that the user never realizes that credentials were just stolen.

Of course, many of the attacks we just discussed deal with an outsider trying to gain credentials. What about people who already have credentials? The greatest threats a company will encounter are from those on the inside – past or present employees and third-party contractors. If care is not taken, those that can do the most damage have already been given keys to pillage the castle while we are not looking. This is why controlling the provisioning and deprovisioning process of access is so important.

All candidates must be properly screened using background checks, especially for sensitive jobs. Security responsibilities for a given position should be described in a job description *before* bringing on an individual, and within the terms and conditions of employment that the individual must sign. During the entire time an individual – employee or a non-employee - is working on-site, all expected security behavior must be well-documented, including the formal disciplinary policy in case of a security breach. When the time comes for the individual to be terminated – either voluntarily or not – a process must be in-place to prevent gaps in removing access and returning equipment.

At least once each year current access levels should be reviewed to ensure that individuals have been given the correct level of access. Too much access can be accumulated as a person moves into new positions, but access for the previous position was never removed.

Questions

1. Which attack iterates through all commonly used words or combinations of characters trying to guess a password?

    A) Rainbow attack

    B) Hybrid attack

    C) Dictionary attack

    D) Brute-force attack

2. Which attack uses a combination of dictionary and brute-force attacks?

    A) Hybrid attack

    B) Dictionary attack

    C) Rainbow attack

    D) Brute-force attack

3. Which attack uses the hashes for all relevant values that are pre-computed?

    A) Dictionary attack

    B) Rainbow attack

    C) Brute-force attack

    D) Hybrid attack

4. Which attack uses a software program that mimics an OS interface to collect credentials?

    A) Dictionary attack

    B) Spoofing at logon

    C) Brute-force attack

    D) Hybrid attack

5. Which attack iterates through every possible character in increasing lengths until a password match is found?

    A) Brute-force attack

    B) Hybrid attack

    C) Rainbow attack

    D) Dictionary attack

Section 6: Security Assessment and Testing Domain

This section will cover how to audit security within an organization. There are entire certifications dedicated to security auditing – such as ISACA's CISA – but we're just going to cover the basics in this domain.

Chapter 51: Audit Strategies

A *security audit* is an assessment of all security controls that protect a set of people, computers, processes and information. To properly perform a security audit, there are 8 steps that must be properly executed.

The Process

First, the *goals* of an audit must be clearly articulated. If the goals are not well-defined, then everything that flows after will fail.

Next, the right *people* must become involved. This includes both IT and the leaders of the business units owning the data and processes. Without both, subsequent decisions will be made in a vacuum resulting in a poor outcome of the audit.

Once we have the goals set and the right people gathered together, the *scope* can be defined. This is a very important step to nail down, since it is virtually impossible to test everything. Therefore, what will be tested and what will not be tested needs to be stated. Some questions to ask include:

- What subnets and systems will be tested?
- Are we going to examine user artifacts (such as logs) or user behaviors (their response to social engineering tests)?
- How will we assess the confidentiality, integrity and availability aspects of the subnets and systems tested?
- What privacy issues will we encounter?
- How will we evaluate the processes, and how far should we take it?

Once the scope has been set and documented, we need to choose the audit *team*. This can be an internal group or we can hire an external third-party to carry out the audit. Some organizations will have no choice but to use an external team due to regulatory requirements - there are a lot of variables to consider in this step, but we will cover that ground separately.

Once the audit team has been chosen, it is time to *plan* the actual audit. Some companies may want to skimp on this step, but if you want the outcome to be on-time and within-budget, don't succumb to this temptation. The executing of an audit could introduce risks into the company that did not previously exist – these need to be identified and documented. Overall documentation of the plan is important so that:

- We make sure that the original goals will be achieved
- The team remembers items that are not in scope
- We make sure that the entire process is repeatable in case issues are discovered requiring multiple iterations, and so that subsequent audits have a solid baseline to compare to

Now comes time to *conduct* the audit. The team must remember to document any deviations from the original plan as well as any discoveries made along the way – these discoveries may result in changing the plan the next time the audit is conducted, and will most certainly affect the reports that are produced at the end. All data collected during the audit must be protected and preserved at least until the reports are finalized – nothing is more frustrating than not being able to support an important conclusion because the original data is no longer around.

Once the audit has been conducted, we need to *document* all results. It is far better to include too much information than not enough.

And finally, we need to *report* the results to the correct audiences. This will normally require multiple reports – a very detailed and technical report for IT, a very detailed but non-technical report for business unit management, and a very high-level summary for executive management. The goal of the reports is to achieve and maintain a strong security posture within the identified scope. Obviously, all original goals must be addressed within the reports as well.

Now that we have gone through the entire process, let's return to selecting the team. Unless regulations (such as SOX) require an external third-party team to conduct the audit, there are quite a few factors involved in making the right choice.

Internal Audit Teams

An internal team is made up of employees or individual contractors who know the inner workings of an organization well.

Pros

- The team is already familiar with inner workings (great depth) and can test the weakest and most obscure parts of the system

- The team is more agile since it is a dedicated to the audit, and can be quickly re-tasked to fit changing priorities

Cons

- The team has intimate internal knowledge and does not represent outside attackers well
- The team will have limited exposure to other approaches to both securing and exploitation (limited breadth)
- Conflicts of interests and possible political agendas can taint the results

Third-Party (External) Audit teams

An external team is brought in for the specific purpose of carrying out an audit.

Pros

- Brings knowledge that internal teams will not have (great breadth)
- Immune to internal conflicts of interest or political agendas

Cons

- NDA required
- Costly – third-parties often simply use high-end scanners to do all work
- Cannot be easily redirected if priorities change
- Requires internal resource to bring them up to speed and supervise work (limited depth)

Service Organization Controls

Service organizations (*SOs*) provide outsourced services, such as insurance claim processing, data centers, ASPs, managed security providers, or credit processing organizations. SOs should be held accountable to passing the same audits that the client company requires for itself. The *American Institute of Certified Public Accounts* (*AICPA*) created the *Statement on Auditing Standards No 70* (*SAS 70*) to make sure that any SO claims to protect a company's assets actually do so. SAS 70 was originally meant for financials, but it has been subsequently stretched to include digital assets as well.

AICPA released a new framework for *Service Organization Controls* (*SOC*) which is defined in SSAE 16 and ISAE 3402. There are 3 types of reports – SOC 1, SOC 2 and SOC 3.

SOC 1 deals solely with financial controls, while both SOC 2 and SCO 3 cover trust services such as security, privacy, confidentiality, integrity and availability. The difference between SOC 2 and SOC 3 is in the level of detail each provides. SOC 2 provides:

- A description of all tests that were conducted
- A very detailed discussion of the test results
- The auditor's opinion of how effective the controls were

SOC 3 simply provides a pass/fail report, and is used primarily as a seal of approval that is used by the company to indicate compliance.

Chapter 51: Audit Strategies

Questions

1. What is an assessment of all security controls that protect a set of people, computers, processes and information?

    A) Control audit

    B) Security assessment

    C) Control assessment

    D) Security audit

2. Which of the following is NOT a disadvantage of using an external audit team?

    A) They can be costly

    B) They cannot be easily redirected in priorities change

    C) An NDA is required

    D) Conflicts of interest may taint the results

3. Which SOC report deals with financial controls?

    A) SOC 3

    B) SOC 4

    C) SOC 1

    D) SOC 2

4. Which of the following best describe a party providing outsourced services, such as insurance claim processing, data centers, ASPs, managed security providers, or credit processing organizations?

    A) Outside services

    B) Third-party service organizations

    C) Service organizations

    D) External providers

5. Which of the following is NOT a disadvantage of using an internal audit team?

    A) The team has intimate internal knowledge and does not represent outside attackers well

    B) An NDA is required

    C) Conflicts of interests and possible political agendas can taint the results

    D) The team will have limited exposure to other approaches to both securing and exploitation

Chapter 52: Auditing Technical Controls

We have previously discussed administrative, physical and technical controls in the Identity and Access Management (IAM) domain, but we are going to revisit them from an auditing standpoint. If you will recall, a technical control almost always has some type of software associated with it, and in order to properly test it, we have to understand what it is intended to accomplish to begin with. Once the purpose is known, the most appropriate auditing approach can be selected. In this section, we will be going through the possible approaches and when each should be used.

Before we dive in, it is important to understand the difference between vulnerability testing and penetration testing:

- *Vulnerability testing* – *identify* vulnerabilities that potentially could be exploited
- *Penetration testing* – *test* vulnerabilities to determine if they really can be exploited

Both vulnerability and penetration testing can be executed in one of three knowledge levels. A *black box test* provides the testing team with no prior knowledge of the environment – the only knowledge gained is that which the team discovers through public resources (such as search engines or WHOIS services) or by scanning. This best simulates an external attacker, but will prevent complete internal coverage of controls. It may also lead to the team inadvertently attacking a critical system.

A *white box test* is the opposite – the testing team has complete knowledge of and complete access to the internal infrastructure. This will result in the most complete assessment, but does not represent very well vulnerabilities and risks from an external or internal attacker.

The final level is a *gray box test*, and is a hybrid of the black and white approaches. The testing team is allowed access to the internal environment but is not given complete knowledge of the systems or privileged credentials. This does not provide full coverage of all internal controls, but does strike a decent balance in representing both an internal and external attacker.

Vulnerability Testing

Before any type of vulnerability testing is started, an agreement must be created defining how far testing will be taken, listing possible side-effects or fallout. While vulnerability testing is non-invasive, it can trip IDS/IPS alarms. This agreement must be signed by management as well as the tester – this applies whether the tester is internal or an external party.

Vulnerability testing may use an automated tool as part of the effort, but no tool will be able to effectively discard false positives and uncover false negatives – only an experienced professional with a deep background in security will be able to accomplish this.

The goal of a vulnerability test is to generate a prioritized list of as many vulnerabilities as possible to reveal the actual security posture of a company, as opposed to the imagined. Management should understand that this report is a snapshot in time, and should be performed annually for low-risk systems up to continuous scans for high-risk assets.

There are 3 types of assessments. A *personnel assessment* reviews employee tasks to identify vulnerabilities in policies and procedures. It should demonstrate how social engineering attack occur and highlight the value of training employees to recognize such activities. It should also ensure policies and procedures that cannot be addressed with physical and technical controls are properly addressed with administrative controls.

A *physical assessment* tests facility and perimeter protection, such as door locks, badge readers, ensuring doors close properly, determining if dumpster diving is a risk, checking fire suppression systems, and examining plenum spaces to ensure proper protection.

A *system and networking assessment* employs an automated scanning tool to search for vulnerabilities, and provides the following:

- Identification of active hosts
- Identification of active and vulnerable services (ports) on hosts
- Identification of applications by banner grabbing
- Identification of operating systems
- Identification of vulnerabilities for discovered operating systems and applications
- Identification of misconfigured settings
- Tests for compliance with host application's usage and security policies
- A foundation for subsequent penetration testing

Banner grabbing examines the content resulting from a specific port scan and attempts to figure out what type or brand of service is running behind that port. _Fingerprinting_ uses a similar tactic to identify specific operating systems or applications.

Some commonly discovered (and exploitable) vulnerabilities include:

- _Kernel flaws_ – if found, this type of vulnerability can give the attacker a great deal of control; the countermeasure is to keep OSs patched and up-to-date
- _Buffer overflows_ – poorly implemented code can allow an attacker to overwrite protected memory, resulting in launching an attacker's code; countermeasures include developer education, using strongly typed languages, and employing automated source code scanners
- _Symbolic links_ – this is a file stub that redirects to another location, allowing a back-door path to access sensitive files; the countermeasure is to ensure that programs and scripts are written to require the full path to the file
- _File descriptor attacks_ – operating systems use numbers to represent open files, and some numbers are always the same, allowing an attacker to control input or output for these files; countermeasures include developer education, performing application security testing, and using automated source code scanners
- _Race condition_ – a program's poor design can put it in a temporary vulnerable condition in which an attacker could force the program to execute an operation out of the intended order; countermeasures include developer education, performing application security testing, and using automated source code scanners
- _File and directory permissions_ – inadvertent system or user errors can result in file or directory permissions being lowered, allowing an attacker to access sensitive information; the countermeasure is to employ file integrity checkers that can alert on these changes before an attacker exploits them

Vulnerability testing should always use multiple automated tools – every tool has its own strengths and weaknesses, and by using multiple tools a tester has a better chance of full coverage. In the same vein, it is better to use multiple testers, as each individual or team will have their own unique experiences – rotating teams allows a company to discover a greater breadth of vulnerabilities.

Penetration testing

Penetration testing is the process of simulating attacks on a network and its systems at the request of the senior management. It addresses all 3 types of controls (administrative, technical and physical) and its goal is to:

- Identify true vulnerabilities (those that can be exploited)
- Figure out the protection existing security mechanisms provide
- Identify how suspicious activity is reported

Penetration testing can be very disruptive in that it can result in the loss of data if the company is not properly prepared and can take systems offline, usually due to DoS attacks. A well-documented agreement should be formalized before any testing is carried out that defines:

- Timeframe when the testing begins and ends
- The extent of testing expressed in terms of named systems, IP addresses and types of attacks
- The parties involved
- Define the level of knowledge testers have about the environment and knowledge the environment (internal staff) has about the testers
- Whether the test is to take place internally and/or externally

All members of the testing team should carry a '_Get Out of Jail Free Card_' – this is a document containing the following information:

- The extent of testing authorized
- Contact information for key personnel
- A call tree in case something goes wrong

This is particularly important when testing physical controls in case the team member is caught or apprehended.

Penetration testing typically follows the following steps, executed in order listed:

- _Discovery_ – footprinting and gathering info about a target (using DNS, WHOIS, etc.)
- _Enumeration_ – port scans and resource identification (i.e. system fingerprinting)

- *Vulnerability Mapping* – identifying vulnerabilities (for perimeter devices, OS, services, and web apps)
- *Exploitation* – gain unauthorized access by exploiting discovered vulnerabilities
- *Report to Management* – creating and delivering documentation of test findings with suggested countermeasures

The type of box testing (black, white or gray) is sometimes referred to as 'knowledge':

- Zero knowledge – black box
- Partial knowledge – gray box
- Full knowledge – white box

To make matters even more confusing, there are 3 descriptors describing the coordination between the testing team and internal staff:

- *Blind* – testers only have public information available, but internal network staff ARE notified an attack is taking place
- *Double-blind* (also called a *stealth assessment*) - testers only have public information available, and internal network staff are NOT notified
- *Targeted* – both external and internal parties coordinate and test specific networks, systems or applications

If user credentials are provided, tests should always start off with the most basic user access to ensure proper testing.

The final penetration testing report should be delivered to management and provide a list of all discovered vulnerabilities along with suggested countermeasures, ordered by risk.

War Dialing

We have already covered *war dialing* several times, but we need to add a few more details. While this activity is usually associated with trying to gain access to a network through a dedicated modem, fax machines are often overlooked. They contain internal modems that can be accessed remotely, and faxes previously received or transmitted can be retrieved.

There are multiple tools available to call all numbers within a given range, and allow the user to customize the behavior in the following manners:

- Only numbers belonging to a specific company
- Call only at night
- Choose numbers within a range at random
- Fingerprint answering hosts
- Attempt simple penetration tests

Postmortem

When the final report has been received, management must then decide what actions to take – this is called a *postmortem*. The list of vulnerabilities should have already been prioritized by the testing team according to the likelihood of exploitation, but that ordering alone should not be used to decide on how to address the issues. The cost to the company of a vulnerability being exploited must be evaluated, as well as the cost to mitigate a given vulnerability. All those factors together will allow management to arrive at an ordered list that can dictate the priority of which issues should be addressed first. Once work has been started to mitigate the vulnerabilities, it is often discovered that either a mitigation cost turns out to be much higher than thought, or the mitigation will provide lower protection than first envisioned. In these cases, it is important to allow the prioritized list to remain organic so that discoveries can be shifted up or down as work progresses.

The environment should be continued to be monitored in-between tests on a scheduled basis, and tests need to be scheduled – a single list should be developed that shows for each item:

- The type of test (network scan, war dialing, penetration test, etc.)
- The frequency (weekly, bi-weekly, monthly, quarterly, annually, etc.)
- The goal and benefit (what the activity does and what it will reveal)

Log Reviews

Ongoing examination of log files is crucial to keeping a network and its systems in line with a proper security posture. A *log review* is the examination of system log files to detect security events or verify effectiveness of security controls. Log files must constantly be fine-tuned to reflect changing security requirements – both due to internal security controls as well as to address new threats from the outside. Log files are usually generated by different systems running on multiple servers, or at a minimum multiple log files on a single server. To be able to construct a complete picture, all log files need to be merged somehow into a single view, and one of the most important factors in doing this is to ensure a constant time value is used for all log files.

To facilitate synchronization of time across a network, the *network time protocol* (*NTP*) was created, and is currently at version 4. It is defined in *RFC 5905* and operates using UDP over port 123 with the contents of the datagram being a 64-bit timestamp. NTP defines a *strata*-based hierarchy of time servers with up to 16 strata being supported, and strata 0 being the most authoritative:

- *Stratum 0* – atomic clocks, GPS, radio clocks
- *Stratum 1* – highly accurate primary time sources with internal clocks directly connected to stratum 0
- *Stratum 2* – network servers such as NTP servers or domain controllers connected to stratum 1
- *Stratum 3 and below* – NTP does not define the exact purpose

An NTP client can simultaneously act as an NTP server for other devices.

Synthetic Transactions

A *synthetic transaction* is any transaction initiated by a script to verify proper execution of a service, or to measure metrics such as latency, speed and availability. Synthetic transactions are usually automated to be executed in well-defined intervals, providing a predictable baseline that can be used for continuous monitoring.

This contrasts with *real user monitoring* (*RUM*) which captures metrics such as delay, jitter and errors from a session conducted by a real person. This is normally carried out by background collection of the metrics on the user device (such as a browser, windows application or smartphone app) which are sent in bulk to a server that stores the information in log files. The results are not predictable, but do provide a window into the real-world user experience of an application or service.

Misuse Case Testing

Unified modeling language (*UML*) is a tool to graphically represent 'use cases', among other uses. This typically is used to show the 'happy path' behavior for a system in which *actors* interact with systems to get productive work done. UML can also be used to illustrate *misuse cases* which depict an attacker executing malicious behavior – the diagram shows attack vectors, actions taken by the attacker and the target of their actions. Misuse cases help developers and architects identify security issues during the development life cycle so that security can be effectively addressed up-front, instead of being bolted on after problems are discovered.

Code Reviews

Source code consists of the lines of software instructions that make up an application. A *code review* is a systematic examination of application source code intended to uncover bad practices, unsafe code and ensure conformation to company standards.

Things that are normally looked for are:

- Not following coding standards
- Unnecessary complexity (remember that security loves simplicity!)
- Unused functions leading to 'code bloat'
- Repeated logic that can be reduced by refactoring
- Opportunities to abstract code into external locations for future reusability

From a security point of view, additional areas should be scrutinized during code reviews. Many times, test code is left in place, resulting in a prime target to be exploited once discovered by a hacker. There have been numerous stories of test code – particularly hard-coded credentials – being left in resulting in a very public breach.

Developers may also install *back doors* to make it easier to debug after an application is deployed, thinking no one will discover it. You are pretty much guaranteed that it will be discovered, and there are plenty of real-world anecdotes proving so.

Developers might comment out code instead of removing it, just in case they need it later, or they want to be able to reference it. When dealing with compiled code, such as inside of server-based applications, this code will be automatically removed. However, any type of script, such as JavaScript, will send all comments to the browser where it can easily be read.

Finally, all user input should always be treated as untrusted and should be sanitized before handling.

Defensive coding is the habit of looking for opportunities for source code to go bad.

Interface Testing

An *interface* is a given set of exchange points between two systems. Interfaces are a great tool for abstracting internal details, making systems more robust by hiding implementation details behind a common and mostly-unchanging communication point. _Interface testing_ is the systematic evaluation of an interface to discover problems.

Any given interface will have a set of 'known good' use cases and 'known bad' use cases – usually these are well-documented and tested. However, right in the middle of these two lives _boundary conditions_ that represent seldom-tested scenarios. For example, a service accepts a 10-digit phone number. Obviously including letters should cause the service to reject the value, but what if we send in an 9-digit phone number? This is where testing often falls down.

Interface testing should include all three – known good, known bad and boundary conditions in an automated fashion. Automation allows a team to consistently and quickly execute tests each time the source code is changed to detect hidden fall out.

Chapter 52: Auditing Technical Controls

Questions

1. What is the activity that looks at content returned from a probe to identify specific operating systems or applications?

    A) Pattern spotting

    B) Fingerprinting

    C) Banner grabbing

    D) Software identification

2. What best describes vulnerability testing?

    A) Prioritizing identified weaknesses by the likelihood of being exploited

    B) Identifying weaknesses that have already been exploited

    C) Proving that a weakness can be exploited

    D) Finding weaknesses that could be potentially exploited

3. Which NTP stratum includes highly accurate primary time sources with internal clocks?

    A) Stratum 0

    B) Stratum 3 and below

    C) Stratum 1

    D) Stratum 2

4. Which testing coordination plan requires testers to have only publicly-available information available, but internal network staff are notified an attack is taking place?

    A) Double-blind

    B) Selected

    C) Blind

    D) Targeted

5. Which of the following is NOT a step typically followed with penetration testing?

    A) Discovery

    B) Lateral movement

    C) Enumeration

    D) Exploitation

Chapter 53: Auditing Administration Controls

Account Management

From a legal perspective, it is important that all employees have read and signed an *Acceptable Use Policy* (*AUP*) in case legal action is required in the future (for prosecution or defense). To ensure all employees have this on-file, a comparison should be made between IT's list of named users and HR's list of AUPs on record.

An attacker's preferred method is to become a user with elevated privileges as soon as possible. This can be done in 1 of 3 ways. First, he can use an existing privileged account by stealing the credentials. This can be mitigated by:

- Enforcing the use of strong passwords
- Requiring 2-factor authentication
- Allow the use of privileged accounts only for specific tasks

The last bullet point – not using privileged accounts for day-to-day tasks – can cause some inconvenience to users, but all operating systems normally provide a mechanism to temporarily elevate privileges if the user has sufficient rights:

- Windows – right-click a program icon and select 'Run As Administrator'
- Linux – type '*sudo*' within a terminal session for command line elevation, or 'gksudo' ('kdesudo' for Ubuntu) to start a graphical application with elevated privileges
- OS X – same as Linux, but the graphical command format is 'sudo open –a {appname}'

Failing that, the attacker can elevate privileges an existing non-privileged account. To counteract such an action, close attention needs to be paid to logs resulting from the modification of existing accounts. Additionally, a change control process should be implemented for elevation of privileges requiring two or more employees to authorize such an action.

Finally, an attacker can create a new account with the desired privileges. Again, close attention should be paid to log files, in this case to entries detailing the creation of an account. As with elevating privileges, a change control process should be required for account creation. Company policies should dictate the default expiration for new accounts, minimum password strength and access for specific groups of users.

Privilege accumulation results when a user account is assigned more rights than are necessary to complete his or her job. Proper change control process can mitigate this condition.

Suspending an account is an important step in account management. Common reasons for doing so are:

- Employee termination
- An account reaches an expiration date
- An employee is on a temporary leave of absence (for example, maternity leave or military duty)

System administrators should periodically compare the list of active accounts with HR's records to ensure an account was suspended or terminated properly. Care should be taken to not delete accounts too soon when an employee leaves - suspension should be immediate, but deletion should be deferred in case some type of investigation into the ex-employee's activities while employed needs to take place.

Backup Verification

Backups are essential to any disaster recovery plan, but are worthless if they do not work when needed. That is why backups need to be periodically verified to ensure they will work at the right time.

There are 3 primary types of data usually involved in backups:

User data files are user-created and maintained files such as spreadsheets or text documents. One of the biggest issues is that users are notorious for storing their files anywhere but the location that is routinely backed up. This makes it difficult sometimes to align backup processes with policies, regulations and laws.

Databases are large files in which server-based processes (such as SQL Server or Oracle) store data. Normally, there are ancillary files that contain related metadata (such as indexes) that must be backed up and restored together. Fortunately, most modern databases provide some type of means to back up the files without taking the database offline. Testing the restoration is usually more difficult as it can be very disruptive; many companies have separate servers that are used to test back up restoration to avoid any type of live disruption.

Chapter 53: Auditing Administration Controls

Mailbox data is contained on mail servers, of which most companies have multiple instances of. Often, these servers back each other up, so that facility needs to be considered. Backups should be compliant with e-discovery (a judicial step of retrieving information used for legal proceedings).

As virtual machines become more and more cost effective, they are being used to some extent as a form of backup. Instead of backing up data in a proprietary format, a snapshot of the entire server is made. This has the added advantage of providing extremely quick restores, often in a matter of seconds.

As noted earlier, the verification of a backup can be very disruptive – as a rule of thumb, the more disruptive it is, the less confident a company can be that it will be effective in time of need. A balance should be achieved between the tolerance of users for disruption and the incurred risk if backups do not work as intended. An inventory of backup data should be maintained along with a schedule designed to ensure each is properly tested and verified. In the case of user data, a company must aggressively enforce policies to save user data to network shares where it can be properly backed up.

Creating a proper test plan for backups includes the following steps:

- *Develop scenarios* that represent specific threats
- *Develop a plan* for each scenario that tests all mission-critical backups
- *Use automation* to minimize the required effort to execute the restore periodically
- *Minimize the impact* on the business so it can be executed regularly
- *Ensure coverage* so that every system is tested, though not in the same test
- *Document* the results so you know what is working and what needs work
- *Fix or improve* any issues you documented

Disaster Recovery and Business Continuity

Business Continuity, or *BC*, is the ability for an organization to continue operating following a serious incident. *Disaster Recovery*, *DR*, is a subset of BC and focuses on getting information systems back up after that incident. Because nothing remains constant, the *Disaster Recovery Plan*, or *DRP*, should be tested regularly – at least once per year - to prove whether the plan works, and if not, what needs work.

Each test should:

- Have a scenario in-mind with a limited scope
- Have what 'success' looks like defined up-front
- Have the timing and duration agreed upon
- List who will participate
- List who will do what
- Define what steps will be taken
- List the hardware, software, personnel, procedures and communication infrastructure that will be tested
- Dictate if movement of equipment will be tested
- Contain written exercise plans

Tests should be carried out in increasing scope:

- *Checklist* – all departments review the DRP and make updates as-needed
- *Structured walk-through* – reps from each department get together and go over the plan end-to-end
- *Simulation* – all people involved take part and walk through to test reaction; only materials available during an actual event are used; stops just before actual relocation or shipment to another facility
- *Parallel* – some systems are moved to the alternate facility and tested to ensure they function properly
- *Full-Interruption* – full execution of the plan until all systems are replaced by the alternative facility

During the simulation, parallel and full-interruptions tests, all communication should take place over mobile phones or walkie-talkies to represent a phone line breakdown. At the end of each test, a full report should be made to upper management.

In addition to training specific to the DPR, other training should be considered:

- CPR
- Fire extinguisher
- Evacuation routes
- Crowd control
- Emergency communication methods
- Shutting down equipment in the correct order
- Redistribution of network resources
- Operation of redundant power supplies

The initial reaction to an emergency is very important to the success of carrying out a DRP – all steps should be followed exactly as planned without skipping to ensure success. Protection of life is always the first step – one person in each group of employees should be assigned the responsibility of ensuring that all other employees are present. Once this has been achieved, the following needs to be considered within the DRP:

- One person should be responsible for notifying authorities
- If the situation is not life-threatening:
    - Shut systems down in orderly fashion
    - Critical systems and data files should be removed
- Identify person/people responsible for interfacing with external parties
- Care must be taken to prevent vandalism, looting and fraud

Maintaining the plan and ensuring it does not become outdated is difficult due to the following factors:

- BCP/DRP is not integrated into the change management process
- Infrastructure and environments change
- Employee structure changes due to reorganizations, layoffs, or mergers
- Hardware, software and applications constantly change
- Employee turnover might be high
- After the plan is done, people feel that their job is done
- Plans do not have a direct line to profitability
- Large plans take a lot of work to maintain

To combat these issues, a company needs to:

- Make BC a part of every business decision
- Make maintenance responsibilities a part of appropriate job descriptions
- Include maintenance responsibilities part of personnel evaluations
- Perform internal audits that include DRP and BCP documentation
- Perform regular drills according to the plan
- Integrate the BCP into the change management process
- Incorporate lessons learned from actual incidents into the plan

Security Training and Security Awareness Training

Security training is the process of teaching security skills to security personnel. The effectiveness of this training can be easily measured by testing the performance of security personnel.

On the other hand, *security awareness training* is the process of explaining security issues to all members of an organization, so an employee may recognize risky situations and know how to respond. The effectiveness of this type of training is measured by the degree of change people exhibit when presented with specific situations.

Social engineering represents the most likely situation in which the average employee will find themselves. This is the process of manipulating a person such that they willingly violate security policies. Examples might be giving away a password, letting an unauthorized person into the building, or being convinced to click a dangerous link. Most people assume social engineering attacks require the attacker to think on the fly, and indeed that is a good skillset to have for this type of attack. However, most attacks are usually designed with a specific individual in mind and thought through well ahead of time.

Social engineering attacks such as phishing, spear phishing, whaling and drive-by-downloads have already been covered in the Communication and Network Security Domain, so we will not revisit those. *Pretexting* is one we have not yet covered, and it occurs when an attacker provides a believable scenario to get victim to give up information – for example the victim receives a phone call from someone claiming to be from customer service who is asking for personal information.

Social media presents a security concern, as employees may inadvertently post information or photos about the workplace. Employees should be trained on the use of privacy settings and encouraged to use them – once information is posted it can never be recalled, even if it is removed from the account. Companies can use Google searches to receive automatic alerts whenever relevant information is posted. To mitigate drive-by-downloads and installation of unapproved software, a whitelist can be used to restrict all downloads except for those on the approved list. File metatags can be used to track information that inadvertently leave the security of the company's intranet, and can possibly be used to identify the individual responsible.

Of course, a company can spend an enormous amount of money on training, but how can the success of such a program be measured? Although a very difficult question to answer, there are a couple of options. The first is to conduct a series of social engineering tests and then take an anonymous survey on the number of times employees fell victim. After awareness training has been conducted, perform the same test and follow-up assessments and compare the results. This will provide a very coarse measurement as some people will not admit to falling prey, even anonymously. The second method is to conduct benign phishing, spear phishing or even whaling attacks with links that lead to page informing the employee the danger of clicking unknown links and possibly even an instructional video. The click-through data is saved, identifying the employee as well as the number of times he or she fell victim. After awareness training, conduct the benign attacks again and measure the results. Repeat offenders who simply will not change their habits can be dealt with on a case-by-case basis.

Companies should have a culture that encourages proper security hygiene. Employees who self-report should feel safe, and actively seek guidance when encountering a suspicious situation. When these activities happen, it is a good indicator that a company's culture has a healthy security posture.

Key Performance and Risk Indicators

A _Key Performance Indicator_ (_KPI_) is a high-level indicator of how well things are going from a security posture point of view. The importance of KPIs cannot be understated – running an ISMS without KPIs to measure the effectiveness is often worse than not having an ISMS at all – it can often lead a company in the wrong direction.

ISO 27004 'Information Security Metrics Implementation' outlines a process by which PKIs can be identified and 'calculated'. First, we need to define some terms:

- _Factor_ – an ISMS attribute that can change over time
- _Measurement_ – a factor's value at a specific point in time
- _Baseline_ – a measurement that provides a point of reference going forward
- _Metric_ – a calculated value derived from:
    - Comparing a current measurement against a baseline
    - Comparing two or more current measurements to each other
- _Indicator_ (PKI) – an interpretation of one or more metrics that communicate the effectiveness of the ISMS

PKIs show at a high level if the ISMS is keeping pace with new threats, or if it is lagging behind - they should be meaningful to a business audience. The best process for generating PKIs is:

- Choose the _factors_ that can show the state of security; find a middle line between the number of factors and how much effort will be required to collect measurements
- Create a plan to periodically capture _measurements_, keeping the period constant; automated collection is the best
- Define _baselines_ for the factors under consideration; figure out which will be compared to a baseline and which will be compared to each other
- Generate _metrics_; automate as much as possible, but human intervention will be required to get the correct information
- Generate _indicators_ and communicate to the stakeholders; reports should start high-level and dig deeper as the report goes on; PKIs should be front and center on the summary

On the other end of the security spectrum are _Key Risk Indicators_ (_KRIs_) – roughly how badly things could go in the future. KRIs represent a threshold that should trigger something when exceeded – if a KRI is ever reached it is a warning sign. The best KRIs are based on an SLE (Single Loss Expectancies). If you recall from earlier domains, an SLE is the currency amount the company can expect to lose per incident. If the KRI ever exceeds a certain threshold expressed in currency, this is a clear sign that security needs additional work.

Chapter 53: Auditing Administration Controls

Questions

1. Which of the following backup data is best described as data contained on mail servers?

    A) Repository

    B) User data files

    C) Mailbox data

    D) Databases

2. Which of the following is carried out by an attacker providing a believable scenario in order to get a victim to give up information?

    A) Convincing context

    B) Social engineering

    C) Manipulating context

    D) Pretexting

3. Which of the following best describes is a written company policy informing users of precautions taken by the company?

    A) Allowable use permissions

    B) Umbrella security policy

    C) Acceptable use policy

    D) Login banner

4. What are the steps for testing a plan, in order?

    A) Prepare, walk-through, simulation, simulated simulation, full execution

    B) Checklist, shallow simulation, shallow execution, parallel, full execution

    C) Prepare, shallow simulation, shallow execution, simulated simulation, full execution

    D) Checklist, walk-through, simulation, parallel, full-interruption

5. Which standard outlines a process by which PKIs can be identified and calculated?

    A) ISO 27003

    B) ISO 27004

    C) ASA 436

    D) NIST 800-32

Chapter 54: Reporting and Management Review

Reporting

Reporting may be the least favored task from a security professional's point of view, but it is the most valued output from the point of upper management. For a report to have an impact, it must be written in language that business people speak, but contain all technical detail required to back up the summarized conclusions.

Technical Reporting

A technical report should be the result of applying a standard methodology to the specific context of the *system under study* (*SUS*). In other words, the report should:

- Document the methodology used
- Describe how the methodology was tailored to the SUS
- Contain the findings
- Recommend controls or changes
- End with an appendix containing the raw data and any automated reports
- Speak to the organization's risk posture

The findings should contain:

- Threats – a list of threats as defined by the *Risk Management Process* (*RMP*)
- Vulnerabilities – each vulnerability should be linked to an identified threat
- Probability of Exploitation- the likelihood the vulnerability will be exploited based on the frequency found elsewhere in similar organizations
- Impact of Exploitation – usually expressed in monetary terms so that it remains aligned with the RMP

Be wary of reports that look auto-generated and emphasize less important flaws if more important ones were not found. Reports should be customized, straight-forward and objective.

Executive Summaries

The executive summary is just as important to a report as the findings themselves. Here is where we pull everything together in one or two pages and communicate the final results in a language that is easy for leadership to understand – non-technical and tied to the company's bottom line – money. Any required changes will require their authorization and support to find the resources to effect change. Because most decisions at this level are most often made based on links to profitability, conclusions should quantify the amount of money each recommendation would potentially save the company. There are 3 approaches to arrive at a monetary value:

- *Cost approach* – the amount it would cost to acquire or replace the protected asset; usually applied to IT assets
- *Income approach* – the amount of revenue the protected asset is expected to contribute based on both the past and future business environment; usually applied to assets directly contributing to the company's mission
- *Market approach* – how much other organizations are paying for the same protected asset; useful only for assets for which companies are willing to be transparent about, or can easily be determined from the marketplace

Once a monetary value has been determined, a residual risk is then calculated after taking into account the protection that the suggested change will affect (See the Security and Risk Management domain for how to calculate Residual Risk). To make a strong argument, the cost of the control must be less (preferably substantially less) than the residual risk.

Important questions to answer in the executive summary are:

- How likely is it that this will work?
- How much will it cost us?
- How much will it save us?

Management Review

A *management review* is a formal meeting held by leadership (all key decision makers) to review the current management systems, and to determine if they are currently meeting the company's needs. One of the systems covered is the ISMS, and that is where we will focus.

Most mature management reviews center around ISO 9000, which defines the *Plan-Do-Check-Act* (*PDCA*) process:

- *Plan* – define the objectives and design the processes to meet those objectives
- *Do* – execute the plan

- *Check* – compare the expected results (from PLAN) to the actual results (from DO)
- *Act* – determine next actions based on CHECK; the next iteration of PLAN will take these into account

Reviews should not look at the technical details, but stay at a high-level and holistically look at the entire organization. As a result, to be effective the presenter needs to be able to eloquently speak the language of businesses leaders.

Reviews need to happen periodically –the more immature an organization or management system is, the more frequently a review should take place. Reviews held infrequently or inconsistently will find themselves reacting to issues instead of being proactive. The length of time to enact changes from the last review should help in deciding when the next review will be held – it does little good to hold another review if the changes have not yet been completed to an appreciable degree.

The inputs to a review are both internal and external audits, including the report we covered in previous sections. Every input should have an executive summary in business language. We will discuss the general order of each review meeting – every organization is different, but this schedule should reflect most reviews held.

First, any open issues or actions from previous review meeting will be reviewed. Issues that were not closed will be covered in more detail, and the blockers should be highlighted. A list of unresolved issues normally is sent to all participants before the review so that attendees are not caught off-guard.

An overview of customer feedback is presented. Depending on the type of customer, an overview of RUM, social media and customer service statistics may be included.

Recommendations for change are presented, with clearly defined links to policy changes or resource allocation requests. It is a good idea to provide a range of choices (3 to 5 is optimal) from doing nothing to doing everything, with in-betweens provided varying on risk, resource requirements and business appeal. Each option should have a monetary value that reflects:

- The cost of the entire life-cycle
- Associated risk
- The impact on existing processes or systems
- Any training requirements
- Complexity side-effects

The leadership will consider the inputs, ask questions, and then decide to:

- Approve as-is
- Approve with changes
- Defer for a time
- Defer for additional work
- Reject

The review will end with an overview of open items, who will address each, and when each is due.

Questions

1. Which PDCA step defines the objectives and designs the processes to meet those objectives?

    A) Act

    B) Plan

    C) Check

    D) Do

2. Which approach is calculated using how much other organizations are paying for the same protected asset?

    A) Market approach

    B) Revenue approach

    C) Income approach

    D) Cost approach

3. Which standard defines the PDCA process?

    A) ANSI 38-1

    B) NIST 544

    C) ISO 9000

    D) ISO 9001

4. Which approach is calculated using the amount it would cost to acquire or replace a protected asset?

    A) Income approach

    B) Cost approach

    C) Market approach

    D) Revenue approach

5. What best describes applying a standard methodology to the specific context of a system?

    A) Technical reporting

    B) Logical analysis

    C) Logical reporting

    D) Technical analysis

Section 7: Security Operations Domain

Security operations take place after a network, system, application or environment has been completed and is running – it keeps things running smoothly.

Chapter 55: Roles, Management and Assurance Levels

Roles

Most people see the role of an operations department as being to keep everything working smoothly, which is true. But there is an often-overlooked ancillary role that the Operations Department fills – that of providing legal cover for the organization. In civil litigation when companies are involved, decisions are made by contrasting the actions of the company against the actions that a prudent man may have made. A *prudent man* is responsible, careful, cautious and practical. In terms of the law, that means that a company must practice:

- *Due care* – taking reasonable precautions
- *Due diligence* – doing everything within one's power to prevent a bad thing from happening

The Operations Department ensures that the company has exercised both due care and due diligence in regard to security.

Administrative Management

Administrative management is the act of managing personnel, and ensures that:

- Separation of Duties is implemented where applicable
- A complete list of roles has been defined, with each role containing a small number of tasks
- All roles have a complete and well-defined description
- Job rotation is enforced where applicable
- Least privilege access is implemented
- Need to know access is implemented
- Access rights are applied appropriately as a combination of least-privilege, security clearance, need to know, resource classification and the mode in which system operate
- Enforces mandatory vacations (ideally of at least 2 contiguous weeks) where applicable

Security and Network Personnel

The security administrator should never report to the network administrator – while the two both desire an efficient and secure network, their respective priorities are different and are often at-odds. The primary goal of a *network administrator* is to achieve a highly available, performant infrastructure that meets user needs, while the purpose of a *security administrator* purpose is to ensure a highly-secure and controlled infrastructure, which often can negatively impact availability, performance and usability.

The duties of a security administrator include:

- Implementing and maintaining security devices and software; default settings seldom effectively work and require monitoring and tweaking
- Carrying out security assessments on a timely basis and providing results to the proper decision makers
- Managing user profiles and access controls
- In MAC environments, maintaining security labels
- Managing passwords according to policy
- Reviewing audit logs

Accountability

Accountability and auditing go together, because without proper auditing, holding users accountable for their actions is not possible. To carry out proper auditing, all access attempts must be logged and reviewed complete with a unique user ID so that actions can be traced back to individuals. Auditing in general should take place in a routine manner – if information is being recorded that no one ever looks at, then either too much information is being captured or someone is not doing their job.

Logs should strike a balance between recording enough information to discover security weaknesses without containing cryptic data that is difficult to decipher, or too much noise. Automated monitoring of logs is extremely helpful – many companies would claim it is crucial, particularly as the size of a network increases.

Questions to access when monitoring logs include:

- Are users accessing data or performing tasks that do not align with their job description? Is so, rights need to be revaluated
- Are the same mistakes being made repetitively? If so, more training may be indicated.
- Do too many users have rights to restricted resources? If so, rights need to be revaluated or roles need to be redefined; more than likely rights accumulation has occurred and needs to be addressed.

Clipping Levels

A *clipping level* is a threshold value at which an alert is generated. Normal day-to-day measurements fall below this value. Once it has been exceeded, further violations are examined to determine if action needs to take place. This allows an administrator to act proactively before further damage is done. The job of monitoring clipping levels is normally done by an IDS, which should remain inconspicuous – otherwise an attacker may attempt to circumvent the IDS and remain under the radar.

Assurance Levels

So how can you be sure that a given product is trustworthy? From a security point of view, there are multiple types of certifications that a product can be awarded, but they will generally fall into 1 of 2 categories.

First, *operation assurance* ensures that a product provides the necessary levels of protection based on its architecture, embedded features, and functionality. This includes the following areas:

- Provides the proper level of access control mechanisms
- Implements separation of privileged and user code
- Supports proper auditing and monitoring capabilities
- Has been analyzed and vetted for covert channels
- After experiencing an unexpected shutdown (crash), it provides trusted recovery

The second category of assurance levels is called a *life-cycle assurance* that follows the development life-cycle of the product. It evaluates a product based on:

- The final design specifications
- If it offers clipping-level configurability
- How well it underwent both unit and integration testing
- The level of configuration management it offers
- If the distribution channel is properly secured and trusted

Chapter 55: Roles, Management and Assurance Levels

Questions

1. Which term refers to doing everything within one's power to prevent a bad thing from happening?

    A) Due care

    B) Due precaution

    C) Due persistence

    D) Due diligence

2. Which term refers to the act of managing personnel?

    A) Administrative management

    B) Human resource management

    C) People administration

    D) Asset administration

3. Which role works to achieve a highly available, performant infrastructure that meets user needs?

    A) Infrastructure administrator

    B) Network administrator

    C) Security administrator

    D) Security manager

4. What is the term describing being responsible, careful, cautious and practical?

    A) Practical man

    B) Pragmatic man

    C) Prudent man

    D) Principled man

5. Which term refers to taking reasonable precautions?

    A) Due precaution

    B) Due care

    C) Due diligence

    D) Due persistence

Chapter 56: Operational Responsibilities

<u>*Operational security*</u> refers to the ability to mitigate the damage resulting from unauthorized disclosure of information – this is accomplished by minimizing the opportunities to do so. Operational security focuses on software and hardware only, as opposed to personnel, and has 3 primary objectives:

- To identify and prevent recurring problems
- To reduce hardware and software failures down to an acceptable level
- To minimize the impact that disruptions or any single incidence might have

To meet these objectives, operation security will look for and respond to 3 types of scenarios. The first is to notice unusual behavior in a system, find the root cause and fix it. For example, if a system that normally runs at around 50% CPU utilization jumps to 100% and remains at that level, then this would be a definite cause for concern. The staff investigating such an incidence must methodically approach the issue to prevent a 'problem just magically went away' scenario – these types of 'solutions' will always return in some from. <u>*Event management systems*</u> can help tremendously - this is a system that collects logs throughout the network and automatically correlates the information.

The second type of scenario that operation security looks for are unexpected software restarts. An <u>*Initial Program Load*</u> (<u>*IPL*</u>) represents software starting up after a controlled or unexpected shutdown – this is commonly referred to as a 'restart' for applications and a 'reboot' for operating systems. IPLs for workstations can be common, but when it comes to servers they should only occur when scheduled or when intentionally executed by an administrator. Causes could be:

- Intentional (but the person did not communicate properly)
- Unexpected (due to a misconfiguration or misbehavior of software or faulty hardware)
- Malicious (for example, an attacker rebooting the system after installation of a Trojan horse)

The third type of scenario is referred to as a <u>*deviation from the standard*</u>. Every system should have a 'know good' baseline, which is the excepted behavior when the system is functioning normally. This should be expressed in quantified terms, such as requests per second, % CPU usage, memory usage, response times, etc. If the periodically measured value of a system deviates significantly from the baseline measurements, an investigation should be launched to identify the issue. It should be noted that after any hardware upgrades all systems running on that hardware should be re-baselined to avoid false-negatives.

Questions

1. Which best describes the ability to mitigate the damage resulting from unauthorized disclosure of information?

    A) Confidential recovery

    B) Leakage closure

    C) Operational security

    D) Security restoration

2. Which best describes a system that collects logs throughout the network and automatically correlates the information?

    A) Log management system

    B) Audit trail analyzer

    C) Event management system

    D) Event correlation manager

3. Which best describes software starting up after a shutdown that was unexpected, intentional but non-malicious, and malicious?

    A) Startup sequence

    B) Live restoration

    C) Original module recovery

    D) Initial program load

4. Which best describes a periodically measured value of a system that deviates significantly from the baseline measurements?

    A) Deviation from the standard

    B) Standard arrived-at

    C) Deviation from the mean

    D) Baseline deviation

Chapter 57: Configuration Management

Operational security includes _configuration management_, which ensures that operations are carried out in the proper security context.

The state of a system must be controlled during certain vulnerable times, including:

- The startup sequence
- Error handling
- The shutdown sequence
- Restoration from a known good source

During these periods the system must ensure that lower privileged processes cannot directly access hardware resources unless authorized by a kernel (higher-privileged) process. Alternatively, kernel processes may act on behalf of the user process instead of temporarily allowing direct access.

A _trusted recovery_ indicates that when a system unexpectedly crashes or shuts down, it is not put into an unsecure state. Crashes normally occur because the system has detected a situation in which it thought it better to halt, shutdown or reboot, as opposed to simply continuing to operate. An OS's response to failure of this type will fall into 1 of 3 classifications:

- *System reboot* – the system shuts down in a controlled manner as a result of a kernel failure; examples might be insufficient memory or invalid data structures
- *Emergency system restart* – the system shuts down in an uncontrolled manner; an example might be a lower-privileged process attempting to access restricted memory, and the system deems it is safer to immediately shut down rather than allow the activity to continue
- *Cold start* – the system shuts down and fails to execute a normal recovery procedure; in this case administrator intervention is required

When a system crashes and a normal recovery procedure fails, the following steps might be taken:

1) *Come up in a single user or safe mode* – OS loads but in a severely restricted mode without advanced services, network access and typically in a non-graphical console UI; the administrator will need to either physically be connected via KVM (keyboard, mouse, video) switches or connect to the serial port.
2) *Fix issue and recover files* – restore corrupted or invalid files to the correct state.
3) *Validate critical files and operations* – if it is determined that files were corrupted or compromised, all configuration and system files should be checked for integrity using hashes or checksums, and the system must be verified against system documentation.

A trusted recovery process should:

- Not allow changes to the boot up drive sequence
- Ensure actions are always written to system logs – separation of duties should prevent the same person from altering system logs and configuration files; otherwise an attacker could alter the state a system starts in and hide the change
- Allow only an administrator to force a system shutdown – privilege escalation would be required to bypass this
- Not allow outputs to be rerouted – rerouting the output of diagnostic tools or the console can allow an attacker to gain valuable information about a system

Aside from a system's state and recovery, configuration management is concerned with both input and output – they must be properly controlled to ensure a secure state. Some input controls are:

- Validating data provided by an external user or process
- Ensuring that all transactions are _atomic_ (they cannot be interrupted between input and output)
- Timestamping and logging all transactions
- Requiring that all configuration files and executable code (such as DLLs, plug-ins or device drivers) are digitally signed and that policies restricting use of code that is not signed or is not trusted are in-place and cannot be overridden by users

On the other end of the mechanism we have the output of a system, which must also be properly controlled by:

- Using hashing or message authentication codes to ensure integrity
- Clearly labeling the sensitivity or classification

Chapter 57: Configuration Management

- Ensuring that if there is no resulting information, the output should state 'no output'; this is to remove any ambiguity of whether a transaction was run, and if it completed or failed

Systems should be *hardened*, a description used for systems in which all features and services not required have been removed or disabled and remaining features have been configured to the most conservative setting that remains usable.

A *gold master* (*GM*) should be created for systems, representing a standard hardened image that:

- Should have all extraneous services and applications removed
- Has been scanned for vulnerabilities
- Has been ideally penetration tested
- Has been configured such that each application service runs under its own user account

Once a GM has been created and vetted, it is cloned to the hard drive for new systems, and then updated as-needed for specific uses.

Finally, configuration management also covers remote access security. Best practices for proper configuration are:

- Require a VPN connection with 2-factor authentication
- Commands and data should never be sent in the clear – use SSH
- Strong authentication should be used for any administrative activity
- Critical systems should not allow remote administration
- The number of remote administrators should be limited

Chapter 57: Configuration Management

Questions

1. Which of the following terms ensures that operations are carried in the proper security context?

    A) Operational assurance

    B) Configuration Management

    C) Configuration context

    D) Security assurance

2. Which of the following terms best describes a system that shuts down in an uncontrolled manner?

    A) Cold start

    B) Warm start

    C) Emergency system restart

    D) System reboot

3. Which of the following is NOT an OS's response to a crash?

    A) Warm start

    B) Emergency system restart

    C) Cold start

    D) System reboot

4. Which of the following terms best describes a system that shuts down in a controlled manner as a result of a kernel failure?

    A) Emergency system restart

    B) Cold start

    C) Warm start

    D) System reboot

5. Which of the following terms best describes a system that unexpectedly shuts down and comes back up in a secure state?

    A) Secure recovery

    B) Failsafe start

    C) Complete recovery

    D) Trusted recovery

Chapter 58: Physical Security

Physical security should always be layered – for example, using outdoor lighting, fences, locked doors and a vault provides 4 layers of defense. Even more protection is afforded when the controls are diversified. An example of *diversity of controls* might be requiring unique keys for all locks, instead of having a single key. Facilities should define two modes of operation – one for 'open' hours during which people are actively entering and exiting the facility, and another mode for 'closed' hours with significantly reduced traffic. Physical security access controls require both physical and technical components. By far the best security mechanisms are personnel, but they are also the most expensive. Security personnel need to be trained on not only what activity is suspicious, but also how to report that activity.

Locks

Access control points can be in 1 of 3 categories:

- *Main* (primary personnel entrance and exit)
- Secondary (such as side doors)
- External (such as doors for delivery)

Many people often consider door locks to be a secure mechanism, but they really are only considered to be *delaying devices* – they will only slow down a determined intruder. When considering the strength of locks, the surrounding area must also be examined such as the door, door frame, hinges and the surrounding wall. For example, the strongest lock on the heaviest door does not good if you can simply punch a hole in the wall next to the door. There are quite a few different types of mechanical locks. A *warded lock* is the simplest, and is represented by your basic padlock with a key. The next step up is a *tumbler lock* which comes in 3 flavors:

- *Wafer tumbler lock* – file cabinet locks - uses wafers instead of pins and is easy to beat
- *Pin tumbler lock* – door lock - the key raises individual pins, allowing the cylinder to rotate
- *Lever tumbler lock* – safe locks - uses moving levers to unlock

Locks vary in degrees of ability to resist destructive forces:

- *Grade 1* - Commercial and industrial
- *Grade 2* - Heavy-duty residential or light-duty commercial
- *Grade 3* – Residential or consumer

A *cylinder lock* has a keyhole and tumbler mechanism contained in a cylinder. They come in 3 levels of security in terms of their resistance to lock picking (opening a lock without the required key):

- Low security – no resistance
- Medium security – some resistance
- *High security* –resistance provided through multiple mechanisms (Grade 1 or Grade 2 locks only)

There are multiple methods an attacker can use to defeat locks, but the most common are:

- *Tension wrench* – an L-shaped tool that manipulates pins
- *Raking* – a tool that applies pressure against pins while quickly removing
- *Bumping* – a tool that uses a bump key to force pins into the right position

Keys must be properly managed throughout their lifetime from being assigned, periodic inventory and final destruction. Most facilities will possess a *master key* that opens all locks, and one or more *submaster keys* that open a specific range of doors.

A different type of mechanical lock is called a *combination lock*. This lock uses one or more internal spinning wheels that require an external spin control to be rotated both clockwise and counterclockwise by the operator. An electrical version has a keypad instead of a spin control.

Cipher locks somewhat resemble electric combination locks in that they also have a keypad, but are small programmable computers. Some features they provide are:

- *Door delay* – if door is held open an alarm triggers
- *Key override* –a specific code can be used to override normal procedures
- *Master keying* –supervisors can change access codes and features
- *Hostage alarm* – a special code can be used to communicate duress

Cipher locks normally support a fail-safe mode in which the door automatically unlocks in the event of a power failure to allow people to escape. Changing codes on this type of locks is important, as the keys will eventually appear faded or worn from overuse of the same code, making it much easier for an attacker to guess the actual code. Upper-end cipher locks are called _smart locks_ and are capable of intelligently making access decisions based on specific conditions such as time of day or specific user codes.

Device locks prevent hardware devices from being stolen or accessed in specific ways:

- _Switch controls_ – covers on/off switches
- _Slot locks_ – secures mobile systems to a stationary component using a steel cable
- _Port controls_ – blocks access to disk drives or USB ports
- _Peripheral switch controls_ – inserts an on/off switch between a peripheral and the system
- _Cable traps_ – prevent removal of I/O devices by passing the device's cable through a lockable unit

Personnel Access Controls

Electronic devices that require authorization before allowing a person into a secured area are called _personnel access controls_. These devices usually read some type of card, but can be biometric-enabled and require 2 factors of authentication. The cards may be memory cards or smart cards, which we have already covered both previously. A _user-activated reader_ is a device that requires a user to initiate interaction, such as by swiping a card. A _system sensing access control reader_ (_transponder_) automatically senses an approaching person and reads the card wirelessly. A proximity detection device that identifies and authenticates a person is called an _electronic access control token_ (_EAC token_).

The biggest threat to personnel access control mechanisms is that of _piggybacking_, in which an unauthorized person gains accessing by using another person's credentials. Normally the individual simply follows an authorized person through a door without providing credentials. Sometimes the term _tailgating_ will also be used - the difference between the two is that piggybacking can occur with the authorized individual's consent, while with tailgating the authorized individual is not aware. Tailgating is a type of piggybacking. In either case the best preventative is to have a security guard present.

External Boundary Protection Mechanisms

Boundary protection mechanisms are used to control pedestrian and vehicle flow, provide different security zones, to provide delaying mechanisms and to control entry points. There are 6 types of control types:

- _Access control mechanisms_ – locks, card access systems, personnel awareness
- Physical barriers – fences, gates, walls, doors
- Intrusion detection – motion detectors
- _Assessment_ – guards, CCTV (anything that requires a human)
- _Response_ – guards and law enforcement
- _Deterrents_ – signs, lighting, environmental design

Fences

Like locks, _fences_ are only considered to be a delaying mechanism at best, but even the sight of fencing acts as a deterrent and provides crowd and access control. At times bushes or trees may be used to hide fences if they are deemed unsightly, but such vegetation over time usually leads to damage. When deciding on the height of a fence, the type of threat being addressed must be taken into consideration. For example, the height of a fence dictates its purpose:

- 3-4 Feet – deters casual trespassers
- 6-7 Feet – too high to easily climb
- 8 Feet or higher – means serious business

A barbed wire top on a tall fence can add to its effectiveness – the tilt of the barbed wire indicates if it is meant to keep people in or out (tilted out keeps people out). Fence posts should be buried deeply in concrete, and on uneven ground the fence should extend into the soil. The material used in the fencing will depend on the expected activity – cutting, climbing or even driving a vehicle through. Wire is measured in units of _gauge_ - the lower the gauge, the thicker the wire. _Mesh_ is measured in terms of the distance between wires – the smaller the rating the more secure it will be. A _perimeter intrusion and detection assessment system_ (_PIDAS_) is a fence that detects vibrations, but has a high false-positive rate. The strength of gates must match the fence, and there are 4 classifications:

- _Class 1_ – residential
- _Class II_ – commercial for public access
- _Class III_ – industrial for limited access

- *Class IV* – restricted access such as a prison gate

Although technically not a fence, a bollard serves a similar purpose- it is a small concrete pillar that prevents vehicles from driving into buildings.

Lighting

While fencing provides a delaying mechanism, *lighting* is equally effective but in a different manner – it is used to deter criminal acts (and prevent lawsuits). When using lighting, there should be no dead areas, and it should provide plenty of contrast between people and the background - so lighter-colored areas need less illumination. The higher the wattage, the more area a light covers, but critical areas must have a light that reaches at least 8 feet in diameter with 2 foot-candles. There are several terms to describe various aspects of security lighting:

- *Glare protection* - lighting should point toward the direction of potential attackers and away from security
- *Continuous lighting* - an array of lighting that provides an even amount of illumination
- *Controlled lighting* - prevents the light from bleeding over into unwanted areas
- *Standby lighting* - used to automatically turn lights on and off so that intruders think people are present
- *Backup lighting* – used in the event of power failure
- *Responsive area illumination* - turns on lighting when an intruder is detected; this results in a high false-positive so CCTV should also be used to allow remote verification if there is an actual problem

Lastly, attackers will want to eliminate any lighting, so lighting controls and switches should be properly protected and locked.

Surveillance Devices

Visual monitoring is normally achieved by using *closed-circuit TVs* (*CCTVs*). These types of systems are very useful, but to properly purchase and install an effective solution, there are several factors that must be taken into consideration:

- *Purpose* – to detect, assess or identify intruders
- *Environment* – internal or external areas
- *Field of view* – large or small area
- *Amount of lighting* – lit areas, unlit areas or sunlit areas
- *Integration* - with guards, IDSs or alarm systems

CCTV systems consist of the following components: camera, multiplexer, monitor and the recording system. The *camera* normally sends its video over a dedicated cable (thus calling it 'closed circuit'), but some systems employ wireless video. A *multiplexer* accepts multiple camera feeds and produces a single video feed to the *monitor*. The signal is simultaneously sent to a recording device that compresses the video into a digital format for later review in case an event occurs that warrants further investigation. Because sitting and watching a monitor can quickly become mind-numbing, the systems commonly employ an *annunciator* when an alert is raised – some type of alert (flashing light or audible warning) to let the guards know to immediately investigate further. The most common type of attack to occur on CCTV is to capture video when nothing is happening and then replay it while activity is going on. A timestamp on the screen can help prevent this.

The most important part of a CCTV system will be the cameras – without a clear image it will be impossible to effectively use the system. So, let's go over that component in detail. Every camera has a *charge-coupled device* (*CDD*) that converts light into an electrical signal.

The lens *focal length* determines how wide or narrow the captured image is. A short focal length results in a very wide-angle view that covers a lot of area, while a long focal length provides a much narrower field of vision, but can provide more detail on objects further away.

A *zoom* can be digital or optical. A *digital zoom* happens after an image is captured – enlarging an area will result in pixilation because the image has already been stored. *Optical zoom*, on the other hand, changes the field of view before the image is captured resulting in greater detail.

The *depth of focus* controls whether objects that remain in focus (not blurry) are close or far away. A shallow depth of focus keeps close objects sharp, while a deep depth of focus allows objects far away to remain detailed.

The *iris* is a mechanism that opens and closes around the lens to limit how much light is let in – too much light and everything turns out white – too little light and everything is black. A *manual iris lens* must be manually adjusted at the camera, while an auto iris lens automatically responds to ambient light and opens/closes as-needed to maintain a useable image. _Lux_ is the term most often used to indicate the minimum amount of light needed for a clear image in dark conditions – the lower the lux value, the less light a camera will need.

Finally, cameras can be mounted in two manners – _fixed mount_ in which the camera must be manually adjusted to point in different directions, and _pan, tilt, zoom_ (_PTZ_), which allows a camera operator to remotely move the camera around as well as to control the zoom level.

Intrusion Detection Systems

An _intrusion detection system_ (_IDS_) is used to detect changes in an environment and raise an alert of some type, and some are often referred to as _perimeter scanning devices_. There are several categories of IDSs:

- _Volumetric systems_ detect changes in an environmental baseline, and are very sensitive
- _Electromechanical systems_ detect a change in some type of electrical or magnetic circuit; used to detect open doors and windows; a pressure pad is another example where weight sets off an alarm
- Photoelectric systems (photometric systems) detect a change in a light beam
- _Cross-sectional photoelectric systems_ use multiple beams of light, usually accomplished by mirrors bouncing the signal several times before reaching the detector; used to detect movement
- _Passive infrared systems_ (_PIRs_) monitors heat waves and detects a change; used to detect people or active tools
- _Acoustical detection systems_ uses microphones to detect changes in volume; these are very sensitive, and traffic and weather can set them off; used for rooms far away from ambient noise
- _Vibration sensors_ detect large vibrations such as drilling, cutting or a destructive force; used for walls and vaults
- _Wave-pattern motion detectors_ send out microwave, ultrasonic, or low frequency waves and expects it to return uninterrupted; used for large rooms

- _Proximity detectors_ (_capacitance detectors_) emit a magnetic field and alerts if interrupted; usually used for small areas such as cabinets or safes; this is an example of an _Electrostatic IDS_.

IDSs can generate a local or remote alert. They are expensive and require human intervention when an alarm is activated, but can be linked to a centralized security system for remote monitoring. They do require a backup power supply, should default to fail-secure, and should be able to detect and resists tampering.

Patrol Force and Guards

By far the best security mechanisms are _security guards_. They are very flexible, provide an excellent response to suspicious activities, provide the human factor for IDS alerts, and are a great deterrent to criminal activity. However, they are also very expensive and sometimes unreliable due to making exceptions to security policies. Guards should clearly understand their duties.

Dogs are an effective lower-cost alternative to human guards because of their heightened sense of smell and hearing as well as intelligence and loyalty. However, they will not be able to tell the difference between authorized and unauthorized people, so they usually need to be accompanied by humans.

Auditing Physical Access

Physical access controls can almost always be configured to produce automated logs, which should be reviewed and monitored by guards daily, and by management on a less-frequent but recurring basis. They are detective, not preventative, and therefore are useful only after an incident has occurred. When reviewing logs, the following information should be present and examined:

- Date/time
- Entry point
- User ID
- If the access was unsuccessful

Chapter 58: Physical Security

Questions

1. Which type of device lock prevents removal of I/O devices by passing the device's cable through a lockable unit?

    A) Peripheral switch control

    B) Cable trap

    C) Port control

    D) Slot lock

2. What concept randomizes controls to increase the chance of compromise?

    A) Defense-in-depth

    B) Diversity of controls

    C) Random layering

    D) Variety layout

3. Which camera feature determines the minimum amount of light needed for a clear image in dark conditions?

    A) Focal length

    B) Iris

    C) Depth of focus

    D) Lux

4. Which grade of lock represents a heavy-duty residential or light-duty commercial lock?

    A) Grade 3

    B) Grade 2

    C) Grade 4

    D) Grade 1

5. What gate strength is used for residential purposes?

    A) Class III

    B) Class 1

    C) Class II

    D) Class IV

Chapter 59: Secure Resource Provisioning

The term *provisioning* references the activities necessary to provide a new service to one or more users. From a security perspective, provisioning must ensure that the service operates in a secure manner as well as securing access to it by users or systems. One of the key dependencies an effective resource provisioning plan has is this - you can't protect what you don't know you have. In other words, we must always have an accurate inventory of both hardware and software assets on-hand.

Tracking hardware in a secure manner might seem to be straightforward, but there are two difficulties that must be overcome. First, we must ensure that when new hardware arrives through the door that it has not already been compromised. *ISO 28000* addresses a *secure supply chain*, and references 3 aspects:

- *Trusted supplier* – the manufacturer and supplier must be trusted to create a secure product
- *Trusted transportation network* – the transportation mechanism between the supplier and our door must be secure
- *Trusted inspection* – before the hardware is allowed into our inventory it must be inspected

Secondly, inventory mechanisms must account for unknown devices that connect to the network, such as phones, tablets, desktop, rogue switches, etc. The most effective method for discovering hard devices attached to the network is to walk the premises, preferably during off-hours, and look for devices.

Like hardware, software must also be inventoried, but software provides an interesting twist. Not only are we concerned about security, but liability issues as well. Unlicensed or pirated software can cause a two-fold problem:

- Software companies want to be paid for using their software, and if employees install unlicensed copies, the company will be held liable for them. The authors of such software can be notified by either disgruntled employees or the software itself 'phoning home' and checking in over the Internet.
- Pirated software is notorious for embedding backdoors or Trojan horses, creating a significant security concern. Additionally, you can't update unlicensed software so security holes remain unpatched.

The solutions to both of the above problems are:

- *Application whitelisting* – only allow authorized software to be downloaded and installed
- *Use gold masters* – IT now knows what is installed on each system
- *Enforce least privilege* – users cannot install software by default
- *Automated scanning* – every device should be scanned to see what it is running on a periodic basis

Configuration management (*CM*) is the process of establishing and maintaining a consistent baseline of all systems. This requires a policy dictating how changes are made, who can do them, how they are approved, how they are documented and how they are communicated to employees. Writing and enforcing such policies is much less effort that trying to fix the damage after the fact. CM applies to environments as well as product development, and before changes are applied, some form of a backup should always be taken.

When dealing with cloud assets, the process is the same, but the number of people involved may differ than if systems were installed within the network. IaaS changes should be limited to a very few number of people in IT, and PaaS is limited to an even smaller number of people because platforms are very often specific services for a very granular task. On the other hand, the number of people capable of making changes in a SaaS can be quite large since high-level tools are often provided for setup and configuration, and the skillset is therefore mush less stringent.

To effectively manage provisioning of any type, a rigid change control process must be designed and enforced for items such as systems, applications, patches, upgrades, policies, bug fixes, reconfiguration, and new devices. Best practices dictate that the following steps be followed:

- Request a change to take place
- Approve
- Document
- Implement (scheduled)
- Test
- Report to management

Questions

1. When dealing with a secure supply chain, which aspect addresses creating a secure product?

    A) Trusted vendor

    B) Trusted export

    C) Trusted inspection

    D) Trusted supplier

2. What term best describes the activities necessary to provide a new service to one or more users?

    A) Rollout

    B) Capability increase

    C) Provisioning

    D) Service accommodation

3. When dealing with a secure supply chain, which aspect ensures that the hardware is not allowed into inventory until inspected?

    A) Trusted delivery

    B) Trusted inspection

    C) Trusted transportation network

    D) Trusted supplier

4. When dealing with a secure supply chain, which aspect addresses the need for the transportation mechanism between the supplier and the delivery door to be secure?

    A) Trusted delivery

    B) Trusted transportation network

    C) Trusted supplier

    D) Trusted inspection

5. Which standard addresses a secure supply chain?

    A) ASE 45-01

    B) ISO 28000

    C) NIST 800-34

    D) ISO 27002

Chapter 60: Network and Resource Availability

Network and resource availability is concerned with one thing - making sure availability is 'available'. It ensures that everything is in place *before* bad things happen. There are 4 primary components:

- *Redundant hardware* – hot/warm swaps waiting in the wings for a failure to occur with little downtime
- *Fault-tolerance* – active backup solutions that kick in automatically with no downtime – these are the most expensive
- *Service level agreements* (*SLAs*) – these must be clearly communicated so that a company can make the correct purchasing decisions
- *Solid operational procedures* – well-documented and enforced procedures to prevent mistakes

When it comes to hardware, one of the most important ways to measure expected failure rates is to use the *Mean Time Between Failure* (*MTBF*). This value measures how long we expect a piece of equipment to continue operating in a usable manner, and is calculated by taking the average time between failures for a given system. Note that adding additional devices does not translate into higher MTBFs – quite the opposite. However, including devices in a redundant manner, such as RAID configurations, does help with reliability. Whereas MTBF implies that the equipment can be repaired, *Mean Time To Failure* (*MTTF*) is a measure of the lifetime of a product. A manufacturer typically provides MTBF for a given product, but if an organization buys a product in relatively high volume and tracks MTBF on its own, the process could reveal products that are underperforming.

Along with MTBF and MTTF, we have *Mean Time To Repair* (*MTTR*), which is the expected amount of time required to get a failed device back into a production state. For RAID, MTTR is the number of hours between noticing that a drive has failed and when the array has completed rewriting data to the new drive. For desktop systems, this value is usually measured in days. If MTTR is too high for a given device, then redundancy should be built in.

A *single point of failure* has a high risk, because if the device fails, any other systems or networks dependent on the device will fail as well. The best defense against this is to ensure proper maintenance, perform regular backups, to and implement some type of redundancy or fault tolerance. To protect against router or switch single point of failures, dynamic routing protocols should be enabled, and multiple provider links should be established. To protect against hard drive failure, a *Redundant Array of Independent Disks* (*RAID*) configuration should be used. RAID has already been covered, but for review here are the most common levels:

- *RAID 0* – striped over multiple drives for performance
- *RAID 1* – mirrored – data is written to 2 drives simultaneously
- *RAID 2* – data striping at the bit level across all drives
- *RAID 3* – data striping with one parity drive at the byte level
- *RAID 4* - data striping with one parity drive at the block level
- *RAID 5* – data is written in disk sector units to all drives along with parity; most common
- *RAID 6* – same as RAID 5 plus a second set of parity on all drives
- *RAID 10* – mirrored and striped across several drives

There are quite a few different options for implementing fail-over and redundancy.

- *Direct Access Storage Device* (*DASD*) is your common magnetic hard drive (RAID is a type of DASD); any location on a DASD may be reached immediately
- *Sequential Access Storage Device* (*SASD*) are devices such as tape drives, where all locations in between the current and target location must be traversed to reach (you must fast-forward a tape drive to get to a specific location)
- *Massive Array of Inactive Disks* (*MAID*) offers storage in the area of hundreds of terabytes and is write-optimized
- *Redundant Array of Independent Tapes* (*RAIT*) is similar to RAID but uses tapes instead of hard drives in a RAID 1 configuration (mirroring). RAIT is a more economical option than MAID when smaller storage requirements are required.
- A *Storage Area Network* (*SAN*) is a very small, high-speed network between multiple storage devices, in which a centralized server reads and writes files among all devices on behalf of clients. SANs provide redundancy, fault tolerance, reliability and automated backups and are generally used when storage in the terabytes

range is required. Because they are self-contained, SANs can leverage tape drives, optical jukeboxes and disk arrays simultaneously.

- *Clustering* is a fault-tolerance technology similar to redundant servers, but where all servers take an active part in fulfilling requests instead of waiting until needed. Clusters are managed as a single system, providing load balancing, availability and scalability and are sometimes referred to as server farms. Clustering is favored over redundant servers since no resources are wasted as they sit idle.
- *Grid computing* allows geographically disparate systems to dynamically join and leave a network focused on a single task. By taking part in this infrastructure, systems with free CPU cycles can take part in a distributed effort for a single cause. SETI was the first project supporting such an effort. In clustering, each node trusts all other nodes, but with grid computing, no one trusts each other and has no central control. FYI, rainbow tables were created using grid computing.

In the event of a failure and all other options have been exhausted, often restoring a backup is the ultimate last step. We have already covered backups in detail, but we do want to talk about *Hierarchical Storage Management* (*HSM*) systems. HSMs provide continuous online backups by combining hard disks and cheaper optical or tape jukeboxes. HSM stores seldom-used files on the slower, or *near-line*, devices while newer data that is accessed more frequently is stored on faster devices. To a user, all data is present as a 'stub', but when the stub is requested, HSM will retrieve the actual data from whichever media it is stored on.

Finally, a note about contingency planning - whereas BCP (Business Continuity Planning) addresses disaster-level events, contingency planning deals with smaller issues such as power outages or server failures. Contingency plans require a written plan to follow during a crisis which should never be trusted until thoroughly tested. The plan should be copied and stored in 3 different locations – the original located on-site, another on-site copy that is protected in a fireproof safe, and a copy that is stored off-site.

Chapter 60: Network and Resource Availability

Questions

1. Which value is a measure of the lifetime of a product?

    A) MTBF

    B) MTTF

    C) MTTD

    D) MTTR

2. Which of the following is NOT something that should be in place in order to ensure network and resource availability?

    A) Fault-tolerance

    B) SLAs

    C) Redundant hardware

    D) Solid guidelines

3. Which level of RAID has data striping at the bit level across all drives?

    A) RAID 0

    B) RAID 2

    C) RAID 3

    D) RAID 1

4. Which level of RAID is the same as RAID 5 plus a second set of parity on all drives?

    A) RAID 3

    B) RAID 10

    C) RAID 4

    D) RAID 6

5. Which type of data storage is represented by storage in the hundreds of terabytes and is write-optimized?

    A) Sequential Access Storage Device

    B) Redundant Array of Independent Tapes

    C) Direct Access Storage Device

    D) Massive Array of Inactive Disks

Chapter 61: Preventative Measures

It is crucial that an IT department has the right tools if they wish to be effective. There are 5 steps to follow to select the appropriate tools:

- *Understand the risk* – you can't eliminate all risks, so only attack the most important ones – this requires a prioritized list
- *Use the right controls* – identifying the risks allows you to identify the controls. One control can mitigate many risks, and that capability should put it at the top of the list. Alternatively, a single risk might require multiple controls, but if the risk is great enough, it may be justified.
- *Use the controls correctly* – once selected, a control must be properly installed and configured. For example, a high-caliber IDS will be rendered inert if placed in the wrong location.
- *Manage your configuration* – configuration management is a must for 3 reasons:
    - Unauthorized or undocumented changes results in risk
    - Forgotten configurations become obsolete over time
    - You will always know the state of your network
- *Assess your operation* – periodically compare your plan to the current threats to ensure they align, carry out control tests using automated tools, and perform pen tests.

Of course, some controls are so pervasive that they will always be needed, such as firewalls. Dedicated firewall appliances are relatively uncommon – the functionality is usually packaged in with routers, load balancers or software solutions. When placing a firewall in a network, the first step is to list all threats a network faces, and then create a sub-list of the threats a firewall can mitigate. This will dictate the location and number of firewalls a network requires. Aside from locations, the rules that firewalls operate on are the most important aspects, and configuration management is an absolute must for maintaining firewalls. Once all above has been accomplished, firewall effectiveness needs to be tested against the original list of threats.

We have already covered IDSs and IPSs in-depth, but they are so important that we need to revisit them again. The 3 types – NIDS (network), HIDS (host) and WIDS (wireless) – have different capabilities and purposes, and all 3 must be considered. Both IDSs and IPSs have the potential to become network bottlenecks, so throughput must be considered. Placement of sensors is critical to the success of such devices – ideally start as close to edge routers as possible while still staying within the network perimeter. False-positives and false-negatives must be taken into account and reduced by establishing a baseline, even with rule-based or signature-based devices. On-going fine-tuning of an IDS/IPS device is always required, particularly when whitelisting (known good) or *blacklisting* (known bad) is used. If an intrusion device has knowledge about devices authorized to operate on a network, it can make more intelligent decisions.

Antimalware (*antivirus*) works by extracting a signature from files and comparing it to a known list of malware that is updated weekly. Most products are effective against more than 90% of known malwares, and are relatively cheap. However, a sophisticated attacker can easily create malware that is invisible to the known list, so if he knows the product a specific company uses, he can craft a package to infiltrate that network and bypass the antimalware products.

Patch management is the process for identifying, acquiring, installing and verifying patches for products and systems. *Patches* are software updates designed to remove a defect or vulnerability in software. Patches can be managed in 2 ways. *Unmanaged patching* is implemented by allowing software to check for patches and updates and applying them. However, this carries a lot of risks:

- *Credentials* – most installations require administrator credentials
- *Configuration management* – it will be easy to lose track of what version is running where
- *Bandwidth utilization* – allowing each software installation to download the patch individually can cause a significant strain on the network
- *Service availability* – servers are seldom configured to utilize this method because patches often take services offline and lead to instability

While unmanaged patching is better than none, it is never better than centralized managing of patches. *Centralized patch management* is best practice and supports 3 different approaches:

- *Agent based* – an agent runs on each device and contacts a central update server
- *Agentless* – one or more hosts connect to each device using network administrator credentials and install updates as-needed (Active Directory objects can be used for this as well)
- *Passive* – a system monitors network traffic and infers the patch levels on networked devices; this is the least invasive but also the least effective

Patches must always be tested before rolling out - virtualization makes this much easier. While testing is ongoing, other controls such as firewall rules, IDS and IPS can be used to mitigate known vulnerabilities. Once testing has been completed, it is best to patch subnets incrementally to reduce risk and to minimize network congestion.

Note that attackers can reverse engineer patches to find the vulnerabilities that the patch addresses – this is a much cheaper way to find zero day vulnerabilities. If an attacker can do this quickly, he might be able to exploit the vulnerability before a company can roll out the patch. Code obfuscation (making it harder to reverse engineer code by making it more difficult to read) is being used by vendors to delay attackers, but it is always a race.

We have already discussed honeypots and honeynets in detail, but we haven't discussed honeyclients yet. A *honeyclient* is a client application that can be used to safely explore malicious web sites or links (usually sent in phishing attacks). The attacker is free to do whatever damage he thinks is happening within the honeyclient, but in fact no damage results because the honeyclient is running inside of a sandbox. Now, a *sandbox* (sometimes called an *emulation buffer*) is an application execution environment that abstracts the code away from the actual operating system, providing an extra layer of protection to be inserted. In this case, the honeyclient sits inside of a sandbox, which then interacts with the host OS, preventing any damage from occurring. This allows someone to sit and watch what happens and figure out how the attacker is trying to operate.

Questions

1. What is the process for identifying, acquiring, installing and verifying updates for products and systems?

    A) Systems maintenance

    B) Secure stance

    C) Patch management

    D) Update acquisition

2. What is the term for only allowing known good entries to pass a filter?

    A) Assertion gate

    B) Negative access

    C) Known allowed

    D) Whitelisting

3. Which centralized patch management approach monitors network traffic and infers the patch levels on networked devices?

    A) Agent based

    B) Passive

    C) Active

    D) Agentless

4. Which centralized patch management approach installs software on each device which contacts a central update server?

    A) Agent based

    B) Passive

    C) Active

    D) Agentless

5. Which of the following is NOT a risk encountered with unmanaged patching?

    A) Service availability

    B) Bandwidth utilization

    C) Credential management

    D) Unauthorized patch application

Chapter 62: Managing Incidents

While the terms 'event' and 'incident' are similar, they have different meanings within the context of security. An *event* is any occurrence that can be observed, verified and documented. An *incident* is one or more related events that negatively affect a company and/or its security posture.

When victimized by a computer crime the environment and evidence should be left unaltered. Instead, the person designated to address incidents should be contacted, as a person unfamiliar with the proper procedures could inadvertently destroy evidence and thereby lessen the chance of a successful prosecution. *Computer Emergency Response Team* (*CERT*) is an organization which is a good resource for incident management processes.

Incident management is both proactive and reactive, and for proper incident handing a policy should be in place for dealing with computer incidents. This policy should be should be clear and concise, and managed by both the legal and security department. It should contain the following information:

- The identity of those possessing the authority to initiate an incident response
- A prioritized list of systems, and if each should be taken offline or continue functioning
- The identity of an *incident response team* consisting of representatives from the business units, HR, executive management, security and IT
- Instructions for employees on when to report an incident
- How employees should interact with external parties

Incident response teams can be 1 of 3 different types:

- *Virtual team* – experts who have other responsibilities within the organization
- *Permanent team* – one or more people dedicated strictly to incident response
- *Hybrid team* – one or more core permanent members with other experts on call as-needed

The incident response team should be properly equipped with the following items:

- A list of outside agencies to contact
- An outline of roles and responsibilities
- A call tree
- A list of computer and forensic experts to contact
- A list of steps to secure and preserve evidence
- A list of items that need to be included in a management report and for legal action
- The prioritized list of systems mentioned in the policy

Incident handling documentation should be a part of the disaster recovery planning, usually as an appendix.

Let's take a slight detour for a second and discuss a *kill chain* - the progression of almost all attacks. It is helpful to understand this model when an attack is underway, as it allows the incident response team to be able to identify how far along the attack is, and what the attacker's next step will probably be. The steps are:

- Reconnaissance – deliberate information gathering
- *Weaponization* – preparing and testing weapons based on reconnaissance
- *Delivery* – delivery of the cyber weapon (95% of cases are via email)
- *Exploitation* – the malicious software is executing on a CPU as a result of delivery
- *Installation* – installation of the real payload in a persisted manner is carried out by the malicious software
- *Command and Control* (*C&C*) – the payload phones home to check in and gather instructions
- Actions on the Objective – the payload carries out the instructions as directed

Now that we understand the attack model, we can discuss how an incident response team would react to a report that an attack is underway. The first step is *Detection*. The primary difficulty with detection of an attack in a network setting is that IDSs produce a lot of false-positives, and can easily hide an attack in the noise. That is why fine-tuning the sensors are so important prior to an attack.

The second step is *Response*. Before any action is taking, the team must first gather data and find the root cause of the attack – the who, how, when and why. During this time management must be kept up-to-date as they will be making decisions going forward. Keep in mind that many log files purge or roll over after just a few hours, so time is of the essence in capturing the log files. The team should create a hypothesis and test it based on the information gathered. If the hypothesis does not match the facts, continue analysis. Once the correct hypothesis has been arrived at, it should be relatively simply to figure out where in the kill chain the attacker currently is.

This leads us to the third step, *Mitigation*. Here, the team contains the damage done or about to be done to the most critical assets first, followed by less critical assets as-needed.

The mitigation (containment) strategy depends on whether the attack was internal or external, the type of assets affected and how critical the affect assets are. The containment steps can be either reactive or proactive:

- Reactive – isolate the system(s), revise firewall rules and ACLs
- Proactive – activate a honeypot

This provides the time necessary to carry out the remaining steps.

The fourth step, *Reporting*, is a little misleading. The initial report that lead the incident response team to start their investigation is part of this step, but it is placed 4th because it is an on-going activity throughout the entire incident response process. What information should be contained within the final report? The NIST SP 800-61 "Computer Security Incident Handling Guide" lists the following

- Summary
- Indicators
- Related incidents
- Actions taken
- Chain of custody
- Impact assessment
- Identity and comments of incident handlers
- Next steps

The fifth step is *Recovery*, but before executing this step all information from previous steps should be gathered - every incident should be treated as if it will eventually end up in court. This step returns all systems to a known-good state. This should almost always involve restoring compromised hosts by reinstalling from a gold image, followed by restoring data from the most recent backup for that host.

The final step is *Remediation*. First, the team should decide which measures executed during the Mitigation phase should become permanent. Secondly, indicators of attack and indicators of compromise should be documented. *Indicators of attack* (*IOA*) represent data that can tell the security team that an attack is underway, while *indicators of compromise* (*IOC*) can tell a response team if a successful attack has already been completed. Both indicators use the same set of data:

- Outbound traffic to a specific IP address or domain
- Abnormal DNS query patterns
- Unusually large HTTP requests or responses
- DDoS traffic
- New registry entries for Windows systems

Questions

1. What is the term describing the progression of almost all attacks?

    A) Kill chain

    B) Attack path

    C) Attack tree

    D) Kill path

2. In which attack step does the payload carry out instructions as directed?

    A) Actions on the objective

    B) Exploitation

    C) Command and control

    D) Weaponization

3. Which incident response team contains experts who have other responsibilities within the organization?

    A) Temporary team

    B) Permanent team

    C) Virtual team

    D) Hybrid team

4. Which attack step delivers the cyber weapon?

    A) Exploitation

    B) Weaponization

    C) Installation

    D) Delivery

5. What is any occurrence that can be observed, verified and documented?

    A) Encounter

    B) Incident

    C) Event

    D) Episode

Chapter 63: Disaster Recovery

For this section, we're going to cover a lot of territory and throw around quite a few definitions. So, let's create a scenario that we can use to describe the various bits of information in a real-world scenario. Let's say that there is a company in Long Beach, CA called 'Fish-n-Bits' that sells fishing equipment, both in a local brick and mortar store as well as through their online e-commerce site – roughly 50% of their revenue is generated through each revenue stream (the store and online). Fish-n-Bits employs 50 people and ships in 75% of their merchandise from Taiwan. They have a small data center in a building behind the storefront, and just hired a new CTO, Marvin, to come in and make sure they have proper disaster recovery plans in-place. Marvin imagines a scenario in which Los Angeles is hit by a 5.6 magnitude earthquake that destroys the store front and the office building behind, and creates a DRP around that scenario. Now back to the good stuff.

We have previously defined the _Maximum Tolerable Downtime_ (_MTD_) as the overall time a company can survive without a given system running in an operational capacity. Unfortunately, when it comes to making purchasing decisions, we need something more granular. So, let's add in a few more definitions that are required for BCP to properly create an effective plan.

The _Recovery Time Objective_ (_RTO_) is the longest time a business can survive without the affected process being restored to acceptable levels. The _Work Recovery Time_ (_WRT_) kicks in once a system is back up and running, but without the required data. WRT is the time required to restore that data and complete all testing prior to going live. If we were to express this as an equation, it would be:

WRT = MTD - RTO

In our example, if the Fish-n-Bits online ecommerce site is down for more than 1 week, the company may not have sufficient funds to provide payroll, resulting in all of their employees leaving. So, the RTO for the e-commerce site is 1 week. In our example, let's assume it will take 2 days to get the e-commerce hardware and network connections back up in an alternate location after an earthquake. That means that WRT is 5 days (7 days – 2 days) – Marvin has 5 days in which to restore the data and get the site live.

Restoring data is a great goal - but how much data was lost between the last backup and when the earthquake struck? The _Recovery Point Objective_ (_RPO_) measures this and is defined as the acceptable amount of data loss over time; essentially the maximum allowable time from the last backup if it were to be restored. In Marvin's case the RPO represents the number of days in which all online orders would be lost. For an e-commerce site this value needs to be in minutes, not days. We will discuss later how Marvin is going to achieve that.

MTD, RTO and RPO values are all calculated during the business impact analysis (BIA). Refer to the Security and Risk Management domain for a refresher. For mission-critical systems that collect data continuously (such as e-commerce sites), tape backups are not an acceptable solution for RPO – redundancy is a much better answer, and we will go further into that in just a bit. For now, just remember that the BCP teams needs to define the recovery processes and this process needs to be continuously re-evaluated to ensure that the MTD is met.

Business Process Recovery

To properly recover a business process, the BCP team must understand the process that needs to be protected in terms of people, assets and how they work together. Succinctly, the following items make up a process:

- Roles
- Resources
- Input and output mechanisms
- Internal workflow
- Time required to complete the process
- How it interfaces with other processes

Facility Recovery

BC must address 3 main types of disruptions:

- _Non-disaster_ – an event having a significant impact on a facility, but remains operational in a reduced capacity
- _Disaster_ – an event that causes the entire facility to be unusable for one day or longer, and an alternate facility is required for the business to continue operating
- _Catastrophe_ – an event that results in the facility being a complete loss, and both short-term and long-term facilities are required

There are 4 options for handling these disruptions. The first is to outsource services during disruptions, including both services and suppliers. The company is still ultimately responsible for continuing operations even if services are outsourced. When entering into an agreement with an outsourced service provider, the company should make sure that:

- The company Is financially viable and has a good BCP record
- That the ability to assure continuity is part of any proposal
- BCP is included with contracts and responsibilities are clearly spelled out
- SLAs are well-defined and realistic
- The outsourced company takes part in internal BCP activities

The second option for handling disruptions is to create a _redundant site_, which is a facility that the company owns and maintains, and is sometimes called a mirrored site. Within this redundant facility all processes are completely synchronized and live at all times. While this is the most expensive option, it is also the most reliable and quickest to spin up in event of a disaster. One alternative to a permanent structure is to use a _rolling hot site_ - a mobile data center contained in a large truck or trailer with self-contained communications capability. Another alternative is to employ a prefabricated building that can be setup and used – both alternatives require dedicated hardware that is always ready to go in order to qualify as a redundant site. Another (very expensive) alternative is to run _multiple processing centers_ wherein two or more centers in different regions are used continuously, and in the event of a local disruption, the services shift to another center. Large cloud providers such as Amazon and Microsoft use this model, but it is very uncommon in small to mid-level businesses.

The third option for handling disruptions is to use a _rented offsite installation_. This is a facility that is maintained by a third-party, but it is dedicated to the company. There are three types of rented (or leased) sites.

The first is called a _hot site_ and is very similar to a redundant site in that it is always ready to go at a moment's notice. The difference is that a redundant site is owned by the company, but a hot site is rented or leased from a third-party, and may or may not have synchronized data. The only missing components in a hot site are data and people – all hardware and software is already present and ready to go. This means that the site can become operational in a matter of hours. If the company has proprietary hardware or software, extra costs will more than likely be incurred monthly. Annual testing is relatively simple – have employees arrive, restore from some backups and start testing. Backup media should be tested periodically at the hot site which is a great way to perform the annual testing.

The second type of rented offsite installation is a _warm site_. This facility does not contain any customer hardware, but is ready to accept servers and people. When required, the company will need to bring in the hardware, configure it and apply data backups – as a result it can take days for the site to become operational. This option is expensive (although not nearly as expensive as a hot site) and is very difficult to test as there is no hardware present. Since all backup restoration devices will be carried in by the company in the event of a disruption, backup media should be tested at the original site. Most companies choose to use a warm site for their disaster recovery plans.

The third type of rented offsite installation is a _cold site_. This is a building with only the basics – it is essentially an empty data center, and can take a week or more to become operational. It is the cheapest solution, but annual testing is not plausible.

Before leaving the subject of rented offsite installations, let's cover several related terms.

- A _service bureau_ provides a rented offsite installation
- A _contingency company_ provides raw materials such as generator fuel or backup communication services
- A _tertiary site_ is a 'backup for the backup', or a Plan B when Plan A fails

Offsite locations must be geographically far enough away such that a single disaster does not affect both locations; the rule of thumb is at least 5 miles, with 15 miles being recommended, and a minimum of 50 to 200 miles for critical operations

The fourth option for handling disruptions is called a _reciprocal agreement_, in which the company enters into an agreement with another company to share their facilities if needed. This is a good Plan B measure, but if it is Plan A, there are a few concerns that should be thought through:

- Usually functional data centers are near their maximum capacity, and sharing a site between two companies could prove disastrous for both
- When making environmental changes in their data center, each company is now constrained by the reciprocal company

- Security is a concern as non-employees will have direct access to sensitive infrastructure
- Agreements are not legally enforceable, so there is no way to know if the other company will follow through until a disaster strikes

The final option for handling disruptions is called a *mutual aid agreement* and is used when 3 or more companies agree to aid each other in times of crisis. In these cases, a written agreement detailing responsibilities should be created with great scrutiny by the IT department.

Human Resources should be included in decisions when selecting offsite facilities, as they must consider the following:

- How to get people to man the backup site
- Costs for temporary housing and food
- Consider if new people will need to be hired, and if so, the skillsets required
- Plans for temporary replacement from an agency should be included

Supply and Technology Recovery

Many times, when we think of backup, only hardware and databases come immediately into mind. But it extends quite further than most of us realize. BCP should provide backup solutions for:

- Hardware
- Communication services
- People
- Transportation of hardware and people
- HVAC
- Security enforcement
- Supplies
- Documentation

BCP planners must intimately understand the company's technical infrastructure, which includes ensuring that documentation matches reality. The BCP process needs to know all hardware required to keep critical processes running, including restoration equipment such as tape readers. It needs to know if the images used to spin up replacements will remain compatible with the new hardware. Not only should BCP documents include details about image restoration, but also step-by-step details in case the image restoration process does not work. Estimates on how long it will take for replacement equipment to arrive should be enforceable via an SLA with the equipment vendor. If using legacy equipment, BCP should ask "Where would replacements come from?" This discovery process has often forced a company to move to COTS (commercial off-the-shelf) equipment.

Software backups must also be considered. Copies of software packages must be stored in an offsite backup location, tested periodically and updated when patches or new versions are rolled out. Software escrow should always be used to ensure purchased library source code is available in the event a third-party company goes out of business or is in breach of a contract.

Choosing a Software Backup Facility

When choosing a facility for storing backup software, the following issues should be considered:

- Can the media be accessed quickly enough?
- What are the operating hours and days of the facility?
- What access controls does it have (physical, administrative, technical) and are they tied to an alarm or police notifications?
- What threats can the facility protect the backup media from (fire, flood, earthquake, theft, etc.)?
- Does it have a bonded transport service to deliver the media during a disruption?
- Does it provide environment controls (temperature, humidity, etc.)?

Documentation on how to use backup software must be created and maintained and should include step-by-step instructions, contact information for people and vendors, a call tree and the person or role responsible for each restoration process. Responsibility for keeping documentation up to date should be assigned to one or more roles and individuals – without accountability it will never happen.

End-User Environment

In the event of a disaster, all server and network infrastructure will need to be restored along with moving the right people into place. However, we have missed a crucial element – the end-users that perform day-to-day operations.

The BCP must decide on how to notify end users, what to tell them and where they should go. Ideally a call tree should be defined to ensure the message is sent out in a timely fashion. Restorative processes should be multi-staged, with most important processes being manned first, and how PCs need to be configured including connectivity requirements should be addressed in the BCP. To help restore end-user operations to normal as soon as possible, it should document how tasks that are normally automated can be carried out manually, and how tasks that are normally carried out over communication lines can be fulfilled using manual processes.

Data Backup Alternatives

The BCP must identify ways to protect and restore data after a disruption occurs, so let's dig in a little deeper on backup and restoration technologies.

Backing up data should mirror how often data changes – a change in files can be detected by looking at the file's *archive bit*, which is controlled by the operating system. A *full backup* should be performed, clearing the archive bit on every file. While full back ups take a fairly long longest time to create and uses a large amount of disk space, they are by far the simplest to restore.

A *differential backup* backs up files that have changed since the last full backup. When a restore is carried out, the full backup is laid down followed by the latest differential backup since the full backup was created. This method takes more time to create than an incremental backup, but takes less time to restore. This is the only backup process that does not clear the archive bit.

An *incremental backup* backs up files that have changed since the last full back up or differential backup, and it also clears the archive bit. When a restore is carried out, the full backup is laid down followed by each differential backup since the full backup was created. While it is the quickest to create, it takes more time to restore than a differential backup because each incremental backup must be laid down in succession, and in the correct order.

Differential and incremental backups can never be mixed, as one clears the archive bit and the other does not. Backed up data should be stored both onsite and offsite; the offsite facility should be far enough away such that a single disaster does not destroy both copies. Onsite backups should be stored in a fire-resistant, heat-resistant and waterproof container. Whichever backup strategy is chosen, it should assume something will go wrong, and provide an alternative method for reconstructing the data. It should also be tested periodically by restoring the data to a secondary system and testing to ensure completeness.

Electronic Backup Solutions

Now that we have discussed the various methodologies for backups, let's talk about how each can be implemented.

Manual backups are costly and error-prone, so an automated solution almost always works better, but does require additional cost. Some automated technologies are:

- *Disk duplexing* is a system having multiple disk controllers for fail-over.
- *Disk shadowing* is a system configuration in which all data is simultaneously written to two disks. *Disk mirroring* is a shadowing option that dictates the two disks have the exact same data and configuration. The drives will always appear as a single unit to the client, and provides online backup storage. This option increases read speed as read requests can operate in parallel between the two disks. It is expensive (as all hard drives must be duplicated) but is a good fit where fault tolerance is required.
- *Electronic vaulting* makes copies of files in real-time as they are modified and periodically writes them in a bulk fashion to an offsite backup facility.
- *Remote journaling* moves the journal or transaction logs (files that contain the delta only) to the offsite facility in real-time, as opposed to operating in batches like electronic vaulting.
- *Tape vaulting* backs up data to a tape, where it is then manually transferred to an offsite facility for storage.
- *Electronic tape vaulting* (or *automatic tape vaulting*) allows data to be transferred to a remote offsite tape backup facility over a connection. Personnel in the remote facility are responsible for swapping tapes when necessary.
- *Database replication* is a capability built into most modern DBs that allow them to automatically replicate their data to a remote instance of the database. *Asynchronous replication* means that for a period of time (seconds to days) the two may be out of sync, while *synchronous replication* provides real-time replication in which the two repositories are never out of sync. Synchronous replication can negatively impact performance.

Note that in a software development environment it is necessary to backup source and object code, just as database data is backed up.

High Availability

High availability (*HA*) refers to a combination of technologies that ensures a system or process is always running. There are several terms associated with HA.

Redundancy provides alternative options in real-time, such as is built into the network at the routing protocol level – if a path goes down, the router selects a different one. *Fault tolerance* is a behavior in which a technology continues to operate as expected even if something unexpected happens. For example, a server crashing after an update reboots and recovers automatically, or a TCP connection retries to send a failed packet, or even a RAID disk with a failed disk continuing.

Failover is a capability a technology must switch 'over' to a working system in case the primary system fails (for example two load balancers with one acting as a hot-swap). *Clustering* is a type of failover in which multiple identical systems are linked in real-time such that if one fails, the other systems take over its responsibilities, such as a clustered database. *Load balancing* is also a type of failover in which multiple identical systems all share in servicing the same types of requests as instructed by some type of centralized connection point. Web farms typically use load balancing, but load balancing differs from clustering in that the cluster coordination is more peer-to-peer - with load balancing an external process coordinates everything.

Reliability is the probability that a system will perform its function for a specific time under specific conditions. High reliability results in high availability. Going back to the concept of a recovery point objective (RPO), RPO represents the restoration of data from some type of backup, and can be addressed through backup tapes, electronic vaulting, replication or RAID. Recovery time objective (RTO) represents restoring each process and can be addressed through clustering, load balancing, mirroring, redundancy and failover.

HA is put into place so that disaster recovery (DR) goals can be achieved in a timelier fashion, but it is not just about technology – it also includes:

- Facilities (cold, warm, hot, redundant, rolling reciprocal)
- Infrastructure (redundancy, fault tolerance)
- Storage (RAID, SAN, mirroring, disk shadowing, cloud)
- Server (clustering, load balancing)
- Data (tapes, backups, vaulting, online replication)
- Business processes
- People

Insurance

Not all threats can be addressed, and that is why we have insurance related to information security. The monthly premiums charged are dependent upon the security measures a company already has in place, and there are several types:

- *Cyber insurance* – insures losses caused by DoS, malware, hackers, electronic theft, privacy-related lawsuits, etc.
- *Business interruption insurance* – if a company is out of business past a specific length of time, insurance will pay for specified expenses and income loss
- *Accounts receivables* – if a company cannot collect on its accounts the coverage covers part or all losses

Insurance should be reviewed annually because threat levels and the business market may change. It should be noted that a company must practice due care or the insurance company may not pay when a claim is submitted.

Chapter 63: Disaster Recovery

Questions

1. What is the overall time a company can survive without a given system running in an operational capacity?

    A) MTD

    B) AIW

    C) RPO

    D) RTO

2. Which of the following is a 'backup for the backup', or a Plan B when Plan A fails?

    A) Tertiary site

    B) Incident location

    C) Contingency company

    D) Service bureau

3. What term refers to a combination of technologies that ensures a system or process is always running?

    A) Redundant availability

    B) High Availability

    C) Instant recovery

    D) Always available

4. What type of disruption is an event that results in a facility being a complete loss, and both short-term and long-term facilities are required?

    A) Disaster

    B) Catastrophe

    C) Black swan event

    D) Non-disaster

5. Which automated backup technology has multiple disk controllers for fail-over?

    A) Disk mirroring

    B) Disk shadowing

    C) Electronic vaulting

    D) Disk duplexing

Chapter 64: Recovery and Restoration

65% of businesses that lose computing capabilities for more than one week go out of business. The BCP is crucial in avoiding such a fate and should define several teams responsible for handling a disaster, each with a designated leader. The teams are:

- Damage assessment team
- Legal team
- Media relations team
- Restoration team (get the alternate site into a functioning environment)
- Relocation team (organizes staff to move to new location)
- Recovery team
- Salvage team (start the recovery of the original site)
- Security team

A BCP has specific phases:

First, a *damage assessment* is executed of the original site to determine next steps. The team responsible for this phase executes the following steps in order:

- Determine the cause
- Determine the potential for further damage
- Identify the affected business functions and areas
- Evaluate the functional level of critical resources
- Identify the resources that must be replaced immediately
- Estimate how long it will take to bring critical functions back online
- If restoration will exceed MTD, declare a disaster and initiate the BCP

Initiating the BCP is not a casual act – it requires that multiple criteria are met as spelled out within the BCP itself. The criteria include:

- Damage to human life
- Damage to state or national security
- Damage to facility
- Damage to critical systems
- Estimated value of downtime that will be experienced

If the BCP is initiated as a result of the first step, the second phase is started in which an alternate site is brought online – this is called the *Restoration phase*.

At the same time (if resources allow a parallel effort), the third phase, *Salvage phase*, is started. This entails bringing the original site back into a production level. It is considered completed when the following criteria have been met:

- Employees will be safe
- An adequate environment has been provided
- Necessary equipment and supplies are present
- Proper communications and connectivity has been restored
- The new environment has been properly tested

The fourth phase is the *Recovery* phase - bringing the company back to full capacity as soon as possible. The BCP should use templates to help each team step through their respective tasks and document findings (NIST SP 800-34 provides examples) to help with this phase.

The fifth and final phase is the *Reconstitution* back into the original site. In this phase, the salvage team:

- Backs up data from the alternate site and restores it to the original (starting with the least critical systems first)
- Terminates temporary operations
- Transports equipment and people to the original site

Remember that a company never leaves the emergency state until it moves back into the original site or a permanent replacement.

Developing Goals for the Plans

Setting a list of goals for the plan is crucial to stay on-track when creating the BCP. Each goal should address:

- Responsibility – each individual should have clearly defined responsibilities
- Authority – clearly define who is in charge
- Priorities – the priority relative to other goals
- Implementation and testing – dry runs must be conducted with the individuals identified above

Implementing Strategies

The final BCP should be distributed in both paper and electronic from and key individuals should keep copies at their homes. The general structure of a BCP plan follows the sections below.

- Initiation phase (overview, goals, definitions)
- *Activation phase* (notifications, damage assessment, plan activation)
- *Recovery phase* (move to alternate site, restore processes, start recovery)
- Reconstruction phase (restore facility, test, move back)
- *Appendixes* (calling tree, system requirements, schematics, other plan types)

You might notice that the appendixes contain 'other plan types'. These include:

- Business resumption plan
- Continuity of Operations (COOP)
- IT contingency plan
- Crisis communication plan
- Cyber incident response plan
- Disaster recovery plan
- Occupant emergency plan

COOP and BCP are the same, but COOP is specific to government agencies.

Chapter 64: Recovery and Restoration

Questions

1. What BCP plan phase brings the company back to full capacity?

    A) Recovery

    B) Damage assessment

    C) Restoration

    D) Salvage

2. What are the five phases of the BCP plan, in order?

    A) damage assessment, salvage, restoration, reclaim and recovery

    B) damage assessment, repair, salvage, reclaim and reconstitution

    C) damage assessment, restoration, salvage, recovery and reconstitution

    D) damage assessment, repair, recover, reclaim and reconstitution

3. What BCP plan phase brings an alternate site online?

    A) Salvage

    B) Restoration

    C) Damage assessment

    D) Recovery

4. What BCP plan phase brings the original site back up to a production level?

    A) Damage assessment

    B) Recovery

    C) Restoration

    D) Salvage

5. What BCP plan phase is executed at the original site to determine next steps?

    A) Salvage

    B) Recovery

    C) Restoration

    D) Damage assessment

Chapter 65: Investigations

Any incident will require some type of investigation to determine what happened and who or what is responsible. Any disruption or disaster should be initially treated as a crime scene – you never know until later what the actual root cause was. Even if a natural disaster has occurred, a malicious party could have used that event to gain access to a company's systems. Every action needs to be carried out with the mindset of 'If this goes to court, will my action help or hinder legal action?"

One of the most important decisions to make early on is whether to involve law enforcement or not. Law enforcement agencies have considerable investigative capabilities and can be quite an asset if included. However, there are a few negatives that need to be considered:

- Once law enforcement is involved, the company may lose control over where the investigation leads
- Secrecy of the event will become part of the public record, and the fallout needs to be considered
- Evidence collected will not be available for a long time (a year or more)

Computer Forensics and Proper Collection of Evidence

Computer forensics deals with the recovery, authentication and analysis of electronic data with the express purpose of carrying out a digital criminal investigation. *Digital forensics* is a superset of computer forensics and includes network forensics, electronic data discovery, cyberforensics and forensic computing. Any result of computer forensic, network or code analysis is called *digital evidence*.

Digital evidence has a short lifetime and must be collected quickly and properly, according to its volatility. Evidence that is stored in *volatile memory*, such as RAM and in caches, must be collected first as it is more at-risk for being lost than evidence stored in non-volatile storage. However, even non-volatile storage, such as hard drives or USB drives, can inadvertently be lost if running processes overwrite them. *Volatile* data includes:

- Registers and cache
- Process tables and ARP cache
- System memory (RAM)
- Temporary file systems
- Special disk sectors

Non-traditional computing devices such as cell phones, laptops, GPS devices and memory cards should be included as containing potential evidence.

The *Scientific Working Group on Digital Evidence* (*SWGDE*) aims to ensure all organizations have a consistent approach to forensics. SWDGE promotes the following attributes that all forensic processes should have:

- Consistency with all legal systems
- Allowance for a common use of language
- Durability
- Ability to cross state and international boundaries
- Ability to instill confidence in the integrity of evidence
- Applicability to all forensic evidence
- Applicability at every level, including that of individual, agency and country

SWDGE also has 6 principles:

1. When dealing with digital evidence, all general forensic and procedural principles must be applied.
2. Upon seizing digital evidence, actions taken should not change that evidence.
3. When it is necessary for a person to access original digital evidence, that person should be trained for the purpose.
4. All activity relating to the seizure, access, storage or transfer of digital evidence must be fully documented, preserved and available for review.
5. An Individual is responsible for all actions taken with respect to digital evidence whilst the digital evidence is in their possession.
6. Any agency, which is responsible for seizing, accessing, storing or transferring digital evidence is responsible for compliance with these principles.

Motive, Opportunity and Means

MOM is an acronym representing the motive, opportunity and means of a crime – all 3 must be addressed to figure out what was behind a crime, as well as to succeed in any subsequent prosecution. We are all probably familiar with the report's mantra for collecting a news story information – who, what, when, where, and why. Crime adds in the 'how', because if it cannot be proven that a perpetrator was capable of committing a crime (the how), he or she cannot be blamed for it from a legal perspective. In short, we must be able to prove the following:

- The crime is the 'what'
- *Motive* – the 'who' and 'why'
- *Opportunity* – the 'where' and 'when'
- *Means* – the 'how'

Computer Criminal Behavior

A criminal's *modus operandi* (*MO*) is the typical pattern a criminal follows in all his or her crimes. Criminals rarely change their MO, so it can act as a 'fingerprint' to help identify the perpetrator. Computer criminals also have an MO, but it deals with the choice of tools, favored targets and how he or she proceeds with the attack.

Locard's exchange principal states that every criminal always takes something from a crime scene, and leaves something behind. This means that we can always know something about the perpetrator by examining the crime scene after the fact - this applies to digital crime as well.

Incident Investigators

Effective incident investigators must be able to differentiate between background noise and suspicious behavior. They also must understand forensic procedures, how to collect evidence properly and the proper approach to analyze an ongoing situation.

There are four types of assessments an investigator can perform (with examples):

- Network analysis
    - Traffic analysis
    - Log analysis
    - Path tracing
- Media analysis
    - Disk imaging
    - Timeline analysis
    - Registry analysis
    - Slack space analysis
    - Shadow volume analysis
- Software analysis
    - Reverse engineering
    - Malicious code review
    - Exploit review
- Hardware device analysis
    - Dedicated appliance attack points
    - Firmware and dedicated memory inspections
    - Embedded OS, virtualized software and hypervisor analysis

The Forensic Investigation Process

The process of collecting evidence can vary, but all should include the following steps:

- Identification
- Preservation
- Collection
- Examination
- Analysis
- Presentation
- Decision

Both of the Examination and Analysis steps above should use an image of the original disk that is a bit-for-bit copy – this is required to identify deleted files, slack spaces and unallocated clusters. A few examples of tools that provide this capability are Forensic Toolkit (FTK), EnCase Forensic and the dd Unix utility. Simple file copying does NOT allow a proper investigation as a lot of information will not be included unless it is contained within a valid existing file.

Access to the crime scene must be controlled and the following steps should be followed:

- Only authorized individuals with basic crime scene analysis knowledge should be allowed access
- Document who is at the crime scene
- Document the individuals who were the last to interact with a system
- If contamination does occur, document it

Original media should have two copies – a *primary image* to be stored in a library and a *working image* to be used during the investigation. The media used to make the images must be completely purged of old data before being used. Hashing should be used to verify integrity between the original and images – if the hashes do not match, then we know that the copy is a modified version of the original and is no longer usable. Making copies of data requires specialized tools to ensure the original is not modified in any way during the copy process.

Normally, after conducting an initial analysis, an investigator will wish to shut down computers that are in a running state – this is required to preserve evidence. However, acquiring evidence from critical systems presents a special problem as they cannot be turned off –

in these cases the evidence must be gathered only while the system continues to run.

Forensic field kits normally contain documentation tools, disassembly and removal tools, and package and transport tools. A *chain of custody* is crucial to digital evidence integrity – this shows a complete history of how evidence was collected, analyzed, transported and preserved. Crime scenes should be photographed, including behind any computer involved in the crime to show cable connections and possible hardware that is attached.

The most common reasons for improper evidence collection are:

- Lack of an established incident response team
- Poorly written policies
- Broken chain of custody

After evidence has been properly collected, it can be analyzed. An investigator will:

- Decide if it is admissible as primary or secondary evidence and establish its source, reliability and permanence
- Compare different sources of evidence to establish a chronological chain of events
- Reconstruct the event based on the evidence

Analysis can take place on-site (*live forensics*), or in a lab (*dead forensics*). The advantage of live forensics is that it will include data found in volatile memory. The final step of the investigation process is to present the findings in a non-technical manner to the proper audience – judge, lawyer, CEO, etc.

What is Admissible in Court?

Normally digital evidence (such as log files) is not admissible in court because it is *hearsay* – meaning it is secondhand evidence. The only way in which hearsay evidence is admissible is if it has firsthand evidence to prove that it is accurate, trustworthy and reliable – in this case the testimony of the person who was responsible for generating the log files. However, that alone is insufficient as well – to truly be admissible the log files must have been generated and collected as part of normal business activities, and not specifically for use in court. It is equally important to be able to show that digital evidence has not been tampered with, which can be established using both a chain of custody and checksums or hashing on the evidence. If digital evidence meets all criteria above, it must still be vetted for content according to the following criteria:

- *Relevant* – it must have a reasonable relationship to the findings
- *Complete* – it must communicate the whole truth
- *Sufficient* (believable) – its validity must be convincing to a reasonable person
- *Reliable* (accurate) – it must be consistent with the facts, and be factual itself

Evidence has a life cycle that must be respected and followed:

- Collection and identification
- Storage, preservation and transportation
- Presentation in court
- Return of the evidence to the owner

If an employee is being charged based on files found on her computer, she could claim that those files were private and cannot be used against her. That is why it is important for companies to conduct security awareness training, have employees sign documents stating they are aware of security policies and to show legal banners when logging in. Continued use by an employee after viewing the login banner provides an implicit acknowledgement by the employee of the contents of the banner.

Surveillance, Search and Seizure

There are 2 types of surveillance that can be associated with computer crimes. *Physical surveillance* includes cameras, guards, and CCTV, while *computer surveillance* is more technological in nature, and can be passive or active. *Passive monitoring* uses network sniffers, keyboard monitors, wiretaps and line monitoring to collect evidence. *Active monitoring* is more invasive and gathers evidence directly. This type of computer surveillance requires a search warrant, or a person must be warned ahead of time that it may occur (such as a logon banner).

The 4th Amendment (unlawful search and seizure) only applies to citizens acting as police agents, so employees may be acted upon by their employer without fear of violating law - however, other privacy laws may still apply. If law enforcement is involved and it is determined that potential evidence is about to be destroyed, a search warrant is not required to confiscate the evidence under a lawful exception called *exigent circumstances.* This allows law enforcement to immediately seize the evidence, and a court will later determine if it is admissible evidence.

Interviewing Suspects

Suspect interviews should be conducted by a trained professional, and only after consulting with legal counsel. Security professionals may be asked to observe or provide input into an interview, but all questions should be prepared beforehand. The interviewer should always be in an employed position that is senior to the interviewee, and held in a comfortable place. Exhibits should be shown one at a time, and rights do not need to be read unless a law enforcement officer is conducting the interview.

Chapter 65: Investigations

Questions

1. What term best describes evidence that is convincing to a reasonable person?

    A) Relevant

    B) Reliable

    C) Sufficient

    D) Complete

2. What is the term used for any analysis taking place in a lab?

    A) Dead forensics

    B) Clean forensics

    C) Post-scene forensics

    D) Delayed forensics

3. Which of the following is NOT a negative consequence of contacting law enforcement after an incident has occurred?

    A) Secrecy of the event will become part of the public record, and the fallout needs to be considered

    B) Crucial evidence may lose integrity due to mishandling

    C) Evidence collected will not be available for a long time

    D) Once law enforcement is involved, the company may lose control over where the investigation leads

4. In terms of computer forensics, what does the acronym MOM stand for?

    A) Motive, opportunity and means

    B) Motive, opening and method

    C) Moment, opportunity and method

    D) Moment, opening and means

5. What is the term describing the digital evidence image to be used during the investigation?

    A) Working image

    B) Active image

    C) Primary image

    D) Checked image

Chapter 66: Liability and Its Ramifications

We have already mentioned the concepts of due care and due diligence several times, but it is such an important subject that we're going to revisit once more with respect to security and prosecution under law. *Due diligence* means that a company properly examined all possible weaknesses and vulnerabilities. *Due care* means that a company acted appropriately based on the findings of due diligence, did all it could reasonably do to prevent a security breach, and ensured that if a breach still happened, steps were taken to acceptably minimize the damage. Sometimes precautions are so obvious that 'due diligence' is not required before 'due care' should be executed. For example, it doesn't take a whole lot of brainpower to know that at least one firewall needs to be installed in front of your web servers.

The execution of due care requires a weighed approach between risk and cost – not all risks need to be addressed if they are sufficiently low relative to the cost of effective mitigation. This assessment does not stop at the outer boundary of a company – the third-party providers of any external services the company consumes in a production capacity should also be taken into consideration from a security perspective. This works both ways – if a Company A provides services to Company B, then Company A needs to make sure it has performed due care/diligence regarding security so that Company B cannot sue it down the road – this is called *downstream liability*. In this example, Company A has a *responsibility* to provide secure services to Company B. At the same time, Company B can hold Company A *accountable* for those services. So, when Company B sues Company A, it is holding Company A accountable. Now, when Company B shows up in court, it will have to show that Company A had a *legally recognized obligation* to protect Company B from security breaches, and this was the *proximate cause* (the obvious cause) of Company B's damages.

To address the above scenarios, the following contracts should be examined from a security perspective:

- Outsourcing agreements
- Supplier chain providers
- System provision, maintenance and support
- Consultancy service agreements (software, hardware, network, etc.)
- NDAs
- Licensing agreements

Before entering into an agreement, the company's security requirements must be understood – otherwise those concerns will not make it into the agreement. A *Request for Proposal* (*RFP*) is the first step in getting a vendor to provide a solution. RFPs should clearly outline security requirements, and the vendor's response should indicate how each requirement will be met. Once contracts have been put into effect, the relationship must be monitored and developed – this is referred to as *vendor management*. A *vendor management governing* process controls this activity, and will dictate what performance metrics and SLAs are required. This process also requires specific meetings to be scheduled, a defined reporting structure to be laid out, and a single individual identified who is ultimately responsible for the relationship.

A company should always be on top of remaining in compliance with applicable laws. This means knowing what laws apply, and what is required for the company to do to remain in compliance with each law. This activity is addressed by a compliance program, which details all internal and external requirements, and will directly drive company activities to meet those requirements. The following steps provide a recipe for creating an effective compliance program:

1. Figure out what laws are applicable (SOX, HIPAA, GLBA, FISMA, PCI DSS, etc.)
2. Decide on a security framework that will address the requirements of each law (COSO, Zachman, ISO 27001, etc.)
3. Choose a risk methodology (COBIT, NIST 800-53, etc.)
4. Put the security framework and risk methodology into action
5. Carry out an audit

Organizations often create *governance, risk and compliance* (*GRC*) programs to align all 3 together – if they all use the same KPIs, it is relatively simple to judge how well they are integrated.

Another aspect of liability is the safety of people, which is almost always *the* most important goal above all others – not just for company employees, but any individual who comes into contact with a company's products or facilities. For example, in cases of fire, how do we allow fire fighters access to all needed areas while still maintaining a good measure of security? Or, in the case of a power loss and people need to evacuate, should locks default to fail-safe (unlocked) or fail-secure (remain locked) when the power source has been removed? It is a constant dance to balance effective security with safety.

Questions

1. What term best describes the obvious cause of a security breach?

    A) Original cause

    B) Initial cause

    C) Proximate cause

    D) Sensible cause

2. What term best describes the first step in getting a vendor to provide a solution?

    A) RFP

    B) INI

    C) ITP

    D) RFI

3. What type of liability does a company take on when it performs services for other companies which may result in a law suit by a customer?

    A) Upstream

    B) Cross stream

    C) Side stream

    D) Downstream

4. What term best describes the alignment of governance, risk and compliance programs?

    A) GRC program

    B) Inter-departmental synergy

    C) Enterprise security

    D) Cross-organization alignment

5. What term best describes monitoring and developing a relationship with a vendor?

    A) Outsourcing diligence

    B) Outsourcing management

    C) Vendor management

    D) Vendor diligence

Section 8: Software Development Security Domain

Most software is approached from a functional point of view first – after all, developers have to create software to meet a user's needs, and a user does not think of security very often. Therefore, security requirements never make it into the list of things to get done. But effective security cannot simply be bolted on near the end of a project – it must be baked in from the very beginning.

Chapter 67: Where Do We Place Security?

Software is responsible for the clear majority of vulnerabilities. Even in networks, it is the software running on switches and routers that can most often be exploited, not the hardware. We can choose to mitigate this reality with two different approaches – either harden the software or harden the perimeter. The perimeter approach is most often chosen because:

- The importance of implementing proper security in software is a relatively new focus
- It is very uncommon to find a software developer who is also a security professional
- Software vendors are trying to get products to market as soon as possible and do not make security a priority
- Customers have become accustomed to receiving software with security flaws that are then patched
- Customers cannot fix the security flaws in software they purchase, so they resort to perimeter solutions

Changing the security posture of software development is difficult because of several factors. First, secure programming practices are not taught in educational institutions. As a result, operating systems and applications have never been built from the ground up to be secure, and in general the software development mindset is not security-oriented. Integrating security as an after-thought is extremely difficult and therefore avoided. In short, software development needs to become 'proactive' regarding security instead of 'reactive' as it is today.

Environment vs. Application

Software controls can be implemented either in the operating system or inside of an application – ideally in both places. Implementation at the operating system level is desirable to ensure a consistent approach, but the OS has no visibility or control of access activities within an application – the OS only kicks in when the application needs to consume some resource that the OS controls. Conversely, implementation of security at the application level provides very granular control, but does nothing for security outside of the application, including any external resource the application requires.

External products and perimeter devices do provide protection, but again, they do not have access to an application's internal logic and cannot protect against poor security implementations within an application. Perimeter devices are also more reactive in nature – they protect best against known vulnerabilities that are discovered over time.

We have stated many times that 'security loves simplicity'. Unfortunately, applications are anything but simple. The more functionality that is packed into an application, the more difficult it becomes to achieve a good level of security hygiene. Restricting the level of functionality is not the answer either – without increasing functionality, the product is less marketable. The only real answer is to implement property security measures from the application design stage.

Implementation and Default Issues

Most software comes with minimal security enabled. Advanced security features must be configured and enabled after installation, making setup easier for the end-user. However, from a security perspective, software should default to 'No Access' which is quite the opposite. Predictably, we now have usability competing with both security and functionality

For example, earlier versions of Windows defaulted to "Allow Access" unless security features were enabled. After many security issues and customer complaints, Microsoft started shipping later versions of Windows with "No Access" as the default. On some OSs, many unsecure services such as NetBIOS, FTP, TFTP and SNMP are enabled in the default installation. These will need to be disabled on most servers.

Security patches are a fact of everyday life for system administrators. But, they are often not installed because the administrator:

- Does not keep up to date on security vulnerabilities
- May not realize the importance of applying patches
- Might fear the patches will cause other problems

Education can address the first two points above, but the third (unstable patches) will always be an issue until vendors perform proper testing of security patches so that administrators have a higher level of trust and are more likely to apply them.

Defining Good Code

Quality is defined as how fit for a purpose something is. Like security, however, quality is usually thought of after the fact when developing software. The keys to ensuring quality are code reviews and interface testing, such as unit and integration testing. Additionally, misuse cases also increase both quality and security.

Software controls can be used to address input, output, encryption, logical flow, methods for performing calculations, interprocess communication, access, and interaction with other software. On the other hand, *security controls* used within software development can be preventative, corrective or detective, and are usually always technical (as opposed to physical or administrative). The security controls selected for software will depend on the application's purpose, the environment in which it will run, the sensitivity of the data it will process, the functionality it will execute and the security policy attached to it. For example, if software will only be run behind 3 firewalls and accessible only by an administrator, it will have fewer security requirements. If it is a publicly-accessible web application it will be subject to quite a few very restrictive security controls.

Chapter 67: Where Do We Place Security?

Questions

1. Which of the following is NOT a reason most commonly used to choose the perimeter approach to software vulnerability mitigation?

   A) It is very uncommon to find a software developer who is also a security professional

   B) The ROI for secure coding is difficult to quantify

   C) The importance of implementing proper security in software is a relatively new focus

   D) Software vendors are trying to get products to market as soon as possible and do not make security a priority

2. Which of the following is NOT a reason that security administrators fail to install patches?

   A) They do not keep up to date on security vulnerabilities

   B) They do not realize the importance of applying patches

   C) They fear the patches will cause other problems

   D) The cost involved in applying patches is tremendous

3. Which term best describes how fit for a purpose something?

   A) Efficiency

   B) Quality

   C) Effectiveness

   D) Usability

4. What two approaches can we take to mitigate software vulnerabilities?

   A) Fix bugs before deployment or after

   B) Harden the software or harden the perimeter

   C) Implement security at the start of a project or near the end

   D) Create our own software or purchase it

5. What are the two places that software controls can be implemented?

   A) In-process or out-of-process

   B) During I&A or after I&A

   C) At the network level or at the host level

   D) In the OS or in the application

Chapter 68: Software Development Life Cycle

The *software development life cycle* (*SDLC*) is concerned with creating a repeatable and predictable process that development teams will follow – this will result in a higher level of product quality, fewer missed deadlines and a lower cost, all while still delivering an acceptable level of functionality.

There are many SDLC models, but all of them have the same basic phases:

- *Requirements gathering* – figure out what the product will do when completed
- *Design* – plan how the product will be put together
- *Development* – put the product together
- *Testing/validation* – make sure the product does what the requirements said it should do
- *Release/maintenance* – ship the product and update as-needed

Project Management

Project management in general ties together all pieces required to deliver a product, and specifically ensures that each phase is addressed properly. *Security management* is one part of project management, in which a security plan is created from the beginning. By starting with the requirements gathering phase, we can ensure security is not something that is bolted on at the end of the project. The plan can reference any required external document such as standards, projects, policies or guidelines. While the security plan is a part of the overall project, it must be able to stand alone and have its own lifetime. The security plan will be referenced after the project has been completed during audits and to validate the product meets specific security objectives.

Software projects being developed for specific customers are usually driven by a *statement of work* (*SOW*) that helps clarify customer requirements. Project management must ensure that it adheres to the SOW closely to avoid *scope creep* – the addition of new requirements that seem to creep out of the woodwork but were not originally envisioned. A *work breakdown structure* (*WBS*) defines the tasks and subtasks that are required to meet the stated requirements. The SDLC depends on the WBS to be accurate.

Requirements Gathering Phase

During the requirements gathering phase, all focus is on figuring out what the finished product should be capable of, what it should look like and how it should behave. Any known limitations and restrictions should be called out during this phase.

From a security viewpoint, the following tasks should be completed by the time the requirements phase ends:

- Security requirements
- Security risk assessment
- Privacy risk assessment
- Risk-level acceptance

Each security task should be examined from the perspective of CIA (confidentiality, integrity and availability). Potential threats and resulting consequences should be enumerated. The data the product will be handling must be examined in terms of privacy – this is called a *privacy risk assessment*, and is followed by assigning a *privacy impact rating* to each data element. While there is not currently a standardized approach to Privacy Impact Ratings, a common categorization scheme is:

- *P1, High Privacy Risk* – PII is routinely handled and stored
- *P2, Moderate Privacy Risk* – PII is handled in a one-time, user-initiated data transfer
- *P3, Low Privacy Risk* – no PII is handled or stored

Clearly-defined risk-level acceptance criteria needs to be developed to ensure mitigation efforts are properly prioritized. In other words, all possible risks will probably not be addressed, so the team should address the most important ones first.

Software requirements can be documented using 3 different models (all 3 models are used together):

- *Informational model* – lists the type of information to be processed and how they are processed
- *Functional model* – lists the tasks and functions an application needs to provide
- *Behavioral model* – lists the states the application will be in during and after specific transactions take place

Design Phase

The design phase takes each requirement and shows how the product will meet it. Many development teams tend to skip this crucial step, resulting in an unstable and insecure product. This phase provides 3 outputs (loosely mapping to the 3 requirements models we just described):

- Data design
- Architectural design
- Procedural design

From a security perspective, the design phase will result in reducing the *attack surface*, which is the portion of the application visible to an attacker. It should be made as small as possible by reducing:

- The amount of code running
- Entry points
- Privilege levels
- Unnecessary services

An *attack surface analysis* is an automated scan of an application resulting in a report. This analysis will look at files, registry entries, data stored in memory, session information, and process and service details. The end goal is to identify and reduce the amount of code and/or functionality that is accessible by untrusted users.

Threat modeling also needs to be carried out, by imagining various malicious scenarios and designing the software to counteract the threats. A *threat tree* is a useful tool to visualize and document various attack vectors into the software – it visually shows each threat and how it is related to other threats.

Development Phase

In the development phase, the design is broken down into scheduled deliverables, and developers get down to work. A *computer-aided software engineering* (*CASE*) tool can often be used to auto-generate code, create automated tests and handle debugging activities.

Writing secure code is not an easy task, and most vulnerabilities result from poor programming practices. Some common mistakes are:

- Not checking the input length to avoid buffer overflows
- Not inspecting code to prevent the use of covert channels
- Not checking/enforcing proper data types
- Not ensuring checkpoints cannot be bypassed by users
- Not verifying proper syntax
- Not verifying checksums

Buffer overflows can result in an elevation of access, or *privilege escalation*. This is the act of exploiting a process or configuration setting to gain access to resources that normally are off limits to the process or user. The most common way to mitigate privilege escalation is to use input validation coupled with ensuring least privilege.

Static analysis is performed during this phase, and is the process of examining the source code for defects or security policy violations. However, a static analysis cannot understand logic flows, so its limitations need to be well understood.

Testing/Validation Phase

Unit testing is a type of automated test that will exercise individual code modules or classes. Experienced developers understand the power of unit tests, while green developers will often attempt to skip this step or at least complain mightily. While unit tests are usually written in parallel or after the source code is laid down, *test-driven development* (*TDD*) is an approach in which the unit test is written first, followed by the source code that will pass the test. If done properly, TDD can result in superior code.

Unit tests simulate a range of inputs and check the resulting output for the expected result – this ensures the code will always run in an expected and secure manner. Unit tests also allow the software to be automatically retested at any point to validate that changes have not introduced new defects. Developers are the world's worst testers when it comes to their own code – whether intentionally or not, they will avoid weaknesses and concentrate on use cases in which their code works well. Therefore, it is crucial that a separate team is responsible for formal testing – this is a form of separation of duties.

Ensuring that an application meets the security objectives stated during the requirements phase is not straightforward. The identified risk must be expressed in terms of a repeatable test that proves that the vulnerability has been mitigated to an acceptable level. Testing should happen in an environment that mirrors the production environment as close as possible.

Penetration testing is carried out in this phase, as well as ensuring the application meets every stated requirement.

The application should be intentionally crashed to see if it comes back up in a secure state. If it will run on different platforms, all platforms need to be tested, including the supported network conditions.

We have discussed unit testing in detail, but that is only 1 of 4 testing approaches that can be used. Here is a list of all 4:

- *Unit testing* – testing individual components
- *Integration testing* – testing multiple components working together
- *Acceptance testing* – testing to ensure the application meets the customer's requirements
- *Regression testing* – after a change, rerunning all previously passing tests to ensure the application is still on solid footing (this is why automated testing is an absolute must)

Security testing should use both automated and manual testing. Automated tests offer wide breadth but only a moderate level of depth. Their value increases if we can simulate unpredictable uses that an actual user might provide - that is why 'fuzzers' are often used. *Fuzzing* is an attack technique in which a large amount of randomly malformed and unexpected inputs is provided to an application. The goal is to cause a failure of some type. Based on these results, an attacker can then customize their own software to leverage the discovered vulnerability. Fuzzing tools are most useful at discovering:

- Buffer overflows
- DoS vulnerabilities
- Validation problems
- Injection weaknesses
- Any other input that can cause a crash, freeze or unexpected errors

By using fuzzing ourselves, we can beat an attacker to the punch and remove many of the flaws this technique will uncover. Manual testing will reveal logic flaws in which an attacker might influence the flow of an application into providing greater access or bypassing authentication mechanisms. Manual testing needs to be carried out by testers skilled in the security area, and sometimes involves the use of social engineering.

Dynamic analysis means that an application is being evaluated in real-time as it is running (remember that static analysis is used to evaluate the source code). In addition to allowing real-time debugging capabilities, dynamic analysis profiles the application and checks for memory leaks or dependencies without having access to the source code.

Any problems found during the testing phase are reported to the development team, who addresses the issues, followed by more testing to ensure the issues were properly fixed. This cycle continues until everyone agrees the application is ready for production. If the application is intended for a specific customer, that customer should perform their own testing and formally accept the product when they are satisfied – this is called *User Acceptance Testing*, or *UAT*. At this point the product is released for production

It is important at this point to cover 2 terms – verification and validation. While closely related, they have a minor but very important distinction:

- *Verification* – does the product meet the requirements as written?
- *Validation* – does the product meet the original goal as it was envisioned?

It is possible for a product to be verified, but not valid due to missed or incorrect requirements. It is extremely unlikely that a product could ever be valid but fail verification.

Release/Maintenance Phase

Once a product has been released into production, more issues are almost guaranteed to appear that were not foreseen. The development team will need to address the issues by creating a *patch*, which will need to be tested and formally accepted, followed by a rollout to the already installed product.

A *zero-day vulnerability* is an issue that does not yet have a resolution. When an issue with software is discovered, it remains a zero-day vulnerability until a patch, update or a configuration change is made available that will address it.

Now that we have covered all SDLC phases, let's quickly go back and review the phases from a strictly security-focused perspective.

- Requirements
    - Security risk assessment
    - Privacy risk assessment
    - Risk-level acceptance
    - Informational, functional and behavioral requirements
- Design

Chapter 68: Software Development Life Cycle

- - - Attack surface analysis
    - Threat modeling
- Development
    - Automated CASE tools
    - Static analysis
- Test/validation
    - Dynamic analysis
    - Fuzzing
    - Manual testing
    - Unit, integration, acceptance and regression testing
- Release/maintenance
    - Final security review

Questions

1. Which term best describes creating a repeatable and predictable process that development teams will follow?

    A) Security management

    B) Software Development Life Cycle

    C) Project Management

    D) SOW

2. Which privacy rating reflects that no PII is handled or stored?

    A) P3

    B) P1

    C) P2

    D) P4

3. Which software development phase figures out what the finished product should be capable of, what it should look like and how it should behave?

    A) Testing

    B) Development

    C) Requirements Gathering

    D) Design

4. Which type of testing focuses on multiple components working together?

    A) Regression

    B) Integration

    C) Unit

    D) Acceptance

5. Which term best describes a tool to visualize and document various attack vectors into the software?

    A) Attack surface analysis

    B) Threat modeling

    C) Attack surface

    D) Threat tree

Chapter 69: Software Development Models

The *build and fix model* is essentially what is used when a development team follows no formal SDLC model. There are no formal requirements or design phases, and it is pretty much a "Let's get to work and see what magically pops out" mindset.

The *waterfall model* employs a linear-sequential life-cycle approach. Phases are laid out in a linear fashion (each phase leads only to a single future phase), and it is sequential in that each phase must come to a complete close before the next phase can begin. The phases are:

- Feasibility
- Analysis
- Design
- Implement
- Test
- Maintain

At the end of each phase, a review is held to make sure the project is still on-track. Once the next phase is started, there is no capability to go back and change the output from a previous phase. The problem with this approach is that it is virtually impossible to know *all* requirements up-front, so the entire process must be completed before changes can be made on the next release. It can work well for small projects in which all requirements can be easily known, but is dangerous for complex projects.

The *v-shaped model* (*v-model*) was developed to address some of the shortcomings of the Waterfall model by allowing testing to start earlier and continue throughout the entire SDLC. This model provides a higher chance of success than the Waterfall model, but not by much.

A *prototype* is a simple model of a complex idea that can be used to vet or explore that complex idea without investing too much time or effort. For example, if a software application has a user interface, it is often very useful to create just enough so that an end-user can 'touch' and play with the prototype to ascertain how useful it will be. Software development identifies 3 different prototype models. A *rapid prototype* creates a 'throwaway' product with just enough functionality to decide whether it is worth pursuing. An *evolutionary prototype* is not intended to be discarded, but rather incrementally improved upon until it reaches full maturity and can be placed into production. An *operational prototype* is the same as an evolutionary prototype but it is designed to be placed into production immediately and 'tweaked' on-the-fly as customer feedback is received.

If you were to take the waterfall method and not worry about knowing all requirements before continuing, you wind up with the *incremental model*. After each iteration of the entire SDLC, the customer provides feedback (i.e. more requirements) and the team goes back to the beginning with the new set of requirements and enhances the previous product. It has 4 phases:

- Analysis
- Design
- Code
- Test

At the end of each iteration, the team delivers an operational product. This model is ideal when risk, complexity, funding or functionality need to be better understood before fully committing to a path.

The *spiral model* also uses an iterative approach but is employed when a focus on risk analysis is desired. It consists of four phases:

- Determine objectives
- Identify and resolve risks
- Development and test
- Plan the next iteration

The spiral model is a good choice for complex projects in which requirements change often.

The *rapid application development* (*RAD*) model is similar to prototyping in that a working product is quickly developed, but the intention is to use the product to elicit requirements, as opposed to using the requirements to build the product. It is a good fit when the customer is unsure of what they want, or requirements are guaranteed to change quickly and often at the beginning of a project. The four steps of RAD are:

- Analysis and quick design
- RAD (build, demonstrate, refine)
- Testing
- Implementation

To this point, the SDLC models have been rigid and inflexible – while they strive to accommodate changing requirements (such as RAD), they are very dependent on following a strict set of steps in the same exact manner each time.

Chapter 69: Software Development Models

A different type of approach is referred to as _agile models_, which is an umbrella term used to refer to various approaches that emphasize incremental product deliveries built on continuous-feedback from the customer. Gone are the linear steps in favor of an iterative mindset that delivers 'just enough just in-time'. Most Agile approaches center on a _user story_ – a simple description of a single feature written by an end-user. A very important distinction to be made is that Agile models do not use prototypes – instead they break the product down into smaller features that are being continuously delivered.

Scrum is the most widely recognized Agile model, as it can handle projects of any size and is very focused on customer feedback. It recognizes upfront that customer needs will never be fully understood and will change, and therefore focus is put on close collaboration with the customer and continuous delivery. The term scrum comes from Rugby in which play is occasionally interrupted – so all players huddle together in a tight formation until someone gets possession of the ball and play continues. The Scrum methodology is the same – it allows for interruptions at clearly defined points, after which everyone gathers back together and puts the ball back into play. The 'clearly defined points' are at the end of each _sprint_, which is a pre-defined interval (usually 2 weeks) during which the customer is not allowed to make changes. But, at the end of each sprint, the customer has the freedom to completely change direction if it so desires. The feature list is put into a _backlog_, which is a prioritized list of user stories (a user story represents a feature), with the ones the customer deems most important at top. At the beginning of each sprint, the development team selects the user stories, starting at the top of the backlog, that it thinks it can deliver in the upcoming sprint.

Extreme programming (_XP_) relies on _pair programming_, in which developers work in pairs, with one developer telling the other what to type. The cleverness of such an approach is that two eyes are constantly reviewing the code as it is being written, which reduces code complexity as well as errors. XP also requires test-driven development (TDD) in which the test is written before any code is laid down, which means the test will immediately fail. Code is added until the test passes, resulting in the fewest lines of code required to meet the test.

Kanban is an Agile approach that stresses a visual tracking of development tasks, resulting in a just-in-time delivery of features. Originally, a _Kanban wall_ was dedicated to Kanban, with sticky notes representing each task and the wall being divided up into vertical sections, with the sections usually being labelled Planned, In Progress and Done. Like Scrum, the list is prioritized from top to bottom so developers will always take the top sticky note in the Planned column when they free up.

The _exploratory model_ is used when the goals of a project are not well-known, but final specifications that the product must meet are known.

The _joint application development_ (_JAD_) method can be used when non-developers are able to dedicate their full time to the project and sit with the development team as work progresses.

The _reuse model_ assumes that existing prototypes have already been created and are progressively enhanced.

The _cleanroom model_ is used when preventing errors and mistakes is the highest priority, and is achieved by using structured and formal methods for development and testing. This is usually employed for extremely high-quality and mission-critical applications that will need to pass a strict certification process.

An _integrated product team_ (_IPT_) is made up of the development team plus representatives from each stakeholder. Think of starting with JAD and then ensure that all representatives are formal members of the team. IPT is also more focused on internal customers than external customers. IPT is not a methodology, but works well with certain methodologies such as JAD or Agile.

Many organizations define 3 roles separately - software development, IT and QA. All 3 are crucial in rolling out successful software for the company, but they are very often antagonistic to each other. Developers don't like QA because they are always finding problems with their code, IT doesn't like the developers or QA because they are always pushing out buggy code, and QA doesn't like either one because IT complains they are too lax and the developers think QA is too strict. In the end, everyone hates everyone else and the software is a disaster.

Fortunately, there is a solution to this problem – have everyone participate in the development process instead of hiding away in their own little world. This is called _DevOps_ and is defined as the intersection between the 3 roles. Not only is everyone happier because of the continued collaboration, but security is the big winner as it is addressed from the beginning because of IT's involvement.

Chapter 69: Software Development Models

Questions

1. Which software development model is used for complex projects in which requirements change often?

    A) Agile

    B) Build and fix

    C) Prototype

    D) Spiral

2. Which Agile concept is a prioritized list of user stories?

    A) Backlog

    B) Sprint

    C) User story

    D) Scrum

3. Which type of prototype creates a product that is incrementally improved upon until it reaches full maturity and can be placed into production??

    A) Incremental

    B) Evolutionary

    C) Operational

    D) Rapid

4. What software development model is used when a development team follows no formal SDLC model?

    A) Incremental

    B) Build and fix

    C) XP

    D) Prototype

5. Which software development model is used when the goals of a project are not well-known, but final specifications that the product must meet are known?

    A) Exploratory

    B) Incremental

    C) Prototype

    D) Cleanroom

Chapter 70: Change Control

Change control is the process of controlling any changes that take place during a product's lifetime and documenting the activities that result. Change control processes should be in place at the beginning of a project or chaos will result. The primary reasons for enforcing a change control process are:

- To have an agreed upon baseline before work starts – any changes may be justifiable additional charges to the customer
- So the development team knows how to deal with changes as they happen
- To ensure changes do not negatively affect other components of the project

Any change must be approved, documented and tested (including regression testing). Changes should go to the librarian, and from there be deployed into production – changes should never be made directly in production.

A common change control process should include the following:

1. Make a formal request for a change
2. Analyze the request
    a. Develop the implementation strategy
    b. Calculate the costs
    c. Review security implications
3. Record the change request
4. Submit the change request for approval
5. Develop the change
    a. Implement the change
    b. Link the changes to the formal change control request
    c. Test the software
    d. Repeat until quality is adequate
    e. Make version changes
6. Report results to management

Change control procedures related to software development are almost always implemented using a commercial software package that provides a certain degree of automation. This *software configuration management* (*SCM*) tool provides traceability throughout the lifetime of the project by tracking change requests as they are entered, approved and delivered to the customer. The source code repository often can implement the SCM functionality and protect the integrity of the source files by managing versioning and synchronization among multiple developers simultaneously.

Versioning keeps track of each change made to a file so that at any point the current copy can be 'rolled back' to a previous version. Versioning systems also keep track of the 'who, what and when' of each change.

Some SCM systems allow more than one developer to work on the same project simultaneously, but with different files. When each developer is through with their changes, the system allows everyone to get back into *synchronization* automatically.

The code repository must be securely protected and allow only authorized users to look at the source code contained within, much less make changes to it. There are several reasons why a company should protect this asset:

- Someone could steal the source code for their own use
- An attacker could look at the source code to find vulnerabilities to exploit later
- An attacker could inject vulnerabilities that can be exploited later

In environments where security is a premium concern, the most effective method for securing source code is to create an isolated network containing all development, test and QA systems and 'air-gap' the whole thing. Unfortunately, remote work will no longer be possible, and it makes it difficult to collaborate with external parties. At the other end of the spectrum is to use a public web-based repository with security built-in. If a company is not willing to trust their intellectual property to an external party, a decent compromise is to internally host the repository and allow remote connectivity through VPN connections.

While we are on the subject of securing source code, companies very often use something called *software escrow* to protect themselves in the event that a partner company goes out of business or violates a contract. This is used when a company purchases a product or outsources the development of a product to another company. Normally, the source code is not delivered – only the *compiled* version that is usable for run-time is delivered. The source code instead is given to a third-party who holds on to it in case something unforeseen happens and the two companies no longer wish to cooperate. In this case, the third-party will release the source code held in escrow to the first company.

Chapter 70: Change Control

Questions

1. Which term best describes keeping track of each change made to a file?

    A) Software escrow

    B) Synchronization

    C) Change Control

    D) Versioning

2. Which term best describes a tool to protect a company in the event that a partner company goes out of business or violates a contract?

    A) Change Control

    B) Software configuration management

    C) Synchronization

    D) Software escrow

3. Which term best describes allowing more than one developer to work on the same project simultaneously, but with different files?

    A) Software escrow

    B) Software configuration management

    C) Synchronization

    D) Change Control

4. Which term best describes a tool providing traceability for a project by tracking change requests as they are entered, approved and delivered to the customer?

    A) Synchronization

    B) Change Control

    C) Software configuration management

    D) Versioning

5. Which term best describes the process of controlling any changes that take place during a product's lifetime and documenting the activities that result?

    A) Versioning

    B) Synchronization

    C) Change Control

    D) Software configuration management

Chapter 71: Programming Languages and Concepts

Computers and people don't speak the same language – while we humans like to use flowery words to describe things such as 'pink' and 'obtuse', computers are perfectly content to stick to binary - 0s and 1s. In fact, that is all that computers can understand. We humans have a tough time communicating in binary, so way back in the 1950s we invented something called a _programming language_ – a language that humans can understand (with difficulty) but that is easily translated into binary so computers can understand it.

There are 3 categories of programming languages. The first is called _machine language_ and is the binary language computers speak. The second category (which we call a _second generation language_) includes only _assembly language_, which is one step above machine language and uses words like 'push' and 'pop' to convey instructions instead of 0s and 1s; it also introduced the concept of 'variables'. An _assembler_ converts assembly language into machine language. Assembly language is still in limited use today, and an attacker will sometimes use assembly to create tightly controlled malicious instructions. Programs written in assembly language are hardware-dependent and are not portable to other processors.

The third category includes everything above assembly language. The _third-generation_ of programming languages started appearing in the late 1960s, and are collectively called _high-level language_s. These languages introduced the familiar 'if..then...else' construct and allowed programmers to focus on abstract concepts instead of pushing bits and bytes around directly. Programs written in third-generation languages are portable so they can run on multiple processors.

Fourth-generation languages (_very high-level languages_) came about and further abstracted the underlying complexity of computers from the programmer. What used to take 10 lines of code in a third-generation language could now be achieved with a single line of code. Structured Query Language (SQL) is included as a fourth-generation language. _Fifth-generation languages_ soon followed, but these did not simply improve on fourth-generation languages – they provided a whole new way of expressing instructions (using visual tools) for computers that are geared towards letting the computer solve problems that a 'programmer' defines – it is called a _natural language_. Because technology has not quite caught up to this level of programming, the reality is that the world still revolves heavily around fourth-generation languages.

Assemblers, Compilers, Interpreters

We have already discussed what an assembler is – it takes assembly language and converts it into machine language. A _compiler_ takes a high-level language and converts it into a machine-level format that is targeted for specific hardware. When we say that a high-level language is portable, we mean that it can be re-compiled for multiple hardware platforms without having to change the source code.

Modern languages, such as .Net and Java, have created yet another level of abstraction from the hardware, and can now be compiled into a hardware-independent format that can be distributed to multiple platforms. However, this is just an illusion since we still have the problem with machine code having to be compiled specifically for a given hardware platform. These languages achieve this 'magic' by compiling the source code to an intermediate format (.Net calls it 'object code' and java calls it _bytecode_), which is then _interpreted_ at run-time by a language-specific platform into machine code. This middle layer is called the Common Language Runtime (CLR) for .Net and the Java Virtual machine (JVM) for java.

Interpreted languages have another advantage than just being platform-independent. Memory allocation and deallocation is automatically carried out by a _garbage-collector_. This is a huge deal over third-generation languages such as C or C++. Many vulnerabilities in these latter languages have resulted from memory leaks cause by allocating memory and then forgetting to deallocate it when the code has finished with it. The garbage-collector automatically performs these steps so it is virtually impossible to create an accidental memory leak. A side-effect of this is that buffer overflows are much less likely to happen in interpreted languages as the automated allocation routines check for these types of anomalies. The C and C++ libraries have no such protection.

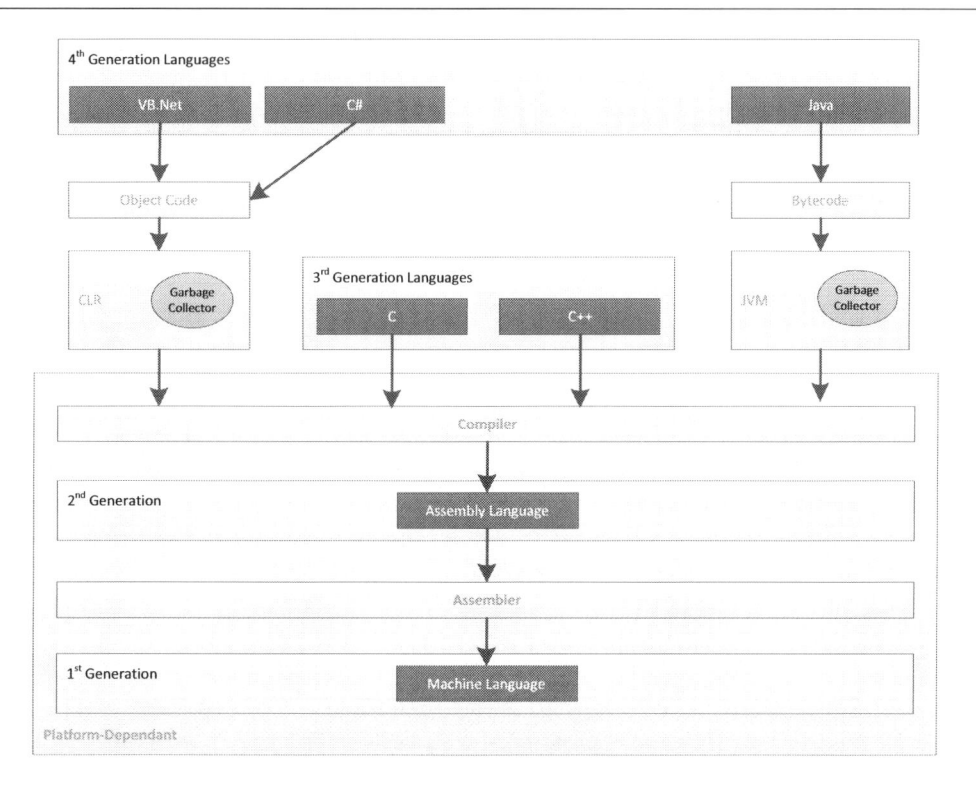

Figure 35: The Evolution of Programming Languages

Object-Oriented Concepts

In the beginning things were simple and all code was *procedural* – it had an entry point, it did some work, and then it exited with some kind of result. Simple perhaps, but very, very messy. Variables were thrown all over the place, and changing a single line of code could cause days of work trying to handle the fallout. Then some bright folks came up with the idea of *encapsulation* – putting all of this code behind walls so that you could only see the bare minimum you needed. And thus, started *object-oriented programming* (*OOP*) – focusing on objects instead of a linear progression of code.

C++, the .Net languages and Java are the best-known examples of OOP. OOP is much less-susceptible to brittleness (a small change requires a great deal of rework and testing). Each object hides it complexity behind an *interface* and provides just enough functionality for outside code to interact with it and no more. OOP is well-suited to mimicking the real-world, so it is great for modeling complex scenarios.

Some of the key terms we need to understand about OOP are:

- *Message* – how outside code communicates and provides input to an object
- *Method* – internal code that is executed in response to a message
- *Behavior* – the results of a message being processed through a method
- *Class* – a collection of methods that define some behavior
- *Instance* – an object is an *instance* of a class
- *Inheritance* – methods from a parent class are *inherited* by a child class
- *Delegation* – if an object does not have a method to handle a message, it will forward (*delegate*) that message to another object
- *Polymorphism* – a characteristic of an object that allows it to respond with different behaviors to the same message
- *Cohesion* – the strength of the relationship between methods of the same class; a high

cohesion means a class limits the scope of what it does, which is better software design
- *Coupling* – the level of required interaction between objects; low coupling means a class is less dependent on another class, which is a better software design
- *Data modeling* – views the data independently from code
- *Data structures* – views the logical relationships between data and how it is presented to code
- *Abstraction* – hides complex details from being seen, leaving only the bare minimum necessary for interaction
- Application Programming Interface (API) – provides a reusable component by abstracting complexity

Questions

1. Which concept best describes hiding complexity behind an interface?

    A) Message

    B) Encapsulation

    C) Procedural

    D) API

2. Which computer language includes the binary language computers speak?

    A) Machine language

    B) Very high-level languages

    C) High-level languages

    D) Assembly language

3. Which term best describes something that humans can understand but is easily translated into binary so computers can understand it?

    A) Encoded instructions

    B) Programming language

    C) Tertiary-speak

    D) Assembly language

4. Which concept best describes an object created from a class?

    A) Linear

    B) Behavior

    C) Method

    D) Instance

5. Which of the following converts a high-level language into a machine-level format that is targeted for specific hardware?

    A) Compiler

    B) Assembler

    C) Interpreted

    D) Bytecode

Chapter 72: Distributed Computing

In our connected world, very few programs are stand-alone – they require some type of connection to software that is running on a remote server. This is the essence of *distributed computing* – a solution that has at least two components separated by a network. Normally the remote component will be a database or set of services. When only two components are used, the architecture is called *client/server* – we have one client, and one remote server (usually a database). Modern systems normally have a third component that sits right in the middle, and we usually call this the 'services layer' or 'mid-tier'. The client will communicate with services, which may or may not communicate with the database or some other subsystem. Any architecture that has 3 or more layers is called an 'n-tier architecture', as there are 3 or more tiers. This section focuses on how those tiers communicate with one another.

A generic term often used is a *Remote Procedure Call* (*RPC*) – this is a generic term for a client invoking a service on a remote computer without the client understanding the details of how the interaction takes place – RPC hides the details. Modern web services are not RPC because the client *knows* the services live remotely.

Distributed Computing Environment

Distributed Computing Environment (*DCE*) is a standard developed by the Open Software Foundation (OSF), and was the first attempt at providing a standard method for distributing computer communication. DCE enables users, servers and resources to be contacted regardless of where each lives by using a *Universal Unique Identifier* (*UID*). It is no longer being used but provided many of the foundational components for later systems.

CORBA and ORBs

One of DCE's primary replacements was the Common Object Request Broker Architecture (CORBA), an open-standard developed by the Object Management Group (OMG). CORBA does not care what platform or language a component is written in – it only dictates how these components communicate to each other by defining the API and communication protocols.

The middle layer of services is contained within objects called *Object Request Brokers* (*ORBs*) – ORBs are responsible for knowing where objects live. In a nutshell, a client requests services from an ORB by giving it the name of the object it is interested in, the requested operation and any necessary parameters. The ORB will locate the object and carry out the request, and when it has completed the request it will return any resulting data.

CORBA objects can be created in any language or format if it aligns with the CORBA standard. The client never needs to know where the object lives - it could live on the same machine or across the world.

COM and DCOM

Microsoft created *Component Object Model* (*COM*) to provide the ability for *interprocess communication* (*IPC*) on a single computer – it can happen within an application or between multiple applications. COM is language-independent but is used for Windows systems only.

Distributed Component Object Model (*DCOM*) extends COM so that it can work over a network in a manner similar to CORBA, but again for Windows systems only. Both COM and DCOM can still be found but has largely been supplanted by the .Net framework.

Object Linking and Embedding (*OLE*) is based on COM and allows objects such as images, spreadsheets and Word documents to be shared on a Windows computer. The object can be *linked* (one program calls another in real-time) or *embedded* (the foreign object is fully contained inside of a native application). OLE was extended to work across networks through ActiveX, which we will cover in just a bit.

Java Platform, Enterprise Edition

Java platform, Enterprise Edition (*Java EE*) was created by Oracle to extend the Java language across the network like CORBA and DCOM, but for Java only. Since Java is platform-independent, Java EE works on multiple platforms and uses the CORBA standard for communications. Keep in mind that CORBA is a standard, DCOM is a Windows-specific technology, and Java EE is a Java technology that implements CORBA.

Service-Oriented Architecture

CORBA and DCOM are still around in a limited capacity in legacy systems, and Java EE is alive and well. However, the entire industry is moving in a direction that moves everything under a standardized envelope that doesn't care about the technology – it only cares about interoperability and standard patterns. That is where a *Service Oriented Approach* (*SOA*) comes in.

SOA is not a technology or standard – it is a pattern, and some even call it a mindset. SOA provides clear-cut patterns to follow when creating services, so that the services layer provides reusable building blocks for any number of applications and currently unknown future uses. Some see SOA simply as a web-based approach to services, and it was created with web technologies in-mind, but it is more of an architectural approach to providing those services.

The idea is to slice functionality up into discrete services that have high cohesion and low coupling (refer to the OOP definitions if these are unfamiliar terms) and expose an abstract interface. The result is a service that is highly reusable, platform-independent, self-describing and client-agnostic. How SOA services are accessed is irrelevant – SOAP, REST and even direct TCP are all just fine as far as SOA is concerned. SOA is 'discoverable' in the same manner as CORBA.

Having said all that stuff about SOA not caring about how it is accessed, the reality is that either SOAP or REST is almost always used. Enterprise organizations currently use SOAP (particularly banks) most of the time, so let's focus on that.

The _Simple Object Access Protocol_ (_SOAP_) is usually based on HTTP, and a Web Services Description Language (WSDL – an XML format) is used to describe the methods and parameters a SOA service offers. A _Universal Description, Discovery and Integration_ (_UDDI_) service provides the ability to 'lookup' a service, and the service itself will provide a WSDL describing the methods that are supported.

SOAP is platform-independent and can communicate using normal HTTP/S ports (80 or 443), so it is easy to access through firewalls. It provides significant security capabilities, but as a result is very 'fat' compared to _Representational State Transfer_ (_REST_), a competing HTTP standard which does not provide any security at all and is very 'lean'.

Mobile Code

Mobile code is any type of code that can be transmitted through a network. It is _not_ a mobile application on a smartphone, nor is it JavaScript files that a browser downloads. Mobile code is a compiled, self-contained component that is downloaded and executed on a client, such as Java Applets or ActiveX controls.

Java is a run-time environment in which bytecode can be executed, and the Java Virtual Machine (JVM) must be installed on a client computer - the JVM will convert the bytecode into machine-language and execute it. Bytecode that is downloaded across the network and executed in the JVM is called an _applet_, and usually runs inside of a browser. Recall that the JVM is a sandbox, meaning that it is a layer between the applet and the operating system. While the sandbox is supposed to prevent the applet from doing bad things, hackers routinely figure out ways to write their own bytecode that will circumvent the sandbox and gain access to local resources they should not be able to get to.

An _ActiveX_ control is like Java Applets, but is specific to Windows machines, and is downloaded in a format specific to the machine. ActiveX is built on COM and OLE, and therefore can allow other applications to execute within the browser through something called a _component container_. There is no sandbox to contain ActiveX controls as there is with Java applets – instead Microsoft relies on digital certificates to authenticate the ActiveX control before installation.

The security issue with ActiveX is that due to the lack of a sandbox the code will execute with the privileges of the current user, and any external application that ActiveX loads will also have the same access. While downloading an ActiveX control initially requires the user to explicitly provide an 'OK', any ActiveX control can download other components without the user knowing it. And unlike Java applets, ActiveX components are stored on the user's hard drive. This provides a perfect storm for compromise and exploitation.

In summary, Java applets rely on the sandbox for security, while ActiveX controls rely on digital certificates before installation. Two vastly different approaches with their own security concerns. Support for ActiveX was officially ended with IE Edge (Windows 10). Due to the increasing popularity of HTML5 and other Web 2.0 features, Java applets also are on their way out. However, both are still present to some degree and need to be monitored.

Chapter 72: Distributed Computing

Questions

1. Which term describes a string of characters that is unique to a system?

    A) RPC

    B) DCE

    C) GUID

    D) UID

2. Which of the following represents a foreign object being fully contained inside of a native application?

    A) Embedded

    B) COM

    C) OLE

    D) Linked

3. What is the best description of a solution that has at least two components separated by a network?

    A) Distributed computing

    B) Remote procedures

    C) Cross-network architecture

    D) Multi-tier application

4. Which of the following allows interprocess communication on a single Windows computer?

    A) DCOM

    B) OLE

    C) IPC

    D) COM

5. Which of the following is an XML document that describes a SOAP service?

    A) SOAP

    B) WSDL

    C) XHTML

    D) REST

Chapter 73: Web Security

Administrative Interfaces

Web-based administrative interfaces are very convenient but dangerous if exposed over the Internet. Access should be limited to local IP addresses only such that a VPN is required. Even better, an *out-of-band* administrative interface should be used, such as using SSH instead of a browser-based interface.

Authentication and Access Control

Due to the conflict of high-security vs. usability, passwords are by far the most common authentication mechanism. Unfortunately, passwords do not prove identity, and usernames can be mined or easily guessed. Many financial organizations require multi-factor authentication – this is implemented by sending a one-time password to the user's registered cell phone. Regardless of the mechanism, it should be obvious that all credentials sent over any network should be TLS-encrypted.

Input Validation

Input validation deals with the consumption of user-provided variables. They can be sent in 2 manners – through the URL or by using input fields within a web page.

URL validation deals with consuming variables provided in the URL sent to a web server. There are 3 types of attacks that can be carried out using URLs. The first is the *path or directory traversal attack* and is also known as the '*dot-dot-slash attack*' because it is carried out by inserting the '../' characters into a URL. The '../' command instructs the web server to walk back up one level from the directory where the current web page is located. For example, if the URL:

'http://www.mydomain.com/pages/../../../c:\windows\system32'

is sent to a web site where the site is located in the local folder 'c:\inetpub\www\mydomain\pages', the web server might try to send back a list of all files in 'c:\windows\system32', and possibly even execute a program from there. To prevent this, the web server (not our web application, the web server itself, such as IIS or Tomcat) must explicitly check for this type of attack and prevent it by filtering the URL (*URL filtering*).

The second URL-based attack is called *Unicode encoding*, and attempts to defeat URL filtering. Unicode is a standard that allows all characters to be expressed as a hexadecimal equivalent. For example, instead of using the character '/' in a URL, we could substitute '%c1%1c' – this would effectively circumvent any code looking for the '/' character.

The last URL-based attack is called *URL encoding*, and is another way to bypass filtering mechanisms by substituting an alternate method for sending characters. In this instance, the '/' character can be replaced with '%2f'.

Attacks using input fields are also referred to as injection attacks, and come in 2 primary flavors – SQL injection and script injection.

SQL injection occurs when the attacker puts SQL commands into a text field and submits a from. The server then executes the text as legitimate SQL allowing the attacker to run SQL commands directly against the database. This could result in reading, updating or deleting data. In extreme cases a SQL injection attack can result in dropping database tables. To counter such an attack the input values should be scrubbed and cleaned of any SQL-like clauses. Unfortunately, this can often result in some rather ugly-looking content that is permanently disfigured. A much better solution is to use 'parameterized statements', wherein the input is not string-concatenated into SQL and executed – the values are provided as parameters to the SQL engine.

Script injection attacks are the entry point to *cross-site scripting* (*XSS*) attacks, and are normally simply referred to as XSS. With this method, an attacker somehow gets their own script (such as JavaScript) to execute inside of a user's browser. The attacker is now able to access anything the web page can get to including cookies or script variables, and can hijack the session or execute malware, to name a few vulnerabilities. There are 3 ways an XSS attack can be carried out.

Non-persistent XSS vulnerabilities (also called *reflected vulnerabilities*) are employed when the attacker convinces the web server to emit HTML that downloads a rogue script from another site. This is accomplished when the web server 'reflects' back to the browser data that was previously submitted, normally in the form of query parameters embedded in the URL. For example, an attacker could convince a legitimate user to click on a link to a valid web site such as

'www.mydomain.com?search=<link to my evil script here>'

If the web site does not properly filter the input, OR properly format the output, it can generate a page that lists the provided search criteria and embed '<link to my evil script here>' in the HTML that goes back to the browser. The result is that the victim's browser now executes the evil script in the context of a valid web page. Note that Cross-Origin Resource Sharing (CORS) controls will normally prevent this from happening, but there are ways around that as well, such as JSONP. The countermeasure for this attack is to always encode the values from the query line if they need to be emitted back to the browser; for example, turn any '<' characters into valid HTML encoding such as '%3c'. This attack is called 'non-persistent' because it does not require the victim website to persist any type of malicious content – it is perpetrated on-the-fly.

Persistent XSS vulnerabilities occur when an attacker can convince a server to store their data (which is actually a command to download a malicious script, or perhaps straight malicious JavaScript) in a database field. Later, another visitor views a page that contains the attacker's code pulled from the database, resulting in execution of the malicious payload. For example, an attacker posts a message to a forum, and the message contains '<script>alert("I am evil!");</script>'. When another visitor views that forum post, the browser will pop up a scary message as soon as the page is loaded saying 'I am evil!'. The countermeasure for this attack is to always encode the input values before storing in the database; for example, turn any '<' characters into valid HTML encoding such as '%3c'. It is possible to store the raw value and encode at the last minute, but this still leaves the system vulnerable to SQL injection attacks. As noted before, this often results in some rather ugly content, but usability must be weighed against security.

Document object model XSS vulnerabilities leverage the ability to dynamically generate content within the browser using the *Document Object Model* (*DOM*). For example, if a page's script executes 'document.write("You are viewing : " + document.location)', then the following URL can force a message to pop up:

'http://www.mydomain.com? <script>alert("I am evil!");</script>'

The countermeasure for this attack is to either not perform this type of DOM manipulation in a web page, or if it is absolutely necessary, include code to properly encode the value before inserting it into the DOM.

Client-side validation is a normal and valid operation and occurs when client code ensures that all required fields are provided and checks for invalid values. Attempting to submit a from and receiving a message immediately that a required field is missing is an example of client-side validation – the request was never sent to a server but handled locally. Once client-side validation is passed, the request is then sent to the server. While this provides a better user experience, developers often assume that client-side validation is sufficient and forget to perform the same checks on the server. Server code should *never* trust data regardless of what type of client-side validation was performed – hackers can easily bypass browsers and substitute their own values, thereby completely negating any client-side validation.

Parameter Validation

While input validation centers around the server examining and validating values provided from the user before processing them, the server also needs to be concerned about another class of values.

Parameter validation is concerned with the server examining and validating values that are assumed to be beyond the ability of a user to change, such as values stored in a client-side cookie or hidden fields. Many web applications assume that because the browser does not expose these values to the user, they are safe to use. The problem with this approach assumes that an attacker is limited by the browser interface, when he is most certainly not. By using a web proxy on the client machine an attacker can intercept any HTTP traffic (even if it is encrypted with TLS!) and change cookie values, hidden fields, the URL – pretty much anything sent over an HTTP connection can be manipulated, including HTTP header values.

The countermeasure is to:

- Never send any server-side data to the browser and expect it to be to be returned unless it is intentionally supposed to be manipulated by the user
- Execute pre-validation – the client ensures the data is valid before submission to the server; this is optional
- Execute post-validation – the server validates incoming values before trusting them; this is required

Chapter 73: Web Security

Session Management

If a web application does anything more than serving up static HTML pages, it will need to deal with sessions – the ability to tie a browser request with an existing user interaction. While the server can certainly store all data associated with a given session, the connectionless nature of HTTP (and HTTPS) means that the server will rely on the browser to tell it *which* session the browser wants to work with. This is called *session management*, and relies on the server generating a unique session ID the first time a browser connects, and requires the browser to always send back the session ID for any subsequent HTTP request.

The session ID can be stored in a cookie, sent as a hidden input field, or added as part of every URL requested – but it is almost always sent over as clear text unless HTTPS is used. If TLS is not enabled, *session hijacking* can occur in which an attacker sniffs a current session ID and uses it in her own packets. Session IDs should be randomly generated to prevent an attacker from predicting a valid value, and some type of timestamp should be required to prevent replay attacks. Cookies containing session information should contain encrypted data – this will not prevent session hijacking but at least the attacker will be unable to look at information such as shopping cart contents.

Web Application Security Best Practices

Following is a short list of best practices to keep in mind when dealing with web applications:

- *Keep it simple* – security loves simplicity, and the simpler a site is, the easier it is to enforce proper security and detect issues
- *Look at user input* – closely scrutinize areas that allow user input and ensure the values are being properly vetted
- *Look at system output* – look for any places where data is emitted, whether it comes from a database, external systems, input fields, or incoming URLs – it should always be HTML-encoded to prevent XSS
- *Encrypt everything* – any traffic between the server and the browser should be encrypted if it is anything but static HTML pages; cookie contents should also be encrypted
- *Fail securely* – when an error is encountered, always provide a friendly and generic message to the user and never divulge internal details
- *Strike a good security/usability balance* – too much security and users will hate your site; too little security and hackers will love your site
- *Never use security through obscurity* – there is no such thing on the web; either it is in plain site or it needs to be wrapped in proper authentication/authorization measures

Chapter 73: Web Security

Questions

1. Which of the following is an attack carried out by inserting the '/' characters into a URL, causing the web server to access inappropriate directories?

    A) Directory traversal attack

    B) SQL injection

    C) URL encoding

    D) Unicode encoding

2. Which of the following is an attack in which URL characters are encoded as URL characters instead of ASCII text?

    A) SQL injection

    B) Unicode encoding

    C) Directory traversal attack

    D) URL encoding

3. Which of the following is taken advantage of when an attacker convinces a server to store their malicious data in a database field?

    A) Document object model XSS

    B) XSS

    C) Persistent XSS vulnerabilities

    D) Non-persistent XSS vulnerabilities

4. Which of the following results when an attacker gets their own script to execute inside of a user's browser?

    A) Document object model XSS

    B) Non-persistent XSS vulnerabilities

    C) Persistent XSS vulnerabilities

    D) XSS

5. Which of the following occurs when client code ensures that all required fields are provided and checks for invalid values?

    A) Parameter Validation

    B) Session hijacking

    C) Session management

    D) Client-side validation

Chapter 74: Database Management

Access to a database should be based on roles only, not individual user accounts. This limits the damage that can be done if an external attacker gains direct access to the database - he will not be able to proceed further without gaining another set of credentials

Database Management Software

A *database* is a collection of persisted data which users can view and modify as-needed. A *database management system* (*DMS*) is software that exposes the database, enforces access control, provides data integrity and redundancy, and provides procedures for data manipulation.

A database should:

- Ensure consistency among all associated servers
- Provide for easy backups
- Provide transaction persistence (that are durable and reliable)
- Provide recovery and fault tolerance
- Support sharing of data among multiple users
- Provide security controls that implement integrity, access control and confidentiality

Database Models

Databases come in many different models, so we will discuss the most common. A *hierarchical data model* combines records and fields in a tree structure without using indexes. LDAP with its many nodes and flexible structure is one use for this model, but it is useful for any data containing one-to-many parent/children relationships.

A *Relational Database Model* (*RDBM*) uses attributes (columns) and tuples (rows) to store data in 2-dimensional tables. The intersection of a column and a row is called a *cell*. A *primary key* is a field that provides a unique value to every record in the table, and relational databases use *indexes* for searching (which are themselves hierarchical models). RDBMs are by far the most widely used.

The *Network Database Model* is built on the hierarchical data model and is useful for many parent/many children relationships. While it does contain records, and each record has many fields (such as a relational database), the parent and child relationships are defined by something called a *set*.

The *Object-Oriented Database* (*OOD*) is designed to handle multiple data types, such as images, audio, video, documents, etc. Each object contains its own data and methods – whereas an RDBM simply sends back data that must then be understood, an OOD sends back one or more objects that understand themselves.

The *Object-Relational Database* (*ORD*) is backed by a standard RDBM but provides a fronting mechanism to implement additional business logic with an object-oriented programming language. Basically, it's an RDBM with an OOP layer on top for implementing business logic.

Database Programming Interfaces

There are multiple ways in which programming code can talk to various database. The oldest is the *Open Database Connectivity* (*ODBC*), which works with local or remote databases. Applications interact with the ODBC API, allowing the same interface to work regardless of the backend database. ODBC locates the database-specific driver and uses it to translate its common language (SQL) into a database-specific language.

Microsoft invented the *Object Linking and Embedding Database* (*OLE DB*), which separates data into components that run on middleware and works with different databases in real-time. It is a replacement for ODBC and supports non-SQL databases. However, it requires COM for interaction, so is a Windows-only solution. OLE DB is very flexible – it supports different applications accessing different types of data in different locations. It can access any data source - not just databases - so SQL is not required.

ActiveX Data Objects (*ADO*) was released with OLE DB, and is the official API for OLE DB.

Oracle released the *Java Database Connectivity* (*JDBC*), which is essentially ODBC for Java applications. JDBC can leverage ODBC underneath the covers but provides database access for a wide range of databases, including support for direct SQL.

Relational Database Components

All relational databases share some common components, so let's quickly run down a list of terms that describe their architecture.

- Data Definition Language (DDL) – defines the structure and schema
    - *Schema* – table details (properties and data types)

- o *Structure* – everything outside of tables (table size, index size, views, table relationships)
- Data Manipulation Language (DML) – provides access to the data
- *Data Control Language* (*DCL*) – defines the internal organization of the database
- *Ad hoc query language* (*QL*) – allows users to make requests (SQL is based on this)
- *Report generator* – produces printouts of data in a user-defined format
- *Data dictionary* – centralized collection of information about all users, user roles, tables, indexes, privileges, etc.; used to provide access controls
- *Primary key* – a unique value across all records in a table, used for indexing
- *Foreign key* – a relationship where Table A has a column that matches a primary key in Table B

Integrity

One common issue all RDBMs face is how to deal with multiple users trying to modify the same data at the same time – this is referred to as *concurrency*. To solve the problem, a database can *lock* data so that only one user can modify the value. The locks can be applied at the table, page, row and field level. This ensures that integrity of the data is maintained.

Aside from concurrency, an RDBM must enforce three types of integrity checks:

- *Semantic integrity* – ensures the database's structure remains secure (enforces data types, logical values, uniqueness constraints and operations)
- *Referential integrity* – ensures that all foreign keys reference a valid primary key
- *Entity integrity* – ensures that all primary keys have a unique value within the table

There is another issue closely related to concurrency – how to ensure integrity resulting from transactions. A *transaction* is a sequence of operations performed as a single unit of work. In other words, all operations need to succeed, or none should. Here are some terms dealing with transaction integrity:

- *Rollback* – cancels the current transaction and reverts the database to the state it was before the transaction started
- *Commit* – completes a transaction and executes all changes just made within the transaction
- *Two-phase commit* – for transactions in a distributed environment, all databases make a 'pre-commit', and once all databases have reported back successfully, they all perform a 'commit'
- *Batch processing* – requests for database changes are put into a queue and executed all at once

Online transaction processing (*OLTP*) is used to provide fault tolerance and better performance with clustered databases. OLTP monitors the entire transaction process across multiple systems and takes steps to ensure integrity across all components while making sure the system remains usable by enabling load-balancing if necessary. To do this, OLTP enforces ACID:

- *Atomicity* – all changes take effect, or none do
- *Consistency* – all data remains consistent in all databases
- *Isolation* – transactions execute in isolation until completed
- *Durability* – once the transaction is committed it cannot be rolled back

Databases must provide a mechanism to handle unexpected error states:

- *Savepoint* – periodic save of a database that can be restored in case of severe interruption; can be triggered based on elapsed time, every # transactions, etc.
- *Checkpoint* – a savepoint is triggered when the database fills up a specific amount of memory

From a security perspective, RDBMs have a couple of tricks to ensure access controls are implemented properly:

- *Database view* – a virtual table comprised of one or more underlying tables that restrict or aggregate data according to an access control policy
- *Polyinstantiation* – interactively creating two instances of the same object with different attributes; this is used to stop inference attacks

Data Warehousing and Data Mining

Data warehousing combines data from two or more databases into a single large database, with the goal of providing an aggregated view of the source data for follow-up analysis. The original data sources are operational (updateable), but the data warehouse is used exclusively for analysis. During the aggregation process, redundant information is removed, and the remaining data is properly formatted and correlated. Because of the 'one-stop-shop for all your malicious needs' capability that a data warehouse database affords, security should be more stringent.

Data mining is the process of combing through the data warehouse information and extracting more useful information, called metadata. _Metadata_ is the result of data mining that can show trends and relationships not evident in the raw sources. _Knowledge discovery in database_ (_KDD_) is another term for data mining, but defines three approaches to identify patterns:

- Classification – groups data according to similarities
- _Probalistic_ – identifies relationships and calculates probabilities
- _Statistical_ – identifies relationships and uses rule discovery

Big data is defined as very large data sets that are unsuitable for traditional analysis techniques due to:

- _Heterogeneity_ – data types are not standardized
- _Complexity_ – many different relationships exist between data
- _Variability_ – some sources are verbose while others are sparse
- _Lack of reliability_ – the reliability of the source is not known
- _Volume_ - too much data to be processed by normal means

Big data is put into a data warehouse, but often must use other technologies to carry out data mining such as Hadoop or MapReduce instead of an RDBMS.

Chapter 74: Database Management

Questions

1. Which of the following combines data from two or more databases into a single large database for follow-up analysis?

    A) Metadata

    B) KDD

    C) Data warehousing

    D) Data mining

2. Which of the following is a unique value across all records in a table?

    A) Foreign key

    B) Complex key

    C) Primary key

    D) Relational key

3. Which best describes a collection of persisted data which users can view and modify as-needed?

    A) Database

    B) Storage mechanism

    C) Middleware

    D) Repository

4. Which of the following is Microsoft's replacement for ODBC that can access any data source?

    A) OLE DB

    B) DDL

    C) JDBC

    D) ADO

5. Which of the following puts requests for database changes into a queue, after which they are all executed at once?

    A) Transaction processing

    B) Batch processing

    C) Transaction follow-through

    D) OLTP

Chapter 75: Malicious Software (Malware)

Viruses

A *virus* is a small application that infects software and can replicate itself. Viruses require a host application and carry payloads that cause the real harm.

A *macro virus* is written in a macro language such as Visual Basic or VBScript and is usually associated with Microsoft Office products.

A *boot sector virus* infects the boot sector of a computer, and often hides itself in hard drive sectors that the virus has marked as bad.

A *tunneling virus* intercepts requests for a file and presents a forged version of it instead. This is useful when antimalware software is running – the virus can convince the antimalware that everything is fine and to move along.

A *stealth virus* hides the modifications it has made to files or boot records by acting as a tunneling virus but can also mask the size of the file it is hiding in and even move itself around during antimalware activity to avoid detection.

A *polymorphic virus* can alter its appearance to outwit virus scanners. It will make multiple copies of itself, each with a different appearance so that it magically reappears when the antimalware software thinks it has eradicated it. Appearance changes are carried out by using different encryption schemes or changing their own code by embedding *noise* (bogus instructions) within themselves, or simply changing the sequence of their own instructions.

A *multipart virus* has several components that are distributed in multiple locations on each system, allowing it to spread more quickly.

A *meme virus* is not a real virus, but simply an email that gets spread quickly around the Internet. The harm is in wasted bandwidth and possible fear based on the email's message.

A *script virus* is sent in script from such as JavaScript, VBScript, Microsoft Windows Script Host or any other interpreted language. Often these scripts are downloaded by a web browser, and when launched can cause great damage.

Malware normally has 6 primary components, although not all 6 are always present:

- Insertion – installs itself
- Avoidance – avoid detection
- *Eradication* – removes itself after the payload has been delivered
- *Replication* – makes copies of itself and spreads
- *Trigger* – uses an event to execute the payload
- Payload – carries out its function

Worms

A *worm* is a self-contained program and can reproduce without requiring a host application. Stuxnet was a worm that targeted SCADA software.

Rootkit

After compromising a system, an attacker will normally attempt to escalate privileges to administrator or root-level access. The attacker can then upload a *rootkit* – essentially a bundle of tools that can be used to cause further mayhem, such as installing a backdoor or to start sniffing for credentials.

The rootkit often replaces valid files with tools from this kit, using the legitimate filename to avoid detection. These are called *Trojan programs*, and the real tools that an administrator might use to discover that the system has been compromised are often targeted first. The Trojan version will often appear to run correctly but leave out certain details such as listing the port that is being used for the backdoor. A rootkit may also include a *log scrubber* that removes traces of the attacker's movements from the system log files. More powerful rootkits will replace actual kernel files, as HIDS often do not bother looking at the core files. A kernel-level rootkit has much more power than user-level rootkit. Rootkits can also exist in a system's firmware or even in the hypervisor of a virtual system.

Spyware and Adware

Spyware is malware that exists to simply gather information about a victim. *Adware* is malware that automatically generates advertisements. While adware is not intended to harm a system (it wants to increase sales revenue) it is invasive and can cause privacy concerns.

Botnets

A *bot* is a type of malware that is installed through infected email, drive-by-downloads, Trojan horses or shared media. Bots normally will check in to let the hacker know it has successfully compromised a system, and then lie dormant until it receives further instructions. It is now part of a *botnet*, or a network of bots. The owner of this botnet, commonly referred to as a _bot herder_, controls the systems, usually through the _Internet Relay Chat_ (_IRC_) protocol.

Botnets are commonly used to carry out DDoS attacks, spamming, and brute-force attacks, among others. _Fast flux_ is also used – it is an evasion technique used to continually be on the move by updating DNS entries. The servers that send instructions to a botnet are referred to as _Command-and-Control_ (_C&C_) servers.

Logic Bombs

A _logic bomb_ is a program that is set to go off and execute its payload whenever a specific trigger is activated. The trigger may be a date/time or when a specific action is detected.

Trojan Horses

A _Trojan horse_ is a program that is disguised as another program. Trojan horses often carry out the activity that the original program is designed to, but additionally carries out malicious operations in the background. That way, the user is never aware that malware is running. A _Remote Access Trojan_ (_RAT_) is a malicious program that allows an intruder to access and use a system remotely.

Spam Detection

Spam is the receipt of unsolicited junk email. Detecting spam is an ongoing effort as 'spammers' continually work to evade our best detection efforts.

Bayesian filtering is a technique that applies statistical modeling to the words in an email message to determine how often each is used and in what order, and from that analysis decide if the message is spam or not. Spammers intentionally misspell words or substitute symbols to get past the spam filters.

Antimalware Programs

Companies should have an antimalware policy that provides details on the type of antimalware and antispyware software that should be installed, including configuration parameters.

Many times, a company will install _virus walls_ that scan incoming SMTP, HTTP and FTP traffic for malware. These can be integrated with email servers, proxy servers or firewalls.

Questions

1. Which of the following replaces valid files with malicious alternatives?

    A) Spyware

    B) Trojan programs

    C) Rootkit

    D) Log scrubber

2. Which component of a virus enables it to make copies of itself and spreads?

    A) Eradication

    B) Avoidance

    C) Replication

    D) Insertion

3. What is a small application that infects software and can replicate itself?

    A) Trojan horse

    B) Worm

    C) Viruses

    D) Logic bomb

4. Which of the following is a tunneling virus that can hide the size of its file and move around to avoid detection?

    A) Polymorphic virus

    B) Stealth virus

    C) Tunneling virus

    D) Multipart virus

5. Which of the following is the owner of a botnet?

    A) Bot herder

    B) RAT

    C) C&C

    D) Fast flux

Answers

Chapter 1
1. B
2. B
3. B
4. B
5. B

Chapter 2
1. B
2. A
3. B
4. B
5. D

Chapter 3
1. D
2. D
3. D
4. A
5. B

Chapter 4
1. B
2. B
3. C
4. B
5. A

Chapter 5
1. D
2. D
3. B
4. D
5. A

Chapter 6
1. D
2. B
3. B
4. C
5. C

Chapter 7
1. B
2. B
3. A
4. A
5. B

Chapter 8
1. C
2. D
3. A
4. A
5. D

Answers

Chapter 9

1. D

2. A

3. D

4. B

5. C

Chapter 10

1. C

2. C

3. C

4. A

5. D

Chapter 11

1. B

2. C

3. B

4. D (Granting access authorization is completed after an employee has been hired)

5. C

Chapter 12

1. A

2. D

Chapter 13

1. A

2. D

3. A

4. C

5. D

Chapter 14

1. C

2. B

3. A

4. B

5. B

Chapter 15

1. D

2. A

3. D

4. A

5. B

Chapter 16

1. C

2. A

3. C

4. C

5. B

Answers

Chapter 17

1. D

2. C

3. B

4. D

5. A

Chapter 18

1. B

2. A

3. A

4. A

5. C

Chapter 19

1. B

2. A

3. C

4. A

5. A

Chapter 20

1. B

2. D

3. B

4. A

5. C

Chapter 21

1. A

2. C

3. D

4. C

5. A

Chapter 22

1. A

2. D

3. C

4. C

5. A

Chapter 23

1. C

2. A

3. B

4. B

5. C

Chapter 24

1. D

2. B

3. C

4. C

5. C

Answers

Chapter 25

1. C (It has yet to be broken)

2. B (AES has low CPU and memory requirements)

3. B (NIST added 8 bits for parity, resulting in a 56-bit key size)

4. A (When a mode has only 2 keys, the first and third cycle use the same key)

5. D (It uses 64-bit blocks, not 32-bit blocks)

Chapter 26

1. C (It provides the same services as all three)

2. A (That would be ECC that is found on mobile platforms)

3. C (Key agreement calculates a shared key, while key exchange requires the two parties to exchange the secret key)

4. B (It has been implemented in most operating systems as well)

5. C (Both keys MUST be mathematically related – that is how one can decrypt ciphertext that the other encrypts)

Chapter 27

1. C

2. A (It accepts a string of any length but always produces a string of the same length)

3. B (Since the message is not encrypted, confidentiality is never provided)

4. A (The hash is computed over the entire message only once)

5. B (This method applies at the system level only)

Chapter 28

1. B

2. C

3. A

4. C

5. D

Chapter 29

1. C

2. B

3. D

4. B

5. A

Chapter 30

1. B (Politically motivated is the fourth physical threat)

2. A

3. B

4. B

5. D

Chapter 31

1. B

Answers

Chapter 32

1. B
2. B
3. A
4. D
5. D

Chapter 33

1. B
2. C
3. C
4. C
5. B

Chapter 34

1. C
2. B
3. B
4. A
5. B

Chapter 35

1. C
2. D
3. D
4. B
5. D

Chapter 36

1. B
2. C
3. D
4. A
5. A

Chapter 37

1. B
2. A
3. A
4. C
5. D

Chapter 38

1. B
2. C
3. A
4. D
5. B

Chapter 39

1. B
2. B
3. D
4. B
5. D

Answers

Chapter 40

1. D

2. B

3. B

4. A

5. C

Chapter 41

1. B

2. C

3. B

4. B

5. B

Chapter 42

1. C

2. D

3. A

4. A

5. A

Chapter 43

1. B

2. D

3. C

4. B

5. C

Chapter 44

1. B

2. D

3. D

4. B

5. D

Chapter 45

1. D

2. B

3. D

4. C (The fourth step is accountability)

5. D

Chapter 46

1. B

2. A

3. C

4. A

5. B

Chapter 47

1. C

2. A

3. B

4. A

5. B

Answers

Chapter 48

1. C
2. B
3. C
4. D
5. A

Chapter 49

1. A
2. A
3. B
4. B
5. D

Chapter 50

1. C
2. A
3. B
4. B
5. A

Chapter 51

1. D
2. D
3. C
4. C
5. B

Chapter 52

1. B
2. D
3. C
4. C
5. B (The steps are discovery, enumeration, vulnerability mapping, exploitation and report to management)

Chapter 53

1. C
2. D
3. C
4. D
5. B

Chapter 54

1. B
2. A
3. C
4. B
5. A

Chapter 55

1. D
2. A
3. B
4. C
5. B

Answers

Chapter 56

1. C

2. C

3. D

4. A

Chapter 57

1. B

2. C

3. A

4. D

5. D

Chapter 58

1. B

2. B

3. D

4. B

5. B

Chapter 59

1. D

2. C

3. B

4. B

5. B

Chapter 60

1. B

2. D (Solid operational procedures is the fourth element)

3. B

4. D

5. D

Chapter 61

1. C

2. D

3. B

4. A

5. D

Chapter 62

1. A

2. A

3. C

4. D

5. C

Chapter 63

1. A

2. A

3. B

4. B

5. D

Answers

Chapter 64

1. A
2. C
3. B
4. D
5. D

Chapter 65

1. C
2. A
3. B
4. A
5. A

Chapter 66

1. C
2. A
3. D
4. A
5. C

Chapter 67

1. B
2. D
3. B
4. B
5. D

Chapter 68

1. B
2. A
3. C
4. B
5. D

Chapter 69

1. D
2. A
3. B
4. B
5. A

Chapter 70

1. D
2. D
3. C
4. C
5. C

Chapter 71

1. B
2. A
3. B
4. D
5. A

Answers

Chapter 72

1. D

2. A

3. A

4. D

5. B

Chapter 73

1. A

2. D

3. C

4. D

5. D

Chapter 74

1. C

2. C

3. A

4. A

5. B

Chapter 75

1. B

2. C

3. C

4. B

5. A

Index

1000base-t	149
100base-tx	149
10base-t	149
1G	186
2.5G	186
2G	186
3.5G	186
3DES	100
3G	186
3GPP	186
4G	186
5G	186
6to4	137
802.11	183
802.11a	183
802.11ac	184
802.11b	183
802.11e	184
802.11f	184
802.11g	184
802.11h	184
802.11i	182
802.11j	184
802.11n	184
802.16	184
AAA	3, 213
ABR	170
absolute addresses	66
abstraction	71, 304
abstraction layer	71
academic	20
accept the risk	36
acceptable use policy	238
acceptance testing	294
accepting	36
access	17, 194
access control	194
access control lists	159, 202, 208
access control matrix	212
access control mechanisms	256
access control model	208
access controls	194
access point	181
access triple	78
account management	197
accountability	3, 17, 195, 217
accounts receivables	275
accreditation	82
accuracy	60
ACLs	159, 202, 208
acoustical detection systems	258
acquisition	50
activation phase	278
active attack	112
active monitor	149
active monitoring	282
activex	307
activex data objects	313
actors	235
actual	169
AD	67
ad hoc	181
ad hoc query language	314
adding oracle on downgraded legacy encryption	189
address bus	65
address resolution protocol	150
address space layout randomization	67
ADM	10
administration interface	220
administrative	7, 18
administrative controls	214
administrative management	247
ADO	313
ADSL	176
advanced encryption standard	100
advanced mobile phone system	186
advanced persistent threat	17
advisory	25
adware	317
AES	100
agent	151
agent based	266
agentless	266
aggregation	84
agile models	298
AH	177
AICPA	230
AIDSs	220

Index

AIK	110
ALE	34
algebraic attack	113
algorithm	90
algorithmic logic unit	64
ALU	64
AM	140
american institute of certified public accounts	230
amount of lighting	257
amplitude	140
amplitude modulation	140
amplitudes	181
AMPS	186
analog	140
analytic attack	113
analyzer	220
and	72, 81
annual loss expectancy	34
annualized rate of occurrence	34
annunciator	257
anomaly-based ids	221
anonymous open proxy	164
antimalware	265
antivirus	265
anycast	137
AP	181
API	73, 165
appendixes	278
applet	307
appliances	162
application layer	128, 129, 134
application programming interface	73
application whitelisting	260
application-based idss	220
application-level proxies	162
application-specific integrated circuit	160
APT	17
architecture	64, 67
architecture description	67
architecture development method	10
architecture views	68
archive bit	274
archived	50
ARO	34
ARP	150
arp poisoning	150, 221
arp table cache poisoning	150
AS	156
AS/NZS 4360	33
ASIC	160
ASLR	67
assembler	302
assembly language	302
assess	28
assessment	256
asset value	34
assisted password reset	197
assurance evaluation	81
asymmetric	65
asymmetric algorithms	94
asymmetric dsl	176
asymmetric keys	95
asynchronous	141
asynchronous algorithms	97
asynchronous attack	88
asynchronous otp	200
asynchronous replication	274
asynchronous transfer mode	168, 169
ata encryption standard	100
atbash	90
ATM	168, 169
atomic	252
atomicity	314
attack	29
attack chain	29
attack surface	293
attack surface analysis	293
attack tree	29
attenuation	145
attestation identity key	110
attribute value pairs	213
audit trails	217
auditing	3
auditor	54
audit-reduction tool	217
AUP	238
authenticate	195, 196
authentication	3, 86, 91, 196
authentication by knowledge	199
authentication header	177
authentication server	182, 183
authenticator	182, 183, 202, 203
authorization	3, 91, 201
authorization creep	202
authorized	195
automatic tape vaulting	274
automatic tunneling	137
autonomous system	156
availability	195
availability,	3
available bit rate service	170
avalanche effect	96

Index

AVPS	213
back doors	235
backdoors	88
backends	86
backlog	298
backup	50
backup lighting	257
bandwidth	141
banner grabbing	232
base register	71
baseband	141
baseline	25, 241
basic rate interface isdn	176
basic service set	181
bastion hosts,	163
batch processing	314
bayesian filtering	318
BC	239
BCM	40
BCP	40
bcp committee	41
bcp policy	41
beaconing	149
beamforming	184
BEDO RAM	65
before	183, 226, 262
behavior	303
behavior blocking	222
behavioral model –	292
behavioral trait	198
behavioral-based ids	221
bell-lapadula model	77
best-effort service	170
between	163
BGP	156
BIA	41
biba model	77
big data	315
binding	110
biometrics	198
birthday attack	107
BISDN	176
bit-level parallelism	84
black box test	232
black hole	156
blacklisting	265
blackout	122
Blind	234
block cipher	96
block ciphers	94
block device	72
blocked	70
blowfish	100
bluejacking	184
bluesnarking	184
bluetooth	184
bollards	116
boot sector virus	317
BOOTP	151
bootstrap protocol	151
border gateway protocol	156
bot	16, 191, 317
bot herder	318
botnet	16, 191, 317
boundary conditions	236
boundary protection mechanisms	256
brewer and nash model	78
BRI	176
bridge	159
broadband	141
broadband isdn	176
broadcast	149
broadcast domain	148
brownout	122
brute-force attack	199, 225
brute-force method	91
BSS	181
buffer overflow	67
buffer overflows	66, 233
build and fix model	297
bumping	255
burst edo dram	65
bus topology	147
business continuity	239
business continuity coordinator	41
business continuity management	40
business enablement	10
business impact analysis	41
business interruption insurance	275
bytecode	302
C&C	191, 268, 318
CA	109
cable traps	256
cache memory	66
caesar cipher	90
camera	257
can bus	132
capability	212
capability component	212
capability maturity model integration	12
capability table	212
capacitance detectors	258

Index

CAPTCHA	199
carbon dioxide	124
care-of address	214
carrier	92, 148
carrier sense multiple access	148
carrier sense multiple access with collision avoidance	148
carrier sense multiple access with collision detection	148
cascading errors	32
CASE	293
Cat5	149
Cat5E	149
Cat6	149
catastrophe	271
categories	7
CBC	96
CBC-MAC	106
CBR	170
CCTVs	257
CDD	257
CDDI	149
CDMA	186
CDN	165, 191
cell	313
cell suppression	85
cellular networks	185
central office	176
central processing unit	64
centralized access control administration	213
centralized patch management	265
CEO	53
CER	198
CERT	268
certificate authority	109
certificate revocation list	109
certification	82
CFB	96
CFO	53
chain of custody	282
chaining	96
challenge handshake authentication protocol	178
change control	300
change control analyst	54
channel	168, 181
channel service unit	168
channel service unit/data service unit	168
CHAP	178
character device	72
charge-coupled device	257
checkpoint	314
chief executive officer	53
chief financial officer	53
chief information officer	53
chief information security officer	53
chief privacy officer	53
chief security officer	53
chinese wall model	78
chipping code	181
chips	181
choice	17
chosen-ciphertext attack	112
chosen-plaintext attack	112
CIA	2
CIDR	136
CIO	53
cipher	90
cipher block chaining message authentication code	106
cipher block chaining mode	96
cipher feedback	96
cipher locks	255
cipher-based message authentication code	106
ciphertext	90
ciphertext-only attack	112
CIR	169
circuit	168
circuit-level	162
circuit-switching	168
CISO	53
Civil	18
civil law system	18
civil/tort	18
clark-wilson model	77
class	303
class 1	256
class a	155
class b	155
class c	155
class ii	256
class iii	256
class iv	257
classful	136
classical	136
classification	56
classification levels	50
classless	136
classless interdomain routing	136
clean power	122
cleanroom model	298
cleanup rule	164
client/server	306
client-side validation	310
clipping	217
clipping level	199, 248

closed system 82
closed-circuit tvs 257
cloud computing 84
clustering 263, 275
CM 260
CMAC 106
CMMI 12
CN 195
CO 176
coaxial cabling 144
code division multiple access 186
code of ethics 47
code review 235
cognitive passwords 199
cohesion 303
cold site 272
collection limitation 17
collision 106, 107, 148
collision avoidance 148
collision domains 148
collude 44
COM 306
combi card 201
combination lock 255
command and control 191, 268
command-and-control 318
commercial 20
commit 314
committed information rate 169
committee of sponsoring organizations 12
common 130
common controls 38
common criteria 81
common law system 18
common name 195
community 152
community string 152
compensating control 7
compensating, ... 7
compiled 300
compiler 302
complete 282
complexity 315
component container 307
component object model 306
compression 98
computer and equipment rooms 118
computer architecture 64
computer emergency response team 268
computer ethics institute 47
computer forensics 280

computer is incidental 16
computer surveillance 282
computer-aided software engineering 293
computer-assisted 16
computer-targeted 16
concealment 3
concealment cipher 92
concentrator 159
concerns 67
concurrency 314
confidential 103
confidentiality 3, 91, 195
configuration management 252, 260
confusion 96
connectionless protocol 134
connection-oriented protocol 134
consistency 314
constant bit rate service 170
constrained data items 77
constrained user interface 212
construction 117
contact cards 200
contactless 200
content 85
content distribution network 165, 191
content-based access control 212
contention-based technology 148
context-based access controls 213
context-dependent access controls 85
contingency company 272
continuity planning 40
continuous lighting 257
control 5
control plane 165
control unit 64
control zone 218
controlled lighting - 257
controller area network bus 132
converged protocol 137
cookie 189
cooperative multitasking 70
copper distributed data interface 149
copyright 19
copyright directive 20
copyright law 19
copyrighted 19
core rbac 209
corporate 12
corrective 7
COSO 12

Index

coso enterprise risk management–integrated framework 38
COSO IC 12
coso internal control, ... 12
cost/benefit comparison 32
counter 97
counter-synchronized device 200
coupling 304
covert channel 78
covert storage channel 78
covert timing channel 78
CPO 53
CPTED 115
CPU 64
crime prevention through environmental design 115
criminal 18
criminal law 18
criticality 3, 50
CRL 109
cross certification 109
crossover error rate 198
cross-sectional photoelectric systems 258
cross-site scripting 309
crosstalk 145
cryptanalysis 90
cryptographic hash chaining 217
cryptographic key 200
cryptography 90
cryptology 90
cryptosystem 90
CSMA 148
CSMA/CA 148
CSMA/CD 148
CSO 53
CSU 168
CSU/DSU 168
customary law 18
cyber insurance 275
cyber squatters 154
cyber-physical system 85
DAC 208
damage assessment 277
DAS 149
DASD 262
data 128, 168
data analyst 54
data at rest 28, 58
data bus 65
data control language 314
data custodian 53
data dictionary 314
data encapsulation 135
data encryption algorithm 100
data encryption standard 90
data execution prevention 67
data hiding 71, 74
data in motion 28, 59
data in use 29, 59
data integrity 17
data leak prevention 60
data link layer 129, 130
data mining 315
data modeling 304
data origin authentication 106
data owners 53, 58
data processors 58
data protection directive 17
data quality 17
data remanence 58
data service unit 168
data structures 304
data terminal equipment 168
data throughput 141
data warehousing 314
database 313
database management system 313
database replication 274
database view 212, 314
databases 238
data-circuit terminating equipment 168
data-level parallelism 84
data-over-cable service interface specifications 177
DC 195, 196
DCE 168, 306
DCL 314
DCOM 306
DCSs 86
DDoS 163, 191
DDR SDRAM 65
DEA 100
dead forensics 282
decentralized access control administration 214
default to no access 201
defense-in-depth 7
defensive coding 235
degaussing 58
delayed binding 191
delayed loss 32
delaying devices 255
delaying mechanisms 115
delegate 303
delegation 303

Index

delivery 268
delphi technique 34
deluge 124
demilitarized zones 161
denial of service 135, 162, 191
deny first policy 163
DEP 67
department of defense architecture framework 10
department of veterans affairs information security
    protection act 21
dependent access control 85
depth of focus 257
DES 90, 100
DES-EDE2 100
DES-EDE3 100
DES-EEE2 100
DES-EEE3 100
detection 115, 268
detective 7
deterrence 115
deterrent 7
deterrents 256
development 67
deviation from the standard 250
device driver 72
device locks 256
devops 298
DHCP 150
dhcp clients 150
dhcp snooping 151
diameter 213
dictionary attack 199, 225
differential backup 274
differential cryptanalysis 112
differentiated service 170
diffie-hellman algorithm 103
diffusion 96
digest value 106
digital envelope 95
digital evidence 280
digital forensics 280
digital millennium copyright act 20
digital signal 140
digital signature standard 107
digital signatures 103
digital steganography 92
digital subscriber line 176
digital zoom 257
direct access storage device 262
direct memory access 72
direct sequence spread spectrum 181

directories 195
directory 195
directory service 195
disaster 271
disaster recovery 40, 239
disaster recovery plan 40, 239
discovery 233
discretion 3
discretionary access control 208
disk duplexing 274
disk mirroring 274
disk shadowing 274
disposed 50
distance-vector routing protocol 156
distinguished name 195
distributed component object model 306
distributed computing 306
distributed computing environment 306
distributed control systems 86
distributed denial of service 163, 191
distributed network protocol 3 132
distributed system 84
diversity of controls 255
DLL 71
DLP 60
DMCA 20
DMS 313
DMZs 161
DN 195
DNS 152
dns hijacking 192
dns resolver 153
dns security 153
DNSSEC 153
DOCSIS 177
document object model 310
document object model xss 310
DoDAF 10
Dogs 258
DOM 310
domain 63, 73
domain components 195
domain controller 196
domain grabbing 154
domain name services 152
dominates 208
dongle 218
door delay 255
DoS 135, 162, 191
dot-dot-slash attack 309
double data rate sdram 65

Index

double tagging attack 160
double-blind 234
double-des 100
downstream liability 285
DR 40, 239
DRAM 65
drive-by-download 192
DRP 40, 239
dry pipe 124
dry powders 124
DSD 209
DSL 176
DSS 107
DSSS 181
DSU 168
DTE 168
dual control 44
dual-attachment station 149
dual-homed 163
due care 19, 41, 247, 285
due diligence 41, 247, 285
duplex 129
durability 314
dynamic 151
dynamic analysis 294
dynamic host configuration protocol 150
dynamic ip addresses 150
dynamic link library 71
dynamic mapping 155
dynamic packet-filtering firewall 162
dynamic ports 136
dynamic ram 65
dynamic routing protocol 156
dynamic separation of duty 209
eac token 256
EAL 81
EAP 178
EAP-AKA 179
EAP-FAST 179
EAP-GSS 179
EAP-IKE2 179
EAP-MD5 179
EAP-PSK 179
EAP-SIM 179
EAP-TLS 137, 179
EAP-TTLS 179
e-carriers 167
ECB 96
ECC 104
economic espionage act 22
ecure rpc, or srpc, ... 129
EDGE 186
EDI 167
e-discovery 56
EDLP 60
EDO DRAM 65
EDRM 56
EEPROM 66
egress 161
EK 110
el gamal 104
electrically erasable programmable read-only memory .. 66
electromagnetic interference 122, 144
electromagnetic signals 144
electromechanical systems 258
electronic access control token 256
electronic code book mode 96
electronic data interchange 167
electronic discovery reference model 56
electronic mail gateway 161
electronic monitoring 199
electronic tape vaulting 274
electronic vaulting 274
electrostatic ids 258
elliptic curve cryptosystem 104
email spoofing 154
embedded 306
embedded system 85
EMI 122, 144
emulation buffer 266
encapsulating security payload 177
encapsulation 71, 303
encryption 58, 86
end user license agreement 20
endor management 285
endorsement key 110
endpoint dlp 60
endpoints 86
end-to-end encryption 188
enforcement 17
enhanced data rates for gsm evolution 186
enhanced performance architecture 132
enterprise architecture frameworks 9
enterprise security architecture 10
enticing 223
entity integrity 314
entrapment 223
entry points 117
enumeration 233
environment 257
EPA 132
EPROM 66

Index

eradication 317
erasable programmable read-only memory 66
ESP 177
ethernet 148
EULA 20
european union principles on privacy 17
evaluate 14
evaluation assurance level 81
event 268
event management systems 250
event-based 200
event-oriented 217
every 76
everything 195
evolutionary prototype 297
execution domain 76
executive management, ... 53
executive services 74
executive succession plan 42
exhaustive attack 225
exigent circumstances. 282
expansion 98
expert system 221
exploit 5
exploitation 234, 268
exploited 5
exploratory model 298
exposure 5
exposure factor 34
extended data out dram 65
extends 178
extensible access control markup language 204
extensible authentication protocol 178
extensible authentication protocol transport layer security
 137
extensions 214
external 60
extranet 167
extreme programming 298
facial scan 198
facilitated risk analysis process 33
facility 116
facility safety officer 116
factor 241
Facts 221
failover 275
fail-safe 118
fail-secure 118
failure mode and effect analysis 33
false acceptance rate 198
false rejection rate 198

FAR 198
faraday cage 218
fast ethernet 149
fast flux 318
Fault 122
fault generation 201
fault tolerance 275
fault tree analysis 33
fault-tolerance 262
FCS 168
FDDI 149
FDDI-2 149
FDM 168
FDMA 185
federated identity 204
fences 256
fetch request 65
FHSS 181
fiber distributed data interface 149
fiber-optic cabling 144
field of view 257
fifth-generation languages 302
file and directory permissions 233
file descriptor attacks 233
finger scan 198
fingerprinting 233
fingerprints 198
Fire 117
fire detection 123
fire prevention 123
firmware 65
fixed mount 258
fixed temperature detectors 123
flash memory 66
flooding 191
FM 140
FMEA 33
foam 124
focal length 257
footprint 185
foreign key 314
forwarding plane 165
forwarding proxy 164
fourth-generation languages 302
fractional t lines 167
fragmented 160
frame 131
Frame 28
frame check sequence 168
frame construction 117
frame relay 169

Index

frame relay cloud	169
frames	137
FRAP	33
free-space optics	184
freeware	20
frequencies	181
frequency	140
frequency analysis	94
frequency division multiple access	185
frequency hopping spread spectrum	181
frequency modulation	140
frequency-division multiplexing	168
FRR	198
FSO	184
Full	129
full backup	274
full mesh topology	147
full rbac	209
fully mapped i/o	72
function	7
functional model	292
functional policy	25
fuzzing	294
garbage collector	67
garbage-collector	302
gases	124
gateway	160
gauge	256
general hierarchies	209
general register	64
generic routing encapsulation	177
geographical	157
get	25
get out of jail free card	233
gigabit ethernet	149
glare protection	257
GLBA	22
global system for mobile communication	186
GM	253
gold master	253
governance, risk and compliance	285
grade 1	255
grade 2	255
grade 3	255
graham-denning model	78
gramm-leach-bliley act	22
gray box test	232
GRC	285
GRE	177
grid computing	263
group	201
GSM	186
guidelines	26
H2O	124
HA	275
HAIPE	178
Half	129
hand geometry	198
hand topography	198
handshake	135
handshaking	134
hanging modem	161
hardened	253
hardware segmentation	65
harrison-ruzzo-ullman	78
hash	106
HDSL	176
health insurance portability and accountability act	21
hearsay	282
heat activated	123
Heavy	117
heterogeneity	315
heuristic-based ids	221
HIDS	220
hierarchical data model	313
hierarchical rbac	209
hierarchical storage management	263
high assurance internet protocol encryptor	178
high availability	275
high security	255
high-bit-rate dsl	176
high-level language	302
high-speed downlink packet access	186
high-speed serial interface	170
HIPAA	21
HMAC	106
home ip address	214
honeyclient	266
honeynet	164
honeypot	164, 222
host	136
host based attack	192
hostage alarm	255
host-based ids	220
hosts file	153
host-to-host layer	134
hot site	272
HRU	78
HSM	263
HSPDA	186
HSSI	170
HTTP	189

Index

hub 159
hybrid attack 225
hybrid card 201
hybrid control 38
hybrid dlp 61
hybrid microkernel 74
hybrid microkernel architecture 74
hybrid rbac 209
hybrid team 268
hygrometer 118
hypertext transfer protocol 189
hypervisor 74
i/o using dma 72
IaaS 84, 205
ICMP 151
icmp tunneling 151
ICS 86
ICV 182
IDEA 100
identification 3
identify 232
identity 195
identity as a service 205
identity management 195
IdM 195
IDS 220, 258
ids sensors 150
IEC 9
IEEE 802.1AE 137
IEEE 802.1AF 137
IEEE 802.1AR 137
IGMP 149
ignoring 36
IGRP 156
IKE 177
illogical processing 32
IMAP 154
implement 14
implementation 76
incident 268
incident assessment 115
incombustible material 117
incremental backup 274
incremental model 297
indexes 313
indexing 56
indicator 241
indicators of attack 269
indicators of compromise 269
individual 106
individual participation 17

industrial 19
industrial control system 86
infer 112
inference 85
inference engine 221
information systems risk management policy 28
informational model 292
informative 25
infrastructure as a service 84
infrastructure wlan 181
ingress 161
inheritance 303
inherited 303
initial program load 250
initialization vector 96, 98
in-rush 122
in-rush current 122
installation 268
instance 303
instruction 84
instruction set 72
integrated product team 298
integrated services digital network 176
integration 257
integration testing 294
integrity 3, 91, 195
integrity check value 182
integrity verification procedures 77
intellectual property 19
intellectual property law 19
interface 235, 303
interface testing 236
interior gateway routing protocol 156
internal compartments 118
international data encryption algorithm 100
international electrotechnical commission 9
internet control message protocol 151
internet group management protocol 149
internet key exchange 177
internet layer 134
internet message access protocol 154
internet of things 85
internet protocol security 137, 177
internet relay chat 318
internet small computer system interface 138
internetwork 167
interoperability 60
interpreted 302
interprocess communication 306
interrupt 70
interrupt-driven i/o 72

Index

intersite	137
intranet	167
intrasite	137
intrusion detection system	220, 258
intrusion prevention system	163, 222
inverter	122
IOA	269
IOC	269
IoT	85
ip convergence	138
ip fragmentation attack	164
ip next generation	137
ip telephony device	172
IPC	306
IPL250	
IPng	137
IPS	163, 222
IPSec	59, 137, 177
IPT	298
IPv4	136
IPv6	136, 137
IRC	318
iris257	
iris scan	198
isaca risk it	38
iSCSI	138
ISDN	176
ISMS	9
ISO 15408	81
ISO 22301	40
ISO 27001	9
ISO 27002	9
ISO 27004	45, 241
ISO 27005	33
ISO 27031	40
ISO 28000	260
ISO 31000;	38
ISO 42010	67
isochronous network	172
isolation	3, 314
ISRM	28
issuance	195
issue-specific policies	25
IT 12	
iterated tunneling	178
ITIL	12
IV 98	
IVPs	77
JAD	298
java database connectivity	313
java ee	306
java platform, enterprise edition	306
JDBC	313
jitter	172
joint application development	298
jumbograms	137
kanban	298
kanban wall	298
KDD	315
KDFs	94
kerberos	202
kerckhoffs' principle	91
kernel	65
kernel flaws	233
kernel mode	72
kernel proxy firewall	162
key	90
key agreement	103
key derivation functions	94
key exchange	103
key mixing	98
key override	255
key performance indicator	241
key ring	188
key risk indicators	241
keyspace	90
keystream	96
keystream generator	97
keystroke dynamics	198
keystroke monitoring	218
kill chain	29, 268
knapsack algorithms	104
knowledge base	221
knowledge discovery in database	315
knowledge-based	220
known-plaintext attack	112
knows	306
KPI	241
KRIs	241
L2F	177
L2TP	177
lack of reliability	315
LAN	167
land attack	220
layer 2 forwarding	177
layer 2 tunneling protocol	177
layered	74
layered defense strategy	115
layered operating system	74
LCP	170
LDAP	195
leak	60

Index

leaked	59
lease	150
leash	157
least significant bit	92
least-privilege	202
level parallelism	84
lever tumbler lock	255
life-cycle assurance	248
Light	117
light detector	144
lighting	257
lightweight directory access protocol	195
likely	28
limit register	71
limited hierarchies	209
limited rbac	209
line conditioners	122
line noise	122
linear bus topology	147
linear cryptanalysis	112
link control protocol	170
link encryption	188
linked	306
link-state routing protocol	156
live forensics	282
LLC	129, 130
load balancing	275
Local	159
local area network	167
local organization	71
locard's exchange principal	281
lock	314
log review	234
log scrubber	317
logic bomb	318
logical	147
logical access controls	195
logical address	66
logical link control sublayer	129, 130
logical location restrictions	201
logical topology	147
loki attacks	221
long-term evolution	186
loss	60
Loss	60
loss potential	32
LSB	92
LTE	186
lucifer	90, 100
Lux	258
MAC	106, 129, 130, 208
mac address	150
machine language	302
macro virus	317
macsec	137
macsec security entity	137
MAID	262
mailbox data	239
Main	255
maintain	14
maintenance hooks	88
MAN	169
management information base	152
management review	243
manager	151
mandatory access controls	208
mandatory vacation	44
man-in-the-middle attack	103
mantrap	117
manual iris lens	257
maskable	70
massive array of inactive disks	262
master key	255
master keying	255
master security policy	25
maximum period time of disruption	41
maximum tolerable downtime	41, 271
maximum transmission size	160
MD4	106
MD5	107
mean time between failure	262
mean time to failure	262
mean time to repair	262
Means	281
measurement	241
media	59
media access control address	150
media access control sublayer	129, 130
media access technology	147
meet-in-the-middle attack	113
meme virus	317
memory card	200
memory leak	67
memory leaks	67
memory manager	71
memory mapping	66
memory segment	71
memory types	65
Menu	212
Mesh	256
message	303
message authentication code	106

342

message digest	106
metadata	315
meta-directory	196
method	303
metric	241
metrics	45
metro ethernet	169
metropolitan-area network	169
MIB	152
microarchitecture	72
microdot	92
microkernel	74
microprobing	201
microsoft's point-to-point encryption	177
MIME	188
MIMO	184
ministry of defence architecture framework	10
misuse cases	235
mitigation	269
mixed law	19
MLS	208
MMS	186
MO	281
mobile code	307
mobile ip	214
MoDAF	10
mode transitions	74
model	78
modem	176
modus operandi	281
MOM	280
monitor	28, 257
monoalphabetic substitution cipher	90
monolithic	74
monolithic architecture	73
motive	281
MPLS	137, 160
MPPE	177
MPTD	41
MQV	103
MS-CHAP	178
MTBF	262
MTD	41, 271
MTTF	262
MTTR	262
MTU	160
multicast	137, 149
multifactor authentication	196
multi-homed	163
multilayer devices	160
multilevel security policies	76
multilevel security system	77, 208
multimedia messaging service	186
multimode	144
multipart virus	317
multiparty key recovery	110
multiple in, multiple out	184
multiple processing centers	272
multiplexer	257
multiplexing	130, 167
multiprocessing	65
multiprogramming	70
multiprotocol label switching	137, 160
multipurpose internet mail extension	188
multiservice access technologies	172
multitasking	70
multithreaded	70
mutual aid agreement	273
mutual authentication	183
namespace	195
naming distinctions	71
NAT	155
national institute of standards and technology	11
natural access control	116
natural language	302
natural surveillance	116
natural territory reinforcement	116
NDAs	44
NDLP	60
NDP3	132
near-line	263
need-to-know	202
network	136
network access layer	134
network address	155
network address translation	155
network administrator	247
network based attack	192
network database model	313
network dlp	60
network interface card	149, 181
network layer	129, 130
network protocol	128
network time protocol	235
network topology	147
network-based ids	220
next-generation firewalls	163
NGFWs	163
NIC	150, 181
NIDS	220
NIST	11
NIST RMF	38

Index

NIST SP 800-111 58
NIST SP 800-30 33
NIST SP 800-34 40
NIST SP 800-53 28
NIST SP 800-55 45
NIST SP 800-82 86
NIST SP 800-88 58
NMT 186
noise 317
Noise 145
noise and perturbation 85
noisy 140
nonce 200
non-descriptive 195
non-disaster 271
non-disclosure agreements 44
nondiscretionary 208
noninterference 78
nonmaskable 70
non-persistent xss vulnerabilities 309
nonplenum cable 145
non-rbac 209
nonrecursive query 153
nonrepudiation 91
nordic mobile telephone 186
normalization 56
not 164, 307
notice 17
NTP 235
null cipher 92
number generator 92
OAuth 205
oauth2 205
object 76, 194
object linking and embedding 306
object linking and embedding database ... 313
object request brokers 306
object-oriented database 313
object-oriented programming 303
object-relational database 313
OCSP 109
ODBC 313
OECD 17
OFB 96
OFDM 181
OFDMA 186
office of management and budget 21
OLE 306
OLE DB 313
OLTP 314
OMB 21

one-time pad 91
one-time password 199
one-way function 103
one-way hash 106
online certificate status protocol 109
online encryption 188
online transaction processing 314
online ups 122
onward transfer 17
OOD 313
OOP 303
open 165
open database connectivity 313
open message format 95
open proxy 164
open shortest path first 156
open systems 82
open systems interconnection 128
openflow 165
openid 205
openid provider 205
openness 17
operating system 64, 70
operation assurance 248
operational prototype 297
operational security 250
opportunity 281
optical wireless 184
optical zoom 257
ORBs 306
ORD 313
organizational security policy 25
orthogonal frequency division multiple access 186
orthogonal frequency-division multiplexing 181
OS 64
OSI 128
OSPF 156
OTP 199
outage 122
outgoing 163
out-of-band 309
output feedback 96
overflowing 67
overlapping fragment attack 164
overlays 165
overwriting 58
PaaS 84
packages 81
packet 130
packet fragmentation 137
packet switching, ... 168

Index

packet-filtering 161
padding 98
pages 72
pair programming 298
palm scan 198
pan, tilt, zoom 258
PAP 178
paper records 61
parallel computing 84
parameter validation 310
parameters 66
partial mesh topology 147
partitioning 85
passive 266
passive attack 112
passive infrared systems 258
passive monitoring 282
passphrase 200
password aging 199
password authentication protocol 178
password checker 199
password cracker 199
password file 199
password synchronization 197
PAT 155
patch 294
patch management 265
patches 265
patents 20
path or directory traversal attack 309
pattern-matching 220
payload 92
payment card industry data security standard 22
PBX 161
PCI DSS 22
PCS 186
PDCA 243
peap-v0 179
peapv1 179
penetration testing 232, 233
performance-based approach 115
perimeter intrusion and detection assessment system .. 256
perimeter scanning devices 258
peripheral switch controls 256
permanent team 268
permanent virtual circuit 169
persistent xss vulnerabilities 310
personal communications service 186
personally identifiable information 21
personnel access controls 256
personnel assessment 232

PGP 188
phishing 155
photoelectric 123
phreakers 161
physical 7
physical assessment 232
physical constraint 212
physical controls 215
physical destruction 58
physical layer 129
physical location restriction 201
physical organization 71
physical surveillance 282
physical topology 147
physiological traits 198
PIDAS 256
piggybacking 256
PII 21
pin tumbler lock 255
PING 151
ping of death 191
PIRs 258
PKI 109
plaintext 90
plan 229
Plan 14
plan-do-check-act 243
platform as a service 84
PLCs 86
plenum space 117, 125, 145
plenum-rated cabling 125
point-to-point protocol 170
point-to-point tunneling protocol 177
policies 60
polling 148
polyalphabetic substitution cipher 90
polyinstantiation 314
polymorphic virus 317
polymorphism 303
POODLE 189
POP 154
port address translation 155
port controls 256
port-based network access 182
portlets 204
ports 130, 136
post office protocol 154
postmortem 234
PP 81
PPP 170
PPTP 177

Index

precaution	124	prudent man	247
preemptive multitasking	70	pseudorandom numbers	92
premapped i/o	72	PSP	204
presentation	129	PSTN	172
presentation layer	128, 129	PSW	64
pretexting	240	PTZ	258
pretty good privacy	188	public key infrastructure	109
preventative	7	public key pair	95
PRI	176	public key system	95
primary image	281	public-switched telephone network	172
primary key	313, 314	purpose	257
primary rate interface isdn	176	purpose specification	17
principals	202	PVC	169
privacy	3, 53	QL 314	
privacy impact rating	292	QoS	169
privacy risk assessment	292	qualitative	32
privacy-aware rbac	209	quality	290
private	155	quality of service	137, 169
private branch exchange	161	quantitative	32
privilege accumulation	238	RA 204	
privilege escalation	293	race condition	88, 233
privilege mode	65	RAD	297
probalistic	315	radio frequency identification	200
problem state	65	radio interference	122
procedural	303	RADIUS	213
procedures	26	RADSL	176
process	70	RAID	262
process enhancement	11	RAID 0	262
process isolation	71	RAID 1	262
process life-cycle	13	RAID 10	262
process table	70	RAID 2	262
profile	198	RAID 3	262
program counter register	64	RAID 4	262
program status word	64	RAID 5	262
programmable i/o	72	RAID 6	262
programmable logic controllers	86	rainbow attack	225
programming language	302	rainbow table	199
project management	292	RAIT	262
promiscuous mode	192, 220	raking	255
protection	71	RAM	65
protection profile	81	random access memory	65
protection profiles	81	ransomware	191
protocol analyzer	220	rapid application development	297
protocol anomaly-based ids	221	rapid prototype	297
prototype	297	RARP	151
provisioning	260	RAT	318
provisioning service provider	204	rate-adaptive dsl	176
proximate cause	285	rate-of-rise detectors	123
proximity detectors	258	RBAC	209
proxy firewall	162	RC4	101
proxy server	164, 173	RC5	101

Index

RC6	101
RDBM	313
read password	152
read-only memory	65
read-write password	152
Ready	70
real user monitoring	235
realm	203
real-time analysis	217
real-time transport protocol	173
rebar	117
reciprocal agreement	272
reconstitution	277
recovery	7, 269, 277
recovery phase	278
recovery point objective	271
recovery time objective	271
recursive query	153
redirect server	173
reduction analysis	29
redundancy	275
redundant array of independent disks	262
redundant array of independent tapes	262
redundant hardware	262
redundant site	272
reference monitor	76
referential integrity	314
reflected vulnerabilities	309
register	64
registered ports	136
registrar server	173
registration authority	109
regression testing	294
regulatory	25
relational database model	313
relative address	66
relay	154
relevant	282
reliability	275
reliable	282
religious law	18
relocation	71
remediation	269
remote	159
remote access trojan	318
remote authentication dial-in user service	213
remote journaling	274
remote procedure call	129, 306
rented offsite installation	272
repeater	159
replay attack	113
replication	317
report generator	314
report to management	234
reporting	269
representational state transfer	205, 307
request for proposal	285
requesting authority	204
residual risk	35
resistant material	117
respond	28
response	256, 268
response procedures	115
responsive area illumination -	257
REST	205, 307
restoration phase	277
retention policy	56
retina scan	198
reuse model	298
reverse address resolution protocol	151
reverse proxy	164
RFC 5905	235
RFI	122
RFID	200
RFP	285
rijndael	100
ring topology	147
rings	72
RIP	156
risk	5
risk analysis	32, 33
risk analysis team	32
risk assessment	32, 33
risk avoidance	36
risk management	28
risk management frameworks	38
risk management process	243
risk reduction	36
RMFs	38
RMP	243
roaming	184
robust security network	182
role-based access control	209
Roles	201
rollback	314
rolling hot site	272
ROM	65
root	153
root of trust	110
rootkit	317
rotation of duties	44
rotor cipher machine	90

Index

route flapping	156
routers	159
routing information protocol	156
routing policy	156
RPC	129, 306
RPO	271
RSA	103
RTCP	173
RTO	271
RTP	173
rtp control protocol	173
rule-based ids	221
RUM	235
running	70
running key cipher	92
SA	178
SaaS	84
SABSA	10
safe harbor	17
safe harbor privacy principles (	17
safes	61, 120
sag/dip	122
salt	199
salvage phase	277
SAML	204
SAN	262
sandbox	266
sanitized	59
sarbanes-oxley	202
SAS	149
SAS 70	36, 230
SASD	262
SASL	154
satellite	185
savepoint	314
SCADA	86
schema	313
scientific working group on digital evidence	280
SCM	300
scope creep	292
screened host	163
screened subnet	163
script injection	309
script kiddies	16
script virus	317
scrub	217
Scrum	298
scytale cipher	90
SDH	168
SDLC	292
SDN	165
SDRAM	65
SDSL	176
se linux	209
seclusion	3
second generation language	302
secondary storage	71
secrecy	3
secret keys	94
secure shell	189
secure supply chain	260
security	17, 53
security administrator	53, 247
security assertion markup language	204
security association	178
security assurance requirements	81
security audit	229
security awareness training	240
security domains	203
security effectiveness	11
security event management	218
security functional requirements	81
security governance	45
security guards	258
security information and event management	218
security kernel	76
security label	208
security management	292
security models	77
security perimeter	76
security policy	25, 76
security safeguards	17
security target	81
security training	240
security zones	116
SecY	137
self-healing,	169
self-service password reset	197
SEM	218
semantic integrity	314
sender policy framework	155
sensitive	60
sensitivity	3, 50, 60
sensitivity labels	208
sensor	220
separation of duties	44
sequential access storage device	262
server based attack.	192
service bureau	272
service level agreements	262
service organization controls	230
service organizations	230

Index

service oriented approach	205, 306
service provisioning markup language	204
service set id	181
session	209
session hijacking	221, 311
session initiation protocol	172
session key	95, 103
session layer	129
session management	311
set	313
SHA	107
shadow file	199
shared kay authentication	182
shareware	20
sharing	71
Shell	212
sherwood applied business security architecture	10
shielded twisted pair	144
side-channel attack	59, 112
SIEM	218
signal	140
signal wave	140
signaling system 7	172
signature dynamics	198
signature-based	220
signatures	163
silent rule	164
simple authentication and security layer	154
simple mail transfer protocol	154
simple network management protocol	151
simple object access protocol	205, 307
simplex	129
simplex communication	217
single loss expectancy	34
single mode	144
single point of failure	262
single sign-on	196, 197
single-attachment station	149
SIP	172
situational awareness	218
six sigma	12
SKA	182
SLAs	262
SLE	34
slot locks	256
smart card	200
smart locks	256
smoke activated	123
SMPL	204
SMTP	154
smtp authentication	154
SMTP-AUTH	154
sniffing	192
sniffs	220
SNMP	151
SOA	205, 306
SOAP	205, 307
SOC	230
social engineering	199, 240
social engineering attack	113
socket	136, 161
SOCKS	162
soft token	200
software as a service	84
software attacks	201
software configuration management	300
software deadlock	71
software development life cycle	292
software escrow	300
software piracy	20
software-based guards	208
software-defined networking	165
something	183
SONET	168, 169
SOs	230
source code	235
source routing	159
SOW	292
SOX	202
SP 800-37	38
SP 800-53	11
SPA	159
Spam	318
spam over internet telephony	174
spanning tree algorithm	159
spear phishing	155
special registers	64
SPF	155
Spike	122
spiral model	297
SPIT	174
split dns	153
split duties	110
split knowledge	44
spoofing at logon	225
spread spectrum	181
sprint	298
spyware	317
sql injection	309
SRAM	65
SRK	110
SS7	172

Index

SSD 209
SSH 189
SSID 181
SSL 59
SSO 196, 197
stack 64, 66
stack pointer 65
stakeholder 67
stakeholders 67
stand-alone wlan 181
standard 25
standby lighting 257
standby ups 122
star topology 147
state 221
stateful 156
stateful firewall 161
stateful inspection 161
stateful matching 221
stateful-matching ids 221
stateless inspection 161
statement of work 292
statement on auditing standards no 70 230
static analysis 293
static ip address 150
static mapping 155
static ram 65
static routing protocol 156
static separation of duty 209
statistical 315
statistical attack 113
statistical time-division multiplexing 168
STDM 168
stealth assessment 234
stealth rule 164
stealth virus 317
steganography 92
stegomedium 92
storage area network 262
storage keys 110
storage root key 110
STP 144
strata 235
strategic alignment 10
stream cipher 94, 97
strength 91
strong authentication 196
structure 314
subject 76, 194
subkeys 94
submaster keys 255

subnet 136
subnet mask 136
substitution cipher 90, 94
sudo 238
sufficient 282
supernetting 136
supervisor 53
supervisor mode 65
supervisory control and data acquisition 86
supplicant 182, 183
supposed 148
suppression agents 123
Surge 122
SUS 243
SVC 169
swap space 72
swapping 71
SWGDE 280
switch 159
switch controls 256
switch spoofing attack 160
switched virtual circuit 169
SWOT 41
symbolic links 233
symmetric 65
symmetric algorithms 94
symmetric dsl 176
symmetric encryption algorithms 94
syn flood 135, 191
synchronization 141, 300
synchronized device 199
synchronous 97, 141
synchronous communication method 141
synchronous digital hierarchy 168
synchronous dram 65
synchronous optical network 168, 169
synchronous replication 274
synthetic transaction 235
system 67, 106, 182
system and networking assessment 232
system architecture 67
system authentication 106
system owner 53
system sensing access control reader 256
system under study 243
systems 177
system-specific control 38
system-specific policy 25
TACS 186
tailgating 256
tape vaulting 274

350

Index

target hardening	116
target of evaluation	81
targeted	234
tarpit	164
Task	84
taxonomy	56
t-carriers	167
TCB	76
TCG	110
TCP	134
tcp handshake	135
tcp session hijacking	136
TCP/IP	128
TDD	293
TDM	167
TDMA	186
teardrop attack	164
technical	7
technical controls	215
technology by itself cannot solve any risk	44
telecommunications	127
TEMPEST	218
temporal	157
temporal restrictions	201
tension wrench	255
teredo	137
termination	44
tertiary site	272
test	232
test-driven development	293
the open-group architecture framework	9
third generation partner project	186
third-generation	302
thread	70
threat	5, 29
threat agent	5
threat modeling	28, 293
threat tree	293
tickets	202
timber construction	117
time division multiple access	186
time multiplexing	71
time of day restrictions	201
time slice	70
time to live	136
time-division multiplexing	167
time-of-check/time-of-use attack	88
timing	201
TLS	59, 178
tls portal vpn	178
tls tunnel vpn	178
toc/tou attack	88
TOE	81
TOGAF	9
token device	199
token passing	147
token ring	149
top-level domain	152
total access communication system	186
total risk	35
TPM	110
tracing software	120
trade secret	19
trademark	19
trademark law	19
traffic anomaly-based ids	221
traffic shaping	170
transaction	314
transaction-type restrictions	201
transfer the risk	36
translating	155
translation	159
transmission control protocol/internet protocol	128
transparent bridging	159
transponder	256
transport	129
transport adjacency	178
transport control protocol	134
transport layer	129, 130
transport level security	178
transposition cipher	94
trap	151
trapdoor	103
tree bus topology	147
trigger	317
triple-des	90, 100
trojan horse	318
trojan programs	317
trusted computer base	76
trusted computer group	110
trusted computer system evaluation criteria	76
trusted inspection	260
trusted path	76
trusted platform module	110
trusted recovery	252
trusted shell	76
trusted solaris	209
trusted supplier	260
trusted transportation network	260
TTL	136
tumbler lock	255
tunneling virus	317

Index

twisted-pair cabling	144
two-phase commit	314
type 1 error	198
type 2 error	198
UAC	172
UAS	172
UAT	294
UBR	170
UDDI	307
UDIs	77
UDP	134
UID	306
UML	235
unauthorized	60
unauthorized external	60
unconstrained data items	77
unicast	149
unicode encoding	309
unified modeling language	235
unified threat management	165
uninterruptible power supplies	122
uniqueness	195
unit testing	293, 294
universal description, discovery and integration	307
universal unique identifier	306
unmanaged patching	265
unmapped i/o	72
unshielded twisted pair	144
unspecified bit rate service	170
updates	86
UPSs	122
url encoding	309
url filtering	309
url hiding	153
use	50
use limitation	17
user	54, 182
user acceptance testing	294
user agent client	172
user agent server	172
user data files	238
user datagram protocol	134
user mode	65, 73
user provisioning	198
user stations	86
user story	298
user-activated reader	256
UTM	165
UTP	144
validation	294
value-added network	167
VAN	167
variability	315
variable bit rate service	170
VBR	170
vendor management governing	285
verification	294
vernam cipher	91
versatile memory	110
versioning	300
very high-level languages	302
very small aperture terminal	185
vibration sensors	258
View	67
viewpoint	67
vigenere cipher	90
virtual circuit	169
virtual directory	196
virtual firewalls	163
virtual lans	159
virtual machine	74
virtual memory	71
virtual memory mapping	71
virtual memory paging	72
virtual private lan service	169
virtual private networks	177
virtual router redundancy protocol	156
virtual team	268
virtualization	74
virus	317
virus walls	318
vlan hopping attacks	160
VLANs	159
v-model	297
voice gateway	172
voice over ip	172
voice print	198
voicemail system	172
VoIP	172
volatile	65, 280
volatile memory	280
voltage instability	122
voltage regulators	122
volumetric systems	258
VPLS	169
VPNs	177
VRRP	156
VSAT	185
v-shaped model	297
vulnerability	5
vulnerability mapping	234
vulnerability testing	232

wafer tumbler lock 255
WAM 196
WAN 167
war dialing 176, 234
warded lock 255
war-dialing 225
warez 19
warm site 272
wassenaar arrangement 17
watchdog timer 70
waterfall model 297
wave-pattern motion detectors 258
WBS 292
weaponization 268
web access management 196
web services 205
well-formed transaction 78
well-known ports 136
WEP 181
wet chemical 124
wet pipe 124
whaling attack 155
white box test 232
white noise 218
wide-area network 167
wi-fi protected access 182
wired equivalent protocol 181

wireless networks 181
wireless personal area network 184
work breakdown structure 292
work factor 91
work recovery time 271
working image 281
worm 317
wormhole attack 157
WPA 182
WPA2 182
WPAN 184
WRT 271
X.25 169
X.500 195
XACML 204
xmas attack 220
XOR 91
XP 298
XSS 309
XXX 179
you 135
your 135
zachman 9
zero knowledge proof 104
zero-day vulnerability 294
zombie 16, 163, 191
zoom 257

Made in the USA
San Bernardino, CA
18 October 2018